Educational Theories, Cultures and Learning

A critical perspective

Edited by
Harry Daniels
Hugh Lauder
Jill Porter

with Sarah Hartshorn

Routledge
Taylor & Francis Group

LONDON AND NEW YORK

First published 2009
by Routledge
2 Park Square, Milton Park, Abingdon, Oxon OX14 4RN

Simultaneously published in the USA and Canada
by Routledge
711 Third Avenue, New York, NY 10017

Routledge is an imprint of the Taylor & Francis Group, an informa business

First issued in paperback 2011

Typeset in Galliard by
Bookcraft Ltd, Stroud, Gloucestershire

British Library Cataloguing in Publication Data
A catalogue record for this book is available from the British Library

Library of Congress Cataloging in Publication Data
Educational theories, cultures, and learning : a critical perspective / edited
by Harry Daniels, Hugh Lauder, and Jill Porter.
    p. cm.
    Includes bibliographical references and index.
    1. Educational sociology. 2. Teaching—Social aspects.
    3. Learning—Social aspects. I. Daniels, Harry. II.
    Lauder, Hugh. III. Porter, Jill.
LC191.E427 2009
306.43–dc22   2008043450

ISBN10: 0-415-49118-5 (hbk)
ISBN10: 0-415-68650-4 (pbk)

ISBN13: 978-0-415-49118-1 (hbk)
ISBN13: 978-0-415-68650-1 (pbk)

Educational Theories, Cultures and Learning

Education poses some of the most challenging questions of any profession. Whether we are teachers, policy makers or researchers, the complexity of the practices and policies that we encounter demands careful thought and reflection. The **Critical Perspectives on Education** series includes volumes designed to provoke the kind of thinking that will lead readers to re-evaluate their practices and consider how best they can be justified and improved.

Educational Theories, Cultures and Learning focuses on how education is understood in different cultures, the theories and related assumptions we make about learners and students and how we think about them, and how we can understand the principal actors in education – learners and teachers.

Within this volume, internationally renowned contributors address a number of fundamental questions designed to take the reader to the heart of current debates around pedagogy, globalisation, and learning and teaching, such as:

- What role does culture play in our understanding of pedagogy?
- What role do global influences, especially economic, cultural and social, have in shaping our understanding of education?
- What role does language play in influencing our thinking about education?
- How can we best understand childhood?
- What implications does our view of childhood have for education?
- How do we know what learners know?
- How do learners negotiate the transition between the different phases of education?
- How best can children learn the knowledge we believe should be taught?
- What is a teacher?
- How do teachers learn?
- How do we understand learners, their minds, identity and development?

To help with reflection, the chapters also include questions for debate and a guide to further reading.

Read alongside its companion volume, *Knowledge, Values and Educational Policy*, this book will encourage readers to reflect on some of the key issues facing education and educationists today.

Harry Daniels is Professor of Education: Culture and Pedagogy, Head of the Learning as Cultural and Social Practice Research Programme, and Director of the Centre for Sociocultural and Activity Theory Research at the University of Bath, UK.

Hugh Lauder is Professor of Education and Political Economy, and Head of the Policy and Management Research Group, at the University of Bath, UK.

Jill Porter is Senior Lecturer in Research Methods and Special Education at the University of Bath, UK.

Critical Perspectives on Education

Education poses some of the most challenging questions of any profession. Whether we are teachers, policy makers or researchers, the complexity of the practices and policies that we encounter demands careful thought and reflection. The **Critical Perspectives on Education** series includes volumes designed to provoke the kind of thinking that will lead readers to re-evaluate their practices and consider how best they can be justified and improved.

Educational Theories, Cultures and Learning
A critical perspective
Edited by Harry Daniels, Hugh Lauder and Jill Porter

Knowledge, Values and Educational Policy
A critical perspective
Edited by Harry Daniels, Hugh Lauder and Jill Porter

Contents

Contributors

Robin Alexander is Fellow of Wolfson College at the University of Cambridge and Emeritus Professor of Education at Warwick University, UK.

Sarah-Jayne Blakemore is a Royal Society University Research Fellow at the Institute of Cognitive Neuroscience, University College London, UK.

Guy Claxton is Director of the Centre for Real-World Learning at the University of Winchester, UK, and Professor of the Learning Sciences at the University of Bristol, UK.

Roger Dale is a sociologist of education, who is currently Professor in the Centre for Globalisation, Education and Societies in the Graduate School of Education of the University of Bristol, UK.

Harry Daniels is Professor of Education: Culture and Pedagogy, Head of the Learning as Cultural and Social Practice Research Programme, and Director of the Centre for Sociocultural and Activity Theory Research at the University of Bath, UK.

Fabienne Doucet is Assistant Professor in the Department of Teaching and Learning, Program in Early Childhood Education, at the New York University Steinhardt School of Culture, Education, and Human Development.

Anne Edwards is Professor of Educational Studies, Director of Research and Director of the Oxford Centre for Sociocultural and Activity Theory Research (OSAT) in the Department of Education at the University of Oxford, UK.

Kieran Egan is Professor of Education at Simon Fraser University in British Columbia, Canada.

Michael Fielding is Professor of Education at the Institute of Education, University of London, UK.

Lia B.L. Freitas is Professor of Psychology at the Federal University of Rio Grande do Sul, Brazil.

Sarah L. Holloway is Reader in Human Geography at Loughborough University, UK.

Chris James is Professor of Educational Leadership and Management in the Department of Education at the University of Bath, UK.

William Lachicotte is Research Assistant Professor of Social Medicine, Adjunct Assistant Professor of Anthropology, and Research Associate, FPG Child Development Institute, at the University of North Carolina at Chapel Hill.

Hugh Lauder is Professor of Education and Political Economy, and Head of the Policy and Management Research Group, at the University of Bath, UK.

Yolande Muschamp is Head of the Department of Education at the University of Bath, UK.

Jill Porter is Senior Lecturer in Research Methods and Special Education at the University of Bath, UK.

Anna Sfard is based at the University of Haifa, Israel, and is also affiliated with Michigan State University in the USA (as Lappan-Phillips-Fitzgerald Professor of Mathematics Education) and the Institute of Education, University of London, UK.

Jonathan R.H. Tudge is Professor of Human Development and Family Studies at the University of North Carolina at Greensboro, USA, and has been a visiting professor at several Brazilian universities.

Gill Valentine is Professor of Geography at the University of Leeds, UK.

Willem L. Wardekker is Lecturer in Education at VU University, Amsterdam, the Netherlands, and Professor of Education at Windesheim University of Professional Studies, Zwolle, the Netherlands.

Jack Whitehead is Lecturer in the Department of Education at the University of Bath, UK.

Julian Williams is Professor of Mathematics Education at the University of Manchester, UK.

David Wood is Emeritus Professor at the University of Nottingham, UK, where he served as Professor of Psychology and was the founding Director of the Learning Sciences Research Institute (LSRI).

Heather Wood, who graduated and received her doctorate from the University of Nottingham, UK, has a lifetime interest in the care and development of young children, with a particular research interest in those with sensory disabilities, publishing widely in the fields of infant blindness and childhood deafness.

Acknowledgements

Cartoons by Ros Asquith from the LINES series originally published in *Guardian Education*. Reprinted by permission of the artist.

2.1: Kieran Egan, 'Students' development in theory and practice: the doubtful role of research', *Harvard Educational Review*, 75(1) (Spring 2005), pp. 25–41. Copyright © by the President and Fellows of Harvard College. All rights reserved. Reprinted with permission. For more information, please visit www.harvardeducationalreview.org

2.2: 'Cyberworlds: children in the information age', is adapted from *Cyberkids: Children in the Information Age*, by Sarah L. Holloway and Gill Valentine, © 2003 RoutledgeFalmer. Reproduced by permission of Taylor & Francis Books UK.

3.1: David Wood and Heather Wood, 'Vygotsky, tutoring and learning', *Oxford Review of Education*, 22(1). Reprinted by permission of Taylor & Francis Ltd. (http://www.tandf.co.uk/journals).

Introduction

From Plato to Monday morning

Harry Daniels, Hugh Lauder and Jill Porter

Education poses some of the most challenging questions of any profession. Whether as teachers, policy makers or researchers, the complexity of the practices and policies that we encounter demands careful reflection. *Educational Theories, Cultures and Learning* and its companion volume *Knowledge, Values and Educational Policy* (two volumes in the Critical Perspectives on Education series) are designed to provoke the kind of thinking that will do justice to such complexity. In a world in which policy makers often seek the comforts of magic bullets that solve educational problems with one simple solution, and where commercial companies seek to solve the pressure on teachers' time with off-the-shelf curricula and school improvement packages, these volumes seek to do the opposite: there is no recipe book.

In the daily struggle to keep up with new policy initiatives and increased demands for accountability and the related mountain of paperwork, the fundamental questions that give us our professional moral and practical compass are sometimes overlooked. It is by returning to these questions that we can re-evaluate our practices and consider how best we can justify and improve them.

Within these two volumes we address a number of questions that may appear simple, but very quickly readers will find themselves immersed in debates with themselves and with others. To help with such reflection each chapter poses questions and offers an initial guide to further reading. Many of these questions have been debated from Plato onwards, but they are no less valid now than when first raised. The following are the questions that are addressed in a variety of ways both within and across the sections of the two volumes.

In *Educational Theories, Cultures and Learning*, we ask:

- What role does culture play in our understanding of pedagogy?
- What role do global influences, especially economic, cultural and social, have in shaping our understanding of education?
- What role does language play in influencing our thinking about education?
- How can we best understand childhood? What implications does our view of childhood have for education?
- How do we know what learners know?
- How do learners negotiate the transition between the different phases of education?
- How best can children learn the knowledge we believe should be taught?
- What is a teacher?
- How do teachers learn?
- How do we understand learners, their minds, identity and development?

And in *Knowledge, Values and Educational Policy*, we ask:

- What are schools and what are they for?
- What knowledge should schools teach?
- How are learners different from each other and how are groups of learners different from one another, in terms of social class, gender, ethnicity, and disability?
- What influence does educational policy have on improving schools?
- What influence does research have on our understanding of education and schooling?

These questions are designed to provide a framework for reflection; it is not exhaustive but it attempts to provide what we consider the bedrock questions for educationists. There is one obvious omission and that is values: education always presupposes values. These values are implicit in the systems of education within which we work and in our own practices. In relation to systems of education Allan Bloom (1997, pp. 498–9) makes the point that:

> Every education system has a moral goal that it tries to attain. It wants to produce a certain kind of human being. This intention is more or less explicit, more or less a result of reflection; but even the neutral subjects, like reading, writing and arithmetic, take their place in their vision of the educated person ... Always important is the political regime, which needs citizens who are in accord with its fundamental principles.

These remarks identify why education is seen as so central to modern societies and so controversial. Educational systems make certain assumptions about the nature of the society, human nature and how it develops, and how education can help to foster the dispositions and skills that are considered desirable. Currently, much of the focus in education is on what Grubb and Lazerson (2006) call 'the Educational Gospel', that is, the view that the fundamental task of education is to provide the economic skills for future workers. While some of the issues relating to this question are addressed in the section on 'Learning across boundaries' in *Knowledge, Values and Educational Policy*, it will be clear from other sections in the two companion volumes that education is about much more than just the 'delivery' of workers into the labour market.

The values of an educational system are not always consistent with the practitioners within it, and many teachers reject the idea that their fundamental purpose is to make young people 'fit' for the economy at the expense of aims of individual well-being or social citizenship; this can cause conflicts which raise questions about the purposes of education and the role of the teacher. Here questions about the influence of globalisation and economic competitiveness loom large in policy makers' justifications for educational change.

But if values are caught up in these issues then so is power. Education is often portrayed as a technical matter in which if practice was only improved so many more students could pass their exams. But we know that some groups in society are systematically disadvantaged by education: the progressive expansion of educational systems has not consistently addressed the issues of unequal power and inequality of outcomes in education. In this volume we look at the theoretical and practical issues involved in such inequalities of power in relation to education, asking what progress teachers can make to help redress the problems of inequality they confront. While education may be part of the problem, the asymmetries of power often have their sources in the wider society and in the role of the state; but that insight does not help the teacher on Monday morning[1] when she has to confront the hopelessness and lack of faith that children bring to school as the consequences of inequality.

If education systems presuppose a view of human nature and how it can be changed and developed, then the same is true of the theories and practices of learning. Various theories or approaches to learning have been adopted by state education systems since their inception. This book largely focuses on sociocultural theories of learning, in part because they are assuming an increasingly important position in understanding how children learn. Indeed, learning itself has now taken a central position in education, because where once learners were seen as passive recipients of knowledge now it is recognised that students and teachers are active in the construction of what they learn and the way they come to understand knowledge. This view is consistent with the developing individualisation of society – that is, as individuals break away from established social rules and conventions so they have the possibility of becoming more active in the construction of their lives. But there is also a cultural element to this theory in that culture may be understood as a repository of tools and understandings which, once acquired by individuals, enable new forms of engagement with the world. Access to these cultural tools (words, machines, theories and so on) may be seen as the primary function of schooling. We do not construct knowledge and understanding from some kind of epistemological 'Year 0': rather, we use our cultural historical legacies as the means of moving beyond our immediate experience of the world. Such a social cultural or cultural historical argument is witnessed in many of the chapters in this book. We have asked contributors to be clear about the assumptions which underpin their chapters. This is of particular importance at a time when it appears as if 'we are all sociocultural theorists now'. As ever, underneath this one 'catch-all' descriptor there lies a myriad of different positions.

There have been recent attempts to reduce the professionalism of teachers to that of advanced technicians. For example, in England it can be argued that the state has mandated a particular theory of learning centred on testing and accountability. Under such a system the values and ends of education are set by the state and there is little need for the kind of intellectual and professional reflection that this book encourages. However, state-mandated policies that have used business models as their guide do not have a history of success (Callahan, 1962), and even as we write it seems clear that this model is now under threat.

The questions raised above can only be addressed if we make fundamental assumptions about human nature, learners and the role of institutions such as education. But if we are to achieve coherent and consistent views about these assumptions and how they relate to one another we need to embrace the key theories that seek to understand and explain how education 'works': that is, how views of the learner, pedagogy and schools interact to produce students' identities and outcomes.

There are many different ways in which the idea of a 'theory' can be understood. But the list of questions above provides a good starting point for understanding how we are using the concept. What theories in education do is take some of these questions and show how they can be addressed through a coherent view or perspective. Indeed, at the heart of a well-formed theory lies a world-view as to the role of education in society and the way individuals best learn. For example, there are many theories of learning, each taking a quite different view of human nature. In the work of the celebrated behaviourist B.F. Skinner, human beings were assumed to have no free will but rather learned through a system of environmental stimuli and responses. In his novel *Walden II* he imagined how a utopia could be built from his theory. In contrast, sociocultural theory sees individuals as a product of their history and culture and argues that learning is about building on the engagement with both. In this context human beings are active in the construction of their learning in ways that would have been totally rejected by Skinner. To take a different example, the idea of the Education Gospel assumes that schools are primarily there to socialise students into the world of paid work and to be provide them with the associated skills. But such a view takes no account of the nature of paid work, whether it is exploitative of either individuals or the environment, and it raises questions about whether a focus on paid work precludes the development of critical perspectives that might challenge such a view of schooling.

In contrast to the ambitions of natural scientists, who are seeking a unified theory of everything to explain the origins of the universe, there is no one theory that can provide a full or indeed convincing account of the very many elements that comprise education: it is just too complex for that. Rather, the fundamental task we as educators have to confront is to develop theories in the particular area that is of interest to us, compare them to others and make judgements as to which theories appear the most plausible. Theories typically are in competition with one another. To take the example of behaviourism and sociocultural theory, they make fundamentally different assumptions about human nature. Behaviourism sees human beings as fundamentally passive, determined by the putative laws of stimulus and response. In contrast sociocultural theories see human beings as active but within the context of a particular moment in history. Equally, theories that see schools as fundamentally having an economic function of providing individuals with the skills and outlook to be employable will be quite different from those that argue that such theories uncritically reproduce existing inequalities and forms of exploitation.

In looking at the theories and perspectives adopted in these two companion volumes it will be apparent that theories have different roles. In particular:

- They can guide practice by providing insights, challenging our preconceptions and provoking us to think about education in different ways.
- They can provide explanations.

It would be hoped that we would start by looking at the most plausible explanations for those aspects of education that we are interested in and use those as a basis for guiding our practice, whether as teachers, researchers or policy makers.

How then do we choose which theories to work with? And how do we know which is the best theory in explaining educational relationships at any given moment? These are rather different but related questions. We may choose theories because they provide the best explanations at any given moment, but they may not always give us the insights and the ways of thinking about educational problems that we personally need. In these cases we may choose theories on the basis of our personal view of the world and our values. However, when it comes to competing explanations such as those between different conceptions of learning then there are several questions that we can ask and they centre on the question of how well-formed an explanatory theory is. These include:

- Does the theory provide a particular world-view as to the educational relationships we are interested in explaining?
- How plausible are its fundamental assumptions as regards human nature, society and education?
- Does it give rise to claims that can be empirically researched and tested?
- What is the evidential basis for the theory?
- What are the value implications of holding this theory?

In making judgements about theories, all these questions come into play. Empirical evidence is important, but in studying something as complex as education it is not always clear that the empirical evidence will provide a decisive test of a theory's plausibility, especially in social contexts different from where the theory was originally tested. Therefore, other factors need to be considered, such as the fundamental assumptions a theory makes and the value implications. To return to B.F. Skinner's theory of behaviourism, one of the reasons why it has been treated with scepticism is that it assumes human beings have no free will, with the value implication that they should be treated in a rather paternalistic way in which the environment for their learning is highly structured.

Of course, there are now many computer-based learning programmes that have incorporated elements of Skinner's theory which their proponents will claim are successful – in which case the view of human nature and the value position taken need to be weighed against the empirical evidence. Of course a competing theory may be able to provide a better explanation for the same learning strategies and practices. It is for these reasons that educational issues will always be a matter of debate and analysis.

The structure of the two volumes

Any critical analysis in education will need to take on board the account of theory and its uses that we have given. When reading the chapters in these two volumes, use the questions that we have raised as a guide to understanding and evaluating them.

Educational Theories, Cultures and Learning is divided into three sections. Section 1 presents chapters on the theme of how education is understood in different cultures. The primary purpose of this section is to raise questions about the assumptions we make about education in our own cultures. We often assume that education and our experience are simply a given, that it can be no other way. But the moment we see that education can be understood quite differently a fundamental challenge is posed to the taken-for-granted assumptions we often make about it. In Section 2, the chapters deal with the theories and related assumptions we make about learners and students and how we think about them. Here, readers will find, for example, contrasting chapters on the role of neuroscience in understanding learners and how children are socially constructed. Section 3 looks more explicitly at how we can understand the principal actors in education – learners and teachers.

Knowledge, Values and Educational Policy is divided into five sections. Section 1 asks fundamental questions about what schools are for and what should be taught in them. There are many ways of approaching such questions, and here philosophical, psychological and sociological theories are brought to bear. Section 2 presents chapters on one of the newest areas of interest: learning across boundaries. The more learning is seen not only as the preserve of education but as an activity which is as important at work or in the home the more the question of how we might learn across boundaries assumes significance. Section 3 examines issues of diversity and equity. One of the best-documented facts about outcomes of education is that they are unequal in relation to social class, gender, ethnicity and disability. Here there are two issues: why do these patterns of inequality exist, and how can they best be addressed? The chapters in this section take a range of perspectives on these issues from the global trends identified by Raz Rassool through to the more specific questions of pedagogy identified by Kris Gutierrez and Barbara Rogoff. Section 4 locates these issues in terms of policies and practices within school. This section presents a range of conflicting perspectives on the nature of policy and its effects on school. On the one hand, David Hopkins takes the view that government policies provide the levers for school improvement or have done up to a point, whereas Harry Torrance argues the opposing case, while Vivianne Robinson puzzles as to why policies fail. Andrew Stables does not consider schools to be the kind of institution to which policy levers of the kind championed by David Hopkins are applicable. Finally, Section 5 presents a series of reflections on the importance of theory for guiding educational practice and for developing research in education.

These two companion volumes can be seen as an aid to a personal and moral professional journey; it is hoped that they will provide a guide to reflection on the route to be taken.

Note

1   The idea of what teachers should do on Monday morning is taken from Paul Willis (1977). For a discussion of these issues see Lauder *et al.* (2006).

References

Bloom, A. (1997) 'On virtue (Introduction to *The Closing of the American Mind*)', in Halsey, A.H., Lauder, H., Brown, P. and Stuart Wells, A., *Education, Culture, Economy and Society*, Oxford, Oxford University Press.

Callahan, R. (1962) *Education and the Cult of Efficiency*, Chicago, University of Chicago Press.

Grubb, N. and Lazerson, M. (2006) 'The globalization of rhetoric and practice: the educational gospel and vocationalism', in Lauder, H., Brown, P., Dillabough, J.-A. and Halsey, A.H. (eds), *Education, Globalization and Social Change*, Oxford, Oxford University Press.

Lauder, H., Brown, P., Dillabough, J.-A., and Halsey, A.H. (eds) (2006) *Education, Globalization and Social Change*, Oxford, Oxford University Press.

Willis, P. (1977) *Learning to Labour*, Farnborough, Saxon House.

Section 1

How education is understood in different cultures

Introduction

Hugh Lauder

(Cartoon by Ros Asquith)

This section raises fundamental questions about the nature of education and educational change. Developing a comparative understanding of the similarities and differences in education, teaching and the curriculum in national cultures enables us to reflect upon the assumptions we make about:

- the purposes of education;
- the nature of teaching and the curriculum;
- the way we think about the learner;
- the global forces that bring about convergence and divergences in educational systems.

By examining the assumptions we make about education we can take a first step in asking whether our educational practices are justified. This is a first step because it enables us to be reflective and critical about our role as educators. The second step is to ask whether there are better ways of engaging in teaching and learning. But this step needs to be informed by the forms of thought that structure our understanding as well as the political, social and economic interests that influence our practice.

A consideration of these factors enables us to identify not only the assumptions we make about our educational practices but the limits and possibilities for change.

Alexander's chapter exemplifies these issues. He is concerned with pedagogy, by which he means not only the acts of teaching but also the thinking behind the decisions we make in teaching and our justifications for them. Pedagogy, in his view, is an intellectual as well as technical practice. His paper opens by asking why it is that the question of a comparative pedagogy has been ignored in Britain, although the neglect of a sophisticated comparative pedagogy is largely true of all Anglo-Saxon intellectual educational traditions. In part, the answer to this question is that an adequate framework for understanding pedagogy has not previously been developed. However, in this paper Alexander develops a model for the comparative analysis of pedagogy which he argues can be seen as being influenced by three levels: the classroom; the educational system and related policies; and culture and the self – the role played by values and the way they influence the construction of teaching acts.

As well as a model for comparative analysis this framework allows teachers to think through the assumptions and justifications they make in their own practice. Here the questions that this model prompts are:

- What view of the learner do I take?
- How does education relate to society?
- Which levels are most important in influencing my practice?

The paper by Roger Dale raises the equally profound question of whether there are aspects of globalisation and the modern age (modernity) which create pressure towards convergence in pedagogy and the curriculum in developed and developing nations. Alexander's comparative analysis points in the direction of significant differences in the assumptions underlying pedagogy in different countries, but that does not mean that there are forces external to the views of teachers which are influencing the nature and structure of pedagogy. Dale seeks to tease out the various factors that make for convergence and divergence by critically examining a leading theory on education and globalisation, 'world polity' theory, which explains convergence on the basis of a common set of universal values, drawing on Western modernity, that now permeate education systems at a global level. The central argument of this theory is that there is a supranational ideology of modernity which has determined similarities in the curriculum across most countries. As Dale notes, 'At the core of [this ideology] lies "rational" discourse on how the socialisation of children in various subject areas is linked to the self-realisation of the individual and, ultimately, to the construction of an ideal society.'

The significance of this view is that it addresses one of the fundamental questions in education: what should be taught? It is a question that resurfaces in many of the papers in this book (see Young and Nash). But the answer given by the world polity theorists is paradoxical: on the one hand they argue that the curriculum is imposed by this modernist ideology, irrespective of whether it actually addresses a country's needs, while on the other they see it as part of a rational discourse that can enable self-realisation, which presupposes a degree of individual freedom.

Anna Sfard's paper comes at the fundamental questions concerning education from a different angle. Her paper is concerned with the way we think and talk about education. She notes that much of our discussion about education is impregnated with metaphors. For example, she notes three uses of metaphorical language that we typically take for granted in education: the idea that students *construct* their knowledge, that they may have *learning disabilities* and that, as teachers, we seek to *give* students better *access* to knowledge. There are more subtle examples, the more obvious being associated with metaphors of growth. We think of children growing not only physically but psychologically and talk about them reaching their potential, as if there is some kind of ideal end state that we are aiming for. Why do we use metaphors? Her answer is that it enables us to develop knowledge but they also shape our thinking and our actions. The problem is one of judging how apt and thereby useful any given metaphor in education may be. In turn if our knowledge claims are impregnated with metaphors then how certain are our knowledge claims about pedagogy? Different answers are given in chapters of this book. For example, David Hopkins is confident that the system of pedagogy and assessment used in England has created improvements in educational outcomes as measured by tests. By the same token, similar state-mandated pedagogies in the United States may be considered to have also created improvements. But the chapters by Torrance and Robinson, in different ways, contest the basis for such confidence.

What is clear from these chapters is that education, and pedagogy in particular, is an irreducibly intellectual project. It requires comparative analysis, which in turn can illuminate philosophical and theoretical insights across the disciplines of psychology and sociology and related empirical research. In these respects the idea that pedagogy is just about teaching techniques, a view that is taken by some policy-makers, is fundamentally misguided as the issues raised by the chapters in this book demonstrate.

1.1 Pedagogy, culture and the power of comparison

Robin Alexander

Introduction

This chapter asks why pedagogy, which is at the heart of the educational enterprise, has been largely ignored in British comparative enquiry. Pedagogy is defined as 'the observable act of teaching, together with its attendant discourse of educational theories, values, evidence and justifications'. This definition opens the window to a comparative analysis which focuses on pedagogy as ideas which *enable* teaching in the classroom, *formalise* it as policy and *locate* it in culture. By this process a genuine comparative analysis of pedagogy is made possible which can distinguish the universal in pedagogy – its various *acts*, *frames* and *form* – from the culturally specific ways that these are applied. For teachers, one advantage of such an approach is that it enables critical reflection on what may seem to them as the 'natural' or given way of teaching. It also brings to the fore the sometimes unexamined values by which their practice is informed.

The neglect of pedagogy in comparative enquiry

Pedagogy is the most startlingly prominent of the educational themes that British comparativists have ignored. In the millennial issue of the UK journal *Comparative Education*, Little noted just 6.1 per cent of the journal's articles between 1977 and 1998 dealt with 'curricular content and the learner's experience' as compared with nearly 31 per cent on themes such as educational reform and development (Little, 2000, p. 283); Cowen asserted that 'we are nowhere near coming fully to grips with the themes of curriculum, pedagogic styles and evaluation as powerful message systems which form identities in specific educational sites' (Cowen, 2000, p. 340); and Broadfoot argued that future comparative studies of education should place much greater emphasis 'on the process of learning itself rather than, as at present, on the organisation and provision of education' (Broadfoot, 2000, p. 368).

If the omission is so obvious, one might ask why comparativists have not remedied it. There may be a simple practical explanation. Policy analysis, especially when it is grounded in documentation rather than fieldwork, is a cheaper, speedier and altogether more comfortable option than classroom research. As a less uncharitable possibility, but echoing Brian Simon's 'Why no pedagogy in England?' (Simon, 1981), we might suggest that a country without an indigenous 'science of teaching' is hardly likely to nurture pedagogical comparison: cherry-picking and policy borrowing maybe, but not serious comparative enquiry (Alexander, 1996).

Or perhaps pedagogy is one of those aspects of comparative education which demands expertise over and above knowledge of the countries compared, their cultures, systems and policies. I rather think it is, especially given the condition which Simon identified. One can hardly study comparative law or literature without knowing at least as much about law or literature as about the countries and cultures involved and about the business of making comparisons; the same goes for comparative education. Pedagogy is a complex field of practice, theory and research in its own right. The challenge of comparative pedagogy is to marry the study of education elsewhere with the study of teaching and learning in a way that respects both of these fields of enquiry yet also creates something which is more than the sum of their parts.

New territories, but old maps

Little's framework for mapping the literature of comparative education, referred to above, differentiated *context* (the country or countries studied), *content* (a list of thirteen possible themes), and *comparison* (the number of countries compared). Trying to place my *Culture and Pedagogy* (Alexander, 2001) within this framework underlines pedagogy's marginal status in mainstream comparative discourse. This study used documentary, interview, observational, video and photographic data collected at the levels of system, school and classroom. The study's 'context' was England, France, India, Russia and the United States. Its 'comparison' was across five countries (a rarity). However, its 'content' straddled at least six of Little's thirteen themes without sitting comfortably within any of them, and the educational phase with which it dealt – primary education – did not appear at all in that framework (nor, strikingly, did the terms 'teaching' or 'learning', let alone 'culture' or 'pedagogy').

There is a further reason why the content of this research maps so imperfectly onto Little's framework: the latter does not accommodate studies that cross the boundaries of macro and micro. *Culture and Pedagogy* – as the title suggests – acknowledges Sadler's hoary maxim that 'the things outside the school matter more than the things inside ... and govern and interpret the things inside' (Sadler, 1900), yet Little's framework implies the need for singularity – national *or* local, policy *or* practice, the system *or* the classroom – rather than dialectic. In this respect, comparativists may be somewhat behind the larger social science game, in which the relationship between social structure, culture and human agency has been 'at the heart of sociological theorising' for well over a century (Archer, 2000, p. 1).

Pedagogy does not begin and end in the classroom. It is comprehended only once one locates practice within the concentric circles of local and national, and of classroom, school, system and state, and only if one steers constantly back and forth between these, exploring the way in which what teachers and students do in classrooms reflects the values of the wider society.

That was one of the challenges which *Culture and Pedagogy* sought to address. Another was to engage with the interface between present and past, to enact the principle that if one is to understand anything about education elsewhere one's perspective should be informed by history. So while the comparative journey in *Culture and Pedagogy* culminates in an examination of teacher–pupil discourse – for language is at once a powerful tool of human learning and the quintessential expression of culture and identity – it starts with accounts of the historical roots and developments of primary education in each of the five countries, paying particular attention to the emergence of those core and abiding values, traditions and habits which shape, enable and constrain pedagogical development.

Defining pedagogy: the shifting sands of educational terminology

So far a definition of pedagogy has been implied. It is time to be more explicit, though only after sounding a warning about terminology, for one of the values of comparativism is that it alerts one to the way that the apparently bedrock terms in educational discourse are nothing of the sort.

Thus it may well matter, in the context of the strong investment in citizenship which is part of French public education, that *éduquer* means to bring up as well as formally to educate and that *bien éduqué* means well brought-up or well-mannered rather than well schooled ('educate' in English has both senses too, but the latter now predominates); or that the root of the Russian word for education, *obrazovanie*, means 'form' or 'image' rather than, as in our Latinate version, a 'leading out'; or that *obrazovanie* is inseparable from *vospitanie*, an idea which has no equivalent in English because it combines personal development, private and public morality, and civic commitment, while in England these tend to be treated as separate and even conflicting domains; or that *obuchenie*, which is usually translated as teacher-led 'instruction,' signals learning as well as teaching. It is almost certainly significant that in English (and American) education 'development' is viewed as a physiological and psychological process which takes place independently of formal schooling whereas Russian teachers define 'development' transitively, as a task which requires their active intervention: in the one context development is 'natural' while in the other it is more akin to acculturation. Similarly, in the Anglo-American tradition the most able child is defined as the one with the greatest potential, while in Russia's Soviet pedagogical legacy it is the least able, because he/she has furthest to travel towards goals which are held to be common for all children (Muckle, 1988; Alexander, 2001, pp. 368–70).

Such terms hint at more than the comparativist's need to be sensitive to the problems of language and translation. They also subtly align the educational agenda along culturally distinctive lines even before one starts investigating the detail of policy and practice. In the cases exemplified above, both *l'éducation* and *vospitanie* inject suggestions of public morality and the common good into the discourse in ways which subliminally influence the recurring discussions about school goals and curricula in France and Russia; while the Russian notions of 'potential' and 'development' each imply – and indeed impose – strong teacher agency and responsibility in a way which their more passive and individualistic English and American connotations do not. Thus, the popular Anglo-American notion of teacher as 'facilitator' would make little headway in those continental European countries where school learning without direct teacher intervention and instruction is inconceivable.

The consciousness intimated here also implies a model of pedagogy, and a course for comparative pedagogical analysis, which are as far removed as they can be from the polarising of 'teacher-centred' (or 'subject-centred') and 'child-centred' teaching which too often remains the stock-in-trade of such accounts of pedagogy as are available in the comparative literature, for this polarity is specific to certain cultures only (Alexander, 2006). Perhaps the most damaging residue of this sort of thinking can still be found in the reports of those international development agencies which commend Western 'child-centred' pedagogy to non-Western governments without regard for local cultural and educational circumstances (or indeed for recent advances in the psychology of learning and teaching, or for the findings of classroom research).

That touch of waspishness apart, we would do well to be no less cautious about another boundary problem here. In the literature on culturally-located views and models of teaching, generalised 'Asian', 'Pacific Rim', 'Western', 'non-Western' and 'European' 'models' of teaching and learning feature prominently and confidently (Reynolds and Farrell, 1996; Stevenson and Stigler, 1992; Clarke, 2001). If we recognise that the geographical and cultural coverage of 'Asian' is too broad to have descriptive validity for the analysis of teaching, we should be no less aware of the hegemonic overtones of 'Western'. Does 'Western' encompass South as well as North America? Does it include some European countries while excluding others? With its implied validation of a particular world-view, tellingly captured since 2003 in the Old/New Europe name-calling of the Bush administration, 'Western' may well exacerbate rather than supplant the pedagogy of opposition, fuelling a self-righteous occidentalism every bit as pernicious as Said's orientalism (Said, 1979).

As our core educational concept, 'pedagogy' lies linguistically and culturally on sands at least as treacherous as these. In the Anglo-American tradition, pedagogy is subsidiary to curriculum, sometimes implying little more than 'teaching method'. 'Curriculum' itself has both a broad sense (everything that a school does) and a narrow one (what is formally required to be taught) which comes closer to continental European 'didactics' without capturing the sense in *la didactique* or *die Didaktik* of a quasi-science comprising subject knowledge and the principles by which it is imparted. Curriculum is more prominent in educational discourse in systems where it is contested, less where it is imposed or accepted as a given. In the central European tradition, it is the other way round: pedagogy moves centre-stage and frames everything else, including curriculum and didactics (Alexander, 2001, pp. 540–56; Moon, 1998).

Because the range of meanings attaching to pedagogy varies so much in English – quite apart from differences between English and other languages – we have to be stipulative, and in a way which allows us to use the term for comparative analysis. I prefer to eschew the greater ambiguities of 'curriculum' and the resulting tendency to downgrade pedagogy, and use the latter term to encompass the larger field. I distinguish pedagogy as *discourse* from teaching as *act*, yet I make them inseparable. Pedagogy, then, encompasses both the act of teaching and its contingent theories and debates. Pedagogy is the discourse with which one needs to engage in order both to teach intelligently and make sense of teaching – for discourse and act are interdependent.

A *comparative* pedagogy takes this discourse not one stage but several stages further. It identifies, explores and explains pedagogical similarities and differences across designated units of comparison such as nation states. It thereby exploits opportunities which only proper comparison can provide: teasing out what is universal in pedagogy from what is culturally or geographically specific; informing the development of pedagogic theory; and extending the vocabulary and repertoire of pedagogic practice.

Conditions and frameworks for a comparative pedagogy

We can now propose three conditions for a comparative pedagogy. First, it should incorporate a defensible rationale and methodology for comparing across sites, cultures, nations and/or regions. Second, it should combine procedures for studying teaching empirically with ways of accessing the values, ideas and debates which inform and explain it. Third, because these values, ideas and debates are part of a wider educational discourse and – typically – are located in the context of public national education systems as well as schools and classrooms, a comparative pedagogy should access these different levels, contexts and constituencies and examine how they relate to each other and inform both the discourse of pedagogy and the act of teaching.

The first condition is self-evident and applies to all international comparison, so I say no more about it. About the second and third conditions I need to say rather more.

If pedagogy is shaped by national culture and history, and by the migration of ideas and practices across national boundaries, as by more immediate practical exigencies and constraints such as policy and resources, is it possible to postulate a model of pedagogy, and a framework for studying it, which both accommodates its many forms and variations and rises above the constraints of value and circumstance? Can we devise an analytical model that will serve the needs of the researcher or student in any context? This was the challenge we had to take up in the *Culture and Pedagogy* project, for we needed to make sense of disparate classroom data in a way which showed no obvious bias towards particular, culturally specific accounts of learning and teaching.

The resulting framework has three parts. The first deals with the observable act of teaching; the second with the ideas that inform it; the third with the macro–micro relationship that links classroom transaction to national policy via the curriculum. We start, though, with our definition, consolidated:

> Pedagogy is the observable act of teaching together with its attendant discourse of educational theories, values, evidence and justifications. It is what one needs to know, and the skills one needs to command, in order to make and justify the many different kinds of decisions of which teaching is constituted.

With this our colours are nailed firmly to the international mast. In Britain, if the word is used at all, 'pedagogy' signals merely the teaching act, and the act's informing ideas stand in an at best uneasy relationship to it, as so much 'theory' to be 'applied' (or not). But, unfortunately for the theory/practice dualists, the theory is there whether they like it or not, unless of course they are prepared to claim that teaching is a mindless activity. The task is to explicate the theory, which in teaching we know to be a complex amalgam of sedimented experience, personal values and beliefs, re-interpretations of published research, and policy more or less dutifully enacted.

Pedagogy as practice

Years ago the anthropologist Edmund Leach (1964) argued that the more complex the model, the less likely it is to be useful. With his warning in mind, we start by reducing teaching to its barest essentials:

> Teaching, in any setting, is the act of using method x to enable students to learn y.

In so skeletal a form the proposition is difficult to contest, and if this is so we extract from it two no less basic questions to steer empirical enquiry:

> What are students expected to learn?

> What method does the teacher use to ensure that they do so?

'Method' needs to be unpacked if it is to be useful as an analytical category which can cross the boundaries of space and time. Any teaching method combines *tasks*, *activities*, *interactions* and *judgements*. Their function is represented by four further questions:

> In a given teaching session or unit what *learning tasks* do students encounter?

What *activities* do they undertake in order to address these learning tasks?

Through what *interactions* does the teacher present, organise and sustain the learning tasks and activities?

By what means, and on the basis of what criteria, does the teacher reach *judgements* about the nature and level of the tasks and activities which each student shall undertake (*differentiation*), and the kinds of learning which students achieve (*assessment*)?

Task, activity, interaction and judgement are the building blocks of teaching. However, as they stand they lack the wherewithal for coherence and meaning. To our first proposition, therefore, we must add a second. This unpacks 'in any setting', the remaining phrase in our the first proposition:

Teaching has structure and form; it is situated in, and governed by, space, time and patterns of pupil organisation; and it is undertaken for a purpose.

Structure and *form* in teaching are most clearly and distinctively manifested in the *lesson*. Lessons and their constituent teaching acts are framed and governed by *time*, by *space* (the way the classroom is disposed, organised and resourced) and by the chosen forms of *student organisation* (whole class, small group or individual).

But teaching is framed conceptually and ethically, as well as temporally and spatially. A lesson is part of a larger *curriculum* embodying purposes and values, and reflecting assumptions about what knowledge and understanding are of most worth to the individual and to society. This is part of the force of 'teaching ... is undertaken for a purpose'.

One element remains. Teaching is located in the larger cultural context but students and teachers also create their own microculture. They develop procedures for regulating classroom relationships and behaviour, the equivalent of law, custom, and public morality in civil society. This element we define as *routine, rule and ritual*.

The complete teaching framework (discussed in greater detail in Alexander, 2001, pp. 320–5) is shown in Figure 1.1.1. The elements are grouped under the headings of *frame*, *form* and *act*. The core acts of teaching (task, activity, interaction and judgement) are framed by classroom organisation ('space'), pupil organisation, time and curriculum, and by classroom routines, rules and rituals. They are given form in the lesson or teaching session.

Choices then have to be made about how one analyses each of the elements. These dictate further questions about analytical categories, research methods and technologies which for reasons of space cannot be addressed here. The point at issue is conceptual rather than technical: it concerns not the relative advantages of, say, systematic observation using pre-coded interaction categories to produce quantifiable data and the use of transcripts to sustain close-grained qualitative analysis of discourse, but the viability of this as a framework for researching teaching in any context and by any means.

Pedagogy as ideas

The second part of our framework attends to the ideas, values and beliefs by which the act of teaching is informed and justified. These can be grouped into three domains, as shown in Figure 1.1.2. Private assumptions and beliefs about teaching are not distinguished here from public accounts of the kind which teachers meet while being trained, for all are a

Frame	Form	Act
Space		Task
Pupil organisation		Activity
Time	Lesson	
Curriculum		Interaction
Routine, rule and ritual		Judgement

Figure 1.1.1 A generic model of teaching
(Source: Alexander, 2001, p. 325.)

kind of theory. The object here is not to differentiate theory which is public or private, espoused or in use (Argyris and Schön, 1974) but the themes with which such theories deal. Pedagogy has at its core ideas about learners, learning and teaching, and these are shaped and modified by context, policy and culture. Where the first domain *enables* teaching and the second *formalises* and *legitimates* it by reference to policy and infrastructure, the third domain *locates* it – and children themselves – in time, place and the social world, and anchors it firmly to the questions of human identity and social purpose without which teaching makes little sense. Such ideas mark the transition from teaching to education.

Macro and micro

The element in the framework in Figure 1.1.1 which most obviously and formally links macro with micro is the curriculum. In most systems curriculum is centrally prescribed, either at national level or, as in a federal and decentralised system like the United States, at the levels of state and school district. In few public education systems is control of the curriculum vested solely in the school.

In fact, the curriculum is probably best viewed as a series of *translations, transpositions* and *transformations* from its initial status as a set of formal requirements. At the beginning of this process of metamorphosis is the national or state curriculum. At its end is the array of understandings, in respect of the specified curriculum goals and domains, which the student acquires as a result of his or her classroom activities and encounters. In between is a succession of shifts, sometimes bold, sometimes slight, as curriculum moves from specification to transaction, and as teachers and students interpret, modify and add to the meanings which it embodies. Sometimes the change may be slight, as when a school takes a required syllabus or programme of study and maps it onto the timetable. This we might call a *translation*. Then a school or teacher may adjust the nomenclature and move parts of one curriculum domain into another to effect a *transposition*, which then leads to a sequence of lesson plans. But the real change, the *transformation*, comes when the curriculum passes from document into action and is broken down into learning tasks and activities and expressed and negotiated as teacher–student interactions and transactions.

Classroom level: ideas which enable *teaching*

- Students   characteristics, development, motivation, needs, differences.
- Learning   nature, facilitation, achievement and assessment.
- Teaching   nature, scope, planning, execution and evaluation.
- Curriculum   ways of knowing, doing, creating, investigating and making sense.

System/policy level: ideas which formalise *and* legitimate *teaching*

- School   e.g. infrastructure, staffing, training.
- Curriculum   e.g. aims, content.
- Assessment   e.g. formal tests, qualifications, entry requirements.
- Other policies   e.g. teacher recruitment and training, equity and inclusion.

Cultural/societal level: ideas which locate *teaching*

- Culture   the collective ideas, values, customs and relationships which inform and shape a society's view of itself, of the world and of education.
- Self   what it is to be a person; how identity is acquired.

Figure 1.1.2 Pedagogy as ideas (theories, values, beliefs and justifications) (Source: Adapted from Alexander, 2004, pp. 11–12.)

However faithful to government, state or school requirements a teacher remains, teaching is always an act of curriculum transformation. In this sense, therefore, curriculum is a 'framing' component of the act of teaching, as suggested by figure 1.1.1, only before it is transformed into task, activity, interaction, discourse and outcome. From that point on it becomes inseparable from each of these. In the classroom, curriculum *is* task, activity, inter-action and discourse, and they are curriculum.

Figure 1.1.3 schematises this process, and ties it into the families of 'frame', 'form' and 'act' from the model of teaching in Figure 1.1.1. Together with Figure 1.1.2, the frame-works provide a basis for constructing a reasonably comprehensive empirical account of pedagogy at the level of action, and for engaging with the attendant discourses.

Of course, the macro–micro relationship is about much more than state–school curric-ulum transmission or transformation. For a start, the process is complicated by the existence of more levels than bipolar formulations like 'macro–micro' or 'centralisation–decentralisa-tion' allow. Regional and local tiers of government have their own designated powers, or strive to compensate for their lack of these by exploiting their closeness to the action, and local agency manifests itself in many other guises, both formal and informal, beyond the governmental and administrative. In the *Five Cultures* data, the importance of these inter-mediate levels and agencies provided a corrective to Margaret Archer's classic account of the development of state education systems (Archer, 1979). A proper explanatory account of pedagogical discourse needs to engage with this more complex arena of control and action if it is to move out of the straitjacket of linear models of teaching as policy-enactment and education as unmodified cultural transmission. Here the work of Giroux (1983) and Apple (1995) provides the necessary moderation to the stricter reproductionist line taken by Bowles and Gintis (1976) or Bourdieu and Passeron (1990).

Specification	National, state or local curriculum	1	
Translation	School curriculum	2	**Frame**
Transposition	Class curriculum and timetable	3	
	Lesson plan	4	
Transformation	Lesson	5	**Form**
	Task	6	
	Activity	7	**Act**
	Interaction	8	
	Assessment	9	

Figure 1.1.3 Curriculum metamorphosis
(Source: Adapted from Alexander, 2001, p. 552.)

Such an account also needs to treat the somewhat mechanistic concept of 'levels' itself with a certain caution, for once we view pedagogic practice through the profoundly important lens of values we find – as Archer shows in her later work (1989) – that the relationship between structure, culture and (pedagogic) agency is more complex still.

Values

Values, then, spill out untidily at every point in the analysis of pedagogy, and it is one of the abiding weaknesses of much mainstream research on teaching that it tends to play down their significance in shaping and explaining observable practice. Latterly, the idea of 'value-free' teaching has been given a powerful boost by the endorsement by several Anglophone governments of school effectiveness research (which reduces teaching to technique and culture to one not particularly important 'factor' among many) and by its adoption, across the full spectrum of public policy, of the crudely utilitarian criterion, 'what works'. Teaching is an intentional and moral activity: it is undertaken for a purpose and is validated by reference to educational goals and social principles as well as to operational efficacy. In any culture it requires attention to a range of considerations and imperatives: pragmatic, certainly, but also empirical, ethical and conceptual (Alexander, 1997, pp. 267–87).

Clearly, a value-sanitised pedagogy makes as little sense as culture-free comparative enquiry. Yet values can all too easily be neglected, and the problem may reflect the accident of technique rather than conscious design. Thus, an account of classroom interaction in Kenyan primary schools (Ackers and Hardman, 2001) uses Sinclair and Coulthard's (1992) discourse analysis system, which reduces spoken discourse to a hierarchy of ranks, transactions, moves and acts with little regard to its meaning and none to its sociolinguistic context. The Kenyan study is illuminating, yet if the chosen procedure is problematic in linguistic terms, it may be doubly so in a comparative study of teachers in one country undertaken by researchers from another.

In the rather different setting of a seminar on the American East Coast, a participant viewed one of the *Culture and Pedagogy* lesson videotapes[1] and condemned the featured American teacher for 'wasting time' when she negotiated with her students rather than directed them. The teacher concerned was highly experienced, and perfectly capable of delivering a traditional lesson and imposing her will upon the children. But she chose not to, because her educational goals included the development of personal autonomy and choice and she believed it necessary for children to learn, the hard way if necessary, how to master time rather than have it master them. This teacher was expressing in her practice not only her private values, but also those embodied in the policies of her school, school district and state. These values should have been the seminar participant's first port of call.

The issue here was not one of simple professional competence but of how, in a culture which stands so overtly for individual freedom of action, the diverging individualities of 25 students in one classroom can be reconciled with common learning goals. For this example was but the tip of a values iceberg, a continuum in which the observed American pedagogy stood at the opposite extreme to what we observed in Russia and India. On the one hand confusion, contradiction and inconsistency in values; on the other, clarity, coherence and consistency (inside the classroom at least – what we saw on the streets of post-Soviet Russia told a different story, but then our teacher respondents were very clear that their task was to hold the line against the rising tide of lawlessness and anomie). It is this inherent cultural dissonance, as much as simple executive competence, which explains many of the startling contrasts in the practice, and in the apparent efficiency of the practice, with which such values were associated.

This example, too, may help us with our earlier asides about Sadler and cultural borrowing and lending. For perhaps it is the degree of compatibility at the level of values which sets the limits to what can be transferred at the level of practice. A pedagogy predicated on teacher authority, induction into subject disciplines, general culture and citizenship will sit uneasily, at best, with one which celebrates classroom democracy, personal knowledge, cultural pluralism, and antipathy to the apparatus of the state. And vice versa. This simple proposition, which can readily be tested in practice, eludes the policy-borrowers, who presume that 'what works' in one country will work in another. Thus until Russian education succumbed to resource starvation following the economic collapse of the mid-1990s, Russian children continued for a while to outperform those of the United States in mathematics and science, despite the massive disparity in funding between the two countries' education systems (Ruddock, 2000; World Bank, 2000). Yet in pursuit of ideology rather than educational success the World Bank and OECD dismissed Russian teaching as 'authoritarian' and 'old-fashioned' and pressed for a more 'democratic' and 'student-centred' pedagogy (World Bank, 1996; OECD, 1998).

Temporal and spatial continuities

So the explication of values is a sine qua non for a comparative pedagogy. Such analysis can reveal continuities as well as differences. Although an offspring of revolution, French public education retains features which recall its pre-revolutionary and ecclesiastical origins (Sharpe, 1997), and the conjunction of institutional secularism and individual liberty is not without its tensions, as is shown by the recurrent crises over *l'affaire du foulard* (the scarf in this case is the Muslim *hijab*, occasionally the *chador*). The more obvious Soviet trappings of Russian education have been shed, but the abiding commitment to *vospitanie*, and the emphasis in schools and classrooms on collective action and responsibility allied to unambiguous teacher authority, not to mention the methods of teaching, show the more clearly that the continuities here are Tsarist as well as Soviet. The continuities in India reach back even further, and we found at least four traditions – two of them indigenous (Brahmanic and post-Independence) and two imposed (colonialist and missionary) combining to shape contemporary primary practice in that vast and complex country (Kumar, 1991).

In England, the twin legacies of elementary school minimalism and progressive idealism offset government attempts at root-and-branch modernisation. The one still shapes school structures and curriculum priorities (and government is as much in its thrall as are teachers), while the other continues to influence professional consciousness and classroom practice. Indeed, in seeking to win over a disgruntled teaching force the UK government's post-2003 Primary National Strategy sought to soften its statist image by appealing directly to the progressivist virtues of 'enjoyment', 'creativity' and 'flexibility' in a booklet which combined large print, jolly language and pictures of smiling children (DfES, 2003; Alexander, 2004). Some saw through this ploy; many others did not.

Jerome Bruner reminds us, too, that in our pedagogical theorising

> we are still drawing rich sustenance from our more distant, pre-positivist past. Chomsky acknowledges his debt to Descartes, Piaget is inconceivable without Kant, Vygotsky without Hegel and Marx, and 'learning theory' was constructed on foundations laid by John Locke.
>
> (Bruner, 1990, pp. x–xi)

This kind of intellectual genealogy was most strongly visible in Russian pedagogy, partly because of the overall consistency of practice and partly because those whom we interviewed were themselves fully aware of the roots of their thinking; for this is a pedagogy in which – unlike in England – education theory and history are held to be important. Thus, if Russian pedagogy owes much, via Vygotsky and his disciples, to Hegel and Marx, it owes no less to a tradition of pedagogic rationality which reaches back via Ushinsky to Comenius and Francis Bacon. And it is a familiar truth that Lenin and Stalin built directly on the Tsarist legacy of political autocracy, nationalism and religious orthodoxy, thus securing fundamental continuities amidst the chaos (Lloyd, 1998; Hobsbawm, 1995). In interview, one of our Russian teachers spoke readily about the influence on her pedagogy of Vygotsky (1896–1934), Ushinsky (1824–71) and Kamenski (Comenius, 1592–1670), not to mention a host of post-Vygotskians such as Davydov, Elkonin and Leont'ev and academics at the local pedagogical university. How many British teachers have this depth of historical awareness or interest in what, beyond the immediacies of personal values, public policies and classroom circumstances, might inform their teaching?

Temporal continuities such as these shape contemporary educational practice and set limits to the character and speed of its further development, notwithstanding the ahistorical zeal of government modernisers. The spatial continuities place within our reach an important prize, that of differentiating the universal in pedagogy from the culturally specific.

Versions of teaching

Again, it is not possible to list all the cross-cultural resonances we encountered in the *Five Cultures* research. However, overarching these were six versions of teaching and three primordial values which we briefly summarise.

1   *Teaching as transmission* sees education primarily as a process of instructing children to absorb, replicate and apply basic information and skills.
2   *Teaching as initiation* sees education as the means of providing access to, and passing on from one generation to the next, the culture's stock of high-status knowledge, for example in literature, the arts, humanities and the sciences.
3   *Teaching as negotiation* reflects the Deweyan idea that teachers and students jointly create knowledge and understanding in an ostensibly democratic learning community, rather than relate to one another as authoritative source of knowledge and its passive recipient.
4   *Teaching as facilitation* guides the teacher by principles which are developmental (and, more specifically, Piagetian) rather than cultural or epistemological. The teacher respects and nurtures individual differences, and waits until children are ready to move on instead of pressing them to do so.
5   *Teaching as acceleration*, in contrast, implements the Vygotskian principle that education is planned and guided acculturation rather than facilitated 'natural' development, and indeed that the teacher seeks to outpace development rather than follow it.
6   *Teaching as technique*, finally, is relatively neutral in its stance on society, knowledge and the child. Here the important issue is the efficiency of teaching regardless of the context of values, and to that end imperatives like structure, economic use of time and space, carefully graduated tasks, regular assessment and clear feedback are more pressing than ideas such as democracy, autonomy, development or the disciplines.

The first is ubiquitous, but in the *Five Cultures* data it was most prominent in the rote learning and recitation teaching of mainstream Indian pedagogy. French classrooms provided the archetype of the second, but it also surfaced in Russia and India, and – though often under professional protest at the primary stage – in England and the United States (its more secure pedigree in English education perhaps lies with Matthew Arnold and the independent and grammar school traditions). Teachers in the United States frequently argued and sought to enact both the third and the fourth versions of teaching, often with explicit obeisance to John Dewey and Jean Piaget. Those in England, subject to the pressures of the government's national literacy and numeracy strategies, still made much of developmental readiness and facilitation though rather less of democracy.

Meanwhile, drawing explicitly on Vygotsky's maxim that 'the only good teaching is that which outpaces development', our Russian teachers illustrated the pedagogy of intervention and acceleration (5) which was diametrically opposed to facilitation and developmental readiness. At the same time, they, like teachers across a wide swathe of continental Europe, drew on much the older tradition (6) of highly structured lessons, whole class teaching, the breaking down of learning tasks into small graduated steps, and the maintenance of economy in organisation, action and the use of time and space (Comenius, 1657, pp. 312–34).

The trajectory of recent pedagogical reform shows interesting permutations on these. Thus, under the Government of India District Primary Education Programme, Indian teachers were urged to become more democratic (3) and developmental (4) (Government of India, 1998). The language of developmentalism and facilitation also found its way into policy documents in France and Russia (Ministère de l'Education Nationale, 1998; Ministry of General and Professional Education, 2000). In contrast, English teachers were being urged to emulate the continental tradition represented by (6), notably through the espousal of 'interactive whole class teaching' in the UK government's literacy and numeracy strategies (DfEE, 1998, 1999). These are deliberate acts of pedagogical importation. How far the alien can accommodate to the indigenous remains to be seen.

A distinctly continental European tradition has already been implied. The *Five Cultures* data enables the idea of broad pedagogical traditions which cut across national boundaries to be consolidated. In this research, the great cultural divide was the English Channel, not the Atlantic. There was a discernible Anglo-American nexus of pedagogical values and practices, just as there was a discernible continental European one, with Russia at one highly formalised extreme and France – more eclectic and less ritualised, though still firmly grounded in structure and *les disciplines* – at the other. India's pedagogy was both Asian and European, as its history would suggest.

Primordial values

Teachers in the five-nation study also articulated, enacted or steered an uncertain path between three versions of human relations: *individualism, community* and *collectivism*:

- *Individualism* puts self above others and personal rights before collective responsibilities. It emphasises unconstrained freedom of action and thought.
- *Community* centres on human interdependence, caring for others, sharing and collaborating.
- *Collectivism* also emphasises human interdependence, but only in so far as it serves the larger needs of society, or the state (the two are not identical), as a whole.

Within the observed classrooms, a commitment to *individualism* was manifested in intellectual or social differentiation, divergent rather than uniform learning outcomes, and a view of knowledge as personal and unique rather than imposed from above in the form of disciplines or subjects. *Community* was reflected in collaborative learning tasks, often in small groups, in 'caring and sharing' rather than competing, and in an emphasis on the affective rather than the cognitive. *Collectivism* was reflected in common knowledge, common ideals, a single curriculum for all, national culture rather than pluralism and multi-culture, and on learning together rather than in isolation or in small groups.

These values were pervasive at national, school and classroom levels. We are familiar with the contrast between the supposedly egocentric cultures of the west, with the United States as the gas-guzzling arch-villain, and the supposedly holistic, sociocentric cultures of south and east Asia. Though there is evidence to support this opposition (Shweder, 1991) it is all too easy to demonise one pole and romanticise – or orientalise – the other. But I think when it comes to pedagogy the tripartite distinction holds up, and it seems by no means accidental that so much discussion of teaching methods should have centred on the relative merits of whole class teaching, group and individual work.

In France this debate can be traced back to arguments at the start of the nineteenth century about the relative merits of *l'enseignement simultané, l'enseignement mutuel* and *l'enseignement individuel*[2] (Reboul-Scherrer, 1989). As a post-revolutionary instrument for fostering civic commitment and national identity as well as literacy, *l'enseignement simultané* won. Only now, reflecting decentralisation and the rising tide of individualism, has its hegemony begun to be questioned.

Individualism, community and collectivism are – as child, group and class – the organisational nodes of pedagogy because they are the social nodes of human relations. However, divorcing teaching as technique from the discourse of pedagogy as we so often do, we may have failed to understand that such core values and value-dissonances pervade social relations inside the classroom no less than outside it; and hence we may have failed to understand why it is that undifferentiated learning, whole class teaching and the principle of bringing the whole class along together 'fit' more successfully in many other cultures than they do in England or the United States, and why teachers in these two countries regard this pedagogical formula with such suspicion. For individualism and collectivism arise inside the classroom not as a clinical choice between alternative teaching strategies so much as a value dilemma which may be fundamental to a society's history and culture.

But the scenario is not one of singularity. Human consciousness and human relations involve the interplay of all three values and though one may be dominant, they may all in reality be present and exist in uneasy tension. Nowhere was this tension more evident than in the United States, where we found teachers seeking to reconcile – and indeed to foster as equivalent values – individual self-fulfilment with commitment to the greater collective good; self-effacing sharing and caring with fierce competitiveness; and environmentalism with consumerism. Meanwhile, in the world outside the school rampant individualism competed with the traditional American commitment to communal consciousness and local decision-making; and patriotism grappled with anti-statism. As the teacher interviews and lesson transcripts show, such tensions were manifested at every level from formal educational goals to the everyday discourse of teachers and children (Alexander, 2001, pp. 201–6 and 490–515).

Conclusion

If globalisation dictates a stronger comparative and international presence in educational research generally, there is a no less urgent need for comparativists to come to grips with the very core of the educational enterprise, pedagogy. Such an enterprise, however, demands as much rigour in the framing and analysis of pedagogy as in the act of comparing. In this chapter I have drawn on a five-nation comparative study of primary education to postulate principles and frameworks for a new comparative pedagogy. Pedagogy is defined stipulatively as the act of teaching together with its attendant discourses, ideas and values. The analysis of this discourse requires both that we engage with culture, values and ideas at the levels of classroom, school and system, and that we have a viable and comprehensive framework for the empirical study of teaching and learning. The interlocking models of pedagogy, teaching and curriculum in Figures 1.1.1–1.1.3, which were initially developed to frame the *Culture and Pedagogy* data analysis and have since been elaborated, link national culture, structure and policy with classroom agency; but they also allow for the structure–agency relationship to be played out within the micro-cultures of school and classroom.

The focus here is not on the detailed findings of the *Five Cultures* research but on the potential of its analytical framework to support the much-overdue development of a comparative pedagogy. But in arguing the centrality of culture, history and values to a proper analysis of pedagogy, and in applying the chosen frameworks, tools and perspectives to five countries rather than just one or two, we can open up other important domains: that of the balance of change and continuity in educational thinking and practice over time; and of pedagogical diversity and commonality across geographical boundaries. In so doing, we not only are forced to re-assess the Sadlerian resistance to educational import–export; we also come closer to identifying the true universals in teaching and learning. A properly conceived comparative pedagogy can both enhance our understanding of the interplay of education and culture and help us to improve the quality of educational provision.

Notes

1   With the permission of the teacher concerned.
2   Simultaneous teaching (whole class), mutual (collaborative group) and individual (one to one). Actually, *l'enseignement mutuel* referred initially to the Lancasterian monitoring method, but this updating seems legitimate.

References

Ackers, J. and Hardman, F. (2001) 'Classroom interaction in Kenyan primary schools', *Compare*, 31(2), pp. 245–62.

Alexander, R.J. (1996) *Other Primary Schools and Ours: Hazards of International Comparison*, Warwick, CREPE.

—— (1997) *Policy and Practice in Primary Education: Local Initiative, National Agenda*, London, Routledge.

—— (2001) *Culture and Pedagogy: International Comparisons in Primary Education*, Oxford, Blackwell.

—— (2004) '"Still no pedagogy?" Principle, pragmatism and compliance in primary education', *Cambridge Journal of Education*, 34(1), pp. 7–34.

—— (2006) 'Dichotomous pedagogies and the promise of cross-cultural comparison', in A.H. Halsey, P. Brown, H. Lauder and J. Dillabough (eds), *Education, Globalization and Social Change*, Oxford, Oxford University Press, pp. 722–33.

Apple, M.W. (1995) *Education and Power*, London, Routledge.

Archer, M.S. (1979) *Social Origins of Educational Systems*, London, Sage.

—— (1989) *Culture and Agency: The Place of Culture in Social Theory*, Cambridge, Cambridge University Press.

—— (2000) *Being Human: The Problem of Agency*, Cambridge, Cambridge University Press.

Argyris, C. and Schön, D. (1974) *Theory in Practice: Increasing Professional Effectiveness*, San Francisco, Jossey-Bass.

Bourdieu, P. and Passeron, J.-C. (1990) *Reproduction in Education, Society and Culture*, London, Sage.

Bowles, S. and Gintis, H. (1976) *Schooling in Capitalist America: Educational Reform and the Contradictions of Educational Life*, London, Routledge.

Broadfoot, P. (2000) 'Comparative education for the 21st century: retrospect and prospect', *Comparative Education*, 36(3), pp. 357–72.

Bruner, J.S. (1990) *Acts of Meaning*, Cambridge, MA, Harvard University Press.

Castells, M. (1997) *The Power of Identity*, Oxford, Blackwell.

Clarke, P. (2001) *Teaching and Learning: The Culture of Pedagogy*. New Delhi, Sage.

Comenius, J.A. [1657] tr. M.W.Keatinge (1896) *The Great Didactic*, London, A. and C. Black.

Cowen, R. (2000) 'Comparing futures or comparing pasts?', *Comparative Education*, 36(3), pp. 333–42.

DfEE (1998) *The National Literacy Strategy: A Framework for Teaching*, London, Department for Education and Employment.

—— (1999) *The National Numeracy Strategy: A Framework for Teaching Mathematics from Reception to Year 6*, London, Department for Education and Employment.

DfES (2003) *Excellence and Enjoyment: A Strategy for Primary Schools*, London, Department for Education and Skills.

Giroux, H.A. (1983) *Theory and Resistance in Education*, London, Heinemann.

Government of India (1998) *DPEP Moves On: Towards Universalising Basic Education*, Delhi, Government of India Ministry of Human Resource Development.

Hobsbawm, E.J. (1995) *The Age of Extremes: The Short Twentieth Century 1914–1991*, London, Abacus.

Kumar, K. (1991) *Political Agenda of Education: A Study of Colonialist and Nationalist Ideas*, Delhi, Sage.

Leach, E. (1964) 'Models', *New Society*, 14 June.

Leach, F. and Preston, R. (2001) Editorial, *Compare*, 31(2), pp. 149–50.

Little, A. (2000) 'Development studies and comparative education: context, content, comparison and contributors', *Comparative Education*, 36(3), pp. 279–96.

Lloyd, J. (1998) *Birth of a Nation: An Anatomy of Russia*, London, Michael Joseph.

Ministère de l'Éducation Nationale (1998) *Bâtir l'école du XXI siècle*, Paris, Ministère de l'Éducation Nationale.

Ministry of General and Professional Education of the Russian Federation (2000) *National Doctrine of Education in the Russian Federation*, Moscow, Ministry of General and Professional Education.

Moon, R. (1998) *The English Exception: International Perspectives on the Initial Education and Training of Teachers*, London, Universities Council for the Education of Teachers.

Muckle, J. (1988) *A Guide to the Soviet Curriculum: What the Russian Child is Taught in School*, London, Croom Helm.

OECD (1998) *Review of National Policies for Education: Russian Federation*, Paris, Organization for Economic Co-operation and Development.

Reboul-Scherrer, F. (1989) *Les premiers instituteurs, 1833–1882*, Paris, Hachette.

Reynolds, D. and Farrell, S. (1996) *Worlds Apart? A Review of International Surveys of Educational Achievement involving England*, London, TSO.

Ruddock, G. (2000) *Third International Mathematics and Science Study Repeat (TIMSS-R): First National Report*, London, DfEE.

Sadler, M. [1900] 'How can we learn anything of practical value from the study of foreign systems of education?', in J.H. Higginson (ed.) (1980), *Selections from Michael Sadler: Studies in World Citizenship*, Liverpool, Dejall and Meyorre.

Said, E. (1979) *Orientalism*, London, Vintage.

Sharpe, K. (1997) 'The Protestant ethic and the spirit of Catholicism: ideological and instructional constraints on system change in English and French primary schooling', *Comparative Education*, 33(3), pp. 329–48.

Simon, B. (1981) 'Why no pedagogy in England?', in B. Simon and W. Taylor (eds), *Education in the Eighties: The Central Issues*, London, Batsford, pp. 124–45.

Shweder, R.A. (1991) *Thinking Through Cultures*, Cambridge MA, Harvard University Press.

Sinclair, J.McH. and Coulthard, M. (1992) 'Towards an analysis of discourse', in M. Coulthard (ed.), *Advances in Spoken Discourse Analysis*, London, Routledge, pp. 1–34.

Stevenson, H.W. and Stigler, J.W. (1992) *The Learning Gap: Why Our Schools are Failing and What We can Learn from Japanese and Chinese Education*, New York, Simon and Schuster.

World Bank (1996) *Russia: Education in the Transition*, Washington, DC, World Bank.

—— (2000) *Entering the 21st Century: World Development Report 1999–2000*, New York, Oxford University Press.

Reflective questions

1 In what ways does a comparative pedagogy of the kind outlined in this paper help you to understand your own pedagogy in terms of the primordial values, versions of teaching and ideas at different levels that constitute it?

2   Why do you think a comparative analysis of pedagogy has been until recently ignored in British comparative research?
3   Would participation and observation and systematic analysis of classrooms in another country help to illuminate your own pedagogy?

Further reading

Alexander, R.J. (2001) *Culture and Pedagogy: International Comparisons in Primary Education*, Oxford, Blackwell.
—— (2008) *Essays on Pedagogy*, London, Routledge.
Alexander, R.J., Broadfoot, P., and Phillips, D. (1999) *Learning from Comparing: New Directions in Comparative Educational Research, Vol. 1: Contexts, Classrooms and Outcomes*, Oxford, Symposium Books.
Alexander, R.J., Osborne, M., and Phillips, D. (2000) *Learning from Comparing: New Directions in Comparative Educational Research, Vol. 2: Policy, Professionals and Development*, Oxford, Symposium Books.

1.2 Pedagogy and cultural convergence

Roger Dale

Introduction

'Education' has been seen as a key test of the globalisation thesis, on the grounds that if education, as the most 'national' of institutions, grounded in, and the key means of reproducing, national cultures, is being globalised, then there must be some substance and importance to the idea of globalisation. If this is so, it is even more the case with pedagogy, arguably the most culturally bound of the elements making up education; hence the focus and purpose of this chapter will be to see whether and what changes there have been in pedagogy, whether they can be put down to globalisation, and what they may tell us about 'cultural convergence' on a global scale.

This chapter begins by setting out a minimal distinction between pedagogy and teaching, and between pedagogy and curriculum. It then addresses what might be entailed by the notion of 'convergence' in this context, asking specifically 'what converges, over what period and at what scale(s)', and what drives any such convergence(s). Following this, it discusses the main theoretical approach that argues for a more or less, if incomplete, convergence of pedagogy at a global scale, the so-called 'world polity' theory, which explains this convergence on the basis of a common set of universal values, drawing on Western modernity, that now permeate education systems at a global level. The paper then develops further the basis of some of the critiques of the world polity approach, largely that it tends to abstract pedagogy from the wider 'Education Complex' of which it is a crucial but not independent or autonomous component, and which sets limits to and shapes possibilities for pedagogy; the outcome of these multiple and multi-scalar relationships is referred to as the 'pedagogic space'.

Pedagogy and teaching

It will be helpful to begin with a brief definition of pedagogy. It is now quite widely accepted that pedagogy means something more than and different from 'teaching'. In a nutshell, it means being able to give an *account* of, and *justification* of, the practices of teaching. Alexander's definition, which stood him in good stead through his immense study of *Culture and Pedagogy* (in which, incidentally, the word 'convergence' does not appear in the index) can be broadly accepted: 'Pedagogy is best defined ... as the act of teaching together with the ideas, values and collective histories which inform, shape and explain that act' (Alexander, 2005, p. 2). It is crucial to note, however, that pedagogy never 'stands alone'; as we will show below, it always takes place within particular 'spaces', which selectively filter and shape the forms it can take. Pedagogy is also different from curriculum. The simple distinction is that curriculum is about the content of the message, and pedagogy is the means by which it is conveyed. However, pedagogy makes a rather more significant contribution than might be inferred from that simple statement. There is a pervasive sense that pedagogy is more than a mere relay of messages determined elsewhere; it makes an independent contribution that is more than merely technical. That is to say that the *way* we teach itself affects – indeed is part of – what is learned; with pedagogy, often 'the medium is the message' – we learn from *how* we are taught as well as from *what* we are taught. To put it another way, the difference between curriculum and pedagogy might be compared to that between Coca-Cola and McDonald's; with the former you receive a *product*, that is in principle available anywhere (albeit 'curriculum' is a rather more complicated entity than a fizzy drink); with the latter, you become part of a *service*, a form of organisation in which the mode of delivery is itself part of the experience.

The remainder of this chapter will proceed as follows. I will discuss next what is meant by 'convergence', and how it will be addressed in the chapter, before moving on to discuss the best-known theory of curricular and pedagogic convergence, that of the world polity theorists. I will suggest that persuasive though they are at one level those theorists neglect the influence of the wider contexts of pedagogy. These contexts are represented here as making up an Education Complex, which sets the outlines of the pedagogic space, the opportunity structures within which pedagogy operates. I conclude by suggesting that current changes in globalisation are powerfully affecting the different elements of the Education Complex and their relationships, and that consequently we may be seeing a convergence in pedagogic space, which may or may not lead to convergence in pedagogic practice and discourse.

Convergence

The idea of convergence, whether of practices and/or policies, inputs and/or outputs, has become a common feature of discussions about globalisation and its 'impact upon' education. It seems to stand as a kind of default assumption that globalisation is a homogenising force because by definition it applies to and affects the whole world. Globalisation is often, at least implicitly, taken as a 'common external force' that has effects on all national education systems, as well as on myriad other phenomena, and 'the degree of convergence' between them becomes a key 'test', or register, of the impact of globalisation on a range of institutions, discourses and practices. However, as I shall argue below, this is an excessively simple conception of how globalisation works, and a misleading one.

As a first step to 'complicating' the issue, we need to ask two sets of questions about convergence. What is said to converge, over what period and at what scale(s)? And what do we understand by 'convergence'?

In terms of the first question, in the brief discussion of pedagogy above, we distinguished three distinct areas, or moments, of possible convergence of pedagogies – practices, justifications of those practices, and the spaces which frame those practices and justifications – and those will be our focus in this chapter. The temporal scale we have in mind begins with the fall of the Berlin Wall in 1989, which can be taken as the iconic act that made possible the era we know as neoliberal globalisation. And in terms of scale, in an era of globalisation it is crucial to be mindful of other scales than the national. This does not, of course, mean that the national scale can be ignored – far from it; the national remains the most important scale of educational activity, but it is no longer the only scale of such activity, or the only level at which we may discern changes in education (see Dale, 2005).

In terms of the second question, it is crucial to recognise that – like globalisation itself – convergence has also been used in rather different ways, for instance as an analytic category, describing a process, and as a political project. It is also a rather loose concept, so as a start, it will be helpful to draw on the very useful elaboration of some of the key issues involved provided by Colin Hay (2000). Hay distinguishes four senses in which convergence is used: *input* convergence; *policy* convergence; *process* convergence; and *output* convergence. However, it is important to note that he assumes a *national* scale of convergence, and, as we have just pointed out, this is neither a necessary nor a helpful assumption. Hay also insists that there are no necessary relationships between the types of convergence: input convergence need not imply policy convergence, for instance, nor output convergence be seen as a consequence of process convergence. This is not to say, either, that they are necessarily independent of each other, rather that any relationship between them has to be demonstrated rather than assumed. So, we need to be clear which form(s) of convergence are being assumed when we are discussing pedagogy and convergence, as well as to be clear whether particular changes in pedagogy are to be seen as the source of, or the consequence of convergence, or both, or neither.

Input convergence, convergence in 'the pressures and constraints placed upon an economy' (Hay's examples are taken from the economic field, but that does not limit their relevance to education, *mutatis mutandis*), closely resembles what might be central to most definitions of globalisation: in many understandings globalisation at least connotes 'external pressures and constraints', albeit of a quantitatively or qualitatively different kind. In the field of education it is possible to identify, in an era of neoliberal globalisation, a common set of assumptions that underlies the work of, and is propagated by the leading international organisations that work in the field of education (the World Bank, the OECD and the WTO; see Dale, 2008).

Education sectors are often seen to display forms of *policy* convergence in the education area, whether that be through processes of policy borrowing, harmonisation, or imposition (see Dale 1999). The existence of particular global, one-size-fits-all models of development, aid and their relationship (promoted and promulgated by the World Bank in particular) has been widely noted (see e.g. Robertson *et al.*, 2007). Equally fully documented is the failure of those policies to bring about a successful model of change around which developing countries might converge. If we were to be cynical, we might say that where these policies have broadly converged is around a lack of improvement to education systems, but even the most cynical would be hard put to demonstrate that this convergence on failure was the intended result of the policy.

Output convergence refers to 'convergence in the consequences, effects and outcomes of particular policies' (Hay, 2000, p. 514). One especially interesting form taken by output convergence in education across the world is to be found in the results of the PISA tests. Here we find the emergence of clusters of countries achieving similar performance on the PISA tests, which might be seen as 'converging' on a particular performance level, particularly if we take their performance on TIMSS tests as the point of origin from which convergence might be measured. Thus, we find an unusual and highly heterogeneous group together (converging?) at the top of the PISA tables – Finland, Australia and Hong Kong, for instance. Given this heterogeneity, it is interesting to speculate what might be learned about nation states' performance on the PISA tests from this evidence of convergence, since there seem few common elements across the successful countries' education systems. It seems highly unlikely that it is caused by process convergence in the area of pedagogy, but it is clear that it has become a basis for policy convergence, or at least emulation, around especially the Finnish model of pedagogy.

We consider *process* convergence – 'convergence in the processes sustaining the developmental trajectories of particular states' (Hay, 2000, p. 514) – last in this series, both because it seems the form of convergence where we are most likely to find pedagogy involved and because it is where the most compelling arguments for convergence in the area of pedagogy have been advanced.

World polity theory and the convergence of pedagogy

The outstanding example of converging paradigms at a global level is the work of the world polity theorists (e.g. Meyer *et al.*, 1992). It meets all the criteria for an effective theory of the relationship between globalisation and education – a clear theory of globalisation and of education, and a theory of the relationship between them (see Dale, 2000). This work demonstrates very clearly that, over the course of the twentieth century, as new education systems emerged around the world they described themselves in terms of a standard set of curricular categories, to the point where the 'same' subjects appeared in all education systems.

The central argument of the world institutionalists is that the institutions of the nation state, indeed the state itself, are to be regarded as essentially shaped at a supranational level by a dominant world – or Western – ideology, rather than as autonomous and unique national creations. Here, states have their activity and their policies shaped by universal norms and culture. The values of this universal culture are those of Western modernity; they centre on progress and justice and are associated with the construction of the ideas of the state and the individual.

The argument may be summarised as follows. The rapid spread of national educational systems and the striking but surprising degree of curricular homogeneity that we observe across the societies of the world, irrespective of their location, level of development, or religious and other traditions, cannot be explained by the functional, national-cultural, or rational-instrumental theories that have dominated the study of educational systems or the curriculum hitherto. They derive first of all from the very model of modern 'stateness' that has spread especially rapidly since 1945, with the newly decolonised states seeking to demonstrate that they were 'real' states by emulating and adopting the institutions that characterised existing states, such as education, and by following in particular the curricular 'scripts' that those states had developed, the structure of which is 'closely linked to the rise of standardized models of society and to the increasing dominance of standardized models of education as one component of these general models' (Benavot *et al.*, p. 41). Here, the curriculum is seen as everywhere drawing on supranational educational norms and conventions based on the values of Western modernity, rather than resulting from policies framed to address the needs of particular societies. The definition of legitimate knowledge to be taught in schools, and the selection and hierarchical organisation of such bodies of knowledge, are thus by and large 'externally' prescribed:

> At the core of the prescription lies a 'rational' discourse on how the socialization of children in various subject areas is linked to the self-realization of the individual and, ultimately, to the construction of an ideal society. This discourse is highly standardized and universalistic in character.
>
> (Cha, 1992, p. 65)

Thus we can see the claim of world polity theorists is to have demonstrated the nature and extent of 'output' convergence of at least curriculum categories on a global scale, reflecting a common 'input', drawing on the same broad set of values, as the same patterns of curriculum spread – or are spread – effectively to all the countries of the world. However, this does not in itself constitute 'process' convergence; world polity theory does indeed have a theory of process convergence. It sees it occurring through the *diffusion* of the principles and scripts of (for instance) curriculum through the activities of professional bodies, international organisations such as the OECD and World Bank, and international surveys such as TIMSS and PISA. As McNeely and Cha (1994, pp. 2–3) put it:

> The principles, norms, rules, and procedures of the wider system are enshrined in these organizations, and they have become carriers of the culture of the world polity … they reflect the more binding and universal influence of the global system and operate in a variety of ways to effect the institutionalization of world ideologies, structures and practices at the nation-state level and they attribute 'a certain amount of causal efficacy' to international organizations in bringing about the convergence of national education practices.

World polity theories and pedagogy

The arguments of the world polity theorists have more recently been applied to pedagogy (see Baker and LeTendre, 2005; LeTendre *et al.*, 2001). LeTendre *et al.* drew on the survey and case study data of the third TIMSS (Trends in International Mathematics and Science Study) to study how far differences in teachers' work are accounted for by national-cultural variations and how far by what they call 'global cultural dynamics' (a concept with very clear connections with the world polity theorists). The issue is generated, for them, by debates on whether and how far the strong national 'cultural' factors that seem to underlie and account for the greater success of Asian countries on the TIMMS can be adapted for use in US classrooms. Their basic argument is that such questions to a degree miss the point, because there is at least as much evidence for 'schools not reflect(ing) or simply transmit(ting) culture but themselves (being) the product of a cultural dynamic', and that this cultural dynamic is found in 'global institutions that transect and shape local, regional, or national versions of institutions (i.e., schools)' (LeTendre *et al.*, 2001, p. 4). This is clearly very close to the world polity theorists' ideas, as 'rationality, along with its offshoots of marketization, individualization, bureaucratization, and homogenization, plays the tune that all modern global institutions march to, but it itself is a cultural product and acts as such throughout the social system' (ibid., p. 5). So, the global dynamic perspective suggests that 'all local, regional and/or national cultures are responding to a global cultural environment', a very strong claim for convergence of pedagogy as a process.

Their findings do not wholly bear out this claim. They argue on the one hand that 'teachers in modern nations such as Japan, Germany and the U.S. [the countries they compared] go about their jobs in highly institutionalized social settings where their identities are shaped by the existing institution and where the patterns of their work are driven by the rules and procedures of the specific school (organization) in which they work and the larger institution of schooling' (ibid., p. 11), but on the other that 'the broader role of the teacher … (and) basic differences in overall teacher work patterns may have impacts on the specific enactment of core instructional practices in the classroom' (ibid., p. 12).

There are five important points to be made here. The first is that there is little or no attempt to discuss national-cultural differences more broadly, and how they might be related to any perceived similarities and differences in teachers' work (though some of this may be inferred). The second point is related: that the perceived similarities do seem to be rooted in *common institutional arrangements* – what we will refer to below as the 'grammar of schooling' – which essentially constrains teachers to operate in rather similar ways, and that it is to the nature of these constraints rather than teachers' selection of pedagogic techniques as responses to them that we should be paying attention to clarify possible convergence of pedagogy. The third is that the specified 'basic differences in overall work patterns' include 'the fact that Japanese teachers teach comparatively few periods, specialise in math, and have ample planning time' (ibid.), which would seem, *prima facie*, to be highly significant differences in terms of pedagogy that are at least variations on the global cultural script. Fourth, there is no attempt to relate the differences of outcomes in terms of TIMSS 'success' in the three countries to the similarities and differences between them at the level of teachers' work. Finally, and most importantly, the discussion remains at the level of teacher practices, and to a lesser degree, teacher beliefs. The possibility that as well as being related to different practices and beliefs, the perceived similarities and differences may have been related to different conceptions of 'pedagogic space' is not considered. It is to this consideration that I now turn.

Pedagogy, pedagogic space and the Education Complex

Pedagogies do not arise spontaneously or voluntarily. They always arise in particular pedagogic spaces that are shaped by what I will refer to as the 'Education Complex'. By pedagogic spaces I mean something like the opportunity structure presented for the exercise and operation of pedagogy, for what is expected of pedagogy, by the wider complex of which it is part – and that also, of course, includes existing pedagogic spaces. The 'existing institutional arrangements' pointed to by LeTendre *et al.* as significant factors in 'converging' teachers' practices cross-nationally are one important example of how pedagogic space is shaped by factors outside the school. That example also shows that the nature and forms of pedagogic spaces do not determine how they will be filled; they operate, as it were, as exclusive rather than inclusive, proscriptive rather than prescriptive, mechanisms.

Thus, the idea of 'education' as a complex made up of multiple elements seems fundamental to a full appreciation of the place and variation of pedagogy. The suggestion that what counts as 'education' is shaped by both economic and political factors seems something of a commonplace, too obvious to mention, and yet its importance and significance are rarely fully recognised (and here I include my own work). What will briefly be discussed in this section, is something of an 'owl of Minerva' insight,[1] meaning that we only begin to understand something when it has ceased to exist in the forms we have become used to. Recognising the independent (and mutually irreducible) contributions of economic and political factors in the shaping of education has more recently given way to, or been joined by, a recognition based on the practices of educational governance and management since the last quarter of the twentieth century, that there are other independent and non mutually reducible elements involved in constituting 'education', and it is these I refer to as the Education Complex. Five such elements are distinguished: the core problems of capitalism; the discourses and practices of modernity; the conditions of schooling; the governance of education; and the relationship of education to the nation. These elements combine, in different and *changing* ways (separately and in their mutual relationships), to provide the interpretive structures through which 'education' takes place in contemporary societies. They constitute the means of defining education and its purposes, and the means through which it will be delivered. I will now briefly discuss each element in a little more detail.

The core problems of capitalism

I have argued elsewhere (see Dale, 1989) that the key to understanding education systems lies in recognising their relationship to the core problems of capitalism, that it cannot itself provide and that it needs an institution like the state to provide. These core problems are: ensuring an infrastructure for continuing accumulation and economic development, such as the provision of a diversely skilled labour force; ensuring a level of social order and social cohesion; and legitimating the inherent inequalities of the system. I suggested that the solutions to these problems were as likely to be mutually contradictory as mutually complementary (streaming is a good example here; it is claimed to enhance the identification and development of academic strength, thus serving the accumulation purpose, but at the same time it is widely perceived as unfair, thus threatening the legitimation purpose), and that attempts to resolve these contradictions lay at the heart of education policy. Essentially, these problems may be seen to set the limits of the possible for education systems, not in the sense that they *prescribe* particular curricula, for instance – capitalism has shown itself capable of living quite comfortably with a range of different social preferences and movements, for instance, feminism, and has successfully lived with a wide range of different education systems – but in the sense that they effectively *proscribe* what is not in the interests of capital. Such limits are difficult to predict, and may only be recognised when they are breached, but their reality is reinforced by the increasing mobility of capital, which permits rapid shifts from educational regimes deemed to be insufficiently supportive.

Modernity and education

Due to lack of space, the reader is referred for this section to the discussion of the world polity theorists above, and the way that they have most effectively outlined and elaborated the relationship between education and modernity.

The organisation of education

'Education' does not 'just happen'; it has to be made to happen, in particular ways, for particular purposes, to serve particular ends and interests. So, the first point to be made about the organisation of education is that it rests on an assumption that education is delivered through schooling; this is made most evident, perhaps, by the specification of the Millennium Development Goal for Education as access to primary schooling. In its dominant form as schooling, education has minimally to be funded, provided and regulated; above all, for this section, it has to be organised. That organisation may take the form of children sitting under a tree reciting a song, or sitting in front of computer screens in specially designed rooms, but in each case their co-presence, and the circumstances under which they meet, are not spontaneous, but have to be organised (and this applies even with one-to-one tutorials). It is possible to identify major features of this organisation, which have been usefully described as constituting a 'grammar of schooling' (Tyack and Tobin, 1994). These include, according to one recent historical account:

> the timetable, the division of the day into lessons and playtime, terms and holidays, the architecture of the school, its furniture, classroom layouts, pupil numbers, the age and subject-based grade-school system, the internal school hierarchy, the panoptic gaze, recurrent sanctions, such as exams and prize days [which might be seen more broadly as parts of a system of rewards and punishments], and so on ...
>
> (Depaepe *et al.*, 2000, p. 11; quoted in Brehony, 2002, p. 178)

This grammar has an independent (that is, not reducible to, or transformable in the face of, particular political or policy changes in education) framing effect on what is possible in schooling. For Tyack and Tobin, it is made up of such familiar classroom (itself a major enabling and shaping feature of schooling) elements as (note that the indefinite article is used in this list; it is the framework, not particular realisations of it, however dominant, that constitutes the grammar – just as 'grammar' does not limit the meaning of a sentence): a structure of subjects; a schedule of classes; a system of age grouping; a given duration of a 'class'; a grading system; curricular materials.

We need also to add to this list another rather less visible set of assumptions that enable education, in various ways. The first is that it is, or should aspire to be, universal. Participation in education is the only compulsory requirement of citizens, and the expectation that all will be treated at least formally equally is deeply embedded in the institutional forms of schooling. Second, schooling is typically seen as a job for professional experts, with a dedicated teaching force – and this in itself has major consequences for the provision and experiences of education (see Robertson, 1999) and in particular, of course for issues of pedagogy. And third, there is a set of mutual obligations in the relationship between the school and the society. This takes a wide variety of forms, but central among them is how mutual accountability is established and recognised.

This set of organisational assumptions and practices has grown up around the development of mass schooling and has come to be seen as defining it, to become, in effect, education as practised. One crucial question here concerns the depth of the embeddedness of these enabling practices, which can be seen as a major constraint on the possibilities of education. It has often been remarked that while most other professions have been transformed over the last two centuries, education is still organised on fundamentally the same basis, so that, for instance, it is easy to identify a building as a school from any period over the past two centuries.

It is important to try to identify why that is so. It is often put down to simple inertia, but that explanation is unsatisfactory, question-begging and misleading; it forces us to ask what causes the inertia, and how it might be overcome, rather than to problematise the idea of inertia in this context.

We can point to four elements in particular that combine to limit deep structural change in education. The first is that all organisations operate according to a logic of appropriateness rather than a logic of rationality.[2] Put very simply, this means that the first question to be asked about any proposed innovation, for instance, is not 'How effective will it be ?' or 'How can we make it work?' but 'How can it be accommodated to the way we do things around here?'. It may be objected that if this theory is valid, it is valid for any organisation, so what makes education different? The answer is to be found in the second element, the lack of an agreed technical basis for the work of teaching and education in general. As Meyer *et al.*, (1992, p. 71) put it, 'Education is of great value, but there is no technically known way to do it best – the situation is ideal for the operation of processes of fashion, of imitation, and thus of diffusion.' The third element is the sheer complexity of the Education Complex, the massive range of things that education is expected to do. Schools are unique holders of, and responsible for, numerous, frequently contradictory, mandates. One consequence of this is that radical change in one area is likely to have deleterious effects in another area, which can lead to stand-offs and stasis. The final, and perhaps the most important, element is that a very wide range of what would now be called 'stakeholders' have an interest (in the sense of 'investment' as well as, or rather than, in the sense of 'fascination') in education, and these are deeply embedded and tenaciously defended. A very relevant example here is the interests of the teaching force, and how it has been represented through teacher trade unions (see Robertson, 1999).

The governance of education

This refers to the ways that education sectors have been defined and governed. It has come to be assumed that this necessarily means a state-run education system, but that is now very clearly open to challenge, and indeed, was never the case across large parts of the world. There are different sets of activities involved in governing education, different agents carrying them out, and different scales at which the governance of education operates, so that rather than assuming the governance of education is necessarily the sole responsibility of the national state, it can now be seen to be part of a functional, scalar and sectoral division of labour (Dale, 2002), which has major implications for the definition of pedagogic spaces.

Education as the repository of national tradition and identity

National education systems have been regarded as the key institutions of nation building, economic development and citizenship. They are and have been the major means by which societies seek to define, reproduce and ensure their national distinctiveness, to strengthen their national economies, to address their social problems, to influence the distribution of individual life chances. It is this image of 'Education' that most people have in mind when they think about the issue. It provides the grist for national education politics. These national traditions and issues grow from nationally specific path dependencies (policies and practices that take their form from what has gone before); one especially interesting path dependency derives from whether a national education system preceded or followed industrialisation, for instance (for a highly detailed comparative analysis of these processes see Archer, 1979). Another important area where national path dependencies are significant is in the definition of a national education 'sector'. Is pre-school education, for instance, part of 'Education', 'Health' or 'Family policy'? And what are the consequences for education of its being linked within a single ministry with the Church, as in Norway and Greece?

Conclusion

The basic argument here is that pedagogy is linked with, and related to, each of these elements separately, and to the particular collective forms they take, and that it is at this level that we may see indications of changing patterns of globalisation creating pressures for convergence of pedagogical space.

It used to be assumed that these collective forms – Education Complexes – would be found exclusively at national (or, in the case of some federal states, sub-national) level, but that is, almost by definition, no longer the case in an era of globalisation. As has been hinted above, we find changes in each of the elements of the complex separately, and these combine in ways that alter the shape of the pedagogic space. The core problems are now dominated by accumulation to a qualitatively different degree, where it has been possible to argue that accumulation becomes its own legitimation, on the grounds that if economies can grow everyone ultimately benefits through the 'trickle-down effect' (see Robertson and Dale,

2002). Further, and even further-reaching in its implications, it has been suggested that the current state of education, like other institutions of modernity, is fundamentally a reflection of and a response to the changing nature of the relationship between capitalism and modernity. This is partly reflected in the arguments above that while the case for curricular and pedagogic convergence around a common set of values, discourses and institutions is quite plausible, any such convergences do not exhaust what we have called the pedagogic space; rather, they interact with other elements of the Education Complex from which the pedagogic space emerges, and within which they operate. To put it very briefly, this means that, following Boaventura de Sousa Santos, it is crucial to the understanding of the current global predicaments to distinguish between the trajectories of capitalism (as found currently in the form of neoliberal globalisation) and Western modernity, which are

> two different and autonomous historical processes ... [that] have converged and inter-penetrated each other ... we are living in a time of paradigmatic transition, and, consequently, ... the sociocultural paradigm of modernity ... will eventually disappear before capitalism ceases to be dominant ... partly from a process of supersession and partly from a process of obsolescence. It entails supersession to the extent that modernity has fulfilled some of its promises, in some cases even in excess. It results from obsolescence to the extent that modernity is no longer capable of fulfilling some of its other promises ...
>
> (Santos, 2002, pp. 1–2)

This separation means that the institutions of Modernity, in which education has been central, can no longer be seen as offering the best possible set of extra-economic institutions for capitalism, and may be seen as in serious need of repair – a formulation that could be useful as a means of coming to grips with the myriad apparently random, malevolent, cunningly planned or heralding-a-brave-new-world changes that we observe (see Dale, 2007). We might also combine issues of the organisation and governance of education, since over the past two decades we have witnessed major changes as governance, especially in the form of New Public Management (see, e.g. Kettl, 1997), has come to shape and limit the options and possibilities for organisation of education – for instance, through audit procedures, benchmarks, targets, ex post accountability, in ways that do not merely alter but redirect the organisation of education, with particular and direct consequences for pedagogic space. And finally, while the national level remains as important as ever, it faces new pressures not only from multinational governance but also from such 'collateral' effects of globalisation as major waves of immigration.

Together, then, it is possible to argue that we are witnessing forms of at least 'input convergence', and some policy convergence, that are impacting on pedagogy, bringing about not just changes to the pedagogic spaces of education systems, but *convergent* changes. However, whether these will lead to similar or convergent changes in pedagogic practices and discourses – which is very clearly and explicitly the ultimate intention of some present policies – remains an open question: globalisation may shape spaces but it does not determine practices.

Notes

1   The reference is to Hegel's famous dictum that the 'owl of Minerva [signifying wisdom] only leaves its nest at dusk'.

2 'The logic of appropriateness is a perspective that sees human action as driven by rules of appropriate or exemplary behavior, organized into institutions. Rules are followed because they are seen as natural, rightful, expected, and legitimate. Actors seek to fulfill the obligations encapsulated in a role, an identity, a membership in a political community or group, and the ethos, practices and expectations of its institutions. Embedded in a social collectivity, they do what they see as appropriate for themselves in a specific type of situation' (March and Olsen, 2004, p. 1).

References

Benavot, A., Cha, Y.-K., Kamens, D.H., Meyer, J.W. and Wong, S.-Y. (1992) 'Knowledge for the masses: world models and national curricula, 1920-86', in J.W. Meyer, D.H. Kamens and A. Benavot (eds), *School Knowledge for the Masses*, Brighton, Falmer.

Brehony, K.L. (2002) 'Researching the grammar of schooling: an historical view', *European Educational Research Journal*, 1, pp. 178–89.

Cha, Y.-K. (1992) 'The origins and expansion of primary school curricula: 1800-1920', in J.W. Meyer, D.H. Kamens and A. Benavot (eds), *School Knowledge for the Masses*, Brighton, Falmer.

Dale, R. (1989) *The State and Education Policy*, Buckingham, Open University Press.

——— (1999) 'Specifying globalization effects on national policy: a focus on the mechanisms', *Journal of Education Policy*, 14(1), pp. 1–17.

——— (2002) 'The construction of a European education space and education policy', paper presented to European Social Fund Exploratory Workshop on Globalisation, Educational Restructuring and Social Cohesion in Europe, Barcelona, 3–5 October.

——— (2005) 'Globalisation, knowledge economy and comparative education', *Comparative Education*, 41(2), pp. 117–49.

——— (2008) 'Neoliberal capitalism, the modern state and the governance of education', *Tertium Comparationis*, 13(2), pp. 183–98.

——— (2007) 'Repairing the deficits of modernity; the emergence of parallel discourses in higher education in Europe', in D. Epstein *et al.* (eds) *World Yearbook of Education 2008: Geographies of Knowledge, Geometries of Power: Framing the Future of Higher Education*, pp. 14–31.

Depaepe, M., Dams, K., De Vroede, M. *et al.* (2000) *Order in progress': Everyday Educational Practice in Primary Schools, Belgium, 1880–1970*, Leuven, Leuven University Press.

Kettl, D. (1997) 'Global revolution in public management: driving themes, missing links', *Journal of Policy Analysis and Management*, 16(3), pp. 446–62.

LeTendre, G.K., Baker, D.P., Akiba, M., Goesling, B. and Wiseman, A. (2001) 'Teachers' work: institutional isomorphism and cultural variation in the U.S., Germany, and Japan', *Educational Researcher*, 30(6), pp. 3–16.

March, J. and Olsen, J.P. (2004) *The Logic of Appropriateness*, University of Oslo, *ARENA Working Papers* WP 04/09.

McNeely, C. and Cha, Y.-K. (1994) 'Worldwide educational convergence through international organizations: avenues for research', *Education Policy Analysis Archives*, 2(14); online at http://epaa.asu.edu/epaa/v2n14.html, accessed 27 November 2008.

Meyer, J.W. and Kamens, D.H. (1992) 'Conclusion: accounting for a world curriculum', in J.W. Meyer, D.H. Kamens and A. Benavot (eds), *School Knowledge for the Masses*, Brighton, Falmer, p. 171.

Meyer, J.W., Kamens, D.H. and Benavot, A. (1992) *School Knowledge for the Masses: World Models and National Primary Curricular Categories in the Twentieth Century*, Philadelphia, Falmer Press.

Robertson, S.L. (1999) *A Class Act: Changing Teachers' Work, Globalisation and the State*, London, Routledge.

Robertson, S.L. and Dale, R. (2002) 'Local states of emergency: the contradictions of neo-liberal governance in education in New Zealand', *British Journal of Sociology of Education*, 23(3), pp. 463–82.

Robertson, S.L., Novelli, M., Dale, R., Tikly, L., Dachi, H. and Alphonce, N. (2007) *Globalisation, Education and Development: Ideas, Actors and Dynamics*, London, DfID.

Santos, Boaventura de Sousa (2002) *Toward a New Legal Common Sense*, London, Butterworths.

Reflective questions

1   Would it be a good thing for pedagogies to converge in a global era? What would be the pros and cons, and for whom?
2   In what main ways do the grammar of schooling and pedagogy affect each other?
3   If we accept the idea of a globally framed 'pedagogic space' what possibilities are there for national, local, or school level initiatives and innovations in pedagogy?

Further reading

Bonal, X. and Rambla, X. (2003) 'Captured by the totally pedagogised society: teachers and teaching in the knowledge economy', *Globalisation, Societies and Education*, 1(2), pp. 169–84.

Hartley, D. (2006) 'Excellence and enjoyment: the logic of a "contradiction"', *British Journal of Educational Studies*, 54(1), pp. 3–14.

Jacklin, H. (2004) 'Discourse, interaction and spatial rhythms: locating pedagogic practice in a material world', *Pedagogy, Culture and Society*, 12(3), pp. 373–98.

Luke, A. (2004) 'Teaching after the market: from commodity to Cosmopolitan', *Teachers College Record*, 106(7), pp. 1422–43.

1.3 Metaphors in education

Anna Sfard

Introduction: there is more to metaphor than meets the eyes

Metaphor in *education*? In a poem – yes; in novels or journal articles – yes; in orators' inspired speeches – yes; but in education? The unruly linguistic move that brings surprise and stirs emotions – what does it have to do with propagating established forms of activity and rules of conduct, which education is all about? Aren't teaching and learning too serious a business to allow for frivolity like this?

These days, many writers challenge the view of metaphor as a mere literary gimmick and argue that metaphors are, in fact, everywhere and, yes, also in education. In this chapter, an even stronger claim is made: without metaphors, human beings would not be what they are. As it turns out, metaphors underlie our ability to explore new territories and build new knowledge. They shape our thinking, and through thinking, they mould our actions. As such, they are also full of pitfalls. While this claim is generally true, it is of particular importance in education. Here, our choices of metaphors may affect nothing less than human lives. In what follows, after a brief discussion of what metaphors are, I focus on their role in educational research and practice. Special attention is given to the question of how to utilize metaphors as props and how to make sure that they do not turn into traps.

Metaphor: what is it and why do we need it?

Metaphor as 'discursive transplant'

In the search for metaphors, one needs to listen carefully to what people are saying. Indeed, metaphor is a discursive construct – it is a particular way of making assertions. Some metaphors are easy to notice. Thus, for example, the appearance of the words *like* or *as* is one of the most reliable signs of their presence. To realize this, it suffices to take a closer look at expressions such as *an atom is like a solar system, she was brave as a lion* or *teaching is like growing a garden*.[1] But metaphor can be present in a text even if unannounced with any special linguistic marker. When one says that she found a book *indigestible*, we do not imagine this person pushing printed pages into her mouth and then processing them in her intestines; and when one states that she is *love-sick*, we do not propose to rush her to a hospital. The common property of these and the former metaphorical expressions is that in all cases a word from one thematic domain has been embedded in another one, thus entering a network of new linguistic relations. For instance, we transplanted terms from the discourse on gardening into the discourse of education, and those from the discourse on food and digesting into the one on books and reading. This is, indeed, what metaphors are all about:

they are transplants[2] from one discourse to another.[3] Having said this, I am now in a position to make a number of claims about what metaphors do to us and to our lives.

Metaphors are catalysts of new knowledge

Like any transplant, a metaphor is not a mere add-on; rather, it is often a source of a whole new way of speaking, that is, of a new discourse. As such, it is a source of new ways of seeing things. To say it metaphorically, discursive crossbreeding may result in a new discursive species. This happens much more often than we may readily realize. Dislocating words from their 'native' discourses into unexpected contexts is a common occurrence. As we go on using the familiar words in unfamiliar linguistic settings, we construct new discourses and thus new conceptual systems.

In this process of discursive expansion, our perceptual experiences are primary building materials. Under a close scrutiny, traces of language that pertain to the perceptual and the bodily are visible even in the most abstract of our concepts. Consider, for example, expressions such as *transfer of learning* or *grasping a meaning*, both of which sound so familiar that we may have difficulty recognizing their metaphorical origins. And yet, since these expressions make use of the verbs *transfer* and *grasp*, it is clear that they both have been inspired by discourses on physical actions with material objects. As shown in these examples, metaphors often cross the borders between the physical and the mental, between the concrete and the abstract.

Figurative projections also cross boundaries that separate the intuitive and the formal. Conveyed through language from one domain to another, metaphors enable conceptual osmosis between colloquial and scientific discourses, letting our primary intuition shape scientific ideas and letting the formal conceptions feed back into the intuition. Indeed, these days, philosophers of science agree that metaphors play a central, constitutive role also in research. In fact, no kind of scientific endeavour would be possible without them (Hesse, 1966; Ortony, 1993). What has been traditionally regarded as merely a tool for a better understanding and for more effective explaining of scientific theories is now recognized as these theories' primary source – as a mechanism through which one becomes able to organize new experiences in terms of the previous ones.

The idea that new knowledge originates in old knowledge deserves some elaboration. Although it has been promoted by all theoreticians of human development, from Piaget to Vygotsky to contemporary cognitive scientists, the question of how the old is transformed into the new remained a vexing puzzle. The quandary was first signalled by Plato in his dialogue *Meno* and came to be known later as *the learning paradox* (Bereiter, 1985; Cobb *et al.*, 1992; Sfard, 1998). Although seen in many different disguises throughout history, the question has always been the same: how can we want to acquire knowledge of something which is not yet known to us? If we can only become cognizant of a thing by recognizing it on the basis of the knowledge we already possess, then nothing that does not yet belong to the assortment of the things we know can ever become one of them. Conclusion: creating new discourses – or knowledge – is inherently impossible.

The recent work on metaphors as agents of discursive (conceptual) change offers a way out of this entanglement. Metaphors function as harbingers and catalysts of such change, owing their constitutive power to the fact that familiar words, even if transplanted into a new context, can still be used according to at least some of the old rules (think, for example, about your own ability to get an initial sense of what is being talked about when you come across a familiar colloquial term, such as *strain* or *messenger*, in a hitherto unfamiliar scientific context, where they appear in such expressions as *cognitive strain* or *messenger DNA*).

Once the metaphorical term is introduced into the 'target' discourse, the rules of its use, as well as those of the discourse into which the metaphor was inserted, are mutually adjusted, resulting in a whole new form of talk – and possibly a new scientific theory!

Metaphors shape our thinking

Since the seemingly innocent act of transplanting a familiar word into an unfamiliar context may, in fact, be a beginning of a new form of communication, choosing a metaphor is a highly consequential activity. In fact, it may amount to no less than an upheaval in the way we understand the world. Indeed, since thinking can be conceptualized as *communication with oneself*, the way we talk is the way we think. Saying that metaphors shape our discourses is thus tantamount to saying that they shape our thinking.[4]

The special power of metaphorical expressions lies in the fact that even their very first appearance in an unusual context makes us feel as if we already knew a great lot about the phenomena they describe. When we say, for example, that *teaching is like growing a garden*, many of the statements about gardening known as true are now unreflectively taken as true also for teaching. Thus, for example, the gardening metaphor entails a tacit assumption that the general trajectory of student learning, just like the growth of a plant, is inscribed in genes and that our role as teachers is to provide the child with optimal conditions for the realization of this biologically determined potential.

You may be so accustomed to this latter vision of learning and teaching that it may appear to you as an unassailable truth about the world, and by no means a mere product of a metaphor. Thus, how about the following thought exercise: could you think about some other metaphors with which you would like to describe teaching? Do these other metaphors lead to the same conclusions about the teacher's role in student's learning? If you manage to implement the task you will see that when the metaphor changes, your understanding of how things work is also likely to change. Greek historian and essayist Plutarch was obviously aware of the difference a metaphor can make when he made the following disclaimer: 'A mind is a fire to be kindled, not a vessel to be filled.' You may wish to reflect on the change in our thinking about thinking that takes place when the latter metaphor for mind is supplanted by the former.

Metaphors shape our actions

Because metaphors shape our thinking, they are bound to shape our practical actions too. Indeed, our thinking mediates all our moves: we usually think about what and how to do before making any actual step – and this may be true even if one's conduct appears 'thoughtless'! This simple truth has been encapsulated in the following statement by the Soviet psychologist Lev Vygotsky: 'The gist of human activity is in the dialectic unity between speech and the activity of solving practical problems' (Vygotsky, 1978, p. 24).

To become aware of the impact of metaphors on our practical actions, think about how the shift from the metaphor *mind-as-a-vessel-to-be-filled* to *mind-as-a-fire-to-be-kindled* may affect one's way of teaching. Suppose you are a history teacher and you would like the students to learn about Punic Wars. If you are guided by the mind-as-vessel metaphor, the odds are that you will spend your time in the class at the blackboard, trying to 'transmit' to the students your own knowledge: telling them about what happened, filling them with facts, dropping names and dates. If, on the other hand, you ground your thinking, and thus your teaching, in the mind-as-fire metaphor, you are likely to make some deliberate attempts to 'kindle' your students' curiosity. Rather than just telling them historical facts, you would first ask them to study the map of the Mediterranean in the third century BCE, encouraging them to reflect on territorial aspirations of the then powerful Carthaginian empire and the gradually expanding Rome. You would then suggest that they put themselves in the shoes of either Romans or Carthaginians and think about what their leaders would be likely to do. Indeed, curiosity, like a fire, does not need more than being kindled to do its work.

Metaphors do their work from behind the scene

The upshot of what has been said so far is that, for better or worse, metaphors are behind almost anything we say, think or do. It is only rarely, however, that we recognize the metaphorical connection. More often than not, we take metaphorical entailments for granted and, unaware of their genesis, treat them as facts of life which are nobody's to question. This makes some of our guiding 'truths' inaccessible to critical inspection.

While in force for any kind of metaphor, this statement is particularly relevant for 'extinct' ('dead') metaphors – for those figurative expressions the metaphorical origins of which have long been forgotten. Indeed, 'discursive transplants' are at their most powerful when they lose their 'foreign' identity. Metaphor of object, discussed below, is one of those implicit and extremely influential metaphors that pervade all our discourse. Because of its far-reaching educational consequences, it deserves our special attention.

The metaphor of object

The very ubiquity of the metaphor of object makes it practically transparent to discourse participants. Its invisibility is also due to the fact that the things we say with its help are not easily translatable into 'literal' statements. This metaphor, as many others, has its roots in our tendency for picturing the abstract and inaccessible in the image of the material and tangible. In what follows, after explaining its nature and the reasons for its omnipresence, I argue that in educational context the metaphor of object is a rather mixed blessing.

Objectifying discourses

Consider, for example, the following words, related to learning and thus central to educational discourses: *concept* (or *conception*), *knowledge*, *learning disability*, *abstraction*. Although none of these terms is pointing to a concrete, tangible object, each one of them does seem to refer to a certain self-sustained, well-delineated entity existing at a certain location, possibly in a human head, and enjoying a permanence similar to that of material objects. The object-like effect is attained through the special linguistic forms in which the words usually appear, and which are very close to forms used in descriptions of the material world. Compare, for instance, the three expressions on the left that deal with mental activities, to the three on the right that speak about actions with material objects:

1a Two of my students *constructed* similar *conceptions of fraction.*	**1b** Two of my students *constructed* similar *Lego towers.*
2a He cannot cope with the topic because he *has* a *learning disability.*	**2b** He cannot help with my luggage because he *has* his own *bags* to carry.
3a We have to *give* our students a better *access to* mathematical *abstraction.*	**3b** We have to *give* our students free *access to* the *National Museum.*

Although only half of the sentences deal with tangible things (Lego tower, bags, museum), in all six of them people are said to act on, or to be somehow directed or constrained in their action by an entity which, even if perceptually inaccessible, is implied to have an independent existence, of sorts. The main point I am trying to make here is that the metaphor of object is not a mere substitution for a more literal formulation of the same 'things', but rather is what creates these 'things' in the first place. My argument goes as follows: to begin with, the entities to which we point with the words *conception, learning disability* or *abstraction* are not anything that can ever be observed directly; instead, what we see while conducting a *(mis)-conceptions* survey or when running *learning disability* diagnostic tests is *people in action*. It is only when we are describing our impressions that we turn to entities the presence of which is likely to escape anybody but those who act as expert observers. The act of *objectification* – of translating a discourse about *doing* into a discourse about *being* or *having* – may be exemplified with the following three translations:

4a In the majority of school tests and tasks dealing with fraction she regularly *did well* and *attained* above average scores. → **4b** She *has a good conception* of fraction.

5a In the majority of school tests and tasks she regularly *did well* and *attained* above average scores. → **5b** She *is a good student.*

6a He *cannot cope* with even the simplest arithmetic problems in spite of years of instruction. → **6b** He *has a learning disability.*

Once we objectify a discourse, we no longer notice the metaphorical nature of the objectified terms; rather, we see these terms as speaking about things-in-the-world that are not any less present and real than what we can see with our eyes or touch with our hands. Like with words such as *Lego tower, bag,* or *museum*, we feel that the use of the words *conception, learning disability,* and *abstraction* is a matter of world-imposed necessity, not of linguistic choices; and if the claim about the metaphorical nature of the latter notions is difficult to accept, it only shows how successful we have all been in the project of objectifying!

The metaphor of object in educational discourse

At a closer look, all our discourses are replete with objectifying metaphors, and the specialized disciplinary discourses are no exception. To verify this claim, it suffices to recall such scientific terms as *energy, momentum,* or *speed*, all used in physics to describe motion of bodies; or terms such as *number* or *functions*, which are objectifications of the mathematical procedures of counting and of set-to-set mapping, respectively; or expressions such as *ego, superego, belief, attitude, intention, IQ, mental schema,* or *personality*, used in psychology in describing and explaining human actions.

In the context of education, it is useful to have a closer look at the discourse on cognition. Its objectifying quality is manifest in the definition offered by *Webster's New Third International Dictionary*: although described as a process, cognition is said to result in 'knowledge about perceptions and ideas'. This is echoed by the *Collegiate Dictionary*, which defines cognition as 'the mental faculty or process by which knowledge is acquired'. These definitions are reminiscent of Plutarch's 'mind as a vessel to be filled' metaphor: they make us think of knowledge as a kind of material, of human mind as a container, and of the learner as becoming an owner of the material stored in the container (see also Johnson, 1987).

In view of this, it does not come as a surprise that the *Collins English Dictionary* defines *learning* as 'the act of gaining knowledge'. From this definition, learning emerges as the activity of transferring some entities from one place to another. The metaphor of *learning-as-acquisition* is consonant with our thinking about knowledge as composed of smaller entities. Such decomposability and, conversely, gradual constructability, are salient properties of tangible things. Among the components of knowledge one can list such objects as *concept, conception, idea, notion, misconception, meaning, sense, schema, fact, representation, material, contents.* There are equally many terms that denote the action of making such entities one's own: *reception, acquisition, construction, internalization, appropriation, transmission, attainment, development, accumulation, grasp.* The teacher may help the student to attain her goal by *delivering, conveying, facilitating, mediating* and so on. Once acquired, the knowledge, like any other commodity, may now be *applied, transferred* (to a different context) and *shared with others.*

To recap, the objectifying quality of traditional discourses on cognition and learning expresses itself in the fact that they dichotomize human doings and present them in the dual terms of processes such as *thinking, cognizing* or *learning*, on the one hand, and of the products of these processes, such as *knowledge, concepts, ideas*, on the other hand. All these pertain to an individual learner who is the sole implementer of the processes and the exclusive collector of the products. Being denoted with nouns, the products emerge from these accounts as phenomena more permanent than the processes that brought them into being and also as fully separable from these activities, in that each one of them is now believed to be 'constructible' or 'acquirable' in many different ways. Let me now reflect on gains and pitfalls of educational discourses that picture human processes in this objectified way.

The gains of objectification in educational discourse

Objectified discourse has at least two important advantages over its unobjectified counterpart: it is more parsimonious and it increases our ability to make sense of our experience.

Gain 1: Communicational parsimoniousness and accumulativeness of achievement

The act of discursively turning our own actions into object-like entities vastly increases the effectiveness of communication. To see how it happens, just have another look at the sentences 4a, 5a, and 6a above and notice the relative brevity of their objectified counterparts 4b, 5b, and 6b. Metaphor of object, therefore, makes communication more economical, and thus increases its effectiveness. You can now say much more with much less. Having squeezed lengthy narratives about processes into succinct utterances about objects you may also proceed to new levels of complexity, telling stories about how different processes interact and how they can be improved or combined one with another. Objectifying may thus be the very technique that renders our communication its unique power to accumulate achievement. It is this periodic 'compression' of our discourses that comes with objectification that allows each generation of humans to begin shaping its unique forms of activity from where the former generations left off rather than reinventing the wheel every time anew.

Gain 2: Effectiveness of the discourse as a tool for sense-making

The effectiveness of the metaphor of object as a tool for understanding what is going on and for organizing our subsequent practical actions stems from the fact that it helps us to deal with incessant change. Our relations with the world and with other people are fluid, sensitive to our every action. Objectifying is an attempt to 'make the moment last' – to collapse a video clip into a generic snapshot. It is grounded in the experience-engendered expectation, indeed hope, that in spite of the ongoing change, much of what we see now will repeat itself in a similar situation tomorrow. Consider, once more, sentences 4a, 5a, and 6a on the preceding pages. Although seemingly equivalent, their objectified versions in the right column (4b, 5b, 6b) seem to encourage somewhat different interpretations. In the former type of utterances, the fleeting, the passing, and the changing give way to the relatively permanent, immutable, and ever-present. This, in turn, gives rise to the reassuring conviction that tomorrow we will be able to step into the same river again.

Objectification, therefore, makes us able to cope with new situations in terms of our past experience and gives us tools to plan for the future. Objectifying sentences are not only concise, but also reassuring. Saying *She has a mathematical gift (potential)* makes us confident that the next time this person is charged with mathematical tasks, she will perform to our satisfaction. More generally, objectifying is the ongoing attempt to overcome the transitory nature of our experiences and to gain the sense of security. While objectifying, we overcome distance in time and in space – we 'fold up' the fourth dimension and make the absent present.

In the light of all this, one cannot help concluding that objectification is not anything we could easily give up.[5] This said, we need also to remember that the spectacular gains of objectification are not risk-free.

Pitfalls of objectified educational discourse

As effective as objectifying techniques are in natural sciences, they may be less than helpful when applied to people and their actions. As explained below, there are at least four ways in which excessive objectification of educational discourse can undermine the utility of this discourse and may even bring harm to those toward whom our educating efforts are directed.

Pitfall 1: Overgeneralizations

When talk about processes is replaced with talk about objects, many different forms of actions, e.g. solving certain types of mathematical problems, may be described with the same noun, e.g. *misconception*. This economizes our talk but diminishes its differentiating power. Of necessity, this new talk is bound to gloss over many differences, some of which may be of vital importance. Thus, when we speak of learning in terms of externally given intel- lectual 'goods' that wait 'out there' to be 'acquired', we expect that the goods themselves and the processes of making them one's own will be more or less the same across different settings. There is quickly accumulating empirical evidence that contradicts this expectation. Research tells us about people who, although diagnosed as having a certain 'conception', would soon display behaviours that are at odds with this conception. There is ample evidence showing that task implementation is highly sensitive to the situations in which the activity is performed, to the history of the activity, and to the cultural background of the performers.[6] This undermines the tenets on cross-cultural and cross-situational behavioural invariants in which the acquisitionist discourse is grounded.

Pitfall 2: Logical entanglements

By objectifying, we often entangle ourselves in controversies which have every appearance of disagreements about the 'correctness' of one's world-view but, in fact, cannot be resolved by appeals to empirical evidence. The mechanism that produces the illusion of controversy over facts, while simple, is also mostly invisible: following objectification, we often interpret statements about discursively constructed entities as statements about objects-in-the-world, existing independently of the discourse. This 'ontological collapse' may result in at least two types of complications. First, the objectified talk about human doings may lead to tauto-logical statements disguised as causal explanations. For example, we are likely to say that a child's repetitive failure in mathematics is *caused* by her *learning disability*. And yet, what was identified as the *cause* for the child's invariably unsatisfactory actions is nothing more than the label inspired by properties of the actions. These properties have been objectified and thus presented as in a sense separate from the actions. No value was thus added by the learning-disability 'explanation'. Second, in 'low-resolution' discourse, in which diverse forms of actions may hide under the same objectifying description, such as grades or diag-noses, the differences between individual forms of activity practically disappear. Obviously, overlooking the differences largely diminishes the chances for effective interventions.

Pitfall 3: Self-fulfilling prophecies

Grades and labels such as *learning disabled* may become harmful in yet another way. Although constructed on the basis of one's former actions, they are usually read as statements about the subject's future. The objectified descriptions, which more often than not take the form of statements about one's *abilities* or *potentials*, tend to function as self-fulfilling prophe-cies. Indeed, words that make reference to factors that outlast actions have the power to make one's future in the image of one's past. As agents of continuity and perpetuation, the objectifying descriptions deprive a person of the sense of agency, restrict her sense of responsibility and, in effect, exclude and disable just as much as they enable and create. In particular, when the effectiveness of learning is seen as determined by such personal givens as *potentials, gifts* or *disabilities*, failure is likely to perpetuate failure and success is only too likely to beget success.

Pitfall 4: Normative influences

The metaphor of learning-as-acquisition bears a tacit normative message: it makes the activity of learning into the pursuit of personal possession, comparable to the activity of accumu-lating material assets. Such commodification makes learning into a competitive endeavour, subject to rules not unlike those that govern the pursuit of material goods. It turns school into an arena of power games, where the learner is jolted back and forth by other people's competing interests.

Disobjectifying educational discourse: learning as participation

In response to the much debated weaknesses of objectified educational discourses, a new metaphor for learning has been gaining much visibility for some time now. Perhaps the most salient sign of its presence is the disappearance of such objectifying terms as 'concept' or 'knowledge'. The terms implying an existence of permanent entities are being replaced with words such as 'knowing', 'practising', 'participating' that indicate action. Within this new educational discourse, learning is said to be induction into historically established forms of collective activity (or discourse). The basic tenet is that the learner must gain experience in implementing the activity together with people more skilled than herself, before the activity becomes 'her own', that is, she is able and willing to perform it on her own while solving her own problems. For this reason, some writers replace the word *learner* with the term *legitimate peripheral participant* (Lave and Wenger, 1991), where the word *peripheral* indicates that the participation skills are not yet fully developed and the adjective *legitimate* softens the message and signals the acceptability of this incipient form of participation.

The metaphor of *learning-as-participation* that underlies this new educational discourse should probably be considered as a complement to the acquisition metaphor rather than as its competitor. Although the new metaphor scores high on those accounts on which the older one fails, the reverse is true as well: the participation metaphor shows relative weakness in the areas of the other metaphor's particular strengths. Because participationists refuse to squeeze descriptions of complex human processes into concise but oversimplified stories about permanent entities, their narratives cannot possibly be as thrifty, elegant and supportive of generalized statements as those of the acquisitionists. For the same reason, participationists' stories are not nearly as conducive as their acquisitionist counterparts to the soothing message of stability and predictability. On the other hand, participationists outperform acquisitionists on many of those accounts on which one's ability to inform and improve educational practice seems to depend. First, the same features that sometimes make participationist descriptions messier increase the differential power of these descriptions and thus prevent overgeneralizations. Participationist high-resolution portrayal of learning makes us more aware of individual needs and possibilities. As such, it is a more promising basis for instructional design. Second, in the discourse that avoids dichotomizing and does not stipulate unobservable entities, there is little danger of the logical entanglement typical of objectifying discourses. Third, participationist stories that make no reference to stabilizing entities and permanent traits are much less likely to perpetuate failure. Finally, the normative message of participationist descriptions and analyses is just the opposite of the one carried by the metaphor of object: participationism stresses the value of being a part of collective and favours collaboration over competition.

Conclusion: let one thousand metaphors bloom

Metaphors have emerged from the above account as a double-edged sword: on the one hand, they are among those basic mechanisms that make our advanced thinking possible; on the other hand, they keep our imagination within the confines of our former experience and conceptions, and if not operationalized, they can lead to inconsistent, confusing uses of words and an unhelpful vision of human processes. Since we live by our metaphors, we need to optimize these metaphors' benefits and minimize their risks.

There is more than one way to do so. As a user of metaphors, you may benefit from the following advice. First, be always aware of your metaphors – try to elicit them and then handle them with care. Remember that when speaking with metaphors you may be saying things you did not intend to say, and since what you say is what you get, you may end up not getting what you wanted. Second, be accountable for the way you speak: operationalize your metaphors – be explicit about how you use words and how your uses correspond to those of other interlocutors. Third, let one thousand metaphors bloom. There is no better cure for unwanted entailments of one metaphor than another metaphor's alternative entailments. Above all, however, be always mindful of the possibility that the things you believe are products of metaphors you select rather than empirically verifiable truths imposed by the reality itself. As the creator of your world rather than its mere ventriloquist, you have as much responsibility for as freedom in shaping your own and other people's lives.

Notes

1   Some experts on rhetoric may argue that this figure of speech, one that states a *similarity* of one thing to another rather than their *equivalence*, is called *simile*, not metaphor (this distinction, let me remark, is famously difficult to make: note that similes can also be said without the words *as* and *like*: *an atom is a (miniature) solar system*, *teaching is growing a garden*, etc.). In this article, however, where the focus is on the question of how non-routine linguistic associations inform our thinking, this distinction is irrelevant. Thus, the word metaphor will be used here inclusively, to denote simile as well.

2   Note the recursive nature of the definition of metaphor as 'discursive transplant': metaphor has been defined with the help of a metaphor! As stated by Paul Ricoeur, 'The paradox is that we can't talk about metaphor except by using a conceptual framework which itself is engendered out of metaphor' (Ricoeur, 1977, p. 66).

3   Some authors speak about metaphor as a *mapping from one conceptual domain to another*. It was Michael Reddy (1993, first published 1978) who, in the article 'Conduit metaphor', alerted us to the ubiquity of metaphors and to the fact that they come in thematic clusters. Using as an illustration the notion of *communication*, he has shown how words characteristic of one discourse may take us in a systematic way to another, seemingly unrelated one. In his example, he spoke about the figurative projection from the discourse on *transport* to that on *communication*. Since Reddy's seminal publication, what came to be known as *conceptual mappings* has turned into an object of a vigorous inquiry (Sacks, 1978; Lakoff and Johnson, 1980; Lakoff, 1987, 1993; Johnson, 1987).

4   For the elaboration and the history of the idea of thinking as self-communication see Sfard and Lavie, 2005; Sfard (2008). Let me stress: because communication does not have to be verbal, the communicational definition of thinking does not imply that all our thinking is in words. Note also that the word *discourse* is used here as any type of communication, not necessarily linguistic. This said, much of our thinking is verbal, and even non-verbal (e.g. pictorial or gestural) communication is affected by how we talk.

5   In mathematics, the effect of the 'ban on objectification' would be particularly dramatic. Just imagine we can count, but we did not objectify the discourse on numbers: we do employ number-words for counting, but do not use them as nouns supposed to signify self-sustained objects. In this situation, there is no possibility of impersonal propositions such as $3 + 4 = 7$ (or, in words, *three plus four make seven*) because the number-words *three*, *four*, and *seven* do not function as nouns. In such situation, how do we express the general numerical truth encapsulated in the brief symbolic statement $3 + 4 = 7$?

6   See e.g. studies on market sellers (Cole, 1996), tailors (Lave and Wenger, 1991), street vendors (Nunes *et al.*, 1993), dairy warehouse loaders (Scribner, 1997), shoppers and weight-watchers (Lave, 1988) and nurses (Hoyles and Noss, 2001).

References

Bereiter, C. (1985) 'Towards the solution of the learning paradox', *Review of Educational Research*, 55, pp. 201–26.

Cobb, P., Yackel, E. and Wood, T. (1992) 'A constructivist alternative to the representational view of mind in mathematics education', *Journal for Research in Mathematics Education*, 23(1), pp. 2–33.

Cole, M. (1996) *Cultural Psychology*, Cambridge, MA, The Belknap Press of Harvard University Press.

Hesse, M. (1966) *Models and Analogies in Science*, Notre Dame, IN, Notre Dame University Press.

Hoyles, C. and Noss, R. (2001) 'Proportional reasoning in nursing practices', *Journal for Research in Mathematics Education*, 32, pp. 4–27.

Johnson, M. (1987) *The Body in the Mind: The Bodily Basis of Meaning, Imagination, and Reason*, Chicago, The University of Chicago Press.

Lakoff, G. (1987) *Women, Fire and Dangerous Things: What Categories Reveal about the Mind*, Chicago, The University of Chicago Press.

Lakoff, G. (1993) 'The contemporary theory of metaphor', in A. Ortony (ed.), *Metaphor and Thought*, 2nd edn, Cambridge, Cambridge University Press, pp. 202–50.

Lakoff, G. and Johnson, M. (1980) *The Metaphors We Live By*, Chicago, The University of Chicago Press.

Lave, J. (1988) *Cognition in Practice*, Cambridge, Cambridge University Press.

Lave, J. and Wenger, E. (1991) *Situated Learning: Legitimate Peripheral Participation*, Cambridge, Cambridge University Press.

Nunes, T., Schliemann, A.D. and Carraher, D.W. (1993) *Street Mathematics and School Mathematics*, Cambridge, Cambridge University Press.

Ortony, A. (ed.) (1993) *Metaphor and Thought*, 2nd edn, Cambridge, Cambridge University Press.

Reddy, M. (1993) 'The conduit metaphor: A case of frame conflict in our language about language', in A. Ortony (ed.), *Metaphor and Thought*, 2nd edn, Cambridge, Cambridge University Press, pp. 164–201.

Ricoeur, P. (1977) *The Rule of Metaphor*, Toronto, Toronto University Press.

Sacks, S. (ed.) (1978) *On Metaphor*, Chicago, The University of Chicago Press.

Scribner, S. (1997) 'Mind in action: a functional approach to thinking', in M. Cole, Y. Engström, and O. Vasquez (eds), *Mind, Culture, and Activity: Seminal Papers from the Laboratory of Comparative Human Cognition*, Cambridge, Cambridge University Press, pp. 354–68.

Sfard, A. (1998) 'On two metaphors for learning and on the dangers of choosing just one', *Educational Researcher*, 27(2), pp. 4–13.

—— (2008) *Thinking as Communicating: Human Development, the Growth of Discourses, and Mathematizing*, Cambridge, Cambridge University Press.

Sfard, A. and Lavie, I. (2004) 'Why cannot children see as the same what grownups cannot see as different? Early numerical thinking revisited', *Cognition and Instruction*, 23(2), pp. 237–309.

Vygotsky, L.S. (1978) *Mind in Society: The Development of Higher Psychological Processes*, Cambridge, MA, Harvard University Press.

Reflective questions

1   Choose a page in one of the chapters in this volume (the page should contain continuous text, not list of references or table of contents). Identify on this page all the words and expressions that seem to have metaphorical origins. In each case, try to answer the following questions:

   a   Can the metaphorical expression be replaced by another, more 'literal' one? Can it be operationalized, that is, defined with the help of publicly identifiable characteristics?

   b   What are the possible entailments of the metaphor? Do all of them match the present context, in your opinion? Are they all desirable?

   c   Is any of the identified metaphors the metaphor of object? If not, look at the text again. The odds are you will find one!

2   Does the change from the metaphor of acquisition to that of participation make a difference in school teaching? In other words, does it matter, in your opinion, whether the teacher thinks about students' learning as *acquiring something* (acquisition metaphor) or as *perfecting their participation in certain well-defined, historically established forms of activity*? To answer this question, think about a specific school subject and look for possible differences between 'acquisitionist' and 'participationist' teaching of this subject.

Further reading

Lakoff, G. and Johnson, M. (1980) *The Metaphors We Live By*, Chicago, The University of Chicago Press.

Ortony, A. (ed.) (1993) *Metaphor and Thought*, 2nd edn, Cambridge, Cambridge University Press.

Sfard, A. (1998) 'On two metaphors for learning and on the dangers of choosing just one', *Educational Researcher*, 27(2), pp. 4–13.

Section 2

The person in education

Introduction

Jill Porter

(Cartoon by Ros Asquith)

This section is challenging in that it invites the reader to consider very different approaches to the study of the pupil or student in education. It raises important questions for the reader about the relative place of different theories of explanation, and the role of empirical research as a driving force in seeking to validate or extend our understanding. Inevitably this raises important questions for the reader about the values and assumptions that underpin their own educational practice and provision.

The starting place for this journey is a paper by Egan who, having charted the contribution of theorists to the educational process, in particular the contributions of Plato, Rousseau, Spencer and Piaget, notes that the principles that have greatest currency in education (moving from the concrete to the abstract, starting from what the child knows, starting from the simple and moving to the complex) are not based on empirical research. Indeed he argues they are logically flawed (by definition it being impossible to always start from what the child knows). He argues that there has been a failure of science to inform education, that methods used to test out theories have been problematic, not least because of the difficulty in separating the 'what' from the 'how'. The questions we ask and the answers we seek are inextricably tied. However his point is that it is inappropriate for education, saturated in values with widely different goals to attempt to mimic science. Instead we should return to basic conceptual work and 'generate educational theories of development' which will enable us to understand the ways in which children's understanding of the world changes over time.

This largely historical reflection is followed by a chapter by Holloway and Valentine who invite us to recognise that children and cyberspace are 'symbols of the future' and by implication our understanding of childhood must be seen within the context of the affordances of technology. At the core of their analysis is an account of childhood as a socially constructed identity, one that has changed over time with definitions which are often context-specific and gendered. As they demonstrate with reference to technology, increased interest in researching childhood and giving children a voice has led to attention to the ways in which children create their own positions in space, and their own, often local, cultures. These can be understood in the context of different geographies, sites of negotiation with adults, where issues of risk and safety as well as power-struggles play a role. The authors reject the notions that there are separate real and virtual worlds as they argue 'the social and the technical always co-develop' in a transforming and transformative relationship and therefore we need to understand children in the information age.

Williams takes contrasting views of the learner and the learning process to illustrate the importance of recognising the institutional and political context of learning. He explores analogies of the way we might see the learner, as a 'climber of a building' as an 'acquirer of knowledge' or as someone who is engaged in a shared social practice. His analysis highlights the interrelationship between learning and assessment, where for example notions of progression in understanding (may or) may not underpin the hierarchical organisation of assessment levels. If the economy of the learning organisation is about auditable knowledge outcomes, the motivation for the learner will be about investing in the accumulation of this capital. Limitations are also noted in approaches that seek to assess through using functionally related tasks such as those used internationally in the PISA model where the problem is artificially set in a context that is independent of any social or cultural settings. These examples see the object of the educational activity to be 'results', positions on a league table, rather than an outcome of functional knowledge. He concludes that to understand the learner we need to understand the learning process as framed within a social, cultural historical and political context.

In contrast to the other chapters in this section, Blakemore draws our attention to biological contributions to accounts of development and change in a chapter that looks at the evidence for how the brain continues to develop during adolescence. She presents evidence to suggest that parts of the brain experience more than one sensitive period with a second wave during which the organisation of synapses in the frontal cortex, and the number of synapses in the frontal lobe change. These areas are both noted for their contribution to higher order planning and inhibiting behaviour. These developments are contemporaneous with changes in cognitive functioning including a dip in some aspects of social cognition. This research provides an interesting challenge to the way we seek to explain adolescent behaviour. This is a relatively new field and the contribution of neuro-imaging techniques to research suggests there could be rapid advances to our knowledge that could well change our expectations of the timing and content of formal schooling. The challenge for those working within a sociocultural perspective of development is to link the social processes with these new understandings that concern physiology.

We should not forget that young people themselves are important contributors to our understanding of the learner in education. There is a wide diversity of activities that are encapsulated under the term student voice, and Fielding provides an overview of different frameworks which categorise these in terms of participation, purposes and power relations. He puts forward his own framework of questions to 'interrogate espoused and actual practice' in order to expose the gap between the way in which practices are operationalised and the development of agency in young people. He invites the reader to look back at the ideological assumptions that underpin practices, to re-consider their purposes and values and recognise the ways in which these inform practices including those which might best be described as covert. He provides a rich source of guidance to the literature on methods of gathering pupil views with a particular focus on using visual technologies and students-as-researchers before turning to consider contemporary challenges. How do we best ensure that we seek to represent the plurality of voices? How will teachers recognise the informal offerings of student voice in blogs and web-sites? How will this inform the development of new inter-generational dialogues where teachers and students 'make meaning of their lives together'? This is clearly an important time since student voice could in effect be regenerative for state education, depending on how we see the value and legitimacy of their views.

Taking a contextualist approach to understanding transition periods in children's lives, Tudge, Freitas and Doucet hold that we need to take into account the differences between groups in relation to their social, economic political, cultural and historical nature and also fundamentally what counts as 'the end-point of development'. They draw on Vygotskian theory to consider the importance of the child's social environment to understand how they are influenced by the world around them and on Bronfenbrenner to inform a detailed examination of the spatial context, the micro-, macro- and exosystems in which the child is situated. Using this analysis they pose a number of fundamental questions to ask if we are to consider within-society cultural differences, recognising that children may be part of several cultural groups. The culturally relativist nature of this position suggests that the research studies he describes provide illustrative accounts of the influences on children during the transition process rather than any causal account of how to smooth the process. They provide a series of questions to support teachers in thinking not simply about the personal characteristics of the child but also their local and cultural context and in doing so reveal the true complexity of their account of preparing children for transition. Finally they make a strong case for the dialectical nature of this process with teachers learning from pupils to inform the types of activities and interactions that are given prominence and ask how well teachers are prepared or supported in achieving this.

So how do we view the individual in education? We invite you in reading this section to consider the following broad questions. Do we look for commonalities in the way for example the biological approach seeks to map out the functioning of the human brain? Do we take a broad lens that seeks to understand the learner within a wider context, shaped by political, economic, cultural factors which may indeed recognise the multiple world-views held by learners? Are these informed by the voice of the student and if so how does this dialogue inform our provision, including how children and young people are supported through important stages of transition in their lives?

2.1 Students' development in theory and practice

The doubtful role of research

Kieran Egan

A starting point for this examination of educational research during the past 75 years will be the reception, dismissal, hesitant acceptance, enthusiastic adoption, and apparent decline in the influence on education of Jean Piaget's ideas about development. Piaget's career conveniently spans the 75-year history of the *Harvard Educational Review*. However, his career is a conceptual rather than a sequential starting point for the topics to be discussed. The difficulties found in various theories of development in education form the focus for this article, and they exemplify some little considered but very serious problems for the ambition to bring scientific methods to the study of education. To put this topic into context, I briefly consider the main influences of developmental ideas prior to Piaget's work. This involves discussing the way Jean-Jacques Rousseau set in place the basic assumption on which development in education has been considered ever since, and the particular emphasis generated by the largely forgotten influence of the ideas of Herbert Spencer.

Perhaps Rousseau's, Spencer's, and Piaget's theories do not provide the best lens through which to view the contribution science was expected to make to education by those who most enthusiastically promoted a scientific approach to educational phenomena. Each theorist has always been somewhat suspect to the more self-consciously 'scientific' researchers in education. But the move from one to the other and the increasingly pointed arguments about how to expose the nature of spontaneous development help me describe something of my own trajectory in responding to educational research during the past three decades or more. I came to North America just as the Piaget boom was getting under way, and I was an early enthusiast of his work. The way his theory worked from children's 'illogical' answers was so refreshing, and to me so brilliant. He also seemed to offer a much better understanding of the developmental process itself, and a better understanding of the educational interventions that would be congruent with children's spontaneous development.

I taught the introductory psychology of education course in my home university for a few years, and the more I taught Piaget's theory and its educational implications, the more I became skeptical about those claimed implications. In time I became increasingly skeptical about the theory itself, and then, running out of control, I became skeptical of most of the course content and especially of the claims made for the relevance to education of the psychological theories and research I was teaching. I think part of the problem was that so much of what I was teaching seemed to have very little grasp of the everyday reality of schools and the great diversity among students. As time went on, I began to wonder why so much research over such a long period of time did not seem to be having much purchase on education. Science surely ought to be able to do a better job of dealing with the phenomena of the field. It had worked wonders in other areas, so why was it so sluggish in dealing with education? I was familiar with many of the responses to this question, but came to be persuaded that the problem lay in something little commented on. I also began to wonder if many other educational researchers considered the question – 'Has empirical research clearly benefited education?' – to be an *empirical* question. Despite grounds for some doubt about the general success of the enterprise, from general and depressing achievement data reported in such papers as the *New York Times* and the *Los Angeles Times*, and in works such as Ravitch and Finn (1987), it seemed an assumption that the answer would be positive. For so large an enterprise, there was little apparent attempt to address what surely should be one of the more energetically engaged questions.

Initially, like many researchers, I thought that the scale of research and research funding was paltry compared to the scale of the problems that we were expected to solve. I was also attracted to the view expressed by many researchers that the problem lay with teachers who were not attending adequately to all the knowledge that research was making available to them. But I began increasingly to recognize that many of the teachers in my classes were bright and committed people, and if this knowledge generated by research was having so little effect on their practice, maybe there were other explanations for its apparent irrelevance (apart from my incompetence as a teacher). I began to explore alternative explanations for the apparent failure of science to have much impact on education. I will describe briefly something of the path I followed with regard to developmental ideas.

Empirical or ideological bases for change?

One of the puzzles I faced in exploring developmental theories was that I could not locate any obvious set of changes in educational practice that came in response to particular empirical results. The degree of influence of Piaget's theory on teaching methods and the curriculum, for example, seemed unrelated to empirical results of testing it. But let me approach the problem the way it came to bother me.

Early educational theories such as Plato's recognized that children's thinking is immature and that it becomes more sophisticated as children grow older. That increasing sophistication, however, was generally seen as a product of the social interactions in which children learned valuable knowledge from adults. Without more or less formal tuition, people remained intellectually childlike. In the common ancient Greek view, this was also the condition of adult 'barbarians' (a Greek coinage derived from the way foreign speakers sounded to them: 'bar bar bar bar'). That is, the minds of children were seen to have much in common with the minds of barbarians due to both groups not having received the formal instruction that would make their thinking more sophisticated. While there are suggestions in the premodern era of what today we generally take to be psychological development, such ideas were never clearly distinguished from the sense of development tied in with learning specific kinds of knowledge. For example, Plato – and, in fact, pretty well every other educational thinker before Rousseau – recognized that certain forms of theoretic abstractions became prominent in students' thinking in early adulthood. In the premodern world this was seen as something that happened to knowledge when the individual had accumulated a sufficient amount of it. The valuable knowledge that produced these desirable effects formed the core of an educational curriculum. It did not happen to the minds of those who had not learned that curriculum. This remains a plausible view, though it has largely been displaced by newer conceptions of psychological development.

Jean-Jacques Rousseau (1712–78) offered an alternative view, whose radical nature we sometimes do not notice because we have come to take it completely for granted. In 1762 he published, in novel form – a rather odd novel, to be sure – *Émile, ou De l'éducation*.

In this romance involving a boy reared apart from society, Rousseau introduced a set of revolutionary ideas that are a part of most modern educators' conception of education and that still guide much educational practice. Most significantly for present purposes, Rousseau suggested that the mind goes through its own distinctive developmental process, and the particular knowledge the student learns is only incidental to this development. Indeed, teaching the classical curriculum can interfere with the mind's spontaneous developmental process. He argued that the mind was a bit like the body; both go through regular stages of development, as long as they receive the appropriate environmental supports. For education, Rousseau argued, it was crucial to understand the spontaneous developmental process so that the teacher could conform to it and support it by providing the appropriate exercises, experiences, and knowledge. This is very much the dominant view today. It has led to what has been called a 'biologized' view of the mind (Morss, 1990), for which it seems perfectly normal to use words like 'growth' and to think of the mind as going through stages of spontaneous development. To those influenced by Rousseau, the mind ceased to be seen simply as an epistemological organ and came to be seen also, and to some exclusively, as a psychological organ. That is, instead of seeing the mind as made up of nothing other than the knowledge it has learned, people now see it as engaging in a range of psychological processes that are independent of the particular knowledge acquired.

In the premodern period, the kind of knowledge that was considered most valuable for building a sophisticated mind was summed up in the classical curriculum, in which Latin and Greek, philosophy, history, and theology formed the main pillars. The high status of this kind of knowledge was further undermined by the psychological approach embodied in the ideas of Herbert Spencer (1820–1903), who offered a distinctive shaping to ideas about psychological development. Most people in education today vaguely recognize Spencer's name, associating him perhaps with his curriculum-driving question, 'What knowledge is of most worth?' This neglect of Spencer is perhaps understandable, given his association with the extreme social Darwinist ideas that went out of fashion toward the end of the nineteenth century, but is also astonishing, given his massive influence on education in North America. His book *Education: Intellectual, Moral, and Physical* was published in New York in 1860. By the end of the 1860s the book had been reprinted 15 times by seven different publishers. Over the next few decades it sold hundreds of thousands of copies. It was the widest selling and possibly the most influential book on education published in North America during the period when US public schools were being formed. Virtually everyone involved in education read it (Cremin, 1976; Egan, 2002).

Spencer influenced a number of modern conceptions of development. He became perhaps best known as an advocate of new evolutionary ideas. The problem was that his own conception of evolution was essentially Lamarckian. Jean-Baptiste de Lamarck (1744–1829) had proposed the first comprehensive theory of evolution in his *Philosophie zoologique* of 1809, in which he argued that changes occurred in species over time as acquired characteristics were passed on to their offspring. For example, if a species moved to a new environment in which stretching the neck was necessary to get food, the longer neck would be passed on to its children. Spencer was convinced that Lamarck's account of evolution was correct, and he never really understood the importance of Darwin's theory.

Spencer claimed to have brought to the concept of development what Rousseau had lacked – a scientific theory, derived from evolution. A related idea that Spencer contributed to educational thinking was the idea of progress. His Lamarckian view of evolution and his observation of the regularities that govern all the processes he studied led him to believe that 'progress is not an accident, not a thing within human control, but a beneficent necessity'

(1851, p. 65). Spencer's essay on progress was among his most influential; it imbued many with a sense of great confidence that somehow the most fundamental processes of nature and society were providing a guarantee that we were moving gradually toward a more perfect world. Spencer tied ideas about evolution, development, and progress tightly together. The most powerful movement in education in North America, Progressivism, took its cue and its name from Spencer's central arguments.

Twentieth-century psychology inherited a conception of development that was intricately connected to a nineteenth-century conception of progress. Modern theories of cognitive development are most commonly 'hierarchical integrative' – that is, each stage or phase of development contains, elaborates, and builds on the developments of the previous stage or stages. Consequently, each stage entails an addition without any sense that something might be lost in the process of 'development' (Egan, 1997).

Spencer aimed to show how learning, development, and the daily activities of the classroom were subject to laws. The task for the scientific educator was to discover those laws and to let them shape educational practice for the benefit of children and teachers. Spencer's scientific agenda for educational research generated great optimism and set much of the agenda for educational research throughout the twentieth century. His own belief was that the progress he found in evolution was also evident in human history, and that children's development would recapitulate that progressive process. Spencer believed that he had found a scientific basis for recapitulation, unlike, say, Johann Friedrich Herbart (1776–1841), whose ideas about recapitulation Spencer considered based merely on imprecise intuition. He proposed recapitulation as a central principle for education. Spencer (1928 [orig. 1911]) argued that the 'education of the child must accord both in mode and arrangement with the education of mankind, considered historically' (p. 60). He believed that the child goes through, in a few years, the same process that took our ancestors millennia. By studying the process of mankind's historical progress one can discover principles for both methods of instruction and the curriculum. As with some of Spencer's other ideas, while many took up the underlying principle of a scientific approach to educational phenomena, the particular case of recapitulation ran into various forms of opposition. But the scientific approach to educational research was expected to 'reveal pedagogic possibilities now undreamed of' (Hall, 1904, p. 222).

Spencer's ideas about development led to the formulation of some common instructional principles. In particular, Spencer promoted the idea that teachers should begin with the simple and move to the complex, begin with the concrete and move to the abstract, and begin with the known and move gradually to what is unknown. Spencer (1928 [orig. 1911]) also claimed that 'in education the process of self-development should be encouraged to the uttermost. Children should be led to make their own investigations, and to draw their own inferences. They should be *told* as little as possible, and induced to *discover* as much as possible' (p. 62). Superficially, some of these principles will seem familiar from the works of such people as Johann Heinrich Pestalozzi (1746–1827), Herbart, and Rousseau himself. And, certainly, these educators had considerable influence, especially Herbart, whose five steps for planning instruction were very widely used in America during the latter part of the nineteenth century and into the twentieth. What Spencer offered, however, was a coherent 'scientific' account of education that was tied into a set of ideas that applied also to the physical and social worlds. It was the systematic vision that Spencer developed at encyclopedic length in a huge range of areas of inquiry that gave his work its compelling force, particularly in American education (Egan, 2002).

Education, Spencer wrote, had been most often conducted by forcing irrelevant information into the minds of reluctant children by methods that were patently barbarous. He proposed we should instead draw on new scientific principles to make the process efficient as well as pleasant for the child. In the past, education had dealt with subjects that held their place in the curriculum by dint of tradition and the pretensions to an ornamental culture of a leisured class; instead, he argued, we should make the curriculum of direct relevance and utility to the lives our students would actually lead. In the past, schooling was centered on the knowledge written in texts or authorized by teachers, whereas Spencer believed that the child's own developing needs and expanding activities should be central to the curriculum and to teachers' efforts. No doubt these ideas will appear familiar, even if they are not associated primarily with Herbert Spencer.

What is curious about some of these claims is the degree to which they follow assumptions derived from beliefs or ideology rather than research. The status of claims such as the notion that we should begin teaching with the known and gradually expand to the unknown, or with the simple and move to the complex, or the concrete to the abstract, will occupy us later.

Piaget's reception

Piaget's long career, neatly framing the 75 years of this set of inquiries, began when he became a student of Pierre Janet in Paris. Janet had been strongly influenced by Spencer's ideas through the American, James Mark Baldwin. The influence of Spencer's 'biologized' conception of development, his intricate connections between development and progress, and his assumptions of how one might go about establishing a scientific image of the developmental process are all clear in Piaget's work. Piaget's first books were translated into English about 75 years ago, including *Judgement and Reasoning of the Child,* which appeared in London in 1928, and *The Child's Conception of the World,* which appeared the following year in New York. While there was considerable scholarly interest in Piaget's work, it did not initially spur much in the way of curriculum development activities. Also, in a climate dominated by behaviorism, Piaget's unusual methodology and analyses of children's performance of odd tasks did not have a significant impact on mainstream thinking about development. Also, of course, the dominant theoretical issues of the day concerned the curriculum battles being waged between traditionalists and progressivists, and Piaget's ideas initially seemed to have nothing much to say to these.

By the 1950s, in Lawrence Cremin's words, 'The more fundamental tenets of the progressives had become the conventional wisdom of American education' (1976, p. 19). While the language of education might have become progressivist, this did not mean that everyday practice had correspondingly changed. But the force of Cremin's observation apparently is not often recognized. The language of education in North America from the 1950s on became infused with progressivist assumptions. Even so, modern progressivist reformers think that education is dominated by an unmovable conservatism. The voices that receive the most enthusiastic response among educational researchers are those that promise to bring basic progressivist principles into practice. For example, if one were to look at the most influential modern voices in education, those that seem to bring us closer to realizing the progressivist promise for education are the most eagerly attended to: Eliot Eisner, Howard Gardner, Maxine Greene, and Nel Noddings all offer new insights into the meaning of the progressivist vision and how to bring it to realization. Those progressivist principles promised to make education more humane by adapting it to students' 'natural' or spontaneous forms of learning and development. Progressive educators believed that scientific procedures could uncover what these processes were and devise compatible pedagogical methods.

Piaget's theory quickly gained an enormous audience when it was introduced in the context of Jerome Bruner's report of the Woods Hole conference, which was published in 1960 as *The Process of Education*, as supporting the progressivist aims of making education more humane, scientifically supported, and efficient. The older, 'scientifically established' principles of education were considered a failure when the beeps of the Soviets' Sputnik were first heard around the world.

The trajectory of Piaget's reputation and the influence of his ideas on education have followed a curious route. During the 1960s his work became widely known among educational scholars, and its implications for education were explored. Among the many books that brought his work to the attention of American psychologists and educators during this period one might note John Flavell (1963), Hans Furth (1970), David Elkind's studies and his book of 1976, and Richard Ripple and Verne Rockcastle's edited book of 1964, along, of course, with a steady flood of books from Piaget and his collaborator, Barbel Inhelder. Piaget's name began to appear in curriculum documents in many states in the late 1960s and 1970s, often accompanied by a note that his ideas about children's development deserve some attention. In the 1970s and early 1980s, his developmental theory began to have a serious impact on curriculum revisions around North America and Europe, and his name was commonly found in such documents with more or less elaborate sketches of his 'stages of development'. By the late 1980s, his name appeared less and less in such documents, while his often unattributed theory was represented simply as how children developed. What was at first represented as a theory that might be of some interest had almost entirely lost its status as a theory. Piaget had become almost invisible in such documents, but his ideas remained fundamental to the definition of child development and its implications for practice (Roldão, 1992). Since the 1990s, Piaget's general reputation has suffered from increasingly compelling criticisms, yet his theory's influence on curriculum documents and teacher-education texts marches on. For example, *Time* magazine notes, 'Although not an educational reformer, he championed a way of thinking about children that provided the foundation for today's education-reform movements' (Papert, 1999, p. 104). Also, it seems fair, still, to accept Susan Sugarman's 1987 judgment that 'despite appearances to the contrary, Piaget's ideas and overall approach continue to dominate much of developmental psychology' (p. 241), and even more so, developmental ideas in education.

If one were to look at research on Piaget's theory in education, one would not find that the rise of his reputation coincided with sets of positive empirical tests of the theory from the 1960s to the 1980s. On the one hand, researchers consistently replicated Piaget's classic conservation experiments, though there were irregularities in results and much argument about the criteria for what counted as conservation, for example. But in general, Piaget's genius in attending closely to the peculiar answers children gave to his questions led to a genuine revolution in theorizing about their intellectual development. For millennia people had been hearing the odd logic of early childhood and had usually dismissed it as a kind of intellectual froth to be blown away by more mature forms of thinking. Piaget made it a cornerstone of his theories. As a scientific theory, however, Piaget's frameworks rested on a set of experiments that remained somewhat contentious. In many of the experiments, for example, instructions were given orally, and many found it difficult to conclude whether what the experiments were disclosing was a common sequence of language development or the development of underlying operative structures, as Piaget claimed. Despite such doubts about Piaget's methodology, no competing theory provided more insights into intellectual development. On the other hand, the enthusiasm for Piaget's work was much stronger in education than even in psychology. Projects and programs in curriculum and instructional methods were under way across the continent. Much of this educational work was uninformed by reliable research that showed comparisons between Piagetian programs and others. What research there was suffered the usual problem: the programs that were to be compared were not simply different means to an agreed and common end; the methodological difference also reflected different educational objectives. It had gradually become clearer during the 75 years we are looking at that in education, following a physical science model of comparing alternative treatments just did not deliver the kind of results expected. Progressivist methods, for example, might well be found to be less 'efficient' in achieving particular results, compared with forms of 'programmed learning'. But, progressivists pointed out, the acquisition and memorization of particular knowledge was not the only educational aim. As Dewey had pointed out, in education the aim is tied up in the method used; one uses progressivist methods because they are a part of what you are trying to achieve educationally, not simply because they are the most efficient method of ensuring memorization of some knowledge.

Even so, some large-scale research projects were attempted, comparing programs whose teachers had been trained in Piagetian methods with the results of regular schools teaching the same curriculum. Charles Brainerd reviewed four large comparative studies and concluded that the evaluation data, which included children's performance on concrete-operational content and a range of fairly standard Piagetian activities and also standardized achievement tests (see Brainerd, 1978), 'have failed to show any differences between Piagetian instruction and other curricula' (p. 298). Indeed, in one of the Piagetian schools that was compared with a traditional school, Brainerd concluded that 'those few comparisons which revealed differences tended to favor the traditional group' (1978, p. 293).

A theory that promised to show how a scientific approach to development could revolutionize pedagogy ought to show better results. Piagetian writings for teachers commonly made strong claims about the results that would follow if teachers attended to the theory and shaped their instruction and curricula accordingly. Such knowledge of the process of development would have, in a continuing echo of G. Stanley Hall (1904), 'pedagogical possibilities now undreamed of' (vol. 2, p. 222). The odd feature, of course, is that the inconclusive results of Piagetian research seem to have had little impact on the enthusiastic reception of Piaget's ideas in education.

Empirical science and conceptual analysis in studying education

A background hum to these explorations – a bit like the background radiation from the Big Bang – came from Ludwig Wittgenstein's brief but rather pointed observations about the state of psychology. Wittgenstein's claim follows from the recognition that there is no such identifiable thing as 'the scientific method'. Science proceeds by working out sets of questions that can be addressed to particular kinds of phenomena to result in certain kinds of answers. Phenomena, questions, and acceptable answers are intricately tied together. The problem with psychology, Wittgenstein said, was that 'the existence of the experimental method makes us think we have the means of solving the problems which trouble us; though problem and method pass one another by' (1963, p. 232).

If that was the background hum, an observation more in the foreground about scientific research in education was the guidance offered by its theories. The main source of my growing skepticism about Piaget's theory, and then about many others I had been teaching, was tied up with another of Wittgenstein's observations about psychology. He characterized the psychology of his day as suffering from a defect that might also be directed at much current educational research: he saw a combination of 'experimental methods and *conceptual confusion*' (1963, p. 232; emphasis in original).

Lev Vygotsky (1997) made an argument similar to Wittgenstein's, which also helped me understand why so much of the work that was based on psychological theories seemed to have so little purchase on educational phenomena:

> A concept that is used deliberately, not blindly, in the science for which it was created, where it originated, developed and was carried to its ultimate expression, is *blind*, leads nowhere, when transposed to another science. Such blind transpositions, of the biogenetic principle, the experimental and mathematical method from the natural sciences, created the appearance of science in psychology which in reality concealed a total impotence in the face of studied facts (p. 280).

While that may seem an overwrought judgment about psychology in general, it captured what was bothering me about psychology's contributions to basic educational concepts, such as 'learning' and 'development'.

Take the conclusions that Spencer derived from his developmental theory, that learning and teaching should move from the simple to the complex, the concrete to the abstract, the known to the unknown. Are these ideas supported by scientific research? They are taken for granted by nearly everyone in education as far as I can tell, but how did they get that status?

What bothered me most about Piaget's theory was not the methodological issues, but rather the fact that educators seemed to use his progress-dominated theory to support principles similar to those that Spencer had articulated. For example, Piaget's theory was used to support practices based on the principle that the teacher should move from the 'concrete' to the 'abstract'. This is a principle that came to be embodied in the social studies curriculum, beginning with the local, empirical environment and moving gradually to more distant, conceptually grasped environments – stimulated, again, by Spencer – and it has led to the insistence on beginning with 'hands-on' activities and manipulation of objects prior to conceptualization about them. However, given the definition of those two terms in Piagetian theory, in which later stages incorporate the achievements of the earlier ones, how could the abstract have preceded the concrete? That is, in some degree the sequence seemed not a matter for empirical verification; it is true by definition of the terms (Phillips and Kelly, 1975). Similarly, Piaget also implied that the developmental direction from the simple to the complex and from the known to the unknown was supported by empirical research based on a scientific theory.

Consider the ubiquitous principle that one must move from the known to the unknown: 'If I had to reduce all of educational psychology to just one principle, I would say this: The most important single factor influencing learning is what the learner already knows. Ascertain this and teach him accordingly' (Ausubel, 1968, p. 235). There is something conceptually confusing about such claims resulting from psychological research.

First, if this is a fundamental principle of human learning, there is no way the process can begin. That is, the principle sets one into an infinite regress looking for prior learnings. Now obviously that is not what the researcher or teacher uses the principle for, but if the principle is to make sense we need to be able to discover some starting point for the process. That we cannot do this in any sensible way should alert us that something is wrong with the principle.

Second, if novelty – that is, things unconnected with what is already known – is the problem for human learners, reducing the amount of the novelty does not solve the problem. And if we can manage some novelty, why can we not manage more? That is, the principle tells us to tie new learning to old learning because, it implies, students cannot grasp things that are unconnected with what they already know. But if they are to learn *anything* new, which they do all the time, this shows that students can learn things that are, in some degree, however small, unconnected with what they already know. So why insist on a principle whose sole justification is based on something obviously false? (We'll see below why people hold to the principle despite such gaping flaws.)

The third objection is less directed at the principle than at how it has been invariably interpreted in education, and particularly in the construction of the elementary social studies curriculum. Many educators assume that what children know first and best is the details of their everyday social lives. That is, they assume that children's thinking is simple, concrete, and engaged with their local experience. But children also have imaginations and emotions, and these, too, connect with the world. If children's minds are supposed to be restricted to the everyday details of their social lives, why are they full of monsters, talking middle-class animals like Peter Rabbit, and titanic emotions? Elsewhere I have commented (Egan, 1997) on the absurdity of explaining Peter Rabbit's appeal in terms of its 'familiar family setting', when it involves a safe woodland and a dangerous cultivated garden, and death so close, and so on.

Fourth, and this is perhaps a doubtful notion to suggest, a few moments' reflection should make clear that no one's understanding of the world expanded and expands according to this principle of gradual content association. The neat process of gradually 'expanding horizons' might appeal to the curriculum developer concerned that prerequisite knowledge is constantly in place to ensure a smooth progress through the math or science curricula, but if you reflect on how your understanding of the world and human experience has grown, and continues to grow, you will likely find that it is a much messier and more unpredictable and wild process.

One might similarly analyze the three other principles and show that they too are very dubious. What is 'concrete' about children's learning language early on? Perhaps learning the meaning of 'table' might be, oddly, called concrete, but how can learning the meaning of 'and' and 'but' be concrete in any sense? What 'concrete' instruction is required for the child to master such terms? These principles seem to have an odd status, in that they seem almost true by definition, but at the same time they seem full of holes the more closely one analyzes them. I concluded, aided by Jan Smedslund (1978a, 1978b, 1979), that the reason such doubtful principles retained their force in education was due to their being, like most knowledge claims in education – or so it increasingly seemed to me – a mixture of analytic truth and empirical generalization. That is, at some level the principle is true simply because people define its terms to mean something that cannot be other than true. So, in the case of the 'known to unknown' principle, it is understood to mean something like, you do not know whatever you do not know and if you learn something new, it has to fit in with what you can find comprehensible. Put like this, the principle is just a logical truth – you do not have to run an experiment to discover that a person cannot understand something they lack prerequisite knowledge for. At this level, the principle is not very helpful. What would make it interesting are reliable empirical generalizations; that is, research showing conditions that constrain learning that are other than logical truths. We largely lack these in education because researchers commonly mix up analytic elements – things that are true by definition or by logic – with empirical components – things that could be otherwise but are discovered to be true as a result of experiments. By consistently mixing the two, we get claims that are assumed to be empirical generalizations resulting from research but whose generalizability relies heavily on the analytic component hidden in how the principle is formulated.

Smedslund analyzed various pieces of social science research and showed that they were mostly what he called pseudo-empirical; they claimed to have established empirical connections when their positive findings actually relied on prior conceptual connections. A.R. Louch (1966) had shown earlier how much research in psychology had similar defects. He began with the example of Edward Thorndike's 'law of effect', which claimed to have established that people choose to repeat behaviors that have pleasurable consequences. Louch pointed out that the connection between repeating behaviors and expecting pleasurable consequences is not conceptually independent. The two behaviors are analytically tied: what we mean by choosing to repeat behaviors is tied up with what we count as pleasurable consequences. Louch further noted that E.R. Hilgard's list of findings firmly established by psychological research were similar in kind. Hilgard's (1956) first proposition was that 'brighter people can learn things less bright ones cannot learn' (p. 486). But what we *mean* by brightness involves the ability to learn more. Or take a more recent example. In the *How People Learn* project the aim has been to focus on findings that 'have both a solid research base to support them and strong implications for how we teach' (Donovan *et al.*, 1999, p. 12). The basic principles derived from carefully applying these criteria include the finding that: 'To develop competence in an area of inquiry, students must (a) have a deep foundation of factual knowledge; (b) understand facts and ideas in the context of a conceptual framework; and (c) organize knowledge in ways that facilitate retrieval and application' (p. 12). Such claims seem to have a similar character to those above. Clearly a, b, and c are definitional of what we *mean* by competence in an area of inquiry. Empirical research could not have established that one could be competent in an area of inquiry without deep factual knowledge (and how deep is 'deep'?), or without understanding facts and ideas in the context of a conceptual framework, or while organizing knowledge in ways that hindered retrieval and application. It may prove of practical value to spell out the meaning of competence like this, but the spelling out could have been done without the empirical research that is supposed to have established these conditions of competence.

Let me try to expose the problem with these kinds of research 'findings' by giving a simple example. Let us imagine a team of researchers exploring how students learn and memorize information. They might run an experiment that involves the students in learning randomly ordered seven-digit numbers. If one student's randomly assigned number is her telephone number, the results of the experiment would be contaminated by this arbitrary coincidence. But a sufficiently large sample will neutralize the irregular result in this case.

Let us further assume that this experiment with learning random seven-digit numbers is part of a study that is testing the hypothesis that ordered information is more easily memorized and remembered than random or disordered information. An educational implication of supporting the hypothesis, it might be claimed, is that it will help us understand how to present information to students, particularly if we have to organize it in list form. After the experiment, and many others like it conducted with different populations, the researchers might feel confident in claiming that their research has shown that ordered lists are learned more easily than random lists.

But this would be another pseudo-empirical finding. The analytic component concerns the conceptual ties between order and learnability. Our mind's ability to learn and our notions of what counts as ordered are connected before and regardless of whatever research shows about their relationship. If students in the experimental group learned random lists more easily than ordered lists, the researchers would have scanned the lists for some order they had failed to notice earlier. On discovering that, in one case, the supposedly random number was the student's telephone number, they would feel satisfied that they had accounted for the anomalous result. What we *mean* by order is conceptually connected to what we can more readily recognize and learn. No experiment is required to establish the generalization.

In the experimental group, however, there will have been some variability among subjects' learning and memorizing the random numbers. The telephone coincidence is just one dramatic anomaly, but then there will be the case of the numbers that are, for another student, his mother's birth date, and the one that is only a digit different from another student's bank account code, and so on. Certainly not all random numbers will look equally random to all subjects, but these findings are arbitrary. Researchers control for them by having large samples and other methods. What they cannot do, of course, is generalize from these anomalies. Researchers cannot generalize about that student's ability to learn and memorize random numbers or about other students' ability to learn and memorize those particular numbers.

So in the case of this research there is an analytic tie that guarantees a strong positive correlation both between orderedness in the lists and the ease of learning and memorizing and between randomness and difficulty. There is, in addition, a range of arbitrary elements that will have ensured that what counts as ordered for one subject will seem random to another, and a variety of indeterminable arbitrary contaminants in the data. By confusing the two, by failing to distinguish the analytic component from the arbitrary components, researchers will likely treat the results of the study as an empirically established connection. The analytic component, however, generalizes absolutely. The arbitrary elements cannot be generalized at all. Establishing the analytic component does not need an experiment. And the arbitrary elements, which are genuinely empirical, cannot be generalized.

Conclusion

Rousseau's and Spencer's biological model of human development generated a range of assumptions, which continue to influence how teachers are prepared and how children are expected to learn. Although Rousseau's biologized conception of the mind helped to refute the old notion of a metaphysical and mystical mind distinct from the body, his modeling of the development of the mind on that of the body was excessive. It is far from clear, for example, that food's contribution to our bodily development is very like knowledge's contribution to our minds' development. In the latter case, knowledge becomes a constituent of the mind in a way that food does not become a constituent of the body – eating lots of spinach will not make you look more like a spinach, but the mind *is* shaped by the kinds of experience and knowledge it takes in. Spencer's idea of progressive development and learning gave us those ubiquitous practical principles of moving from the known to the unknown, from the simple to the complex, from the concrete to the abstract. Piaget's more elaborated account of the developmental process supported both progressive educational ideas and Spencer's principles. Despite the important contributions of these thinkers, they have left us with some deep dilemmas about the role and value of empirical research in education.

The usual way of representing education's relationship with scientific psychological research is to suggest an analogy – physics : engineering :: psychology : education. The increasingly preferred version seems to be biology : medicine :: psychology : education. But psychology is not a science like physics or biology. And education is unlike engineering and medicine: it is value-saturated in the way engineering is only marginally, and both medicine and engineering do not have radically different goals asserted for their activities in the way that is common in education. Asserting the analogy seems to replace presenting an argument, as though the analogy were pellucid rather than obfuscating.

It is still the case that anything claimed in education without the support of empirical research is dismissed as speculative, or, as the summary of the *How People Learn* project puts it, what is now 'subject to powerful research tools' was in the past 'a matter for philosophical arguments' (Donovan *et al.*, 1999, p. 5). The implication is that cognitive science will now clear up what was formerly mere speculation or philosophical arguments, just as the physical sciences cleared up and displaced speculation and philosophical arguments about, say, the nature of the objects visible in the night sky, the causes of diseases, and so on. It is increasingly unclear to me that this is an accurate way of seeing the relationship between psychology and education. The assertiveness of cognitive scientists in laying a claim on 'science' seems misplaced. Basic conceptual work has been avoided and left undone, and we go ahead with precisely the kinds of confusion that Wittgenstein pointed out some years ago. Methodological sophistication cannot compensate for a lack of conceptual clarity; method and problem pass one another by.

The waning of Piaget's theory has been accompanied by more attention to Vygotsky's ideas. Some of the interesting areas being opened up follow on Vygotsky's ideas about how students pick up cognitive tools as they grow up in a society, and also about his ideas on the development of imagination. This has facilitated research of a primarily analytic kind into the sets of cognitive tools that come along with an oral language, such as stories, metaphor, forming images from words, and so on, and then working out how one can design frameworks for planning teaching that build in these tools. One can similarly analyze the sets of cognitive tools that come along with literacy, such as fascination with the extreme and exotic, association with heroes, engagement by wonder, and so on, and work out how these too can facilitate imaginatively engaging learning. Such an approach leads to quite distinctive conceptions of development, focusing on the kinds of understanding we can construct with our 'cognitive tool kits', and also to new and potent methods of teaching that focus on engaging the imagination. (One source for this work is available at http://www.ierg.net; also see Vygotsky, 1997, 2004.)

Oddly enough, this newer Vygotskian program takes us closer to Plato than to the kinds of conceptions of development that have held sway in education from Rousseau's time through the years of Piagetian dominance. A concern with 'cognitive tools' drives us more in the direction of epistemological constructs than anything like Piagetian operations. A concern with stimulating and developing cognitive tools takes one immediately to analysis of the curriculum content that constitutes the tools in question; that is, from seeing the 'cultural tools' that can become 'cognitive tools' for each child. The continuing dominance of progressivist thinking in North America has led, during the recent period of increasing Vygotskian influence, to slightly bizarre attempts to suggest that Piagetian and Vygotskian theories are coherent or compatible, despite attempts to show how inappropriate such conflations are (Kozulin *et al.*, 2003; Wertsch, 1985, 1991). It is as though – to use Piagetian language – Vygotsky can be accommodated in North America only if he is assimilated to progressivist assumptions. It is of course presumptuous of me to suggest, at a time when progressivist tenets remain almost at the level of presuppositions in educational thinking, that psychological developmental theories of the kind that have dominated educational thinking on the topic are an aberration and they are finally beginning to lose their hold. The lack of any clear empirical demonstration of their benefit to education must, in the end, lead toward their dissolution. In their place, we may hope to see attempts to generate *educational* theories of development, whose character will be more sensitive to the phenomena of education than to those of psychology and which will likely gain sustenance from Plato and Vygotsky rather than Spencer and Piaget. The problem is to find ways to characterize the successive modes in which children make sense of the world and of their experience in a language that leads us directly to distinctive curriculum content and new methods of teaching. (An attempt to frame such a theory may be found, I am only moderately ashamed to point out, in Egan, 1997.)

Acknowledgements

Originally published as Kieran Egan, 'Students' development in theory and practice: the doubtful role of research', *Harvard Educational Review,* 75(1) (Spring 2005), pp. 25–41. Copyright © by the President and Fellows of Harvard College. All rights reserved. Reprinted with permission. For more information, please visit www.harvardeducationalreview.org

References

Ausubel, D.P. (1968) *Educational Psychology: A Cognitive View,* London, Holt, Rinehart and Winston.

Brainerd, C.J. (1978) *Piaget's Theory of Intelligence,* Englewood Cliffs, NJ, Prentice-Hall.

Bruner, J. (1960) *The Process of Education,* Cambridge, MA, Harvard University Press.

Cremin, L.A. (1961) *The Transformation of the School,* New York, Vintage Books.

—— (1976) *Public Education,* New York, Basic Books.,

Donovan, S., Bransford, J.D., and Pellegrino, J.W. (eds) (1999) *How People Learn: Bridging Research and Practice,* Washington, DC, National Academy Press.

Egan, K. (1997) *The Educated Mind: How Cognitive Tools Shape Our Understanding,* Chicago, University of Chicago Press.

—— (2002) *Getting It Wrong From the Beginning: Our Progressivist Inheritance from Herbert Spencer, John Dewey, and Jean Piaget,* New Haven, CT, Yale University Press.

Elkind, D. (1976) *Child Development and Education: A Piagetian Perspective,* New York, Oxford University Press.

Flavell, J.H. (1963) *The Developmental Psychology of Jean Piaget,* Princeton, NJ, D. Van Nostrand.

Furth, H.G. (1970) *Piaget for Teachers,* Englewood Cliffs, NJ, Prentice-Hall.

Hall, G.S. (1904) *Adolescence: Its Psychology and its Relations to Physiology, Anthropology, Sociology, Sex, Crime, Religion, and Education* (vol. 2), New York, D. Appleton.

Hilgard, E.R. (1956) *Theories of Learning,* New York, Appleton-Century-Crofts.

Kozulin, A., Gindis, B., Ageyev, V.S., and Miller, S.M. (eds) (2003) *Vygotsky's Educational Theory in Context,* Cambridge, Cambridge University Press.

Louch, A.R. (1966) *Explanation and Human Action,* Berkeley, University of California Press.

Morss, J.R. (1990) *The Biologizing of Childhood: Developmental Psychology and the Darwinian Myth,* Hove, Lawrence Erlbaum Associates.

Papert, S. (1999) 'Jean Piaget', *Time,* 29 March, pp. 104–6. Available online at http://www.time.com/time/time100/scientist/profile/piaget.html.

Phillips, D.C., and Kelly, M.E. (1975) 'Hierarchical theories of development in education and psychology', *Harvard Educational Review,* 45, pp. 351–75.

Piaget, J. (1928) *Judgement and Reasoning of the Child,* London, Routledge and Kegan Paul.

—— (1929) *The Child's Conception of the World,* New York, Harcourt Brace Jovanovich.

Ravitch, D., and Finn, C.E., Jr. (1987) *What do our 17-year-olds Know? A Report on the First National Assessment of History and Literature,* New York, Harper and Row.

Ripple, R.E., and Rockcastle, V.N. (1964) *Piaget Rediscovered,* Ithaca, NY, Cornell University Press.

Roldão, M. do C. (1992) *The Concept of Concrete Thinking in Curriculum for Early Education: A Critical Examination,* unpublished doctoral dissertation, Simon Fraser University, Burnaby, British Columbia.

Smedslund, J. (1978a) 'Bandura's theory of self-efficacy: a set of common-sense theorums', *Scandinavian Journal of Psychology,* 18, pp. 1–14.

—— (1978b) 'Some psychological theories are not empirical: reply to Bandura', *Scandinavian Journal of Psychology*, 19, pp. 235–52.

—— (1979) 'Between the analytic and the arbitrary: a case study of psychological research', *Scandinavian Journal of Psychology*, 20, pp. 101–2.

Spencer, H. (1851) *Social Statics*, London, Chapman.

—— (1928) *Essays of Education and Kindred Subjects*, London: J.M. Dent (original work published 1911).

Sugarman, S. (1987) *Piaget's Construction of the Child's Reality*, Cambridge, Cambridge University Press.

Vygotsky, L.S. (1997) *The Collected Works of L.S. Vygotsky* (vol. 3, R. W. Rieber and J. Wollock, eds), New York, Plenum.

—— (2004) [1930] 'Imagination and creativity in childhood', *Journal of Russian and East European Psychology*, 42, pp. 7–91.

Wertsch, J.V. (1985) *Vygotsky and the Social Foundation of Mind*, Cambridge, MA, Harvard University Press.

—— (1991) *Voices in the Mind: A Sociocultural Approach to Mediated Action*, Cambridge, MA, Harvard University Press.

Wittgenstein, L. (1963) *Philosophical Investigations* (G.E.M. Anscombe, trans.), Oxford, Blackwell.

Reflective questions

Egan argues that we need to place less reliance on empirical research to understand how children's understanding changes over time and more on developing theoretical explanations.

1   Who or what informs your understanding of progression in children's understanding?
2   What do you perceive as its strengths and limitations?
3   How do you think this influences your teaching?

Further reading

Eraut, M. (2005) 'Editorial: Uncertainty in Research', *Learning in Health and Social Care*, 4(2), pp. 47–52.

Hyslop-Margison, E.J. and Naseem, M.A (2008) *Education Research as Analytic Truths: The Pseudo-Empirical Claims of Empirical Study*, Netherlands, Springer.

Sanders, J.T. (1989) 'Educational psychology: between an epistemic rock and a hard place', *Canadian Journal of Education/Revue canadienne de l'éducation*, 14(2), pp. 220–5.

2.2 Cyberworlds

Children in the information age

Sarah L. Holloway and Gill Valentine

Introduction

In this chapter we introduce the understanding of children and childhood that underpins the way the research was conducted. Then we introduce our understanding of technology by outlining some of the theoretical debates about ICT, drawn from the social studies of technology and geographies of cyberspace.

Cyberspace is one of 'the zones that scripts the future' (Haraway, 1997: 100). Just as industrial technology was seen to transform Western society in the nineteenth century, so many contemporary academic and popular commentators argue that Information and Communication Technologies (ICT) are about to inflict far-reaching economic, social, cultural, and political changes upon the twenty-first century (for an overview see Kitchin, 1998a, 1998b). Most notably, ICT are popularly understood to be about, if they have not already led to, the transformation of work and the production of value, as manufacturing is substituted by information as the dominant form of employment (Marshall, 1997). The opportunities that ICT offer users to access information and communicate with whom they want, freed from the material and social constraints of their bodies, identities, communities and geographies mean that these technologies are regarded as potentially liberating for those who are socially, materially or physically disadvantaged (Turkle, 1995). Likewise, the speed and connectivity of the internet offer scope to facilitate greater participation in the political process, to re-scale politics from the local or national to the global, and to produce more informed democracy. However, these opportunities also bring new risks. Most notably that those who lack technological skills to participate in the Information Age will be excluded from these activities and, unable to exercise their rights and responsibilities, will consequently be denied full citizenship.

Children, as symbols of the future themselves, are at the heart of debates both about how the possibilities that ICT afford should be realised, and about the 'new' dangers that these technologies might also bring for the Net generation. The British prime minister's statement that 'Children cannot be effective in tomorrow's world if they are trained in yesterday's skills' echoes a similar point made in a Labour Party document, *Communicating Britain's Future*. This claims that:

> We stand on the threshold of a revolution as profound as that brought by the inven-
> tion of the printing press. New technologies, which enable rapid communication to
> take place in a myriad of different ways around the globe, and permit information to be
> provided, sought and received on a scale so far unimaginable, will bring fundamental

changes to our lives ... In many ways it will be in education that the greatest potential use for the new networks will emerge.

(The Labour Party, 1995, pp. 3, 18)

While supporting such political aims to advance children's technological literacy, popular commentaries have also highlighted the fact that children may be at risk of corruption from material that they can find on the internet, and abuse at the hands of strangers whom they might encounter in online spaces (Wilkinson, 1995; McMurdo, 1997; Evans and Butkus, 1997). These fears are exacerbated by the fact that parents and teachers – particularly those who are less technologically literate than the young people in their care – have a limited ability to control or filter what children might see and learn on the World-Wide-Web (henceforth WWW). The internet-connected PC, as the latest form of media (following on from television, stereos, console games and so forth) to play an important role in children's peer group relationships (Suss *et al.*, 2001), is also imagined to threaten children's offline activities. Popular concerns have been expressed that using a computer is a solitary and potentially addictive activity, provoking fears that some children might become so obsessed with the technology that they will socially withdraw from the offline world of family and friends (Hapnes, 1996). In doing so it is suggested that they will also miss out on the imaginative opportunities for outdoor play that public space is perceived to offer, putting not only their social, but also their physical well-being at risk (Gumpert and Drucker, 1998; McCellan, 1994). In such ways, ICT are regarded by some as a potential threat, not only to individual children, but also to childhood as an institution because of their potential to threaten childhood 'innocence' and blur the differentiation which is commonly made between the states of childhood and adulthood. Despite these fears in the popular imagination, little is known about how children actually employ ICT within the context of their everyday lives. We suggest that two key factors contribute to this oversight. First, children and young people are a social group that has been relatively neglected by academic research. Sociology has been criticised as an adultist discipline (see the following section), prompting a new theoretical turn in the study of children and childhood (James *et al.*, 1998). A similar accusation has also been levelled at geography (see also the following section). While there is a small but significant literature about children's geographies that dates back to the 1970s (Bunge, 1973; Hart, 1979), it is only recently that research in this sub-field of the discipline has reached a critical mass (Holloway and Valentine, 2004). As such, it is widely acknowledged in the social sciences that as adults we still know relatively little about children's own social worlds. Second, despite the growing importance of ICT in the contemporary Western world, there are surprisingly few empirical studies of how people actually use these technologies in an everyday context. Much of the contemporary writing about cyberspace in the social sciences is theoretical rather than empirically informed. Where research has focused on actual practices, this has tended to concentrate on the growth of online cultures through Multi User Domain (MUD) environments (textual virtual environments created by a programmer or participants) (see, for example, Turkle, 1995). In other words, it has primarily focused on extreme users and utopian visions of virtual life rather than looking at the complex ways that ICT is used, and made sense of, in everyday worlds (Kitchin, 1998a, 1998b).

Introducing children

'Child' appears at face value to be a biologically defined category determined by chronological age. Children are assumed by the nature of their youth to be not only biologically but also socially less developed than adults. The notion of immaturity, for example, is used not only to refer to children's physical bodies but also to their presumed lack of social, intellectual, emotional and practical knowledge and competencies. This less-than-adult status means that childhood is understood as a period in which children have to be schooled in their future adult roles. The process of learning to become an adult takes place not only through the educational system, but also the everyday processes of socialisation that children undergo as part of family and wider civic life. The flipside of being treated as less-than-adults is that children in the West are assumed to have the right to a childhood of innocence and freedom from the responsibilities of the adult world (though in practice poverty, ill-health and so on rob many children of the right to enjoy such a childhood). As such, we, as adults, are charged with the duty both to provide for children in the widest sense (materially, emotionally and so on), and to protect them from dangerous information, situations and people that might pose a threat to their 'innocence' and 'freedoms' (Holloway and Valentine, 2000a).

This essentialist understanding of children as a homogeneous social group defined by their biology, that in turn positions them as 'other' in relation to adults, has been critiqued by academics from across the social sciences. Rather, like many other social identities, 'child' has been demonstrated to be a socially constructed identity. Cultural historians, for example, have shown that the contemporary understanding of children in the West as less developed, less able and less competent than adults (Waksler, 1991) is historically specific (see, for example, Ariès, 1962; Hendrick, 1990; Steedman, 1990; Stainton-Rogers and Stainton-Rogers, 1992). The work of Ariès (1962), whose study of mainly French cultural artefacts has been generalised to the rest of the Western world (Jenks, 1996), is commonly used as evidence of the socially constructed nature of childhood. He demonstrated that in the Middle Ages young people, rather than being imagined as a distinct social category, were actually regarded as miniature adults. It was only in the sixteenth century, when children began to emerge as playthings for adults from privileged backgrounds, that they started to be defined in opposition to adults. It is from the Enlightenment onwards that this understanding of the category 'child', as inherently different from 'adult', has gone on to dominate our social imagination (Jenks, 1996).

Within this understanding of childhood, Jenks points to two different ways of thinking and talking about children. He labels these Dionysian and Apollonian. Dionysian understandings of childhood view children as 'little devils', who are inherently naughty, unruly, and must be disciplined and socialised into adult ways in order to become fully human. In contrast, Apollonian views of childhood, which emerged later, conceptualise children as born inherently 'good', only for the 'natural' virtue and innocence of these 'little angels' to be corrupted by adults as they are socialised into adulthood. These ideas underpin the emergence in the nineteenth century of a concern for the education and welfare of children, which is evidenced in the contemporary provision and/or regulation of much childcare, education and interventionist welfare services. Although notions of the Apollonian child emerged after that of the Dionysian child, the former did not supplant the latter. Rather, both apparently contradictory understandings of the child continue to be mobilised in contemporary Western societies (Stainton-Rogers and Stainton-Rogers, 1992; Jenks, 1996; Valentine, 1996a).

Even though these conceptualisations of childhood draw on essentialist understandings of children as inherently good or bad, by demonstrating the historical specificity of childhood in the Western world they prove that, far from being a biological category, childhood is a socially constructed identity. Yet the boundaries that mark the divide between child and adult are not clearly defined. James (1986) cites a number of legal classifications, such as the age at which young people can consume alcohol, earn money, join the armed forces, and consent to sexual intercourse, to show how the definitions of where childhood ends and adulthood begins in the UK are variable, context-specific and gendered. Such variations are equally evident between countries, and are also contested by different groups of children and adults, providing further proof of the social nature of childhood.

One 'academic' consequence of the social construction of child as less than adult, and childhood as a phase of socialisation, is that research on children has been less valued than that on other topics (Holloway and Valentine, 2000b). In the mid to late 1980s a variety of authors began to bemoan the lack of research on young people. Ambert (1986), for example, identified the invisibility of children in North American sociological research, claiming that this reflected the continuing influence of founding theorists whose preoccupations were shaped by the patriarchal values of the societies in which they lived. She also argued that the system of rewards within the discipline that favours research on the 'big issues' such as class, bureaucracies or the political system contributes to the devaluation and marginalisation of children as a legitimate research subject. Brannen and O'Brien (1995) point out that the position is little different in British sociology, where children and childhood have tended to be ignored, with children only being studied indirectly in subdisciplinary areas such as the family or education. Here, children have tended to be regarded as human becomings rather than human beings, who through the process of socialisation are to be shaped into adults. This understanding of children as incompetent and incomplete 'adults in the making rather than children in the state of being' (ibid., p. 70) means that it is the forces of socialisation – the family, the school – that have tended to receive attention rather than children themselves (James *et al.* 1998: 25).

This relative absence of children from the sociological research agenda is increasingly being challenged. A number of key texts (e.g. James and Prout, 1990; Qvortrup *et al.*, 1994; Mayall, 1994; James *et al.*, 1998) are beginning to define a new paradigm in the sociology of childhood. This recognises children as competent social actors in their own right (beings rather than becomings) and acknowledges children's understandings and experiences of their own childhoods. A growing body of work within the sociology of education is also beginning to draw attention to children's agency in relation to questions of identity and difference in the school setting (e.g. Skeggs, 1991; Dixon, 1997; Epstein, 1997). In making the claim that such work marks an epistemological break with earlier studies, James *et al.* (1998) identify this approach to the study of children as 'the new social studies of childhood'. This name reflects a growing cross-fertilisation of ideas between researchers in a variety of social science disciplines, linkages that have contributed (among other things) to a renewal of interest within geography in children as social actors (Holloway and Valentine, 2000a).

As in sociology, and for much the same reasons, children have not been a traditional focus of concern in geography (see James 1990), alhough, as we suggested earlier, there is a small but significant literature about children's environments that dates back to the 1970s (Blaut and Stea, 1971; Bunge, 1973). This work was marked by two discernible differences in approach that persist today. One, informed by psychology, has focused on children's spatial cognition and mapping abilities (e.g. Blaut and Stea, 1971; Matthews, 1987; Blaut, 1991). The other, inspired by Bunge's (1973) pioneering work on children's spatial oppression (through which he sought to give children, as a minority group, a voice in an adultist world) but more recently informed by new social studies of childhood, addresses children's access to, use of and attachment to space (Hart, 1979).

Geographical research contributes to social studies of childhood by providing evidence for the ways that childhood is constructed differently, not only in different times but also in different places (Holloway and Valentine, 2000b). In classifying work within the new social studies of childhood, James *et al.* (1998) identify an irreconcilable split between research which is global in its focus (e.g. by examining the importance of global processes in shaping children's position in different societies of the world) and that which has more local concerns (e.g. work showing how children are important in creating their own cultures and life-worlds). By employing an alternative, and more thoroughly spatial understanding of global/local, geographical work transcends this dichotomy to reveal a more complex picture. For example, in a study of New York and a village in Sudan, Katz (1993) has demonstrated that local manifestations of global restructuring have had serious, and negative, consequences for children in both locations. At the same time her study illustrates how these 'global processes' are worked out in 'local' places through 'local' cultures. In doing so, Katz shows that the global and local are not irreconcilably split, but rather are mutually constituted.

A second, and related, way in which geographers have examined the spatiality of childhood is by focusing on the everyday spaces in, and through, which children's identities and lives are produced and reproduced (Holloway and Valentine, 2000b). The street, and 'public' space in general, have been key sites of concern in geographical studies of children's access to, use of, and attachment to space. Most recently work has centred on contemporary concerns in North America and Europe about children's presence in 'public' spaces. These are characterised by twin fears, on the one hand, that some (Apollonian) children are vulnerable to dangers in 'public' places, and on the other hand that the unruly behaviour of other (Dionysian) children can threaten adult hegemony in 'public' space (Valentine, 1996a, 1996b). These same fears are also apparent in debates about children in cyberspace. Indeed, Jackson and Scott (1999) argue that notions of risk and safety are increasingly central to the construction of childhood. They write:

> Because children are ... constituted as a protected species and childhood as a protected state, both become loci of risk and anxiety: safeguarding children entails keeping danger at bay; preserving childhood entails guarding against anything which threatens it. Conversely, risk anxiety helps construct childhood and maintain its boundaries – the specific risks from which children must be protected serve to define the characteristics of childhood and the 'nature' of children themselves.
>
> (Jackson and Scott, 1999, pp. 86–7)

Schools are one particular institutional space through which adults attempt to control and discipline children. In doing so, Aitken (1994) argues that they serve wider stratified society, preparing young people to assume roles considered appropriate to their race, class and gender identities. A number of geographical studies have been concerned with these moral landscapes, including both the historical context of Victorian reformatory schools (Ploszajska, 1994) and the contemporary context of primary schools (Fielding, 2000). Contemporary geographical research also illustrates the importance of schools as sites through which gender and sexual identities are made and remade. Hyams (2000) has examined discourses of femininity among Latina girls in Los Angeles, showing how ideas about appropriate femininities both structure, and are contested through, the girls' everyday practices.

The home is a space that has been of particular relevance to feminist geographers who have been concerned with gender relations within households headed by heterosexual couples (see, for example, England, 1996). As such, other members of these families, mainly children but also elders, have often been constructed in terms of the time/care demands they place upon the household rather than in terms of their role as social actors in their own right. Recent work on children and parenting, however, has identified the home as an important site for the negotiation of adult–child power relations (e.g. Aitken, 1994; Sibley, 1995; Valentine, 1999a, 1999b). Indeed, the home itself is a space that is constituted through familial rules that demarcate appropriate ways for children to behave (Wood and Beck, 1990). Some of this research has drawn attention to the power of children's voices within the household. This is not only in terms of their ability to articulate their own identities and desires, but also in terms of their ability to shape the identity and practices of the household as a whole (Valentine, 1999a).

In part, the willingness of parents to acknowledge children as social actors in their own right is a reflection of the value of their offspring to them. Within the context of individualisation Beck and Beck-Gernsheim (1995) suggest that parents feel increasingly responsible for their children and under pressure to invest in their childhoods in order to maximise the children's opportunities and chances of success in adulthood. In doing so parents are not only thinking of their offspring but also of themselves. This is not only because young people can be a conduit for parents to live out their own hopes and ambitions (Beck and Beck-Gernsheim, 1995; Jackson and Scott, 1999) but also because being a 'good' parent is a rewarding identity in its own right. Geographical research has had an important role to play in exploring the connections between childhood and adulthood as discursive constructions and in examining a variety of spatial discourses. A number of studies have identified local communities as important sites through which understandings of what it means to be a 'good' mother or father and specific parenting cultures are developed (Dyck, 1990; Holloway, 1998; Valentine, 1997a). In a less predictable world these definitions are increasingly structured around the ability of parents to protect their children from social and physical risks.

In the case of children's use of ICT adult anxieties about children's use of the internet are heightened by the discursive construction of children's safety online as the responsibility of their parents, yet young people's technical competencies often exceed those who are charged with protecting them. While some parents regard children's skills as a threat to their status as adults, others embrace the opportunities ICT offers to renegotiate their relationships with young people. Debates about children's safety and competence are also negotiated through spatial discourses about the spaces of the home and the internet.

To summarise, therefore, we understand children to be social actors within their own right. We recognise, however, that children's identities are constituted in and through particular places, spaces and spatial discourses (Holloway and Valentine, 2000b). Here we focus on the sites of school, home and cyberspace. At the same time we acknowledge the ways that understandings of childhood can also shape the meaning of these spaces and places. We challenge the split between global and local approaches to childhood by showing how children's everyday use of ICT is situated within the context of shifts in the global economy, and national educational policies and by examining how children's online activities are constituted and interpreted within the context of local cultures.

Introducing technology

In the initial flood of academic and popular commentaries on cyberspace a clear opposition has often been drawn between offline and online worlds, or the 'real' and the 'virtual' (Laurel, 1990; Heim, 1991; Springer, 1991). In such representations the two worlds are viewed as distinct or unconnected from each other and as possessing different, usually oppositional (see Doel and Clarke, 1999) qualities. For some commentators (e.g. Heim, 1991; Thu Nguyen and Alexander, 1996), whom we have termed 'boosters' (Bingham *et al.*, 1999a), 'virtual' space is understood to be an advance on the 'real' world, an opportunity to overcome its limitations. For others (e.g. McLaughlin *et al.*, 1995), whom we label 'debunkers', the 'virtual' is regarded as inauthentic, a poor imitation of the 'real'.

Notably, online worlds have been uncritically celebrated by boosters as disembodied spaces in contrast to the materiality of 'real-world' environments. As such, this technology has been heralded for the possibilities it is perceived to offer its users to escape the constraints of their material surroundings and bodies by enabling them to create and play with online identities (Springer, 1991, Plant, 1996). In these terms the human body is regarded not only as invisible online but also as temporarily suspended such that it becomes a complete irrelevance (Thu Nguyen and Alexander, 1996). In this way, cyberspace is claimed to offer its users an escape from social inequalities – such as racism or gender discrimination – that relate to their embodiment (Turkle, 1995). In a similar vein boosters have also claimed that ICT create new forms of social relationships in which participants are no longer bound by the need to meet others face-to-face but rather can expand their social terrain by meeting others located around the globe online, mind-to-mind. This is a privileging of mind over body that characterises masculinist rationality. Some observers even claim that 'virtual' relationships are more intimate, richer and liberating than offline friendships because they are based on genuine mutual interest rather than the coincidence of offline proximity. In all these representations 'virtual' space is characterised as a space that is not just set apart from everyday life, but also one that offers the possibility to transcend everyday life. It is a zone of freedom, fluidity and experimentation that is insulated from the mundane realities of the material world (Springer, 1991; Laurel, 1990). In Doel and Clarke's (1999) terms it provides a hyper-realisation of the real.

Like the boosters, debunkers also view the 'real' and the 'virtual' as both different and separate worlds. However, for these commentators online worlds are viewed as unambiguously bad. The 'virtual' is conceptualised as a poor substitute for the 'real world'. Disembodied identities are viewed as superficial and inauthentic compared with embodied identities. Likewise, online forms of communication are regarded as fleeting, individualised and one-dimensional exchanges in contrast to the more permanent and complex nature of human engagements in the offline world (McLaughlin *et al.* 1995). ICT users are often characterised as so immersed in online culture that they become detached from their offline social and physical surroundings and consequently their responsibilities in the 'real' world (Wilson, 1997). For example, as we argue above, some commentaries paint a picture of children as so absorbed in their online worlds that they reject 'the real', becoming detached from offline social and familial relationships and withdrawing from public outdoor space into online fantasy spaces. In these understandings the 'real' is represented as a fragile world under threat from the seductive lure of the 'virtual' (Doel and Clarke, 1999).

While boosters and debunkers differ about whether the development of online worlds is positive or negative, what they share is a tendency to regard the 'real' and the 'virtual' not only as different but also as discrete. Research on cybercultures has commonly focused on users' online activities, ignoring the way that these activities remain embedded within the context of the offline spaces, and the social relations of everyday life. Such understanding of the relationship between online and offline worlds is now increasingly subject to critique (see, for example, essays in Crang *et al.*, 1999). For example, the ability to access online space presupposes certain offline material resources, not least access to a computer and the electricity to run it. Given the digital divide in terms of access to ICT both between countries/parts of the world and within them, not everyone is equally positioned to take advantage of online opportunities (Kitchin, 1998a). The importance of the offline spaces in which technologies are accessed has also been highlighted by Wakeford (1999). She refers to cyber-cafes as 'translation landscape[s]', offline spaces through which online spaces are produced, mediated and consumed.

Other writers have disputed imaginings of the 'real' and the 'virtual' in opposition to each other, arguing that 'virtual geography is no more or less "real"' (Wark, 1994, p. vii). In a study of the use of the internet by community organisations in Chicago, Light (1999) criticises the way that ICT are perceived to threaten the vitality of 'real' cities. Her observations suggest that online activities, rather than being set in opposition to the offline world, provide new ways to revitalise people's engagement with the urban environment. Other authors have also begun to question the discourse of disembodiment. Sobchack's (1995) account of experiencing post-operative pain while online exposes the error of the boosters' claims that ICT enable users to transcend their physical bodies. Green (1997, p. 63) observes that:

> Attending only to digital spaces ignores the physicality of technological production and consumption in everyday processes of interaction and the negotiation of meaning that occurs during such encounters. Disregarding this is precisely what has allowed the discourse of disembodiment to become so prevalent in both popular and academic discussions of cyberspace.

Critiques are also emerging of the debunkers' claims that online interactions and relationships are not only distinct from, but also less authentic than, offline encounters. As Smith (1992) comments:

> Despite the unique qualities of the social spaces to be found in virtual worlds, people do not enter new terrains empty-handed. We carry with us the sum-total of our experiences and expectations generated in more familiar social spaces.

Yet, despite the growing unease with the ways that online and offline spaces are often dichotomised, research has so far failed to map the complex ways that online activities are embedded within 'real-world' lives (Kitchin, 1998a).

By examining how children and technology come together, however, we want to reject any simple technological determinism. By technological determinism we mean narratives in which a 'new' technology is presumed to impact (either positively or negatively) on society, replacing what has gone before, and producing a predictable set of effects which are presumed to be more or less the same everywhere (Bingham *et al.*, 1999b). Technologically determinist accounts are commonly apocalyptical in that they usually draw on metaphors of inevitable change in which people are seen as under threat from techno-'shocks' or 'waves' (Thrift, 1996; Bingham, 1996). As such, they ignore the way that the impact of any technology varies according to specificities of time and place, who is using it and their intentions, and the other agendas to which technology may become attached (Thrift, 1996; Bingham *et al.*, 1999b). It is what Bryson and Castell (1994) term an 'artifactual' view, where technology is severed from the normative social context. As Thrift explains:

> What is missing from technologically deterministic accounts ... is any concerted sense of new electronic communication technologies as part of a long history of rich and often wayward social practices (including the interpretation of those practices) through which we have become socially acquainted with these technologies.
>
> (1996, p. 1472)

Despite such criticisms, Winston (1995) observes that technological determinism is still popularly employed to explain material-social change. This is perhaps most apparent in the theorisations of ICT.

Bromley (1997) cautions, however, against adopting the polar position, viewing technology as a 'neutral tool' whose impact is entirely determined by the intentions of its users. Authors who take this approach commonly fall into the trap of assuming that the meanings of technology are stable and unproblematic. This is because they do not acknowledge the interpretive processes that are part of all of the practices through which we become socially acquainted with technologies, from their design, manufacture and marketing, through to their domestication in the home or workplace (Thrift, 1996; Bingham, 1996). In other words, they substitute a technological determinism with a social determinism in which the assumption is that only people have the status of actors (Ackrich, 1992).

Wajcman (1991) labels these two positions use/abuse and social shaping models. Both are based on setting up false and unproductive oppositions between 'technology' and 'society' in which either strong technology impacts on weak society or strong society shapes weak technology (Bingham, 1996). As such, they ignore the mutual implication and complication of bodies and objects.

An alternative approach is offered by scholars from the social studies of technology such as Michel Callon (1991), Bruno Latour (1993) and John Law (1994). These writers argue that we always live among, and are surrounded by, objects, and that these bits and pieces that we enter into assemblage with matter. As such, we need to recast the social to include non-humans. Callon and Latour (1981), for example, point out that it is our use of objects that is one of the things that differentiates us from animals such as baboons. Whereas baboons only form associations and order their social worlds through actions between one body and another, as humans we use a range of objects or 'props' to mobilise, stabilise and order our society. In these terms, agency is not something possessed by humans but rather is an effect generated by a 'network of heterogenous, interacting materials' (Law, 1994, p. 383). It is therefore both precarious and contingent. Callon and Law (1995, p. 484) further demonstrate this point with what they call a thought experiment. Referring to the example of an imaginary office manager called Andrew they write:

> [J]ust imagine what would happen if they took away Andrew's telephone and his fax machine. If they blocked the flow of papers and reports. Imagine what would happen if they shut down the railway line to London and stopped him from using his car ... Then imagine, also, that his secretary were to disappear. And his room, with its conference table, its PC and electronic mail were to vanish.

In other words, the world cannot be unproblematically divided up into 'things' (on the one hand) and 'the social' (on the other) (Bingham, 1996). Rather, in order to understand human activity and society we need 'to take full account of those crowds of non-humans mingled with humans' (Latour, 1988, p. 16).

For these advocates of what has become known as Actor Network Theory (ANT), society is produced in and through patterned networks of heterogeneous materials in which the properties of humans and non-humans are not self-evident but rather emerge in practice. In other words, the social and the technical always co-develop. As Nigel Thrift explains:

> the actors in these actor networks redefine each other *in action* in ways which mean that there are no simple one-to-one relationships from technology to people but rather a constantly on-going, constantly inventive and constantly reciprocal process of social acquaintance and re-acquaintance.

(1996, p. 1485)

This study of children's use of the internet is informed by these ideas. We do not view computers as things 'with pre-given attributes frozen in time' (Star and Ruhleder, 1996, p. 112), nor as objects which impact on social relations in fixed ways producing a predictable set of effects (either as positive like the boosters or negative like the debunkers). Nor do we understand computers to mirror the logic of their designers and manufacturers. Rather, we understand them to be 'things' that materialise for children as diverse social practices and which may thus have as many everyday translations as the contexts in which they are used (Bingham *et al.*, 1999b). In other words, we understand computers and their users to be in a relational process of coming into being, in which each is transforming and transformative of the other (Ackrich, 1992).

Acknowledgements

This chapter is adapted from *Cyberkids: Children in the Information Age*, by Sarah L. Holloway and Gill Valentine, © 2003 RoutledgeFalmer. Reproduced by permission of Taylor & Francis Books UK.

References

Aitken, S. (1994) *Putting Children in Their Place*, Washington, DC, Association of American Geographers.

Ambert, A. (1986) 'Sociology of sociology: the place of children in North American sociology', in P. Alder and P. Alder (eds), *Sociological Studies of Childhood Development*, vol. 1, Greenwich, CT, JAI Press, pp. 11–31.

Ariès, P. (1962) *Centuries of Childhood*, New York, Vintage Press.

Beck, U. and Beck-Gernsheim, E. (1995) *The Normal Chaos of Love*, Cambridge, Polity Press.

Bingham, N. (1996) 'Objects-ions: from technological determinism towards geographies of relation', *Environment and Planning D: Society and Space*, 14, pp. 635–57.

Bingham, N., Holloway, S.L. and Valentine, G. (1999a) 'Where do you want to go tomorrow? Connecting children and the internet', *Environment and Planning D: Society and Space*, 17, pp. 655–72.

Bingham, N., Valentine, G. and Holloway, S.L. (1999b) 'Bodies in the midst of things: relocating children's use of the internet', in S. Ralph, J. Langham Brown and T. Lees (eds), *Youth and the Global Media*, Luton, University of Luton Press, pp. 24–33.

Blaut, J.M. (1991) 'Natural mapping', *Transactions of the Institute of British Geographers*, 61, pp. 387–93.

Blaut, J. and Stea, D. (1971) 'Studies of geographic learning', *Annals of the Association of American Geographers*, 61, pp. 387–93.

Brannen, J. and O'Brien, M. (1995) 'Childhood and the sociological gaze: paradigms and paradoxes', *Sociology*, 29, pp. 729–37.

Bromley, H. (1997) 'The social chicken and the technological egg: education, computing and the technology/society divide', *Educational Theory*, 47, pp. 51–65.

Bryson, M. and Castell, S. (1994) 'Telling tales out of school: modernist, critical and postmodern "true stories" about educational computing', *Journal of Educational Computing Research*, 10, pp. 199–221.

Bunge, W.W. (1973) 'The geography', *Professional Geographer*, 25, pp. 331–7.

Callon, M. (1991) 'Techno-economic networks and irreversibility', in J. Law (ed.), *A Sociology of Monsters: Essays on Power, Technology and Domination*, London, Routledge, pp. 132–61.

Callon, M. and Latour, B. (1981) 'Unscrewing the big leviathan', in K. Knorr-Cetina and A. Cicourel (eds), *Advances in Social Theory and Methodology: Toward an Integration of Micro and Macro Sociologies*, New York, Routledge, pp. 275–303.

Callon, M. and Law, J. (1995) 'Agency and the hybrid collectif', *South Atlantic Quarterly*, 94, pp. 481–507.

Crang, M., Crang, P. and May, J. (eds) (1999) *Virtual Geographies: Bodies, Space and Relations*, London, Routledge.

Dixon, C. (1997) 'Pete's tool: identity and sex play in the design and technology classroom', *Gender and Education*, 9, pp. 89–104.

Doel, M. and Clarke, D. (1999) 'Virtual worlds: simulation, suppletion, s(ed)uction and simulacra', in M. Crang, P. Crang and J. May (eds), *Virtual Geographies: Bodies, Space and Relations*, London, Routledge, pp. 261–83.

Dyck, I. (1990) 'Space, time and renegotiating motherhood: an exploration of the domestic workplace', *Environment and Planning D: Society and Space*, 8, pp. 459–83.

England, K. (ed.) (1996) *Who Will Mind the Baby? Geographies of Childcare and Working Mothers*, London, Routledge.

Epstein, D. (1997) '"Boyz" own stories: masculinities and sexualities in schools', *Gender and Education*, 9, pp. 105–15.

Evans, M. and Butkus, C. (1997) 'Regulating the emergent: cyberporn and the traditional media', *Media International Australia*, 85, pp. 62–9.

Fielding, S. (2000) 'Walk on the left! Children's geographies and the primary school', in S.L. Holloway (ed.), *Children's Geographies: Playing, Living, Learning*, London, Routledge, pp. 230–44.

Green, N. (1997) 'Beyond being digital: representation and virtual corporeality', in D. Holmes (ed.), *Virtual Politics: Identity and Community in Cyberspace*, London, Sage, pp. 59–78.

Gumpert, G. and Drucker, S.J. (1998) 'The mediated home in the global village', *Communications Research*, 25, pp. 422–38.

Hapnes, T. (1996) 'Not in their machines: how hackers transform computers into sub-cultural artefacts', in M. Lie and K.H. Sorenson (eds), *Making Technology Our Own?*, Oslo, Scandinavian University Press, pp. 121–50.

Haraway, D. (1997) *Modest_Witness@Second_Millennium.FemaleMan©_Meets_OncoMouse™*, London, Routledge.

Hart, R. (1979) *Children's Experience of Place*, New York, Irvington.

Heim, M. (1991) 'The erotic ontology of cyberspace', in M. Benedikt (ed.), *Cyberspace*, Cambridge, MA, MIT Press, pp. 59–80.

Hendrick, H. (1990) 'Constructions and reconstructions of British childhood: an interpretive survey, 1800 to present', in A. Prout and A. James (eds), *Constructing and Reconstructing Childhood*, Basingstoke, Falmer Press.

Holloway, S.L. (1998) 'Local childcare cultures: moral geographies of mothering and the social organisation of pre-school childcare', *Gender, Place and Culture*, 5, pp. 29–53.

Holloway, S.L. and Valentine, G. (eds) (2000a) 'Children's geographies and the new social studies of childhood', in *Children's Geographies*, London, Routledge, pp. 1–28.

Holloway, S.L. and Valentine, G. (2000b) 'Spatiality and the new social studies of childhood', *Sociology*, 34, pp. 763–83.

Hyams, M. (2000) '"Pay attention in class... [and] don't get pregnant": a discourse on academic success amongst adolescent Latinas', *Environment and Planning A*, 32, pp. 635–54.

Jackson, S. and Scott, S. (1999) 'Risk anxiety and the social construction of childhood', in D. Lupton (ed.), *Risk and Socio-Cultural Theory: New Directions and Perspectives*, Cambridge, Cambridge University Press, pp. 86–107.

James, A. (1986) 'Learning to belong: the boundaries of adolescence', in A.P. Cohen (ed.), *Symbolising Boundaries: Identity and Diversity in British Cultures*, Manchester, University Press, pp. 151–71.

James, A. and Prout, A. (eds) (1990) *Constructing and Reconstructing Childhood: Contemporary Issues in the Sociological Study of Childhood*, Basingstoke, Falmer Press.

James, A., Jenks, C. and Prout, A. (1998) *Theorizing Childhood*, Cambridge, Polity Press.

Jenks, C. (1996) *Childhood*, London, Routledge.

Katz, C. (1993) 'Growing girls/closing circles: limits on the spaces of knowing in rural Sudan and US cities', in C. Katz and J. Monk (eds), *Full Circles: Geographies of Women over the Life Course*, London, Routledge, pp. 88–106.

Kitchin, R. (1998a) *Cyberspace: The World in the Wires*, Chichester, John Wiley.

—— (1998b) 'Towards geographies of cyberspace', *Progress in Human Geography*, 22, pp. 385–406.

Labour Party (1995) *Communicating Britain's Future*, London, Labour Party.

Latour, B. (1988) 'Visualisations and reproduction', in G. Fyfe and J. Law (eds), *Picturing Power: Visual Depiction and Social Relations*, Oxford, Basil Blackwell.

—— (1993) *We Have Never Been Modern*, London, Harvester Wheatsheaf.

Laurel, B. (1990) 'On dramatic interaction', in R. Hattinger, C. Morgan and G. Schopf (eds), *Ars Electronica 1990, vol. 2, Virtuelle Welten*, Linz, Veritas-Verlag.

Law, J. (1994) *Organising Modernity*, Oxford, Blackwell.

Light, J. (1999) 'From city space to cyberspace', in M. Crang, P. Crang and J. May (eds), *Virtual Geographies: Bodies, Space and Relations*, London, Routledge, pp. 109–30.

McCellan, J. (1994) 'Netsurfers', *The Observer*, 1 February, p. 10.

McLaughlin, M., Osbourne, K., and Smith, C. (1995) 'Standards of conduct on the Usenet', in S. Jones (ed.), *Cybersociety: Computer-Mediated Communication and Community*, London, Sage, pp. 90–111.

McMurdo, G. (1997) 'Cyberporn and communication decency', *Journal of Information Science*, 23, pp. 81–90.

Marshall, D. (1997) 'Technophobia: video games, computer hacks and cybernetics', *Media International Australia*, 85, pp. 700–78.

Matthews, M.H. (1987) 'Gender, home range and environmental cognition', *Transaction of the Institute of British Geographers*, 12, pp. 32–56.

Mayall, B. (ed.) (1994) *Children's Childhoods: Observed and Experienced*, London, Falmer Press.

Plant, S. (1996) 'On the matrix: cyberfeminist simulations', in R. Shields (ed.), *Cultures of Internet: Virtual Spaces, Real Histories, Living Bodies*, London, Sage, pp. 170–83.

Ploszajska, T. (1994) 'Moral landscapes and manipulated spaces: gender, class and space in Victorian reformatory schools', *Journal of Historical Geography*, 20, pp. 413–29.

Qvortrup J., Bardy, M., Sgritta, G. and Wintersberger, H. (eds) (1994) *Childhood Matters: Social Theory, Practice and Politics*, Aldershot, Avebury.

Sibley, D. (1995) 'Families and domestic routines: constructing the boundaries of childhood', in S. Pile and N. Thrift (eds), *Mapping the Subject: Geographies of Cultural Transformation*, London, Routledge, pp. 123–37.

Skeggs, B. (1991) 'Challenging masculinity and using sexuality', *British Journal of Sociology of Education*, 12, pp. 127–39.

Smith, M. (1992) 'Voices from the WELL: the logic of virtual commons', http://www.sscnet.ucla.edu/soc/csoc (accessed 10 January 1997).

Sobchack, V. (1995) 'Beating the meat/surviving the text, or how to get out of this century alive', in M. Featherstone and R. Burrows (eds), *Cyberspace, Cyberbodies, Cyberpunk: Cultures of Technological Embodiment*, London, Sage, pp. 205–13.

Springer, C. (1991) 'The pleasure of the interface', *Screen*, 32, pp. 303–23.

Stainton-Rogers, R. and Stainton-Rogers, W. (1992) *Stories of Childhood: Shifting Agendas of Childhood*, Hemel Hempstead, Harvester Wheatsheaf.

Star, S.L. and Ruhleder, K. (1996) 'Steps towards an ecology of infrastructure: design and access for large information spaces', *Information Systems Research*, 7, pp. 111–34.

Steedman, C. (1990) *Childhood, Culture and Class in Britain*, London, Virago.

Suss, D., Suonien, A., Garitaonandia, C., Juaristi, P., Koikkalainen, R. and Oleaga, J.A. (2001) 'Media use and the relationships of children and teenagers with their peer groups: a study of Finnish, Spanish and Swiss cases', *European Journal of Communication*, 13, pp. 521–38.

Thrift, N. (1996) 'New urban eras and old technological fears: reconfiguring the goodwill of electronic things', *Urban Studies*, 33, pp. 1463–93.

Thu Nguyen, D. and Alexander, J. (1996) 'The coming of cyberspacetime and the end of polity', in R. Shields (ed.), *Cultures of Internet: Virtual Spaces, Real Histories, Living Bodies*. London, Sage, pp. 99–124.

Turkle, S. (1995) *Life on the Screen: Identity in the Age of the Internet*, London, Weidenfeld & Nicolson.

Valentine, G. (1996a) 'Angels and devils: moral landscapes of childhood', *Environment and Planning D: Society and Space*, 14, pp. 581–99.

—— (1996b) 'Children should be seen and not heard: the production and transgression of adults' public space', *Urban Geography*, 17, pp. 205–20.

—— (1997a) '"Oh yes I can." "Oh no you can't." Children and parents' understanding of kids' competence to negotiate public space safely', *Antipode*, 29, pp. 65–89.

—— (1999a) 'Eating in: home, consumption and identity', *Sociological Review*, 47, pp. 491–54.

—— (1999b) 'Being seen and heard? The ethical complexities of working with children and young people at home and at school', *Ethics, Place and Environment*, 2, pp. 141–55.

Wajcman, J. (1991) *Feminism Confronts Technology*, Cambridge, Polity Press.

Wakeford, N. (1999) 'Gender and the landscapes of computing in an internet café', in M. Crang, P. Crang and J. May (eds), *Virtual Geographies: Bodies, Space and Relations*, London, Routledge, pp. 178–201.

Waksler, F.C. (ed.) (1991) *Studying the Social Worlds of Children: Sociological Readings*, London, Falmer Press.

Wark, M. (1994) *Virtual Geography: Living with Global Media Events*, Bloomington, IN, Indiana University Press.

Wilkinson, H. (1995) 'Take care in cyberspace', *The Independent*, 1 December.

Wilson, M. (1997) 'Community in the abstract: a political and ethical dilemma?', in D. Holmes (ed.), *Virtual Politics: Identity and Community in Cyberspace*, London, Sage, pp. 145–61.

Winston, B. (1995) 'Tyrrel's Owl: the limits of the technological imagination in an epoch of hyperbolic discourse', in B. Adams and S. Allan (eds), *Theorising Culture*, London, University College London Press, pp. 225–35.

Wood, D. and Beck, R. (1990) 'Dos and don'ts: family rules, room and their relationships', *Children's Environments Quarterly*, 7, pp. 2–14.

Reflective question

Holloway and Valentine's research suggested that children are able through their competence in using ICT to renegotiate the boundaries of childhood and adulthood at home and school (p. 73). In what ways do you see (or experience) this as challenging to conventional practices in school?

Further reading

Alanen, L. (2000) 'Review essay: visions of a social theory of childhood', *Childhood*, 7(4), pp. 493–505.

Holloway, S. and Valentine, G. (2000a) 'Spatiality and the new social studies of childhood', *Sociology*, 34(4), pp. 763–84.

James, A., Jenks, C. and Prout, A. (1998) *Theorizing Childhood*, Cambridge, Polity Press.

Lee, N. (2001) *Children and Society: Growing Up in an Age of Uncertainty*, Milton Keynes, Open University Press.

Valentine, G. and Holloway, S. (2001) 'Online dangers?: geographies of parents' fears for children's safety in cyberspace', *The Professional Geographer*, 53(1), pp. 71–83.

2.3 The learner, the learning process and pedagogy in social context

Julian Williams

Introduction

In this chapter I will contrast several distinct views of learning and learners: that of the learner as an acquirer of knowledge, that of the learner becoming engaged in a social practice, and that of the learner as a 'climber of a building'. I will then consider the learner and learning in informal contexts (e.g. in 'play', and sometimes in work) versus formal, institutionalised contexts (e.g. in 'study' at 'school', and so on) that demand pedagogy. The latter leads me then to the need for a social analysis of institutions of 'studying/schooling', and to assessment. Taking a particularly interesting case of a new, international assessment system (PISA), I will offer a critical perspective on the model. Similarly, I will examine a teacher's account of pedagogy and learning in a college context, and point out how institutional and political contexts frame learning activity. I will conclude that an understanding of the learner and the learning process requires an understanding of pedagogy in its social, cultural, historical and political context.

How is it that a young child seems to learn their first language effortlessly, absorbing information and vocabulary like a sponge; yet I struggled to pick up conversational French even after many years of 'schooling'. Is it a difference in the 'learner', the difference between the young child and the uncouth adolescent? Or is there something 'different' about the learning processes involved? How is it that learning in school seems to become increasingly difficult for many learners? Why does the population gradually drop out of education feeling at each level they have failed, despite apparently all the powers-that-be declaring the need to 'keep students in education'?

I may not be able to answer all these questions, but any answers demand an understanding of the learner and the learning process. Additionally, they demand an understanding of 'studying' and 'schooling' as particular institutionalised learning activities, and of how these contrast with 'learning' in informal situations. In this chapter I will set out what I see as some of the vital elements of such an understanding.

I draw on a particular theoretical, critical point of view on learning activity as socially, culturally and historically mediated, in contrast with other perspectives found in the literature: behaviourist, cognitivist and – most radical – constructivist views. In the former view the learner is seen as the active 'agent' in culturally 'mediated' activity, and learning arises because of engagement in practice with a community, a social grouping that shares a history and a culture. The learner's participation and engagement with any community involves a process of sharing in the culture, of becoming a member of that community, and hence of acquiring an identity. Let us now unpack some of these metaphors of 'becoming', of 'acquiring' and of 'participating' (see also Sfard, 1998, and this volume).

Models of learning, knowing and identity

In one view, learning consists of acquisition of 'knowledge'. Knowledge consists of objects of learning of different kinds that can be acquired by a learner through some process of mental internalisation, 'into the head', say: facts, concepts, skills, problem-solving strategies and all sorts of capabilities, even ways of speaking or acting, and also perhaps attitudes and dispositions such as confidence or anxiety, likes or disliking. This view is dominant in formal education in schools, where a curriculum typically consists of a specification of such knowledge objects, laid out according to some plan. The fact that knowledge in the institution of school has to be laid down implies the need for an appropriate technology of communication: the curriculum.

In another view, learning is seen as a process of engagement in a social practice, i.e. some joint, socially shared enterprise – tailoring, footballing, bike-riding and so on. One thereby learns by *becoming* a different type of person: one learns to become a tailor, a footballer, a Hell's Angel, or some other kind of person. This view is dominant in informal, and workplace or apprenticeship learning contexts, where there may be no written curriculum (Lave and Wenger, 1991). One typically becomes accepted into some community, whether by rite of passage or otherwise, and the recognition involves the acquisition of a social representation, one acquires a label. This view naturally emphasises the 'identity' of the learner, as given by the social group and the individual to themselves. The engagement of the learner and their motivation to learn is explicit, i.e. it is a matter of who they want to become (Holland *et al.*, 1998).

In fact most learning in practice may benefit from taking both viewpoints. In school, while it may be obvious that there is supposed to be a body of knowledge being learnt – 'arithmetic', 'geography' and so on – one can also see that learners do become engaged in certain social practices with their peers and teachers, too. They turn up to lessons when the bell goes and do the work the teacher specifies, they chat and play in the playground, they submit themselves to evaluations and assessments, attend new classes with different teachers when they progress to a new year, and so forth. In fact they learn a 'hidden curriculum' involving ideologies of knowledge, power, and discipline. That is, they become socialised as 'school-goers' in certain ways with their peers, and not always in ways that are ideally expected or implied as normative by the overt curriculum (see e.g. Willis, 1983). However, even the formal classroom practices involved in 'learning the curriculum' can be regarded from the 'participation in social practice' point of view: learners of arithmetic may learn to 'do sums' that are repetitious of examples provided, they learn to find that the answers are in the back of the book, if stuck to ask the teacher who generally knows it all, and perhaps not to use it much outside school where a calculator will be used. All this might be regarded as the 'social practice of doing school arithmetic'.

On the other hand informal learning and play often involve 'knowledge' in the objective senses too. As one becomes a Hell's Angel, one acquires a code of knowledge about who is in charge, what and how initiation of new members has to be done and so on. Looked at in an objective way, an identity is itself a social representation, and to a representation we can generally attach all kinds of knowledge, of properties, contingencies, and narratives (Moscovici, 1984; Jenkins, 1996). Thus, a tailor can describe many facts, skills and competences they have acquired during their apprenticeship, without which they would not have come to be regarded by 'old-timers' as 'one of us'. However, in informal and apprenticeship systems, the learning is not generally as rigorously or explicitly defined as in schooling, though there may be elements of both, and nowadays we do find that vocational learning is increasingly becoming bureaucratised and 'schooled'.

Finally, let us consider the metaphor of learning as 'climbing' a building, or a tree (of knowledge). The learner progresses from level to level, *acquiring* knowledge and status (the ability to see from higher up) as they 'progress'. This is a commonly used metaphor and structures many curricula into hierarchies of knowledge or competence. In year 9 one might be expected to acquire 'level 6 mathematics' or by the end of a series of music lessons to perform at level 1 competence on a musical instrument. Even in workplaces 'getting your level' can be a rite of passage (Wenger, 1998). This has become a widely used model in both formal, academic 'acquisition' models and in informal, *participatory* competence models. The latter can be seen in the award of 'mastery' levels in apprenticeship, in musicianship, or in gang membership. 'Becoming' a 'level two', a 'master', or a 'hood' is associated with progressing one's identity in relation to the community. And so it is with academic knowledge too: one 'becomes' a graduate, as well as 'acquiring' the knowledge required of a degree course by 'going to uni'.

Towards a cultural-historical theory of learning

I turn aside for the moment to situate my perspective on learning very briefly in relation to others that the reader will find in the literature.

Most theories of learning involve a definition of learning as a change in the learner of some kind: the learner becomes a different person by virtue of having learnt, whether that involves learning a new behaviour (a behaviourist theory, e.g. Skinner), learning new knowledge or ways of knowing (a cognitivist theory, e.g. Gagné) or acquiring some new social status in social practice, such as 'becoming a tailor' (a social theory of learning, e.g. Lave, 1996; Lave and Wenger, 1991).

My critique of most of these theoretical points of view is that they do not adequately place the individual learner and the culture of society in a practical, *dialectical* relationship; though of those just mentioned Lave's account certainly does, and she draws on Marxist traditions to do this. The worst of these perspectives make the learner into a passive 'object' of teaching, even programming, as in behaviourist theories. Only in Vygotsky's cultural-historical approach does the proper relationship emerge, i.e. that of the learner as the 'agent' and society as the 'mediator' of learning activity (Vygotsky, 1978, 1986; Leont'ev, 1978, 1981; Cole, 1996; Roth *et al.*, 2005; Roth and Lee, 2007).

Piaget's constructivism certainly placed the learner as the agent of their learning, but did not theorise the social and cultural as 'mediation'. He was focused on how children develop intellectually, and actually took little interest in pedagogy as such. For Vygotsky and his followers, teaching, and hence pedagogy, are essential to supporting the constructions of the learner, as 'good learning' (in the so-called zone of proximal development) involves the learner in performing with others at a more advanced level than can be achieved alone.

In this approach, then, the learners are active, constructive agents, engaged in work that is of interest and motivating to them, but they acquire the best of the culture by working with others (teachers, or peers/co-workers, co-learners). My own view of this is that learners' motivation is always dual: they are interested in learning new 'scientific' knowledge (Vygotsky's term for all academic, advanced ways of knowing, not just natural 'science' per se), but learners also have non-academic concerns, that is they are also 'interested' in everyday things, whether it be in 'play', in 'being a teenager', in work, or in citizenship, that is, in general, in matters outside of academic 'scientific' knowledge and 'schooling' that tends to encapsulate 'formal' knowledge (Engeström, 1991, 1987). The art of pedagogy lies in capturing the relation between these two motivations: in this view *good* pedagogy engages the learner in activity in the learner's own focus or field of interest, but also shows how 'scientific, academic knowledge' provides a superior way of knowing that empowers the learner therein (see Ryan and Williams, 2007, chapter 9).

Formal and informal contexts, and institutionalisation of learning

Learning through play – and to some extent informal learning generally – typically implies that the learning is driven by the learner in the context of a communal activity, by what they want to learn, or become. Often the motivation to learn is really all that is noticed, and all that matters: processes like trial and error and mimicry are prominent. One joins a walking group and walks, one tries and tries again to ride a bike, one picks up language-in-use as one goes along in life. There is no explicit, formal 'knowledge' specified in advance and no academic, institutional context.

A learning institution implies some social structure, usually hierarchically ordered with vertical power relations that place the learner at a disadvantage vis-à-vis an instructor. Thus, the learner does not define the curriculum, nor the criterion for certification. Rather, from the institutional point of view, the learner becomes the 'object' of the teaching process, and learning is the activity that ensures the institution's objectives of 'learning outcomes'.

The institution in fact is held to account for its success in promoting these learning outcomes, e.g. through measures, indicators and league tables: these audits can become the means by which such institutions are managed, and drive the allocation of resources and personnel in the 'teaching corporation' or school/college. The 'economy' of the institution therefore involves exchanges of auditable 'knowledge commodities' made visible by educational measurement. The bottom line for a college/school is that it is funded – in real money by the economy at large – in relation to its measurable performance against auditable targets that hold it accountable (these may include a basket of indicators, from student satisfaction, to certificated outcomes and proportions of drop outs or exclusions). It is clear in this account that from the institution's point of view the learner's agency is secondary: motivating the learner becomes a means to an end, not the starting point of learning.

However, there is more to this, for even in the potentially alienating institutional context in which learning becomes commodified, the learner must become engaged for learning to take place. Where is the motivation to study what must be studied? The institution has to make some kind of 'contract' with the learner, that studying will be exchanged by certificates that confer status (Chevallard and Joshua, 1991). Learners – if they are to be motivated to engage – must come to believe (at least in post-compulsory education, but the logic applies throughout) that education offers them some form of 'educational capital' that is exchangeable later for some desired goods or status (Bourdieu, 1990).

What is 'hard' about 'studying' or 'schooling' compared to informal learning may be the dissociation, or the distancing, of this larger motivation from the immediate engagement in the learning activity itself, and it is clear that gender, class and ethnicity, inter alia, are implicated in this question (e.g. Bernstein, 1996). For the learner in the studying context, the gain may be long delayed, and some satisfaction from learning may need to come from its immediate use rather than the long-term exchange value it acquires. The art of teaching in this context then follows: effective teaching would seem to require a substitute for the immediate feedback that informal learning usually offers.

Teachers have two means at their disposal. The first is the intrinsic 'use' value of the activity itself as distinct from its intended learning outcomes (e.g. the fact that learning to desk-top publish, say, might be demonstrably, 'authentically' useful for learners' immediate lives as well as a step on the road to a qualification). This approach essentially mimics informal learning within the institutional setting. The second is 'assessment': the feedback to learners about their progress that can serve to reward learners' activity ('Well done, you have learnt your 5 times table and have reached level 4b!'). Assessment-driven education has become almost universal in schooling, and this is one reason why. In the next section I turn to an interesting case of one such system.

A case study of an assessment system: PISA

In this section I want to see how these concepts work in explaining some recent innovations in assessment on the international stage. International testing of students' mathematics and science attainment across countries has been a feature of the educational scene for many years, and by the time that the third Trends in International Mathematics and Science Study (TIMSS) reported, it had reached global extent and was becoming an almost permanent part of the landscape. When these studies report their findings, news stories around the world take note, and politicians appear in the media: usually to complain that 'something must be done'.

One result was the development of a new international assessment approach, with an alternative methodology that produced different results: PISA (Programme for International Student Assessment of the OECD; see PISA, 2003, 2004, 2005 et seq.). Its methodology has a lot in common with previous studies: an essential requirement is that examinees produce a score that indicates a 'level', and a nation's cohort produces an 'average' score that can be put in a league table alongside those of other nations (and so compete for media and political attention). However, its rhetoric claims that its assessments are of 'literacies' using 'authentic' tasks that draw from real-life competences. Thus, for example, the appeal is to a construct of 'mathematical literacy' that is both auditable/measurable *and* has motivational, use value.

For instance, in assessing 'problem-solving', one of the tasks asks the student to diagnose a faulty bicycle pump. In another they are asked to evaluate some information on various drugs and select an appropriate painkiller for George, a 13-year-old asthmatic child with a sprained ankle. At face value, these represent a kind of functional 'literacy', that is the capacity to function in real, authentic situations and contexts.

Turning to the mathematical literacy item used to explain the notion of mathematical modelling and mathematisation, one finds the 'park' problem: where should a street-light be placed to illuminate a park? The park is modelled as a triangle, the area lit is a circle, and the offered solution turns out to be the triangle's circumcentre, that is the point that is equally distant from the three corners of the park – as long as the park is not obtuse-angled, (explains PISA, 2003, p. 26). You have to really think mathematically to imagine a solution like this!

In critiquing PISA I was inspired by a visual metaphor: the Leaning Tower of Pisa herself (Williams, 2005). She is really quite, quite beautiful. When I was a boy I visited Pisa and was very impressed by the Leaning Tower. I recall imagining that one could walk up the tower by spiralling up the outside, and was slightly disappointed by the reality. Later I learned that the inclination of the tower was annually increasing, and engineers feared that it would eventually fall over: they planned to strengthen the foundations to stop this, but they did not straighten it, of course. The tower has become a global spectacle, instantly recognisable around the world. And – significantly – the tower of Pisa had become globally spectacular *because* of its faulty foundations, not despite them.

Figure 2.3.1 The Leaning Tower of Pisa

From the point of view shown in Figure 2.3.1 Pisa is seen to lean to the right, it has six 'levels' with no visible means of ascent, and is the object of post-modern spectacle in the photographs of 'leaning' tourists.

While I find PISA assessment tasks sometimes very seductive, I wonder if in fact they are truly 'authentic': I went in search of a triangular park, and mostly found car parks outside my office. The lights are usually on the edge of the parks, which are usually rectangular. But wait: is the theorem about circumcentres of triangles really anything to do with lighting and parks, or is this a spurious 'motivation' of a curriculum that should be otherwise inspired? The more I thought about it, the less convinced I was that PISA tasks are truly 'authentic': if George was my younger brother I'd ask the pharmacist or doctor for the right drug, wouldn't I? Not that these tasks don't have some value, but 'realistic' might be a better term than 'authentic'. The reason these tasks are 'faulty' and cannot be made authentic, in the end, is that they have to be performed in test-like, paper-and-pencil conditions, and in such conditions the 'real' social, communal context of the activity is necessarily lost. One has to imagine George, one has no social resources (such as pharmacists) available, one cannot 'phone a friend' or even look it up on the internet and so on.

Thus, I argue, the fault in PISA is precisely due to the fact that its *function* is as an international testing instrument for measuring individuals' and groups' attainment, and that is precisely what is required of it to provide its 'spectacular' performance as an auditing, international league-tabling instrument. It is flawed because it is a spectacle, whereas the poor Leaning Tower is spectacular because it is flawed!

Similar critiques of formal, institutionalised educational systems that are driven by assessment are made constantly by those of us who bemoan the increasingly ubiquitous testing, league tables and performance culture, nationally and internationally. Yet audit is here to stay, as a social perspective of educational institutions resourced by the state that holds it accountable shows (Strathern, 2000; Power, 1999).

In the next case study, I will show how pedagogy in regular schooling situations is similarly 'flawed' by the institutional and audit cultures that institutions create.

Teaching in a corporate environment: Colin's story

In this section I draw on some transcript from an interview with a teacher who seems to me to mediate the institutional culture of his college's corporate view of learning outcomes as *exam results* in framing the learning process in his classrooms. The reader is invited to interpret his account of his teaching in this light.

Colin is a teacher of twenty years' experience, and one who has won great respect from the college's senior management because of the results his students get. I knew him some considerable time before because he had been an enthusiast for some innovative curriculum development involving making mathematics accessible and meaningful to students. The interview that I draw on here was conducted after I had observed two different lessons he taught with different classes separated by some time. I found his teaching 'interactive' but formal; this is how he described his teaching to me:

Colin: I mean normally, I, maybe I spend too long, you know, you know my sort of methods, it's nothing, it's old fashion methods, there's a bit of input from me at the front and then I try to get them working, practising questions as quickly as possible, and normally I'd spend quite a lot of time, but it tends to be now literally no more than twenty minutes on an exercise, I mean, some people say that's enough, really, and then, you know, move on to something else. Where in the old days I might have spent more time and have some harder questions at the end consolidating it, but not now. It tends to be as long as they can do the basics, then we'll move on, and we'll come back to it.

One thing that struck me in the lesson I had seen was the way he had simply 'told' the class the key idea for the topic: the formula to add together the terms of a geometric series. There had been no development, discovery, connection-making or even motivation for the topic. But this is a truly beautiful and important topic. It explains a most significant philosophical concept for the first time.

Excuse me while I enthuse, but every educated adult has to hear of 'Achilles and the tortoise' at least once. Achilles – it was argued by Greek philosophers – takes off to run after the tortoise but never quite overtakes him. Why? Because while it takes Achilles 10 seconds (say) to run to the tortoise, by that time the tortoise has moved on. Achilles now has a further one second to run (let's say the tortoise runs at $1/10$ the speed of Achilles, who is having a bad day!) But – as you can readily see – by this time, the tortoise has moved on again. And so Achilles has to keep running for an infinite series of times, presumably infinite in length (in fact 10, then 1, then 1/10, then 1/100 then 1/1000 and so on ... which can be shown to add up to eleven and one ninth seconds). The Greeks knew of course that Achilles *does* catch up with the tortoise, but they thought it a paradox that an infinite number of elements could add up to a finite sum. But this is just what this lesson was 'about': how to sum up an infinite series of numbers.

However, Colin had simply said, 'This is it, believe me, and this is what the examiners want, now let's do these calculations.' I wanted to discover from him how this situation had come about.

He often says he is 'in a rush' and I asked him about this 'rush':

Interviewer: You talk about rushing. I mean, did you feel you were rushing today?
Colin: Oh yeah. This is typical. This is what it's like all year.
Interviewer: All the time ...?
Colin: This is what it's like all the time. Because I feel the pressure on, I've got 25, 26 weeks in a year to get through 3 modules and this is how I feel, which is what I've got to do. You know, *I would not call that teaching, what I did today.* I don't think it is anyway. There might have been one or two good things in there but most of it is just trying to cram things in as fast as possible. And it is a nightmare but this is how it is. You know. *Because at the end of the day, what I get judged on now is results. In September, results. You know, have they got the grades? And if they haven't, my head's on a block.*

So it seems that Colin believes he cannot teach because of the pressure of exams, grades and results – and the institution holds him accountable for these. I later asked him to explain more:

Colin: Yeah, the results are everything ... it's *not necessarily what you as a maths community would want, I don't think.* I mean, this is me speaking here. This is not my department, necessarily, but I do tend to teach to the syllabus now. If it's not on, I don't teach it. I mean, I do try to bring some interest and explain things, if I can, but I do tend to say this is going to be on the exam, it's going to be worth X number of marks, that's why we're doing it. And it's like that because we are ... the main thing is the shortage of time, but also we have a lot of students, I mean, maybe it's me over the years and it's worn me down, who are only doing maths because they have to do it, even at A level, because if they're doing medicine or whatever course, they need to have maths. And, although you try and get some interest, a lot of them, at the end of the day, *the only way I can persuade them to do anything is well it's worth ten marks on the exam paper.*

Thus, he rejects the view of the 'maths community' that he thinks I represent, and to the institutional pressures on him to perform he now adds the pressure from the students, who pressure him to stick to things that 'count' for them. Indeed, he seemed to me ambivalent about the exams, as regards the development of 'understanding' in particular:

Colin: Yeah ... and it is really teaching them the tricks. I mean, I admit, it's a bit like, I teach it the way I was taught really, which was teaching them the tricks. Because with me a lot of the understanding didn't come for maybe years and years and years, and suddenly thought well that's why. I mean, in theory I've done a maths degree, and I'm not a brilliant, I still wouldn't say I'm a brilliant mathematician, and I think a lot of understanding does actually take years. And we haven't got years. I've got twenty-six weeks with the lower sixth and maybe a little bit more with the upper sixth. So I teach them the tricks. I mean, we do try to put the understanding, but you know, some of it is going to be, you take my word for this, it's going to work.

Interviewer: You actually said that at one point in a lesson, I seem to remember...

Colin: I say it a lot, 'Take my word for it.'

Interviewer: 'We haven't time to prove it'?

Colin: Yeah, 'even if you don't believe me, it's true', is one of my standard phrases. 'Even if you don't believe me, it's true, it works, and it should work every time, hopefully ... I could show you a proof of this, but they'll never ask you it, it's what you do with it that the exam board are interested in.' So that's a classic thing now. In the old days I might have spent a bit of time trying to prove it to them.

In this explanation it seemed that Colin's personal history and relation to the 'subject culture' is implicated: he himself experienced his subject as something that took years to understand, and he coped by learning 'tricks'. He therefore sees this as a way out of the pressure he feels under to perform. I pressed Colin on his 'view of understanding', which I felt was ambivalent:

Colin: Well it is, yeah, I mean, it does lead, a lot of the time, it does lead them up the garden path. It tells them what to do, but even despite that some of them still can't; you know, they struggle with it. And unless it's set up exactly as the question was that I've shown them, they can't do it, and that's because they haven't got the deep understanding, and that's my fault, that is, in a sense. Because we've not given them the time to really learn how to, you know, when the question's slightly different, they can't cope with it.

Interviewer: You're a bit ambivalent about understanding.

Colin: Sometimes you say you haven't got the time for it; that it comes later, but other times you say you actually do need it ... Well, they do need it. For some of the questions they do need it. I teach them the tricks and hope that most of the time, that's enough to get them to do the exam questions, but, you know, if they set it in a slightly different way, they haven't got that understanding. Well, some, obviously the better ones pick up on it and they know how to adapt, but the weaker ones just haven't got a [clue?] ... It's been going over their head a bit, certainly since Christmas it's been going over their head.

I concluded that the institution's view of his successful exam results coupled well with his own view of his pedagogic function and the learner as the object of teaching: their learning outcomes are measured by grades, and optimised by tricks that allow them to complete the syllabus and get marks within a very tight timetable. *Understanding* (perhaps the 'use value' in the learning here) plays a subservient and ambiguous role in this process, both for Colin and in his account for his students. On the one hand it is deemed an unnecessary interference for which one does not really have 'time' (perhaps a proxy for priorities) and on the other it comes to be a requirement to progress to the harder parts of the course successfully.

What I see in the above account is Colin working out a professional identity in a culture of institutionalised audit, where the exchange value of the knowledge (in this case mathematics) is highlighted by the institution itself, but also by the students. His own personal history is interwoven with this work of identity, and there is conflict in his account. But the end result, for the moment, is that the learners and their knowledge are objectified as 'results', and the importance of the knowledge for understanding and use is marginalised.

In practice, professional teachers make their identity, drawing on multiple, interweaving discourses that draw on cultural contexts – their agency is mediated by institutional, audit and subject cultures, but they still have agency (and responsibility) too.

Conclusion

In the previous two sections I offered analyses and interpretations respectively that drew on a perspective of learning as a socially, culturally and historically mediated activity. I argued that understanding phenomena such as PISA, or a teacher's account of their everyday work in our audit culture, requires a framing of the institutional, political context through which learning activity is structured. To understand the learner and the learning process in formal contexts, one has to understand pedagogy and its institutionalisation, e.g. through assessment . It is almost never the case that the learner learns 'alone', and the learning process with all its attendant difficulties can only be properly understood in this social and political context.

Acknowledgements

I acknowledge the support of ESRC for the project RES–139–25–0241 in the TLRP Widening Participation Programme which gave rise to this work.

References

Bernstein, B. (1996) *Pedagogy, Symbolic Control and Identity*, London, Taylor & Francis.
Bourdieu, P. (1990) *The Logic of Practice*, Oxford, Polity Press.
Chevallard, Y. and Joshua, M.A. (1991) *La Transposition didactique: du savoir savant au savoir enseigné*, Paris, La Pensée Sauvage.
Cole, M. (1996) *Cultural Psychology: A Once and Future Discipline*, Cambridge, MA, Belknap Press of Harvard University Press.
Engeström, Y. (1987) *Learning by Expanding: An Activity-theoretical Approach to Developmental Research*, Helsinki, Orienta-Konsultit.
Engeström, Y. (1991) 'Non scolae sed vitae discimus: toward overcoming the encapsulation of school learning', *Learning and Instruction*, 1, pp. 243–59.
Holland, D., Lachicotte, J., Skinner, D. and Cain, C. (1998) *Identity and Agency in Cultural Worlds*, Cambridge, MA, Harvard University Press.
Jenkins, R. (1996) *Social Identity*, London, Routledge.
Lave (1996) 'Teaching, as learning, in practice', *Mind Culture and Activity*, 3(3), pp. 149–64.
Lave, J. and Wenger, E. (1991) *Situated Learning: Legitimate Peripheral Participation*, Cambridge, Cambridge University Press.
Leont'ev, A.N. (1978) *Activity, Consciousness, and Personality*, Englewood Cliffs, NJ, Prentice Hall.
—— (1981) *Problems of the Development of the Mind*, Moscow, Progress.
Moscovici, S. (1984) 'The phenomenon of social representations', in R.M. Farr and S. Moscovici (eds), *Social Representations*, Cambridge, CUP, pp. 3–69.
PISA (2003) *The PISA 2003 Assessment Framework*, Paris, OECD.
—— (2004) *Learning for Tomorrow's World*, Paris, OECD.
—— (2005) *School Factors Related to Quality and Equity*, Paris, OECD.
Power, M. (1999) *The Audit Explosion: Rituals of Verification*, Oxford, OUP.

Roth, W.-M. and Lee, Y.J. (2007) 'Vygotsky's neglected legacy: cultural-historical activity theory', *Review of Educational Research*, 77(2), pp. 186–232.

Roth, W.-M., Hwang, S.-W., Lee, Y.J. and Goulart, M.I.M. (2005) *Participation, Learning and Identity: Dialectic Perspectives*, Berlin, Lehmans Media.

Ryan, J. and Williams, J. (2007) *Children's Mathematics 4–15*, Milton Keynes, Open University Press.

Sfard, A. (1998) 'On two metaphors for learning and the dangers of choosing just one', *Educational Researcher*, 27(2), pp. 4–13.

Strathern, M. (ed.) (2000) *Audit Cultures: Anthropological Studies in Accountability, Ethics and the Academy*, London, Routledge.

Vygotsky, L.S. (1978) *Mind in Society: The Development of Higher Psychological Processes*, Cambridge, MA, Harvard University Press.

—— (1986) *Thought and Language*, Cambridge, MA, MIT Press.

Wenger, E. (1998) *Communities of Practice: Learning, Meaning and Identity*, Cambridge, Cambridge University Press.

Williams, J.S. (2005) *The Foundation and Spectacle of [the leaning tower of] PISA*, Melbourne: Proceedings of PME-2005.

Willis, P. (1983) 'Cultural production and theories of reproduction', in L. Barton and S. Walker (eds), *Race, Class and Education*, London, Croom-Helm, pp. 107–38.

Reflective questions

1   I have argued that it is necessary to understand the social context of learning – e.g. institutionalised schooling versus informal learning. Identify two contrasting contexts of learning you have personally experienced: how did these contexts shape your experience of the learning process?

2   I have suggested that there is a contradiction between the 'use value' (e.g. the skills and competences that are likely to be useful, and used) of knowledge being acquired in learning and its 'exchange value' (e.g. the certificate that can be exchanged for a job). How have you experienced this contradiction in your own present or previous academic studies?

Further reading

Sfard, A. (1998) 'On two metaphors for learning and the dangers of choosing just one', *Educational Researcher*, 27(2), pp. 4–13.

Lave, J., and Wenger, E. (1991) *Situated Learning: Legitimate Peripheral Participation*, Cambridge, Cambridge University Press.

Engeström, Y. (1991) 'Non scolae sed vitae discimus: toward overcoming the encapsulation of school learning', *Learning and Instruction*, 1, pp. 243–59.

2.4 Brain development during adolescence

Sarah-Jayne Blakemore

Introduction

Until relatively recently, it was widely believed that the brain ceases to develop after childhood. This belief was based on Nobel prize-winning brain research carried out in the 1950s. This research demonstrated that the animal brain undergoes dramatic reorganisation in the first three years of life (e.g. Wiesel and Hubel, 1965). Moreover, this early period of life was found to constitute a 'critical period' for learning, when the development of sensory and motor regions in the brain depends on experience. This period has been likened to a window of opportunity, after which it closes and is too late for normal brain development, and learning, to occur. The idea that the brain could grow new cells and new connections after the early years was rarely entertained. Educational literature often suggests that the crucial phase of brain development in humans occurs as early as from birth to three years and that during this time children should be exposed to all sorts of learning experiences (cf. Blakemore and Frith, 2005).

However, these early findings have been countered by subsequent research showing that windows for learning and development remain ajar after early critical periods. Indeed, research in the past two decades has revolutionised our knowledge about the brain and its development. This research has demonstrated that the human brain continues to develop during adolescence and beyond. In this chapter, I will describe the developmental processes that occur in certain parts of the brain, in particular the frontal cortex, during adolescence, and the implications of this development for teenagers.

Early brain development

An adult human brain contains about 100 billion brain cells (*neurons*);[1] human babies are born with just as many neurons as adults. However, as babies develop, many changes take place in the brain. Neurons grow, which accounts for some of the change, but the 'wiring', the intricate network of connections between neurons (*synapses*)[2] undergoes the most significant change. Early in development, the brain begins to form new synapses, so that the synaptic density (the number of synapses per unit volume of brain tissue) greatly exceeds adult levels. This process of synaptic proliferation, called *synaptogenesis*, lasts up to several months, depending on the species of animal. Thus, a one-year-old baby's brain contains many more connections than does an adult brain. The next stage of development reduces the surplus synapses to an adult number.

The increase in the number of synapses is followed by a period of synaptic elimination (or *pruning*) in which excess connections whither away. This process is genetically pre-programmed to a large extent – it will happen no matter what environment the baby is in. To a certain extent, however, the species-specific environment influences synaptic pruning, in that frequently used connections are strengthened and infrequently used connections are eliminated. Pruning of synapses is much like pruning of a rose bush: getting rid of the weak branches allows the remaining branches to grow stronger. This experience-dependent process, which occurs over a period of years, reduces the overall synaptic density to adult levels, usually by the time of sexual maturity.

It is believed that synaptic pruning effectively fine-tunes networks of brain tissue and perceptual processes. Synaptic pruning is thought to underlie sound categorisation, for instance. Learning one's own language initially requires categorising the sounds that make up language. Newborn babies are able to distinguish between all speech sounds. Patricia Kuhl at the University of Washington discovered that, by the end of their first year, babies lose the ability to distinguish between sounds to which they are not exposed (Kuhl, 1998). Kuhl's experiments studied babies' perception of two different sounds from the Hindi language between which American (and British) adults are simply unable to distinguish. In an ingenious series of experiments, Kuhl showed that American babies under 10 months could detect the difference between these sounds that American adults could not. After 10 months of age, babies gradually lose this ability (Werker *et al.*, 1981). This is because the American language does not contain those particular distinct sounds, so American babies are not exposed to them. In contrast, babies brought up hearing Hindi at the same age become even better at hearing the distinction between these distinct sounds because they are exposed to them in their language. In this respect, there is nothing unusual about Hindi language sounds: there are many sounds from all languages that non-speakers cannot detect. The inability of many Japanese people to distinguish between 'r' and 'l' sounds is another example of this. Again, Japanese babies can detect this difference, but lose this ability because the Japanese language does not contain distinct 'r' and 'l' sounds. This experience-dependent fine-tuning of sound categorisation may rely on the pruning of synapses in sensory areas involved in processing sound.

Are there critical periods in brain development?

Experiments on animals, starting in the 1950s, showed that sensory regions of the brain go through *critical periods* soon after birth, during which time environmental stimulation appears to be crucial for normal brain development and for normal perceptual development to occur. In their Nobel prize-winning research on brain development, Torsten Wiesel and David Hubel temporarily covered one eye of new-born cats (Wiesel and Hubel, 1965). After about three months, the eye was uncovered and the researchers studied the connections between the two eyes and the brain. They found that this early visual deprivation led to severe deterioration of neuronal connections in the visual areas of the brain and to virtual blindness in the eye that was covered. This is because the brain had received no stimulation from the deprived eye and it had wired itself to receive information only from the other, open eye. By comparison, the same or longer periods of complete visual deprivation had no such effects on the visual system of adult cats, nor on their ability to use the deprived eye to guide their behaviour when it was subsequently uncovered.

This research showing that early visual deprivation has detrimental consequences is often cited as evidence for the importance of stimulation in the first few years of a baby's life. The claim assumes that the time course of synaptogenesis and critical periods are the same for humans as for the animals. However, development in humans is much more protracted than most animals. Second, the claim assumes that the period of synaptogenesis and synaptic pruning is the same in regions of the brain other than the visual cortex. Third, the claim often implies that no learning or brain development can occur after an early critical period.

Subsequent research by Hubel and Wiesel and others has suggested that some recovery of function is possible depending on the specific period of deprivation and the circumstances following deprivation. The shorter the period of deprivation the more recovery of function is possible. In addition, if the animal is trained to use the initially deprived eye after it is uncovered there is some recovery of vision (e.g. Chow and Stewart, 1972). Indeed, most neuroscientists now believe that critical periods are not rigid and inflexible. Rather, they are interpreted as *sensitive periods,* comprising subtle changes in the brain's ability to be shaped and changed by experiences that occur over a lifetime. For some functions to develop normally, the animal must receive appropriate sensory input from the environment at some stage during development. However, this input tends to be very general in nature, including patterned visual stimuli, the ability to move and manipulate objects, noises, and speech sounds and social interaction for human babies. It seems fair to say that the natural environment of most children contains sufficient sensory stimulation for normal brain development. There is no evidence that extra stimulation aids brain development in children who are brought up in typical environments. Furthermore, the parts of the human brain that underlie complex cognitive capacities, such as language and decision-making, seem to have several sensitive periods, many of which continue into adolescence and even early adulthood.

Brain development during adolescence: the first experiments

The experiments described above suggested that development of certain areas of animal brains is particularly sensitive to environmental influence at particular times very early in life. As a consequence of this research, the very idea that the brain might continue to undergo change after this very early sensitive period seemed improbable. Indeed, it was not until the 1970s that research on post-mortem human brains revealed that some brain areas, in particular the *frontal cortex* (see Figure 2.4.1), continue to develop well beyond childhood. The frontal cortex is the area responsible for important cognitive abilities such as the ability to make plans, remember to do things in the future, multi-task and inhibit inappropriate behaviour (known as *executive functions*). The frontal cortex also plays an important role in self-awareness and understanding other people. Peter Huttenlocher, professor of Paediatrics and Neurology at the University of Chicago, collected post-mortem brains from people of all ages, and found that the frontal cortex was remarkably different in the brains of pre-pubescent children and post-pubescent adolescents.

While in sensory brain areas synaptogenesis and synaptic pruning occur relatively early (as described above), Huttenlocher discovered that there is a second wave of synaptic reor-ganisation in the frontal cortex that starts at around the age that corresponds to the onset of puberty (Huttenlocher, 1979). He found that the number of synapses in the frontal lobe is maximal at an age that corresponds to the onset of puberty, after which the number of synapses in the frontal cortex decreases (due to synaptic pruning) throughout adolescence.

Another developmental mechanism that occurs for many decades in the frontal cortex is *myelination*. As neurons develop, they build up a layer of *myelin* on their *axon* (the long fibre attached to each brain cell). Myelin is a fatty substance that insulates the axons and hugely increases the speed of transmission of electrical impulses from neuron to neuron. Whereas sensory and motor brain regions become fully myelinated in the first few years of life, axons

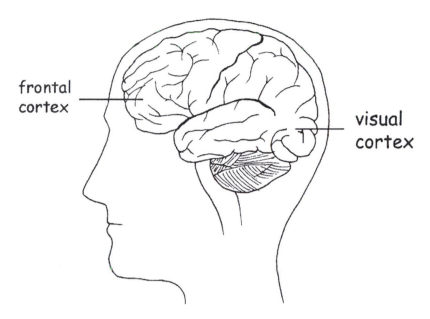

Figure 2.4.1 The location of the frontal and visual cortices.

in the frontal cortex continue to be myelinated well into adolescence in the human brain (Yakovlev and Lecours, 1967). This finding is remarkable because it means that the transmission speed of neurons in the frontal cortex may increase after puberty. In addition, the research demonstrating synaptic pruning in the frontal cortex suggests that fine-tuning of cognitive processes of the frontal lobes should also take place in adolescence. One purely speculative possibility is that sensitive periods accompany this later period of fine-tuning, just as they do for fine-tuning of speech perception in the first 10 months of life (as described for sound categorisation). Just as the environment influences early synaptic pruning, so might it have an impact on the pruning that occurs in the frontal cortex during adolescence. We have no idea whether or not this is the case – there are no tools as yet to look at pruning in the living brain. However, if the environment influences synaptic pruning during adolescence, this has implications for what kind of experiences adolescents should encounter. Recent research from the Institute of Psychiatry in London has shown that adolescents who regularly smoke cannabis have a much higher chance of developing schizophrenia in their twenties (Arseneault *et al.*, 2002). It is possible that cannabis affects brain development during adolescence – but this is pure speculation at this stage.

Brain development during adolescence: recent experiments

Until recently, the structure of the human brain could be studied only after death. The scarcity of post-mortem child and adolescent brains meant that knowledge of the adolescent brain was extremely scanty until very recently. In the past decade, non-invasive brain imaging techniques, particularly Magnetic Resonance Imaging (MRI),[3] have enabled scientists to study development of the living human brain. In the past seven or eight years, a number of MRI studies have provided further evidence of the ongoing maturation of the frontal cortex into adolescence and even into adulthood. These imaging studies have confirmed that the brain changes during the teenage years, first revealed in the cellular studies carried out 20 years earlier (Giedd *et al.*, 1999; Sowell *et al.*, 1999; Paus *et al.*, 2005).

The brain images from the MRI studies show that the amount of white matter in the frontal cortex (amongst other cortical regions) increases between childhood and adulthood. Myelin is made up of fatty tissue and appears white in an MRI scan. Therefore, the increase in white matter seen to occur throughout adolescence may represent the increase in axonal myelination discovered by the cellular studies performed decades earlier. The increase in white matter in the frontal cortex is steady and linear.

In contrast to the steady, linear increase in white matter, at the same time, there is a more complex, non-linear decrease in grey matter in the frontal cortex during adolescence (Giedd, 2004). In the past decade, Jay Giedd and his colleagues at the National Institute of Health in Maryland, USA, have scanned hundreds of children, adolescents and young adults. The results from their studies have shown that grey matter volume in the frontal cortex increases gradually during childhood and peaks at around the onset of puberty: approximately 11 years in girls and 12 years in boys. This is followed by a gradual decrease in the volume of grey matter during adolescence and early adulthood. Grey matter is made up of cell bodies, dendrites and synapses. Therefore, the pattern of grey matter development has been attributed to the increase in the number of synapses, which peaks at the onset of puberty, followed by synaptic pruning during adolescence (first discovered by Huttenlocher in his post-mortem studies described above).

Cognitive changes during adolescence

The frontal cortex changes dramatically during puberty and adolescence and beyond. As mentioned above, this brain region plays a critical role in a host of high-level cognitive abilities such as executive functions, including planning, multi-tasking, inhibiting inappropriate behaviour, and social understanding, including perspective taking and self-awareness. In the past few years, empirical research has looked at the cognitive changes that occur during adolescence (see Blakemore and Choudhury, 2006, for review).

A number of studies have demonstrated that these abilities do undergo refinement during adolescence. Some abilities, including planning and inhibiting behaviour, seem to improve steadily, while others seem to undergo a 'dip' at puberty. A series of experiments carried out in Australia showed that many executive functions steadily improve during adolescence (Anderson *et al.*, 2001). In contrast, a recent study showed that the ability to match an emotional face to an emotion word actually deteriorates at around the age of puberty (McGivern *et al.*, 2002). In this study, a large group of children and adolescents were shown pictures of faces showing particular emotional expressions (happy, sad, angry), or words describing those emotions ('Happy', 'Sad', Angry'), and were asked to specify, as quickly as possible, the emotion presented in the face or word. In a third condition, volunteers were shown both a face and a word, then, after a delay, had to decide whether the facial expression matched the emotional word. The rationale behind the design of the task was that the face/word condition places high demands on frontal lobe circuitry, since it requires working memory and decision-making.

The results revealed that, at the age of puberty onset, at 11–12 years, there was a decline in performance in the matching face and word condition compared with the younger group of children. The results suggest that there is a dip in performance on this kind of task at the onset of puberty. After puberty, from age 13–14, performance improved until it returned to the pre-pubescent level by the age of about 16–17 years. The authors linked this pubertal dip to the increase in the number of synapses in the frontal cortex at the onset of puberty. The idea is that this wave of synaptic proliferation perturbs the functioning of prefrontal cortex, which has to be reorganised into efficient networks by synaptic pruning during adolescence.

A study published in 2006 studied the link between brain development and IQ. In this experiment by Jay Giedd and his colleagues, over 300 children were scanned at least once, and underwent IQ tests, between the ages of 8 and 16 (Shaw *et al.*, 2006). The participants were divided into three groups depending on their IQ: average, high or superior. The results revealed that cortical (particularly frontal cortex) thickness peaks later (at age 13 years) in children with superior IQ, compared with children with average IQ (5.6 years) or high IQ (8.5 years). This is followed in late adolescence by cortical thinning, which is more rapid in the superior IQ group than in the other groups. In other words, although cortical thickening is delayed in the superior IQ group, their cortex thickens and thins faster than the other groups. The authors of this study suggest that the delay in thickening might promote higher IQ because the older the child is, the more complex and varied experiences they can experience at a time when the cortex is growing and malleable.

Development of neural circuitry used for cognitive tasks during adolescence

Functional MRI (fMRI)[4] is used to investigate which brain regions are active when volunteers carry out a certain task. fMRI studies that have investigated functional brain development during adolescence have focused mainly on executive function tasks. Some have shown that activation of frontal cortex increases with age (e.g. Adleman *et al.*, 2002; Kwon *et al.*, 2002; Rubia *et al.*, 2000), while others report decreased frontal activation with age (e.g. Durston *et al.*, 2006; Gaillard *et al.*, 2000; see Blakemore and Choudhury, 2006). The same discrepancy in findings with respect to frontal activity applies to studies that have investigated the development of social cognitive processes during adolescence. However, there is some indication that, for social cognitive tasks, activity in the frontal cortex increases between childhood and adolescence, and then decreases between adolescence and adulthood. For example, female subjects (but not male subjects) showed increased activation in dorsolateral PFC in response to fearful faces between childhood and adolescence (Killgore *et al.*, 2001). A recent study reported increased activity in prefrontal cortex (PFC) (bilaterally for girls; right-sided for boys) in response to fearful faces between age 8 and 15 (Yurgelun-Todd and Killgore, 2006). In contrast, another study of face processing found that attention to a nonemotional aspect of fearful relative to neutral faces was associated with increased activity in orbitofrontal cortex in adolescents compared to adults (Monk *et al.*, 2003). A recent fMRI study investigated the development of communicative intent using an irony comprehension task and found that children (aged between 9 and 14) engaged frontal regions (medial PFC and left inferior frontal gyrus) more than did adults in this task (Wang *et al.*, 2006).

We recently carried out a study to investigate the development during adolescence of the neural systems underlying mentalising ability (Blakemore *et al.*, 2007). We scanned a group of 19 adolescents (aged 11–17) and a group of 11 adults (aged 21–37) while they were thinking about intentional causality (the relationship between intentions and actions) compared with physical causality (the relationship between natural events and their consequences). Neuroimaging research in adults has demonstrated that such 'mentalising' tasks activate a network of brain regions including medial prefrontal cortex (mPFC) and superior temporal sulcus (STS) (Frith and Frith, 2003). While the mentalising network was active in adults and adolescents when thinking about intentions, our study showed that adolescents activated part of the mPFC more than did adults and adults activated part of the right STS more than did adolescents. These results suggest that the neural strategy for thinking about intentions changes between adolescence and adulthood. Although the same neural network is active, the relative roles of the different areas change, with activity moving from anterior (mPFC) regions to posterior (STS) regions with age.

In summary, functional imaging studies have reported mixed findings with respect to changes in frontal activity with age, but there is a hint that activity during certain social cognition tasks might increase during childhood and decrease between adolescence and adulthood.

Implications

In this chapter, I have skimmed the surface of research demonstrating that the brain continues to develop and change during adolescence. The study of the development of the brain beyond childhood is a new but rapidly evolving field with potential applications in education and social policy. The finding that changes in brain structure continue into adolescence and early adulthood has challenged accepted views and has given rise to a recent spate of investigations into the way cognition might change as a consequence.

If early childhood is seen as a major opportunity for teaching, so perhaps should teenage years. During both periods, particularly dramatic brain reorganisation is taking place. The idea that teenagers should still go to school and be educated is relatively new. And yet the research on brain development suggests that education during the teenage years is vital. The brain is still developing during this period, the brain is adaptable, and needs to be moulded and shaped. Perhaps the aims of education for adolescents might change to include abilities that are controlled by the parts of the brain that undergo most change during adolescence. These abilities might include internal control, multi-tasking, planning, and social cognitive skills.

Research on neural plasticity suggests that the brain is well set up for life-long learning and adaptation to the environment, and that educational rehabilitation in adulthood is possible and well worth investment. On the other hand, the research also suggests that there is no biological necessity to rush and start formal teaching earlier and earlier. Rather, late starts might be reconsidered as perfectly in time with natural brain and cognitive development.

Conclusion

Research suggests that adolescence is a key time for the development of regions of the brain involved in decision-making, social processing and self-awareness. This is likely to be due to the interplay between a number of factors including changes in the social environment and in hormonal functioning, structural and functional brain development and improvements in social cognition. Future research should investigate how these factors account for behavioural phenomena that are typical of adolescence.

Notes

1 A *neuron* is the primary cell in the nervous system. Neurons communicate with other neurons by sending electrical impulses from their cell body, down their axon, to their synaptic terminals, which connect with the dendrites of neurons in the surrounding areas.

2 A *synapse* is a gap between nerve cells, across which chemical information is passed in the nervous system. Synapses generally lie along synaptic terminals and dendrites of nerve cells.

3 *Magnetic Resonance Imaging* (MRI) uses a very large magnetic field to produce high-quality three-dimensional images of brain structures without injecting radioactive tracers. A large cylindrical magnet creates a magnetic field around the person's head, and a magnetic pulse is sent through the magnetic field. Different structures in the brain (so-called white matter and grey matter, blood vessels, fluid and bone, for example) have different magnetic properties and therefore they appear different in the MRI image. Sensors inside the scanner record the signals from the different brain structures and a computer uses the information to construct an image. Using MRI, it is possible to image both surface and deep brain structures in great anatomical detail.

4 *functional Magnetic Resonance Imaging* (fMRI) is an imaging technique used for measuring blood oxygen levels in the living brain. When neurons become active they require a supply of oxygen to be carried to them in the blood. It is this oxygen carried in the blood that the fMRI scanner detects because oxygen has magnetic properties. fMRI measures the amount of oxygenated blood that is sent to particular regions in the brain. This information is used to make 'films' of changes in brain activity as volunteers see or hear certain stimuli and do other things, like answer questions or press buttons.

References

Anderson, V., Anderson, P., Northam, E., Jacobs, R. and Catroppa, C. (2001) 'Development of executive functions through late childhood and adolescence in an Australian sample', *Developmental Neuropsychology*, 20, pp. 385–406.

Arseneault, L., Cannon, M., Poulton, R., Murray, R., Caspi, A. and Moffitt, T.E. (2002) 'Cannabis use in adolescence and risk for adult psychosis: longitudinal prospective study', *British Medical Journal*, 325, pp. 1212–13.

Blakemore, S.-J. and Choudhury, S. (2006) 'Development of the adolescent brain: implications for executive function and social cognition', *Journal of Child Psychiatry and Psychology*, 47(3–4), pp. 296–312.

Blakemore, S.-J. and Frith, U. (2005) *The Learning Brain: Lessons for Education*, Oxford, Blackwell.

Blakemore, S.-J., den Ouden, H.E.M., Choudhury, S. and Frith, C. (2007) 'Adolescent development of the neural circuitry for thinking about intentions', in press in *Social Cognitive and Affective Neuroscience*.

Chow, K.L. and Stewart, D.L. (1972) 'Reversal of structural and functional effects of long-term visual deprivation in cats', *Experimental Neurology*, 34, pp. 409–33.

Frith, U. and Frith, C.D. (2003) 'Development and neurophysiology of mentalizing', *Philosophical Transactions of the Royal Society of London B: Biological Sciences*, 358(1431), pp. 459–73.

Giedd, J.N. (2004) 'Structural magnetic resonance imaging of the adolescent brain', *Annals of the New York Academy of Sciences*, 1021, pp. 77–85.

Giedd, J.N., Blumenthal, J., Jeffries, N.O., Castellanos, F.X., Liu, H., Zijdenbos, A., Paus, T., Evans, A.C. and Rapoport, J.L. (1999) 'Brain development during childhood and adolescence: a longitudinal MRI study', *Nature Neuroscience*, 2(10), pp. 861–63.

Huttenlocher, P.R. (1979) 'Synaptic density in human frontal cortex – developmental changes and effects of aging', *Brain Research*, 163, pp. 195–205.

Kuhl, P.K. (1998) 'The development of speech and language', in T.J. Carew, R. Menzel and C.J. Shatz (eds), *Mechanistic Relationships Between Development and Learning*, New York, Wiley, pp. 53–73.

McGivern, R.F., Andersen, J., Byrd, D., Mutter, K.L. and Reilly, J. (2002) 'Cognitive efficiency on a match to sample task decreases at the onset of puberty in children', *Brain and Cognition*, 50, pp. 73–89.

Paus, T. (2005) 'Mapping brain maturation and cognitive development during adolescence', *Trends in Cognitive Sciences*, 9, pp. 60–8.

Shaw, P., Greenstein, D., Lerch, J., Clasen, L., Lenroot, R., Gogtay, N., Evans, A., Rapoport, J. and Giedd, J.N. (2006) 'Intellectual ability and cortical development in children and adolescents', *Nature*, 440, pp. 676–9.

Sowell, E.R., Thompson, P.M., Holmes, C.J., Batth, R., Jernigan, T.L. and Toga, A.W. (1999) 'Localizing age-related changes in brain structure between childhood and adolescence using statistical parametric mapping', *NeuroImage*, 6(1), pp. 587–97.

Werker, J.F., Gilbert, J.H., Humphrey, K. and Tees, R.C. (1981) 'Developmental aspects of cross-language speech perception', *Child Development*, 52(1), pp. 349–55.

Wiesel, T.N. and Hubel, D.H. (1965) 'Extent of recovery from the effects of visual deprivation in kittens', *Journal of Neurophysiology*, 28, pp. 1060–72.

Yakovlev, P.A. and Lecours, I.R. (1967) 'The myelogenetic cycles of regional maturation of the brain', in A. Minkowski (ed.), *Regional Development of the Brain in Early Life*, Oxford, Blackwell, pp. 3–70.

Reflective questions

1   Very little is known about gender differences in neurocognitive development during adolescence. This is an important question because it might have implications for the type, and timing, of education that boys and girls require. It is possible that different educational strategies suit boys and girls because of the different ways their brains are developing. This is a purely speculative idea and remains to be tested. Based on your experience of education, in what ways do you think boys and girls differ in terms of the way they learn?

2   Many things are changing during the teenage years, including hormonal changes, physical changes and the social environment of the child. How hormonal changes are related to brain changes is unknown. The social environment changes dramatically during the teenage years, and this is likely to have profound effects on the brain and cognition. How the social environment interacts with biological factors to influence cognitive behavioural development is an important question that requires further research. Have you any feelings about how these factors interact, and can you think of ways this question might be looked at by researchers?

Further reading

Blakemore, S.-J. (2008) 'The social brain in adolescence', *Nature Reviews Neuroscience*, 9(4), pp. 267–77.

Blakemore, S.-J. and Frith, U. (2005) *The Learning Brain: Lessons for Education*, Oxford, Blackwell.

Howard-Jones, P. (2007) *Neuroscience and Education: Issues and Opportunities*, TLRP Commentary, Swindon, ESRC.

Goswami, U. (2006) 'Neuroscience and education: from research to practice?', *Nature Reviews Neuroscience*, 7(5), pp. 406–13.

Pickering, S.J. and Howard-Jones, P.A. (2007) 'Educators' views of the role of neuroscience in education: a study of UK and international perspectives', *Mind, Brain and Education*, 1(3), pp. 109–13.

2.5 Interrogating student voice

Preoccupations, purposes and possibilities

Michael Fielding

Introduction

Listening with interest

In this chapter, I begin by drawing attention to the range of professional and research activity in listening to the voices of young people that has mushroomed in the last ten years, and explore a number of different typologies and intellectual frameworks that have been developed to try to bring both conceptual coherence and organisational clarity to the wide range of activities and research that come under the rubric of student voice.

I then explore a range of research methods that have been used to elicit and gain access to the views of young people. In addition to underscoring the importance of ethical issues I pay particular attention to two new developments that seem to me to reflect the current zeitgeist. These are the development of visual methods of research and the emergence of the students-as-researchers movement, which locates young people themselves as active partners/agents in the origins, design, process, outcomes and active legacy of research.

In the third section, 'Contemporary challenges', I explore a number of key issues emerging from work in the field. Of these I identify three – the plurality of student voices, the dangers of neo-liberal incorporation, and the debate about consultation and participation – that prompt substantial debate within the professional and research communities. I then explore a further three issues that seem to me to offer promising sites for future development. These are the move towards intergenerational dialogue; the importance of new public spaces and the necessity of narrative engagement; and the need to reclaim radical traditions of state education. The section ends with a brief consideration of what I take to be two fundamental challenges to the presumptions of student voice.

The short penultimate section briefly sets out a small number of 'Permanent dilemmas' that are likely to confront any attempt to listen seriously to the voices of young people in most societies. The final section, 'Making choices', concludes by pointing to the inevitability and desirability of teachers and researchers making choices about the kind of student voice work that sits most comfortably within their own aspirations for school and for the kind of society and the kind of world they wish to live in.

Making sense of student voice: frameworks for understanding and interpretation

Student voice has gained an increasing prominence in the last few years, with special issues of academic journals from Australia, Canada, the UK and the USA, and professional journals from the UK, numerous books and edited collections. However, the considerable range of professional and research activity developing on the ground (e.g. the ESRC [Economic and Social Research Council] project 'Consulting Pupils About Teaching and Learning' and a follow-up ESRC research seminar series 'Engaging critically with pupil voice: children and young people as partners in school and community change') has created what some see as difficulties of interpretation, understanding and potential. Under the broad penumbra of student voice we have

- activities that suggest young people benefit, both socially and academically, from listening to each other's voices whether individually, e.g. through buddying, coaching, mentoring and peer teaching, or more collectively, e.g. as prefects, student leaders and class and schools councils;
- activities in which students are given responsibility for working alongside teachers in engaging with their peers, e.g. student-led learning walks, students as co-researchers and lead researchers, student ambassadors and lead learners; and
- activities in which students express their views on a range of matters, sometimes after collecting and interpreting data, either on individual members of staff, schools teams or departments, or the school as a learning community, e.g. students as observers, students as informants in teacher consultation about effective teaching and learning, students on staff appointment panels, students as governors/school board members, student focus groups and surveys, and students as key informants in the processes of external inspection and accountability.

If all these and more come under the banner of student voice and to some degree trade on its substantial positive resonance in a range of professional, policy and academic contexts how are we to make discriminating judgements about the relative merits and challenges of what are quite palpably disparate activities and forms of engagement?

Participation, purposes and power

This situation has prompted a number of writers to attempt some kind of categorisation to aid in the clarification of what sorts of things come under the portmanteau of student voice and what potential there is for the development or, as some would see it, 'transformation' of the school system. Many have found Roger Hart's ladder of participation (Hart, 1997) very useful in helping to distinguish salient power relations and energising dynamics that range from manipulation, through consultation and participation to co-construction. Following the work of Sherry Arnstein (Arnstein, 1969), Hart suggests an eight-runged ladder ranging from the non-participatory 'manipulation', 'decoration' and 'tokenism' at the bottom through five further rungs of increasing child involvement culminating in the final two that are 'child-initiated and directed' to 'child-initiated, shared decisions with adults' at the top.

Others, mindful of Arnstein's work, have developed typologies of 'voice' according to different processes of articulation and outcome. Thus Mark Hadfield and Kaye Haw distinguish three different kinds of voice – authoritative, critical and therapeutic – that enable us to 'understand the links, both possible and actual, between the construction of "voice" and the practice of action' (Hadfield and Haw, 2001, p. 488).

Mary John acknowledges the importance of Hart's typology, but suggests that there are problems with a ladder metaphor on the grounds that it can be seen as reinforcing traditional notions of patriarchy in which rights are bestowed by the powerful on the less powerful.

Drawing on work from minority groups she argues that we need a 'transformational' model 'which is much more dynamic, which takes account of the politics of child participation and which also encompasses the construction of creative alliances with adults which forms the true basis of an emotional democracy on which ... children's participation must be based' (John, 1996, p. 19). Opting for a bridge-building metaphor she identifies the three key pillars of 'responsibility', 'unity' and 'involvement' as the necessary foundations on which the collaborative work of spanning the chasm between child and adult can take place.

While acknowledging his debt to Hart's work, in his influential 'Pathways to participation', Harry Shier also seeks to go beyond it, and comes up with a very user-friendly device as 'an additional tool for practitioners, helping them to explore different types of participation process' (Shier, 2001, p. 109). In it he articulates five levels of participation, which are then mapped onto a threefold matrix of openings, opportunities and obligations.

My own typology of 'students as data source', 'students as active participants', 'students as co-researchers', 'students as researchers' (Fielding, 2001) and, latterly, 'joint work' is strongly influenced by both Roger Hart and Mary John's work and has been widely used in England, most recently by the National College for School Leadership in its four-year Networked Learning Communities programme.

Interrogating professional and research practices

In most cases the underlying assumptions about participation, purposes and power shape the typologies developed. Thus, in my own work there is a concerted attempt to bring to the surface a set of key questions designed to interrogate espoused and actual practice in ways that force us back to values and purposes. Partnering the 'data source to researcher' typology mentioned above (Fielding, 2001) my framework of questions evaluating the conditions of student voice asks a series of simple but searching questions of various key elements of the processes of student voice engagement and development. Thus, of speaking I ask – 'Who is allowed to speak? To whom? What are they allowed to speak about? What language is encouraged or allowed? Who decides the answers to these questions? How are those decisions made? How, when, where, to whom and how often are these decisions communicated?' Of listening I ask, e.g. 'Who is listening? How and why?' And there are questions underscoring the necessity of skills development; of the fundamental importance of certain attitudes and dispositions; of organisational culture and public spaces for dialogue and discussion; of the necessity of action, and of the need to ask ourselves whether we need new structures and ways of relating to each other. Underpinning these questions, operationalised in a number of subsequent papers, is a worry that student voice is turning out to be a dissembling device directed at purposes that have little to do with encouraging the agency and aspirations of young people.

The same concerns animate a later paper interrogating academic practices, not just the burgeoning student voice work in professional contexts. Here my six questions for interrogating research practices (Fielding, 2004a) are intended to prevent us from slipping unwittingly into unwanted and unwarranted presumptions that oppress or marginalise the standpoints of young people. These underscore the importance of resisting re-description in our own interests, interrogating the impulse to control, questioning the correctness of how we do things now, acknowledging our own discursive locations, facing up to issues of power and the necessity of being open to criticism, and, finally, understanding the dangers of unwitting disempowerment.

Back to basics: inevitable ideologies

What these various typologies in both academic and professional fields are seeking to do is not only distinguish different kinds of practices of student voice so that we have a more differentiated understanding of what it is that is being advocated or deplored. What they are also trying to do, as I have suggested earlier, is to lead us back to purposes, values and ideological assumptions that either inform voice practices or frame them in ways that are not always visible and sometimes deliberately covert. Among those who deliberately address these matters through an interrogation of ideological and theoretical assumptions are Vibert and Shields (2003) and Fielding (2004b), who also grounds the pragmatic expression of ideological assumptions.

Rather than attempt a synoptic overview, other writers prefer to tackle these fundamental issues through a detailed articulation and application of the work of a major social theorist or philosopher. Thus, for example, Madeleine Arnot and Diane Reay draw heavily on the work of Basil Bernstein (Arnot and Reay, 2007), Helen Gunter, Roger Holdsworth and Pat Thomson on Pierre Bourdieu (Thomson and Gunter, 2007; Thomson and Holdsworth, 2003), Sara Bragg on Michel Foucault (Bragg, 2007b), Michael Fielding on John Macmurray (Fielding, 2006), Joe Kincheloe and John Smyth on critical theory (Kincheloe, 2007; Smyth, 2007), and Alison Cook-Sather on feminist theory (Cook-Sather, 2007).

Finding out about what young people think and feel

As with other aspects of student voice there has within the last decade been a revival of interest, not only in researching the lives and experiences of young people, but also in extending and developing approaches to conducting that research. I will touch on some of those substantive developments in a moment, but first I want to briefly draw attention to ethical considerations that are arguably more pronounced in their profile, if not in actual importance, when researching with and on young people.

Ethical considerations

Integral to the process of arriving at either the focus of the research or the design of an appropriate approach, the ethics of working with young people has received increased and sustained attention as more and more fields of enquiry and social practice have come to see the importance of taking account of changes in societal views of the nature of childhood and its consequences for the theoretical and practical frameworks that guide their work. Sara Bragg (2007a) provides an engaging and accessible account of centrally important issues citing a manageable range of key texts.

What is crucial in all this is getting clear about the recurring issues of purposes and power and responsibility that weave their way through any consideration of listening to and working with young people. Ethical considerations thus need to address issues to do with, for example, whether or not the research is in children's interests, the interplay of costs and benefits to them, matters of confidentiality, who is included and excluded from the research, funding and recompense, involvement in research design, clarity of aims, consent, dissemination, and impact on thinking, policy and practice (Bragg 2007a, p. 49).

Developments in research on and with young people

Sara Bragg's highly readable, elegant research review of the literature, *Consulting Young People* (2007a), also has an especially good chapter (Chapter 3) on the range of methods currently used in the consultation process by academic and teacher researchers and by young people working with them in a variety of ways. These include surveys and questionnaires, different kinds of interviews, observation, traditional forms of consultation such as councils and forums, and newer approaches such as suggestion boxes, ideas booths, listening posts and graffiti walls. Bragg also draws attention to creative, non-verbal research and evaluation methods that have become increasingly used in recent years, in part because many felt there was undue emphasis on the spoken word which was in danger of excluding children and unintentionally reinforcing existing marginalisation. Methods such as photography, drawing, collage, multi-media approaches, and audio-recording are increasingly widely and imaginatively used. So too are experiential, multi-faceted approaches such as logs and scrapbooks, guided tours, bedroom culture, toys, drama and role play, vignettes and scenarios.

The range of approaches and the nuanced possibilities opened up here again reflect the energy and expansive optimism running through the field of student voice. Two things strike me as emblematic of much that is characteristic of research with and on young people in an era in which identity and agency combine synergistically with new, especially audio-visual, technology. These are, first, an increasingly wide-ranging body of imaginative, high-quality work which is extending visual approaches into new intellectual as well as new experiential territory. Second, the growing prominence, both among teachers and academics, of an active partnership between young people and adults goes beyond consultation to embrace a participatory mode in which young people's voices are part of a more dialogic, reciprocal way of working.

Valuing the visual

An indication of the increasing level of interest in and use of visual methods in research in general and in listening to the voices of young people in particular comes from a recent special issue of *Discourse* (2007, vol. 8, issue 3). Of the seven papers making up this issue, two explicitly engage with visual methods of research and one other uses visual approaches as a central component of its research design. Pat Thomson and Helen Gunter's paper on students-as-researchers (Thomson and Gunter, 2007) includes a compelling account of the use of photo-elicitation or photo-voice which is designed to stimulate a response in its viewers in ways which reduce shyness and/or reticence and provoke the production of community and local knowledge.

That notion of local knowledge, particularly the local knowledge of the child, is something that Cathy Burke pursues in 'The view of the child: releasing "visual voices" in the design of learning' (Burke, 2007). Acknowledging the apparently contradictory nature of the notion of 'visual voice', she nonetheless argues that it has the capacity to 'draw attention to the overlooked, over familiar and taken for granted in the material and cultural design of schooling' (p. 360). This suggests that young people's experience of their interpersonal and built environments, particularly through their visual engagement with it, has important insights to offer us, not only about schooling as it is and was, but also about schooling as it might be in the future.

Finally, Heather Piper and Jo Frankham's 'Seeing voices and hearing pictures: image as discourse and the framing of image based research' (Piper and Frankham, 2007) provides a sustained examination of the increasing practice of eliciting visual texts from young people. While positive and supportive of the creative potential of such approaches they suggest it is 'now time to problematise the production, distribution, reception, and consumption of all such visual images as research questions, as part of the whole process in which they are deployed' (p. 375).

Visual methods of research with young people are not, of course, new. However, when the kind of taking stock that Piper and Frankham advocate goes hand in hand with a new surge of work and a desire to extend and cross boundaries – see especially Pat Thomson's *Doing Visual Research with Children and Young People* (Thomson, 2008) – one gets a sense that something with a wider resonance is on the move.

Students-as-researchers

If a 'visual turn' in research with and by young people is symptomatic of a social, interpersonal and increasingly political zeitgeist, not merely a technological advance readily available to the person in the street, then it is arguable that 'students-as-researchers' (hereinafter SAR) is an even more iconic phenomenon that also reflects political, not just relational, dynamics of the time. Certainly, the increasing sense that childhood has changed significantly, that young people are legitimate contributors to as well as subjects of the conversations of society, and that the improvement of schooling and other services targeted at the young depends in significant part on the capacity of those services to attend to what young people have to say have a wide-ranging currency.

Broadly speaking there are two forms of SAR, which emerged in its current manifestation in the mid 1990s. One approach, sometimes called 'students as co-researchers', involves teachers identifying issues they wish to explore and seeking the active support of young people, not only in carrying out the research, but also in helping to reflect on its processes, and make meaning from the data gathered so that recommendations for change and future action can be made. In full SAR mode the originating impulse and ongoing dynamic of the research, enquiry or evaluation come from the students themselves. It is the students who, with the support of adults, design and carry out the research and see it through to the often problematic later stages of meaning-making, recommendation, and dialogue with those in positions of relative power or influence to bring about desired changes. In both modes adults and students work in partnership, but, in the former, adult preoccupations and perspectives guide the processes and outcomes, whereas, in the latter, the reverse is the case. Key assumptions underlying both variants are, first, that young people's perspectives are sometimes significantly and interestingly different from those of adults; second, that too often access to those differences is either highly problematic or elusive unless young people are themselves involved in a research design and process that gives space, support, and motivation to enable them to engage with issues that interest them and matter to them; and, third, that if we manage to create conditions of dialogue then reciprocal engagement with those differences may, at least on some occasions, turn out to be mutually enlightening and productive.

Needless to say, with the growth and popularity of student voice, including SAR, with governments (e.g. in North America and the UK) and school leaders/educational administrators (e.g. *International Journal of Leadership in Education*, 2006, vol. 9, issue 4), in the past decade the nature of SAR has become increasingly contested. There are at least four points to make here. Under the umbrella of SAR there are important differences of focus, of age, of university involvement, and, last, but by no means least, of purpose and interpretation.

With regard to focus, there are those for whom SAR is important because it provides space and opportunity for young people to develop skills, dispositions and capacities that motivate and engage them in their school learning. For others, this engagement is not so much about retaining interest in existing school requirements as it is about enabling students to break out of the constraints of required curricula and ask fundamental questions of the society in which they live (e.g. Steinberg and Kincheloe, 1998; Kincheloe, 2007). For yet more others, the interest is less about classroom enquiry than it is an enquiry about teaching and learning in classrooms and other aspects of student experience across the school (Fielding and Bragg, 2003).

With regard to age, within the field and to a lesser extent in the literature, there is a significant age range of those involved including primary/elementary school (e.g. Johnson, 2004); middle school and junior secondary/high school (e.g. Mary Kellett's Children's Research Centre at the Open University – Kellett, 2005); and the pioneering work of Bill Atweh and Leonie Burton (e.g. Atweh and Burton, 1995) involving students on the school/university boundaries.

With regard to university involvement there are some studies which articulate a brief engagement with schools and others which are part of a longer process of capacity building in which schools develop their own SAR capacity (e.g. Fielding, 2001). With regard to matters of purpose and interpretation a great deal depends on which manifestation of SAR one is considering. Certainly, the openly emancipatory, transgressive forms of SAR advocated by Joe Kincheloe are commendably transparent in their values orientation and intentions. With the now increasingly widespread adoption in the UK of SAR as a technique of enquiry questions of values and purposes are regrettably more opaque. As a consequence much of the debate centres on the degree to which SAR, while perhaps not intentionally and not solely a form of neo-liberal incorporation, is nonetheless a clear instantiation of twenty-first century knowledge society working its way through existing systems of schooling. This latter position is persuasively argued by Sara Bragg (2007b). Pat Thomson and Helen Gunter (2007) are slightly more optimistic, and my own work, while acknowledging the power of Foucauldian critiques, nonetheless holds out for the importance of identifying and supporting prefigurative practice (Fielding, 2004b). Despite important differences between us my sense is that we are united in our commitment to the research community developing new forms of engagement that are mutually educative, joyfully energising and permanently restless in their pursuit of a better world.

Contemporary challenges

In the last couple of years there have been various attempts to take stock of some of the key challenges that are facing the new wave of student voice developments that has gained momentum since the mid 1990s (Angus, 2006; Fielding, 2007a and b; Rudduck, 2006; Rudduck and Fielding, 2006; Thiessen, 2007; Thiessen and Cook-Sather, 2007; Whitty and Wisbey, 2007a). From these and from various typologies, frameworks and standpoints mentioned earlier in this chapter a number of recurring issues have emerged.

Among the most pertinent are:

- those that cluster round the deconstruction of the too easily presumed singularity of student voice;
- the debate about student voice as a means of neo-liberal incorporation or democratic renewal;
- disagreements within the field about consultation and participation.

In addition to these, there are a further three issues that seem to me important matters which, if addressed more deliberately, hold out some promise for the development of student voice in directions supportive of democratic renewal. These concern:

- the move towards more inter-generational dialogue;
- the development of vibrant public spaces within schools, and finally;
- the importance of reclaiming radical traditions of state education.

Class, gender and race

There is, of course, no one voice that is authentic or representative of young people and much of the criticism of the resurgence of interest in student voice is concerned with issues to do with class, gender and race. Many of those who have pioneered student voice work as academics and/or as activists constantly and properly remind us of the importance of social class, some of the most compelling writing in this area coming from Australia (see Smyth and McInerney, 2007; Thomson and Holdsworth, 2003) and the USA (e.g. Weis and Fine, 2005; Steinberg and Kincheloe, 1998). Somewhat surprisingly, it is not until fairly recently that the influence of Basil Bernstein's work has begun to make itself heard in the field with writers like Madeleine Arnot and Diane Reay reminding us again and again of the ways in which systems of formal schooling privilege some voices over others, not just in terms of the structures of recognition, but also in the deep codes of communication and understanding that comprise the foundational grammar of engagement on which so much daily encounter and future possibility depends (see especially Arnot and Reay, 2007).

Alison Cook-Sather, one of the North American pioneers of new wave student voice work (e.g. Cook-Sather, 2002) especially within the context of teacher education, reminds us in her recent work (Cook-Sather, 2007) of the contribution of post-structuralist feminists such as Mimi Orner and Frances Maher. In the UK, of particular note is Madeleine Arnot's work on gender (e.g. Arnot, 2006) and Leora Cruddas's work with disadvantaged girls (Cruddas and Haddock, 2003).

Some of the most engaging student voice work on issues of race, as well as on class and gender, comes through, not only in the previously cited work of Michele Fine and Lois Weis, but also in the work of Dana Mitra (Mitra, 2001) and Elena Silva (Silva, 2001; Rubin and Silva, 2003). What strikes me, more particularly about the UK context, are the absences and silences here and, if student voice is to continue to establish a wider credibility among young people, teachers and academics then issues of race will need to be addressed more overtly.

Neo-liberal incorporation or democratic renewal?

At various points in this chapter we have briefly touched on the debate about how we might best read and understand the burgeoning of new wave student voice developments in the decade since the mid 1990s. There are two points to make here. First, this is not an arcane academic debate pertinent to only a relatively small circle of people – it is a matter of profound significance because, according to how and where we position ourselves and, as I emphasise at the end of this chapter, because of the fact that we do need to consciously take a view on these matters of purpose and values, a great deal will follow in terms of where and if we direct our energies and commitments. In addition to those sources mentioned at the beginning of this section other useful texts that wrestle with these matters include, for example, Fielding (2001, 2004b) and Vibert and Shields (2003).

Second, taking a view is likely to become more rather than less important as account-ability mechanisms and the relatively unfettered spaces of the internet increase the stakes for individuals, organisations and, indeed, systems of public provision. In the rush to tick boxes about student involvement that now feature in a number of inspection frameworks, in the proliferation of blogs and websites inviting young people to comment on their teachers and their schools, there are substantial concerns now being expressed, in some cases by major teacher trade unions and professional organisations, about threats to professional integrity and the degree to which the student voice movement is being used for purposes other than the well-being and further learning of young people in schools.

The participation/consultation debate

One aspect of these dilemmas that has recently opened up differences in the field concerns the relationship between those who advocate consultative approaches to student voice and those who champion a more overtly participatory orientation. In the last two years of her life Jean Rudduck, one of the pioneers of student voice as an academic field and as a distinctive and, in her view, potentially transformative approach to school improvement (e.g. Rudduck *et al.*, 1996; Rudduck and Flutter, 2004) became increasingly convinced that energy should be diverted away from what she felt was the sometimes more glamorous, but invariably less important, forms of student participation in schools (Rudduck, 2007). Together with Donald McIntyre (Rudduck and McIntyre, 2007) she argued that participatory approaches were, despite quite other intentions, too prone to the emergence of elite minorities and ephemeral influence. They also argued that, if these kinds of dangers were to be addressed effectively, we need to put energy into the perhaps less alluring and more difficult business of developing practices of teacher–student consultation as part of the familiar realities of daily schooling.

If we attend to the tectonics rather than the surface features of these arguments we come up against some important differences of view that can either be seen as either oppositional or complementary. Certainly, the consultation/participation debate about democracy itself goes back many hundreds of years and the disagreements between contemporary researchers within the field of student voice reflect those longstanding and inevitable differences.

Inter-generational dialogue

In a number of the typologies referred to earlier in this chapter the apogee of their aspira-tions often pointed to the importance not just of young people's involvement but of their engagement with adults on the basis of mutuality, reciprocal learning and joint responsibility. Perhaps understandably, the role of adults and their responsibility to challenge as well as be challenged has taken a back-stage role. What is now beginning to emerge are accounts in which this kind of engagement is explored more overtly (see Thomson and Gunter, 2007). There is also, through the work of researchers like Greg Mannion, a suggestion that at the heart of a genuinely and strenuously intended participatory approach to adult–child relationships must lie new kinds of relationships between them and new spaces in which this loosening of role and relation are explored together (Mannion, 2007). This seems to me to be an important development which Manion articulates convincingly and elegantly. Furthermore, it is one that is linked to my next suggestion which is that we work hard at developing public and semi-public spaces within which adults and young people can make meaning of their lives together.

Re-imagining and rearticulating narrative space in the public realm

One of the most difficult and important recurring issues that the challenge of difference and diversity touched on at the beginning of this section raises concerns how, within those societies that have democratic traditions and aspirations, the richness and range of multiple, fluid, criss-crossing identities come not merely to co-exist but develop a vibrant, respectful and joyous reciprocity. How we understand and respond to this challenge will tell us much about the cultural health of our own circumstances and aspirations.

While there are a small number of historical counter-examples – e.g. St George-in-the-East Secondary School, Stepney, to which I will return in a moment – as things currently stand, shared, public space in schools is heavily managed by adults and there is little evidence of anything approaching the kind of reciprocity I am advocating. There are, however, welcome signs from the work of people like Morwenna Griffiths (Griffiths *et al.*, 2006) and Barry Percy-Smith (2006) in England, and Deirdre Kelly (2003) in the USA, of serious engagement at both a theoretical and practical level with issues of public space in schools. For me this is exciting, not just because this area is so rich in potential, but also because it underscores the importance of a wider and deeper issue that is absolutely central to the nature of a good society at the beginning of the twenty-first century, namely, how we can in formal and informal, public and private spaces develop and nurture what Richard Sennett so beautifully and so insightfully calls a 'sense of sustainable self ... A narrative of identity and life-history in a society composed of episodes and fragments' (Sennett, 1998, pp. 27, 26; see also Fielding, 2006, p. 308).

Reclaiming radical traditions

The last of the six issues emerging from contemporary student voice work – the importance of reclaiming the radical traditions of state education – foregrounds what I see as a major weakness, not only of the professional development and academic practice of student voice but also of both current educational thinking and of the wider intellectual culture of many societies currently influenced by neo-liberal paradigms. This concerns what some teachers have called 'presentism', i.e. an obsession with the imperatives and mindsets of the present utterly disconnected with the past. This is a matter of some consequence since, in the words of Russell Jacoby, 'The inability or refusal to think back takes its toll in the inability to think' (Jacoby, 1997, p. 4). Our history tells us that education is a contested field within which different values and perspectives fight for dominance and allegiance. The radical traditions of state education (see e.g. Apple and Beane, 2007; Fielding, 2005; and Jensen and Walker, 1989) have much to tell us about the past, the present and the future of student voice. While the patient development of sustainable consultation within the rhythms of daily schoolwork is important, so too are those few counter-hegemonic examples that reconfigure those day-to-day routines and encounters and gesture towards quite different realities. Certainly the work of Alex Bloom at St George-in-the-East Secondary School in Stepney in the East End of London (Fielding, 2005) between 1945 and his untimely death in 1955 provides compelling examples of radical student voice practices that remain unsurpassed in England to the present day. Here, in a school that had a significantly negotiated, sometimes mixed-age, curriculum with no ability grouping, no prizes, no competition, no regimentation, and no punishment there was a wide-ranging formal and informal democratic culture with a commensurately sophisticated, highly developed set of democratic structures.

Two fundamental challenges to the presumptions of student voice

In drawing this section on contemporary challenges to a close there are two very difficult, related seams of questions that thread their way through the bedrock of student voice practice, advocacy and research.

The first has to do with the particularity of youth and with the situatedness of students in hierarchical institutions of formal learning such as schools. In other words, there seems in much student voice work to be a presumption that the standpoint and lived perspectives of students gives them distinctive, illuminating and useful insights into the circumstances and processes of formal and informal learning that are (a) difficult for adults in general and teachers in particular to gain access to and (b) often easy for teachers to misunderstand, marginalise or ignore.

The theoretical grounding of this view includes, for example, (a) the foundational beliefs of radical progressive education, (b) a particular version of standpoint epistemology, and (c) contemporary variants of customer- or client-oriented practices as the basis of, among other things, public service reform. Of course, these are all very different and the differences matter because the disparate bases of student voice work will shape the kinds of questions asked and the nature and direction of the advocacy being articulated. As one would expect, confronting these and other justifications and aspirations for student voice are ranged a parallel set of objections. These include those who argue either that the Romantic presumptions of much radical progressivism are untenable; or that the complex, relational, constantly dynamic characteristics of identity seriously undermine standpoint perspectives; or that neo-liberal, market-oriented approaches to education (and much else besides) are immoral, dishonest, and corrosive of human flourishing in a just society.

The second stratum of questions challenge the aspirations of those who see in student voice work the possibility of the transformation of the current system of education and even of society. Part of the difficulty here is being clear about what is meant by 'transformation'. It is a word that tends to be bandied about with much enthusiasm and little intellectual or professional modesty by many of the proponents of new approaches to systemic change. It is also occasionally used by those who wish to create a quite different society, not merely alter currently preferred ways of working. For writers such as these, certain radical forms of student voice are seen as prefigurative practices, as ways of engaging with education that exemplify and anticipate profoundly different futures.

Against reformist versions of transformation the objections tend to be that, hyperbole and over-excitement apart, transformation of all or part of the current system is likely to be less profound than hoped for. More seriously, it is argued that the changes that do in fact take place will almost certainly advance the interests of those in positions of profound power in society and, insofar as this is true, transformation will turn out to be either a duplicitous process or a well-meaning delusion. Against the revolutionary versions of transformation objections tend to come from those who bridle at what they see as a pernicious millennialism or, for those better disposed towards profound social and political change, a charge of a well-meaning but hopeless utopianism that in the end is as delusional as their reformist counterparts.

Permanent dilemmas

While the challenges identified in the previous section will inevitably change over time according to contextual pressures and aspirations there are, arguably, a number of core issues that have a residual intractability. These might, for example, include those to do either with how different societies and religious and social movements (a) regard the learning relationship between young people and adults, regardless of cultural and economic identities or status and (b) seek to realise ideals of human flourishing that rest on quite different configurations of values than those presumed by global capitalism.

Thus, within the context of formal education, there is always likely to be a tension between those who regard the standpoints and perspectives of the young as, by virtue of their youth and inexperience, of limited value or legitimacy and those who take a view that sees the characteristic and very different virtues and capacities of young people as a source of creativity, providing we attend to the conditions within which those views are elicited, discussed and developed.

There is also always likely to be a permanent tension between those who place the imaginative and serious commitment to listening to the voices of young people within quite different political and religious frameworks. The foundational characteristics of those positions will inevitably play themselves out either through the contrasting approaches valorised by particular societies and nation states or through the ongoing disputes, discussion and differences within those particular entities. Many would, of course, argue that such persistent contestation is both inevitable and desirable: inevitable because key notions like 'education' and 'childhood' are examples of what some philosophers have called 'essentially contested concepts', i.e. concepts about which agreement will never be reached because the dynamic of contestation is part of what characterises their meaning; desirable because the prospect of a single, totalising ideological framework is one that is unlikely to lead to the betterment of humankind.

Certainly my own view is that the respectful articulation of these deep disagreements is especially important at a time when the international ascendancy of neo-liberalism perennially announces the end of ideology or even history itself. My earlier advocacy of the radical traditions of state education could, of course, be seen as a useful repository of ideas and practices to aid the next surge of capitalist regeneration. However, it could also be read, as I would hope it would, as an invitation to organise our lives on the basis of quite different principles and values from those that express the covert presumptions of the present.

Making choices

There is evidence to suggest that, as a field of professional and academic enquiry, student voice work is entering a particularly interesting phase of its development that reflects wider changes, some of which have transnational significance. It seems likely that it will become more rather than less important in many post-industrial societies across the world for a range of reasons. These have broadly to do with different dispositions and drivers that shape the necessity of any society understanding, motivating, and controlling those who are to be the inheritors of the present and the architects of a more distant future. Some of these drivers will be energised by negative desires to confine, control and manipulate young people and, perhaps somewhat paradoxically, certain groups of adults, including teachers. Other drivers will be energised by positive desires to encourage, enable and liberate and, in so doing, elicit a responsive adulthood that welcomes not a return to childhood but a remaking of the present and a revisioning of the future that sings a song of hope and joyful possibility.

In the end where we choose to put our energies and the issues we choose to tackle will depend on (a) the policy contexts and dominant ideologies that both constrain and enable the spaces within which we pursue this work, (b) our own values and dispositions, and (c) our willingness to locate those values and dispositions within a tradition of thought, action and struggle that helps us to read the historical forces and conjunctures that confront us.

For some readers this may seem overly complex and too far removed from the energising, immediate contexts of classrooms and the daily buzz and busyness of schools and other formal contexts for learning. I understand this response and have some sympathy with it. However, whether we wish to understand better how we might go about listening with care, respect and openness to the young people with whom we work, or whether we wish to do all this and go beyond it in the spirit of a quite different future is a choice we cannot avoid. The kind of teacher we are, the kind of research we do, depends in significant part on how we understand these choices, how we make them, and, of course, which ones we actually make.

References

Angus, L. (2006) 'Educational leadership and the imperative of including student voices, student interests, and students' lives in the mainstream', *International Journal of Leadership in Education*, 9(4), October/December, pp. 369–79.

Apple, M. and Beane, J. (2007) *Democratic Schools: Lessons in Powerful Education* (2nd edn), London, Heinemann.

Arnot, M. (2006) 'Gender voices in the classroom', in B. Skelton, B. Frances and L. Smulyan (eds), *Sage Handbook on Gender and Education*, London, Sage, pp. 407–22.

Arnot, M. and Reay, D. (2007) 'A sociology of pedagogic voice: power, inequality and pupil consultation', *Discourse*, 28(3), September, pp. 311–25.

Arnstein, S. (1969) 'A ladder of citizenship participation in the USA', *Journal of the American Institute of Planners*, 35(4), pp. 216–24.

Atweh, B. and Burton, L. (1995) 'Students as researchers: rationale and critique', *British Educational Research Journal*, 25(1), pp. 561–75.

Bragg, S. (2007a) *Consulting Young People: a Review of the Literature*, London, Creative Partnerships.

—— (2007b) '"Student voice" and governmentality: the production of enterprising subjects?', *Discourse*, 28(3) September, pp. 343–58.

Burke, C. (2007) 'The view of the child: releasing "visual voices" in the design of learning environments', *Discourse*, 28(3) September, pp. 359–72.

Cook-Sather, A. (2002) 'Authorizing students' perspectives: towards trust, dialogue and change in education, *Educational Researcher*, 31(4), pp. 3–14.

—— (2007) 'Resisting the impositional potential of student voice work: lessons for liberatory educational research from poststructuralist feminist critiques of critical pedagogy', *Discourse*, 28(3), September, pp. 389–403.

Cruddas, L. and Haddock, L. (2003) *Girls' Voices: Supporting Girls' Learning and Emotional Development*, London, Trentham.

Discourse (2007) *Special Issue: Beyond 'Voice': New Roles, Relations, and Contexts in Researching with Young People*, 28(3), September.

Fielding, M. (2001) 'Students as radical agents of change', *Journal of Educational Change*, 2(3), Summer, 123–41.

—— (2004a) 'Transformative approaches to student voice: theoretical underpinnings, recalcitrant realities', *British Educational Research Journal*, 30(2), April, pp. 295–311.

—— (2004b) '"New wave" student voice and the renewal of civic society', *London Review of Education*, Special Issue on 'Education for Civic Society', 2(3), November, 197–217.

—— (2005) 'Alex Bloom: pioneer of radical state education', *Forum*, 47(2 and 3), pp. 119–34.

—— (2006) 'Leadership, radical student engagement and the necessity of person-centred education', *International Journal of Leadership in Education*, 9(4), October/December, pp. 299–313.

Fielding, M. (2007a) 'Beyond "voice": new roles, relations, and contexts in researching with young people', *Discourse*, 28(3), September, pp. 301–10.

Fielding, M. (2007b) 'Jean Rudduck (1937–2007) "Carving a new order of experience": a preliminary appreciation of the work of Jean Rudduck in the field of student voice', *Educational Action Research*, 15(3), pp. 323–36.

Fielding, M. and Bragg, S. (2003) *Students as Researchers: Making a Difference*, Cambridge, Pearsons.

Griffiths, M., Berry, J., Holt, A., Naylor, R. and Weekes, P. (2006) 'Learning to be in public spaces: in from the margins with dancers, sculptors, painters and musicians', *British Journal of Educational Studies*, 54(3), September, pp. 352–71.

Hadfield, M. and Haw, K. (2001) '"Voice", young people and action research', *Educational Action Research*, 9(3), pp. 485–99.

Hart, R.A. (1997) *Children's Participation: The Theory and Practice of Involving Young Citizens in Community Development and Environmental Care*, London, Earthscan.

International Journal of Leadership in Education (2006) *Special Issue: Student Voice*, 9(4), September–December.

Jacoby, R. (1997) 'Revisiting "Social amnesia"', *Society*, 35(1), November–December, pp. 58–60.

Jensen, K. and Walker, S. (eds) (1989) *Towards Democratic Schooling*, Milton Keynes, Open University Press.

John, M. (1996) 'Voicing: research and practice with the silenced', in M. John (ed.), *Children in Charge: Children's Right to a Fair Hearing*, London, Jessica Kingsley, pp. 3–24.

Johnson, K. (2004) *Children's Voices: Pupil Leadership in Primary Schools*, Nottingham, National College for School Leadership.

Kellett, M. (2005) *How to Develop Children as Researchers: A Step by Step Guide to Teaching the Research Process*, London, Paul Chapman.

Kelly, D. (2003) 'Practising democracy in the margins of the school: The Teenage Parents Program as feminist counterpublic', *American Educational Research Journal*, 40(1), pp. 123–46.

Kincheloe, J. (2007) 'Clarifying the purpose of engaging students as researchers', in D. Thiessen and A. Cook-Sather (eds), *International Handbook of Student Experience in Elementary and Secondary School*, Dordrecht, Springer, pp. 745-74.

Mannion, G. (2007) 'Going spatial, going relational: why "listening to children" and children's participation needs reframing', *Discourse*, 28(3), September, pp. 405–20.

Mitra, D. (2001) 'Opening the floodgates: giving students a voice in school reform', *Forum*, 43(2), pp. 91–4.

Percy-Smith, B. (2006) 'From consultation to social learning in community participation with young people', *Children, Youth and Environments*, 16(2), pp. 153–79.

Piper, H. and Frankham, J. (2007) 'Seeing voices and hearing pictures: image as discourse and the framing of image-based research', *Discourse*, 28(3), September, 373–87.

Rubin, B. and Silva, E. (eds) (2003) *Critical Voices in School Reform*, New York, Routledge.

Rudduck, J. (2006) 'The past, the papers and the project', *Educational Review*, 58(2), May, pp. 131–43.

—— (2007) 'Student voice, student engagement, and school reform', in D. Thiessen and A. Cook-Sather (eds), *International Handbook of Student Experience in Elementary and Secondary School*, Dordrecht, Springer, pp. 587–610.

Rudduck, J. and Fielding, M. (2006) 'Student voice and the perils of popularity', *Educational Review*, 58(2), May, pp. 219–31.

Rudduck, J. and Flutter, J. (2004) *How to Improve Your School: Giving Pupils a Voice*, London, Continuum.

Rudduck, J. and McIntyre, D. (2007) *Improving Learning Through Consulting Pupils*, London, Routledge.

Rudduck, J., Chaplain, R. and Wallace, G. (1996) *School Improvement: What Can Pupils Tell Us?* London, Fulton.

Sennett, R. (1998) *The Corrosion of Character: The Personal Consequences of Work in the New Capitalism*, New York, Norton.

Shier, H. (2001) 'Pathways to participation: openings, opportunities and obligations', *Children and Society*, 15(2), pp. 107–17.

Silva, E. (2001) '"Squeaky wheels and flat tires": a case study of students as reform participants', *Forum*, 43(2), Summer, pp. 95–9.

Smyth, J. (2007) 'Toward the pedagogically engaged school: listening to student voice as a positive response to disengagement and "dropping out" study', in D. Thiessen and A. Cook-Sather (eds), *International Handbook of Student Experience in Elementary and Secondary School*, Dordrecht, Springer, pp. 635–58.

Smyth, J. and McInerney, P. (2007) '"Living on the edge": a case of school reform working for disadvantaged adolescents', *Teachers College Record*, 109(5), May, pp. 1123–70.

Steinberg, S. and Kincheloe, J. (eds) (1998) *Students as Researchers*, London, Falmer.

Thiessen, D. (2007) 'Researching student experiences in elementary and secondary school: an evolving field of study', in D. Thiessen and A. Cook-Sather (eds), *International Handbook of Student Experience in Elementary and Secondary School*, Dordrecht, Springer, pp. 1–76.

Thiessen, D. and Cook-Sather, A. (eds) (2007) *International Handbook of Student Experience in Elementary and Secondary School*, Dordrecht, Springer.

Thomson, P. (ed) (2008) *Doing Visual Research with Children and Young People*, London, Routledge.

Thomson, P. and Gunter, H. (2007) 'The methodology of students-as-researchers: valuing and using experience and expertise to develop methods', *Discourse*, 28(3), September, pp. 327–42.

Thomson, P. and Holdsworth, R. (2003) 'Democratising schools through "student participation": an emerging analysis of the educational field informed by Bourdieu', *International Journal of Leadership in Education*, 6(4), pp. 371–91.

Vibert, A.B. and Shields, C. (2003) 'Approaches to student engagement: does ideology matter?', *McGill Journal of Education*, 38(2), Spring, pp. 221–39.

Weis, L. and Fine, M. (eds) (2005) *Beyond Silenced Voices: Class, Race and Gender in United States Schools*, Albany, NY, State University of New York Press.

Whitty, G. and Wisby, E. (2007) 'Whose voice? An exploration of the current policy interest in pupil involvement in school decision-making', *International Studies in Sociology of Education*, 17(3), pp. 303–19.

Reflective questions

If you are considering a research approach which involves young people, or if you are reflecting on research writing and development work that has tried to engage them in significant ways, it is worth asking and reflecting on at least five clusters of questions.

1 *Purposes* Why is involving young people something to be seriously considered in this particular project at this time?
2 *Ontology* Is there such a thing as a young person's standpoint and, if there is, why should we pay attention to it?
3 *Epistemology* What can young people tell us that we don't already know or that we cannot find out via other means?
4 *Roles* In what ways and to what degree does the research require and enable young people to take an active role in its design, execution, interpretation and final recommendations?
5 *Identity* How does the research engage with issues of identity and difference, not only among young people but also in a context of increasing fluidity between notions of childhood and adulthood?

Further reading

Arnot, M., McIntyre, D., Pedder, D. and Reay, D. (2004) *Consultation in the Classroom: Developing Dialogue about Teaching and Learning*, Cambridge, Pearsons.

CYPU (2003) *Working Together: Giving Children and Young People a Say*, available online at http://www.dfes.gov.uk/consutlations/downloadableDocs/239_2.pdf.

Davies, L., Williams, C., and Yamashita, H. with Ko Man-Hing, A. (2007) *Inspiring Schools: Case Studies for Change – Taking Up the Challenge of Pupil Participation*, London, Esmee Fairbairn Foundation/Carnegie UK.

Davies, L. and Yamashita, H. (2007) *School Councils – School Improvement: The London Secondary School Councils Action Research Project*, London, Esmee Fairbairn Foundation/Carnegie UK.

DCSF (2008) *Working Together: Giving Young People a Say*, London, DCSF.

Educational Action Research (2007) *Special Issue: Pupil Voice*, 15(3).

Educational Review (2006) *Special Issue: Pupil Voice*, 58(2), May.

Forum (2001) *Special Issue: Student Voice*, 43(2).

Kirby, P. (1999) *Involving Young Researchers: How to Enable Young People to Design and Conduct Research*, York, Joseph Rowntree Foundation.

Kirby, P. and Bryson, S. (2002) *Measuring the Magic? Evaluating and Researching Young People's Participation in Public Decision Making*, London, Carnegie Young People's Initiative.

Kirby, P., Lanyon, C., Cronin, K. and Sinclair, R. (2003) *Building a Culture of Participation: Involving Children and Young People in Policy, Service Planning, Delivery and Evaluation*, London, Department for Education and Skills.

Improving Schools (2007) *Special Issue: Pupil Voice*, 10(1).

MacBeath, J., Demetriou, H., Rudduck, J. and Myers, K. (2003) *Consulting Pupils: A Toolkit for Teachers*, Cambridge, Pearsons.

McGill Journal of Education (2003) *Special Issue on The Challenge of Student Engagement: Beyond Mainstream Conceptions and Practices*, 38(2), Spring.

NCSL (nd) *Pupil Involvement in Networked Learning: A Tool for Helping Pupils and Teachers to Create a Vision of Pupil Involvement in School Improvement, Learning and Teaching*, Nottingham, National College for School Leadership.

Robinson, C. and Fielding, M. (2007) *Children and their Primary Schools: Pupils' Voices* (Primary Review Research Survey 5/3), Cambridge, University of Cambridge Faculty of Education.

Rudduck, J., Demetriou, H., and Pedder, D. (2003) 'Student perspectives and teacher practices: the transformative potential', *McGill Journal of Education*, 38(2), Spring, pp. 274–87.

Whitty, G. and Wisbey, E. (2007b) *Real Decision Making: School Councils in Action*, London, DCSF.

Websites

Save the Children Fund: www.savethechildren.org.uk
School Councils UK: www.schoolcouncils.org
Teachers TV: www.pupil-voice.org.uk/Teachers-TV-pupil-voice-week.doc.

2.6 The transition to school

Reflections from a contextualist perspective

Jonathan R.H. Tudge, Lia B.L. Freitas and Fabienne Doucet

Introduction

The first day of school arrives. Some of the children enter in tears, others with excited looks on their faces, and yet others come into the classroom with tentative steps, a mixture of holding on to someone's hand and looking around to see whether there are friends to be made. For the teachers, too, the first day of the new school year can be a time of excitement, of challenge, or a feeling of 'same old, same old'. Although the first day of school may not be a good predictor of children's eventual success or failure, the transition to school itself is one of the most important changes that occur in the lives of young children. Children who make this transition smoothly may be on an easier road to success than those for whom the transition is more troublesome.

In this chapter we therefore reflect on ways in which to help children and teachers negotiate this transition. The vast majority of the research that has been conducted on this topic focuses on the transition to school from the school's perspective: what can be done to help children be prepared for school entry? Much of this research deals with issues of 'school readiness' or examines the nature and quality of children's preschool experiences. Other researchers examine the steps that can be taken to encourage parents to understand and support the school's goals, both before the children arrive in school and during the children's first years in school. Our primary goal, however, is to explain how a contextualist perspective may help both children and their teachers make the transition go smoothly. We therefore first describe what we mean by contextualism and briefly discuss two major contextualist theories – those of Lev Vygotsky and Urie Bronfenbrenner – before discussing how this contextualist perspective can be incorporated into the classroom.

The transition to school

There are various ways to think about children making the transition to school. Some people talk about 'school readiness', often thinking about children possessing the types of basic skills, particularly in literacy, that will enable them to succeed. Others describe the same concept, but from the point of view of the children's overall cognitive development, with less attention paid to specific skills. Yet others will focus on the children's social competence – are they ready to interact with other children and their teacher in appropriate ways, can they sit still and listen during story time and so on. Some will argue that preschool institutions should work directly to prepare children for the transition, by teaching them the types of skills that they will need once they enter school, and others will argue that the best way to prepare children for school is to allow them to play actively with interesting materials in conjunction with other children.

Alternative ways of thinking focus on the role that teachers can play in easing the transition; this often involves meeting parents and explaining to them what will be expected of their children once they are in school, and then trying to keep contact with the parents during the children's first years of school. It is also possible to think of changing what goes on in school to fit changing perceptions of children. This can happen both at the level of a specific classroom or school (individual teachers making changes because of the way they perceive the types of children who are entering the school) and also at the societal level, as when growing awareness of Piaget's views of children's development led to changes in the types of activities that commonly occurred in preschool and primary school classrooms.

These are just some of the possible ways in which we could think about easing the transition of children to school. It would be nice to say that research has clearly demonstrated that one of these approaches, or a combination of approaches, is the most effective. Then we could just apply it, and children would be much more likely to make an easier transition. One of the reasons why there is no such clear demonstration is that people disagree about what would count as a clear demonstration, largely due to their basic assumptions about the world.

Our guiding assumptions

Within the areas of education, psychology and human development there are three basic assumptions, or 'world hypotheses' (Pepper, 1942), known as mechanism, organicism and contextualism. Each of these world-views differs in its set of beliefs about the nature of reality (ontology), about how one can know reality (epistemology) and how one can appropriately test that knowledge (methodology). Mechanists hold that there is a single reality that, even if it cannot be known, is testable in the sense that hypothetical aspects of reality can be tested and proved to be incorrect. (Mechanists believe that aspects of reality can never be proven, because some contrary fact may subsequently come to light, and so the 'best' theories or facts are those that have not yet been proven incorrect.) The methods used by mechanists generally emphasize tightly controlled experimental designs to allow the testing of cause–effect hypotheses or the use of forced-choice questionnaires. Pepper noted that the 'root metaphor' of mechanists is the machine, with its reliance on cause–effect relations.

Organicists, too, hold that there is a single reality to be known, but believe that it can never be known by carefully controlling relevant variables in an experimental design, because simple cause–effect relationships do not exist. Instead organicists talk about the 'emergent properties' of all aspects of reality; reality emerges in a systemic or dialectical way from the complex interplay of all relevant factors. Water is made up of hydrogen and oxygen, but what emerges from their interaction is something that is more than the sum of the two elements. In the same way, human development is a phenomenon that emerges from interaction between aspects of the developing individual and that individual's context, both social and physical. However, organicists believe that endpoints (or most mature aspects) of development can be specified and that development, particularly in the period from birth through adolescence, occurs in a specified order. The root metaphor that Pepper ascribed to organicism is the human body.

Contextualists hold that there is no single reality to be known, but a variety of different realities, each of which depends on the specific social, economic, cultural and historical nature of the group under consideration. Like organicists, contextualists see reality as an emerging property of relevant factors (individual, context and time), but differ from organicists in that they believe that what counts as the 'endpoint' of development varies across different contexts. Pepper's root metaphor for contextualism was the historic event. However, the world-view's name and its metaphor are misleading. Those who fit within this world-view clearly do not hold that context *determines* development, although it plays an important role; furthermore, what Pepper actually meant by 'historic events' are typically occurring activities. He noted that only verbs should be used in giving instances of the metaphor; children playing, adults preparing dinner, people talking with friends. Historic events include 'the event alive in its present' such as 'incidents in the plot of a novel' (1942, pp. 232–3).

Given the different ontological, epistemological and methodological positions that these three groups take it is not surprising that what counts as evidence from one of their world-views is not considered relevant by proponents of another. In other words, using mechanistic methods to 'test' some aspect of an organicist or contextualist theory makes no sense; nor does using contextualist methods to 'test' a mechanist theory. What counts as evidence for a successful transition to school is thus likely to vary considerably as a function of the world-view within which the research is being conducted.

Contextualism

We have written a good deal about the various assumptions of these three world-views because we want to show how contextualist theories can help us understand better the transition to school and improve the transition itself. Contextualist theories, of which the best known are those of Bronfenbrenner (e.g. Bronfenbrenner, 2005; Bronfenbrenner and Morris, 1998, 2006) and Vygotsky (1987, 1993; see also Tudge and Scrimsher, 2003), have at their centre the types of activities that people engage in regularly (Tudge, 2008). However, the nature of the activities varies.

What types of activities do contextualists have in mind? Vygotsky is most widely known for his writing about activities that create a zone of proximal development, as when a child interacts with a more competent adult or peer. Bronfenbrenner also focused on activities likely to lead to success, namely 'processes of progressively more complex reciprocal interaction between an active, evolving biopsychological human organism and the persons, objects, and symbols in its immediate external environment' (Bronfenbrenner 2001/2005, p. 6). He argued that these 'proximal processes' are effective when they continue regularly over time.

These activities, important though they are, vary according to the specific characteristics of the individuals who are engaging in those activities, the nature of the setting where the activities are taking place, and both the cultural and temporal contexts in which the activities occur.

What is meant by 'individual characteristics'? Vygotsky (1931/1937, 1934/1987, 1935/1994) argued that they are socially formed; however, he never viewed the social world as separate from but inclusive of the individual. Children's biological and behavioural attributes influence people around them to respond in certain ways, and vice versa, continuing a process of interaction that started with conception. Bronfenbrenner (1995; Bronfenbrenner and Morris, 2006) provided more detail about these personal characteristics, which he subdivided into demand, resource and force characteristics, each of which, in different ways, influences the surrounding context. And so, long before children start school, they both are influenced by the world around them and influence it because of the individual characteristics, socially formed, that they bring to any situation. The same is true, of course, of their parents and teachers.

Parents and teachers, as is true of any of the other individuals, objects and symbols with which children are in contact, are an important part of the context, but context, in any contextualist theory, is far broader than those people and things with which developing individuals have immediate and direct contact. Despite the amount of attention given by

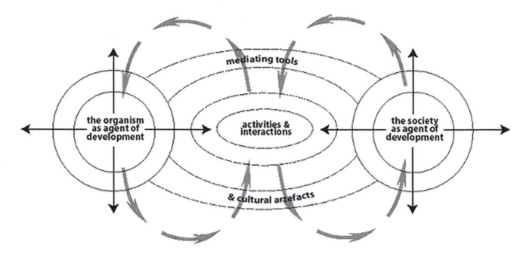

Figure 2.6.1 Lev Vygotsky's view of how both the organism (the individual, developing over ontogenetic time) and society (the sociocultural world, as developed over historical time) interact via tools and artifacts (the skills and technologies available within the cultural context) in the course of activities and interactions. Adapted from Edwards (2007).

scholars to Vygotsky's concept of the zone of proximal development, Vygotsky's theory is termed a *cultural-historical* theory because interactions within the zone of proximal development can only be understood by taking into account the culture, as it developed over historical time, within which those interactions are taking place (Cole, 2005; Daniels, 2005; Tudge and Scrimsher, 2003). From the moment of birth infants are enveloped in a social world that includes the various objects and technologies (mediating tools and artefacts) that are available in the culture (e.g. pram, crib, cradleboard or carrying cloth, for keeping infants secure, participating in storytelling, reading books, or watching DVDs, as ways of learning the culture). Figure 2.6.1 provides a view of the active and interactive nature of the relations between individual and social world as envisioned by Vygotsky.

Bronfenbrenner's theory makes these varying aspects of the social world somewhat more explicit than did Vygotsky. Bronfenbrenner's view of the spatial context included the microsystem (the contexts, such as home, school or workplace, in which activities and interactions take place), the mesosystem (relations among two or more microsystems), the exosystem (a context in which the developing individual is not situated, but which nonetheless has an important indirect effect) and the macrosystem (cultural groups and societies). Bronfenbrenner did not describe the temporal context, or chronosystem, in as much detail as he did the spatial context, but clearly it reflects the fact that cultures and societies are always undergoing change: historical events are interrelated with shifting values and beliefs, which are then expressed within microsystems. A representation of a microsystem, in which the active individual interacts with available people, objects and symbols, and how the microsystem fits within the other 'systems' in Bronfenbrenner's theory, is provided in Figure 2.6.2.

The macrosystem, for Bronfenbrenner, as is true for culture in Vygotsky's theory, plays a critically important role. He defined the macrosystem as a context encompassing any group ('culture, subculture, or other extended social structure') whose members share value or

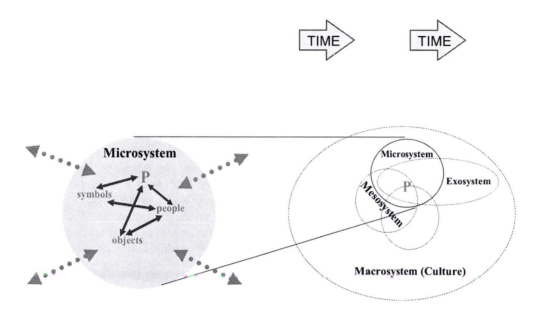

Figure 2.6.2 Urie Bronfenbrenner's PPCT model. The active *Person* (P) engaging in *Proximal Processes* with people, symbols and objects within a microsystem, in interaction with other *Contexts*, involving both continuity and change over *Time*. Reproduced from Tudge (2008).

belief systems, 'resources, hazards, lifestyles, opportunity structures, life course options and patterns of social interchange' (1993, p. 25). Why is culture so important? Weisner (1996) wrote that if we want to know how a child will develop the most important thing to know is his or her cultural group, because once we know that we can make inferences about the types of values and beliefs that child will be exposed to, the typical range of activities, access to resources, institutions with which he or she will interact, social relationships and a whole range more. Is it considered appropriate, in the given cultural group, for an adult to play with a child? Are books widely available, are the adults typically literate, and is schooling or literacy considered important for children? Are the adults physically and emotionally available to their children, or are they too pressured by the demands of multiple jobs (or the need to find some sort of work) to play with or read to their children? Are the prevailing beliefs such that older siblings are given primary responsibility for caring for those who are younger? These questions are all relevant to culture.

It is probably easy to see the likely influence of culture on activities and interactions when thinking about society-wide differences – our own research, for example, shows that preschool-aged children in the United States, Kenya and Brazil have some clearly different patterns of activities and interactions (Tudge *et al.*, 2006). However, it is just as important to examine within-society cultural differences, such as race (a term we are using to denote a social category linked to skin colour), ethnicity or social class; in the research just mentioned, the intersection of race and class was necessary to make sense of the differing patterns of activities and interactions that we observed. Moreover, in related research, the activities and interactions of preschool-aged children of middle-class and working-class backgrounds in the United States, Russia and Estonia had differential effects on their teachers' perceptions of their competence once they had entered school (Scrimsher and Tudge, 2003; Tudge *et al.*, 2007).

Our definition of a cultural group is a group that shares similar values, beliefs, social institutions, access to resources and sense of identity, and attempts to pass on those values, beliefs and so forth to the next generation. Ethnic groups and social class groups within any given society can thus be considered cultural groups to the extent that they fit this definition. The situation becomes more complex, therefore, as individuals cannot be thought of as being part of just one cultural group but of several – English, working-class, of Punjabi background – with their sense of identity at any given moment influenced by the current comparison group (English, when thinking about Punjabi friends who immigrated to Canada; Punjabi, when thinking about Gujeratis; working class, when comparing with Punjabi middle-class individuals).

Weisner (1996) could have added, of course, that knowing the historical period is equally important, given that cultures are not static phenomena. As we noted above, values about schooling and beliefs about the types of experiences that young children should get in school have changed dramatically over the course of time in any given society (Beatty, 1995; Freitas *et al.*, 2008; James *et al.*, 1998; Tudge, 2008). This is why contextualist theories involve a dynamic interaction between individual and context, with context viewed in both spatial and temporal terms.

Development of our position

Our position has become increasingly dynamic and interactional, if not dialectic, as we have thought more about the implications of contextualism. We would like to show the ways in which contextualism can help us think better about the transition to school and, in the process, make that transition easier for more children. First, however, it would be worth examining at least some of the research literature on this topic. In what follows we will rely primarily on research conducted in the United States. Given our theoretical position, we clearly do not believe that the American context is applicable elsewhere, but will use it simply as illustrative of the situation in a specific geographical and temporal context.

As Mangione and Speth (1998) argue, we can think of the transition in terms of horizontal and vertical continuity or discontinuity. A good deal of research in the United States has focused on the vertical axis, or trying to arrange continuity between children's prior-to-school experiences and those they will encounter in school. Much of that work has focused on children's experiences in child care, and specifically child-care quality. Some of this research has focused on the impact of structural characteristics, such as age and sex, group size, teacher–child ratio, as well as teachers' training, experience and length of time within the child-care classroom (e.g. Gullo and Burton, 1992, 1993; Magnuson *et al.*, 2004). Other researchers have tried to assess what actually occurs within classrooms, such as the nature of adult–child and child–child interactions, and the ways in which children are encouraged to become involved in activities (e.g. Cassidy *et al.*, 2005; National Institute for Early Education Research, 2005). The research evidence seems clear: the higher the quality of the child-care experience, the better children do following school entry (Barnett, 1995; Field, 1991; Howes, 1990; Howes *et al.*, 1992; NICHD Early

Child Care Research Network, 2003; Phillips *et al.*, 2000; Ramey *et al.*, 1999; Shonkoff and Phillips, 2000).

A second approach to vertical continuity is to focus on aspects of the home environment, examining the links between such things as child-rearing practices and subsequent school performance. The literature on the transition to school has dealt far less with the home environment than that of earlier child-care experiences, but the results are similar. There appear to be clear links between aspects of the child's home life (such as authoritative parenting, children's autonomy, the quality of the parents' relationship, both with one another and with their children, and the children's perceptions of those relationships, access to books, children involved in conversations with adults, and so on), and the children's transition to school (Bradley, 1995; Christian *et al.*, 1998; Clarke and Kurtz-Costes, 1997; Cowan *et al.*, 2005; Dickinson and Tabors, 2001; Hart and Risley, 1995, 1999; Parker *et al.*, 1999; Snow *et al.*, 1991).

Horizontal continuity, as the name suggests, deals with concurrent links between home and school, the idea being that when teachers and parents are working towards the same ends and using similar approaches children will do better making the transition to school and succeeding in school than when parents are unaware of what their children's teachers are doing and/or working at cross-purposes. Horizontal continuity may be achieved by such things as parents being encouraged to take an active role (at least up to a point) in their children's schooling, helping their children with homework, coming to meet their children's teachers both at designated times ('open house' nights) and when their children are perceived as having problems or needing extra help. There is not a good deal of literature on this subject, at least in the United States, but what there is describes the clear value in such continuity (see, for example, Comer, 1993; Comer *et al.*, 1996; Epstein, 1986, 1996; Gutman and McLoyd, 2000; Haynes and Comer, 1996; Hoover-Dempsey and Sandler, 1995; Pianta and Cox, 1999).

The central goal behind the vast majority of this research is to suggest ways of making the transition to school easier by ensuring that children are ready for school – by supporting or changing the types of experiences that they have in the years before they go to school and those they have in their first years of schooling. In other words, the approach is what has been termed 'top down' or 'schoolocentric' (Doucet, 2008; Graue, 1992; Graue *et al.*, 2001; Lawson, 2003). This approach received a significant boost from America's first President Bush, in 1989, when six goals for education were set forth, the first of which declared that 'by the year 2000, all children in America will start school ready to learn' (Action Team on School Readiness, 1992, cited in Shepard *et al.*, 1998, p. 128).

It is difficult to know how such a goal can be achieved by legislative effort alone, and the fact that the new century arrived without any significant alteration in children's school readiness should make us view the statement with caution. It is also worth pointing out that the wording of President Bush's panel could have been reworded to state: 'By the year 2000, all schools will be ready to learn about the children who populate their classrooms and the families that raise those children' (Doucet and Tudge, 2007, p. 314). Perhaps we should be thinking more about 'ready schools' than 'ready children' (National Education Goals Panel, 1998; see also Murphey and Burns, 2002; Pianta *et al.*, 1999). However, rather than taking a position either of modifying children to fit them into schools or of modifying schools to fit them to the children it surely makes more sense to use an approach that incorporates both positions. And that is precisely what a contextualist perspective allows us to do.

How to understand the transition to school from a contextualist perspective

As described above, at the centre of any contextualist theory are the activities that typically go on between the developing individuals of interest (children entering school) and the other important people with whom those individuals interact (e.g. other children, parents, relatives and teachers). The nature of the activities and interactions can only be understood by taking into account the individual characteristics of the people concerned and aspects of the context – local, cultural and temporal. We will consider each of these aspects in turn, although all aspects are necessarily intertwined from a contextualist point of view.

What, then, are the typical activities and interactions in which a child, a young boy for example, participates soon after entering school? Mostly they will be activities that his teacher has organized, depending (in part) on her views of what is appropriate for children of this age and what it is that she hopes to accomplish. The same is true, of course, for the types of interactions that she wants to encourage, both between her and the children and between the children themselves. In other words, her own background, experience, likes and dislikes, comfort level and so on play a key role in arranging these activities and interactions.

At the same time, the way in which these activities and interactions occur are related to the background, experience, likes and dislikes and so on of each child. What experience does this boy have with the types of activities that his teacher has prepared? If he has had some experience, has he enjoyed it, found it too difficult, or been bored by it? Is he ready for the activity, cognitively speaking, or is it too simple? And as for the interactions, what are his prior experiences with such things as sitting in a large circle, waiting his turn to talk or listening while his teacher speaks? To what extent has he been accustomed to being told exactly what he has to do, been used to responding to questions the answers to which are obvious to the questioner, or learned that 'I'd rather that you didn't …' means 'Don't'. Has he had many prior experiences playing with many other children, and what has been the nature of those experiences? Is he an active type, eager to engage in different activities and engage with the other children, or is he more passive, one who waits to be drawn into activities and interactions?

It is impossible to answer these questions by focusing simply on the personal characteristics of the individuals involved, but we need to consider their contexts, both local and cultural. The school itself is a good place to start – where is it situated, how old is it and how old are the materials in it, how much money is available for teachers' salaries, new materials and so on? From the British point of view these may seem odd questions – but in the context of the United States they are far from odd, given that some schools have more than twice the funding, per child, than do others, with similar differences in teachers' salaries across different school districts even within the same region of the country (Kozol, 1992, 2005). Children's involvement in activities and interactions, both with their teachers and their peers, is likely to be different in a school that is well equipped, in a pleasant neighbourhood, with small class sizes, with teachers who feel themselves well paid than in a poor, run-down school, bursting at the seams, with inadequate facilities and poorly paid teachers.

But equally one has to consider the homes from which the children come. Is the setting one that allows time for joint play, storytelling, or reading? Is the environment chaotic or calm? Are the available adults involved in another activity (preparing a meal, watching television) while their children want to engage with them? If so, are the children encouraged and invited to participate in the adults' activities? Are reading materials easily available in the home? Are the adults interested in reading with their children and, if so, in what way? Do children and adults exchange stories about the day or about past experiences? Setting characteristics, as well as individual characteristics, are clearly important in influencing the way in which activities and interactions occur.

So too are the broader aspects of context. Even staying within the confines of a single country, given the way in which we defined culture earlier, we could discuss variations among different ethnic groups, racial differences, recency of immigration, religious affiliation, or social class. Here we focus on the latter, drawing on Mel Kohn's (1977, 1995) view that parents' prior educational and current occupational experiences have a profound impact on their child-rearing values. Kohn's argument is that although parents want to raise their children to succeed, working-class and middle-class parents tend to have different approaches, based on their educational and occupational conditions of life. Those who need to be self-directing and think for themselves at work are much more likely to value self-direction and autonomy in their children; by contrast, those who succeed at work primarily by carefully following the rules that others have decided are more likely to value children who also carefully do what they are told. In Kohn's view, therefore, authoritarian and authoritative child-rearing styles are not primarily personal characteristics (Baumrind, 1989) but are related to socioeconomic conditions of life; a more inductive, authoritative approach is likely to fit better with values favouring the development of children's self-direction, whereas a more controlling, authoritarian approach makes more sense given a goal of raising children to follow others' rules.

Obviously there are parents from both social classes who, temperamentally, are more inclined to lay down the law whereas others favour drawing children into the decision-making process. Similarly some children from both social classes seem be more temperamentally suited than others to try to achieve self-direction despite what their parents might wish. Cleary it would be a mistake to view social classes (or any other cultural group) as homogeneous. Nonetheless, systems of values and beliefs that are widespread throughout a cultural group also have a profound impact on the ways in which parents in that group try to raise their children.

But the situation is yet more complex, because children clearly are influenced by other people than their parents, and many, as we know, have had child-care experiences with teachers and other children alike. As described earlier, there are relations between the quality of the child care and the ease of the child's transition to school. But the quality of child care is not so easily ascertained, once we accept the notion that different groups within any given society have different goals for raising their children. And it is just as easy to see clear variations in the types of child-care experiences provided to working-class and middle-class children as it is to see variations in their home lives. Again we will draw on the US situation, although precisely the same arguments have been made with regard to societies as diverse as China, Japan and Brazil (Freitas and Shelton, 2005; Freitas *et al.*, 2008; Tobin *et al.*, 1989).

During the nineteenth century, coinciding with the rise of industrialization in the United States, day-care services were made available for some (but far from all) of the children of indigent and/or poor, but working, families. These services were designed essentially to take care of children whose parents were viewed as unwilling or unable to do so or, as in the case of the kindergarten, to socialize the children of immigrants into the American way of life (Freitas *et al.*, 2008; Scarr and Weinberg, 1986; Tobin *et al.*, 1989; Weber, 1969). The very name ('day care') denotes the fact that children were there to be taken care of during the day in order to allow parents to work. The aim was clearly to serve economic, and not educational, ends. However, during the same historical period, a different type of setting was being established for the children of middle-class and wealthy families – kindergartens whose purpose was to provide educational and social experiences for the children who attended for just part of the day.

The impact of these roots is still felt today. Admittedly, day-care facilities have gone beyond the simple provision of care to serve educational goals; this is seen most clearly in the various programmes designed to help the children of the poorest families, such as the federal Head Start programme, established in 1965, Early Head Start (started 30 years later, for 3-year-olds) and the rapidly growing number of state-wide pre-kindergarten programmes (Gilliam and Zigler, 2004; Love *et al.*, 2005).

However, as Scarr and Weinberg pointed out: 'In contrast to the nursery schools of the 1950s, most Head Start programs emphasized education more than development – or more precisely, learning to learn' (1986, p. 1143). The focus in many of these programmes is on the 'basics' of education – learning the 'skills' of early literacy and early numeracy and, equally important in the eyes of the teachers, learning to pay attention, follow instructions and obey the school norms. This approach to school readiness is clearly quite different from middle-class approaches to early education that are based more on ideas of the 'whole child' who learns through play and whose interests are supported and extended (Heath, 1983; Lubeck, 1985; Lubeck *et al.*, 2001).

Two things are noteworthy. The first is that historical time is important; children's experiences are not simply influenced by their geographic and social context but also by their historical context. Not only does it matter *when* children are born (to be cared for during the day, in the nineteenth century, and to be given a 'head start' in the basics to give them, supposedly, a better chance at competing with their middle-class peers, at the start of the twenty-first century), but also historical origins continue to be influential.

The second noteworthy aspect is that parents' child-rearing values and beliefs seem to be mirrored in the types of child-care settings that their children frequent. This is perhaps not surprising; parents who value their children growing up to be relatively self-directing will be unlikely to choose (assuming they have a choice, both financially and in terms of availability) a child-care facility in which the children are encouraged simply to learn to obey and follow directions. Parents who think it important for their children to learn respect and discipline will be far happier choosing this type of setting. In other words, the very notion of what is to count as quality varies – what is viewed as high quality by one group (even within a single society) may not be so viewed by members of another group.

We should stress that this contextualist position is not one of simple relativism, in which any set of values and beliefs is as good as any other, but what Lourenço (1992) termed 'cultural relativism'. Within any given society, such as the United States, in terms of contemporary markers of cognitive and social development and of school success, the research evidence seems fairly clear (see, for example, Dickinson and Tabors, 2001; Hart and Risley, 1995, 1999). But one cannot simply assume that all cultural groups, even within one society, therefore subscribe to the same set of values and beliefs; there are historically formed reasons for the variations, and each set has both strengths and weaknesses for children's development.

Just by looking at social class variations in a single country, we can thus see deep-seated differences in the values, beliefs and experiences of children arriving in school. The issue becomes more complex when we consider the other sources of variation, such as ethnicity, religion, skin colour and so on, and the intersections among them. What then are the implications for the vertical continuity that helps children's transition to school? Continuity is least likely to be found when the teacher's background (by virtue of social class, ethnicity, race, religion, etc.) is different from that of the child (Crozier, 1998; Delgado-Gaitan, 1991; Lareau, 1989, 2002).

In societies in which there is a good deal of *de facto* segregation (whether by race, ethnicity, social class, or religion) perhaps there is less of a problem; working-class children, for example, will simply go to working-class schools. But there is a problem if that society, at the current time, accepts an ideology of schools providing an equal education, or of no child being 'left behind' as in contemporary discourse in the United States. Teachers, moreover, by virtue of their own education and their current occupation, are more likely to have middle-class values and beliefs. Cooney (1995) reported, for example, that even in an area of the United States with a wide range of different ethnic and social class groups, the schools there clearly reinforced the values, interests and expectations of just one group – white and middle class. This is hardly surprising, given that success (at least as measured by income and status) is more clearly attained by this group than by any others. But we should be extremely cautious about accepting one set of values and beliefs as a societal ideal, with alternative sets viewed as a deficit (Doucet, 2008; Lawrence-Lightfoot, 2003).

Shortcomings, dilemmas and tensions

To this point we have laid out what we mean by contextualism and our view of a contextualist approach to the transition to school, relying primarily on Vygotsky's and Bronfenbrenner's contextualist theories. Both theories have their shortcomings, however. Vygotsky never defined what he meant by culture and paid minimal attention to the processes whereby differences among cultural groups are transformed into variations in children's developmental experiences. He also did not focus on what the individual brings to the process of development.

Bronfenbrenner, building on Vygotskian and Lewinian foundations, was far more explicit about the impact of children themselves on their own development, and laid out a clearer differentiation of layers of context than did Vygotsky. However, despite his treatment of the macrosystem as a culture or subculture, he failed to take seriously the implication of different cultural groups having different values and beliefs, and therefore of encouraging different types of activities and interactions ('proximal processes' in his terminology). Instead he implicitly accepted mainstream white middle-class practices as the ideal to be attained. (For a more detailed assessment and critique of the theories, and the discussion of a more inclusive contextualist theory, see Tudge, 2008.)

The primary dilemma of a contextualist approach to the transition to school is, surely, the difficulty of applying it in practice, at least in contemporary society, as we will now attempt to illustrate. Returning to our example of a boy entering school, what sort of activities and interactions are going to be most helpful to his doing well? His teacher's first goal needs to be to understand his past experiences and his current attitudes and abilities. Although some understanding can be gained from meeting his parents, knowing whether he attended child care (and its nature), and assessing his cognitive and social skills, what is really needed is better and different communication between teacher and child.

Vygotsky's concept of the zone of proximal development is particularly relevant. Unfortunately, too many scholars continue to translate the crucial Russian word *obuchenie* as 'instruction' rather than the more accurate 'teaching/learning' when describing interactions within the zone (Tudge and Scrimsher, 2003). Instead we should think of a bi- (or multi-) directional interchange between child and teacher, in which a zone of proximal development is created in the course of interactions in which both can teach and learn. Our boy can certainly teach his teacher about his past experiences, if he is given the chance, and his teacher can certainly teach him better after having learned from him. The types of activities and interactions in which he then engages can then be related to both his strengths and his weaknesses. As we have argued elsewhere, 'children, while teaching their teachers about themselves and their ways of thinking, are likely to become more drawn into the process of learning' (Doucet and Tudge, 2007, p. 312) and it is often the case that teachers learn best when teaching (Tudge and Scrimsher, 2003). Our view is thus very similar to that of Paulo Freire, who defined 'liberating education' as education in which 'the teacher is no longer merely the-one-who-teaches, but one who is himself taught in dialog with the students, who in their turn while being taught also teach' (1998, p. 53).

For this to happen, of course, it would help for both teacher and child to be interested in this type of teaching and learning process, and some are more temperamentally suited to it than are others. But we also need to look outside the classroom. To what extent are teachers prepared to teach in a way that not only is highly individualized and time-consuming but also requires a degree of humility about how much needs to be learned from one's pupils as one teaches them? This depends in part on the type of education that students have while becoming teachers; it would obviously be helpful if teaching/learning experiences of the type described above were a regular feature of their interactions with their own lecturers and professors. But it also depends on what contemporary society thinks is important: What are its values? How great is the concern that all children are helped to make a successful transition to school? What resources will be given to the education system to ensure that children and teachers can create zones of proximal development in the ways we have suggested? To what extent will head teachers support teachers who try a different approach to interactions with children and the provision of varied types of activities?

At present we are doubtful that these questions can be answered in a way that we think would be valuable. However, cultures and societies are forever undergoing change, and change, in part, comes from the activities of individual members of those cultures and societies. From a contextualist perspective, it is never enough to expect the context to determine the nature of activities and interactions, but for individual actors to play their role in changing their context.

Acknowledgements

For providing the time to write this chapter, the first author would like to thank the University of North Carolina at Greensboro for the award of a year-long Research Assignment and the Psychology programme of the Federal University of Rio Grande do Sul, Brazil, for the invitation to spend a year as Visiting Professor with financial support generously provided by CAPES (Coordenação de Aperfeiçoamento de Pessoal de Nível Superior). We would also like to thank David Darts for his help producing Figure 2.6.1.

References

Barnett, S. (1995) 'Long-term effects of early childhood programs on cognitive and school outcomes', *Future of Children*, 5, pp. 25–35.

Baumrind, D. (1989) 'Rearing competent children', in W. Damon (ed.), *Child Development Today and Tomorrow*, San Francisco, CA, Jossey-Bass, pp. 349–78.

Beatty, B. (1995) *Preschool Education in America: The Culture of Young Children from the Colonial Era to the Present*, New Haven, CT, Yale University Press.

Bradley, R.H. (1995) 'Environment and parenting', in M.H. Bornstein (Vol. and Series ed.), *Handbook of Parenting, Vol. 1: Biology and Ecology of Parenting*, Mahwah, NJ, Lawrence Erlbaum Associates, pp. 235–61.

Bronfenbrenner, U. (1993) 'The ecology of cognitive development: research models and fugitive findings', in R. Wozniak and K. Fischer (eds), *Development in Context: Acting and Thinking in Specific Environments*, Hillsdale, NJ, Erlbaum, pp. 3–44.

—— (2005) 'The bioecological theory of human development', in U. Bronfenbrenner (ed.), *Making Human Beings Human: Bioecological Perspectives on Human Development*, Thousand Oaks, CA, Sage, pp. 3–15, (first published in 2001).

Bronfenbrenner, U., and Morris, P.A. (1998) 'The ecology of developmental processes', in W. Damon (Series ed.) and R.M. Lerner (Vol. ed.), *Handbook of Child Psychology, Vol. 1: Theoretical Models of Human Development* (5th edn), New York, John Wiley, pp. 993–1028.

—— (2006) 'The bioecological model of human development', in W. Damon (series ed.) and M. Lerner (vol. ed.), *Handbook of Child Psychology, Vol. 1: Theoretical Models of Human Development*, 6th edn, New York, John Wiley, pp. 793–828.

Cassidy, D.J., Hestenes, L.L., Hegde, A., Hestenes, S. and Mims, S. (2005) 'Measurement of quality in preschool child care classrooms: an exploratory and confirmatory factor analysis of the early childhood environment rating scale-revised', *Early Childhood Research Quarterly*, 20(3), pp. 345–60.

Christian, K., Morrison, F.J. and Bryant, F.B. (1998) 'Predicting kindergarten academic skills: Interactions among child care, maternal education, and family literacy environments', *Early Childhood Research Quarterly*, 13(3), pp. 501–21.

Clarke, A.T., and Kurtz-Costes, B. (1997) 'Television viewing, educational quality of the home environment, and school readiness', *Journal of Educational Research*, 90(5), pp. 279–85.

Cole, M. (2005) 'Cultural-historical activity theory in the family of socio-cultural approaches', *International Society for the Study of Behavioural Development Newsletter*, 47(1), pp. 1–4.

Comer, J.P. (1993) *School Power: Implications of an Intervention Project* (2nd edn), New York, The Free Press.

Comer, J.P., Haynes, N.M., Joyner, E.T. and Ben-Avie, M. (eds) (1996) *Rallying the Whole Village: The Comer Process for Reforming Education*. New York, Teachers College Press.

Cooney, M.H. (1995) 'Readiness for school or for school culture', *Childhood Education*, 71(3), pp. 164–7.

Cowan, P.A., Cowan, C.P., Ablow, J.C., Johnson, V.K. and Measelle, J.R. (eds) (2005) *Family Context of Parenting in Children's Adaptation to Elementary School*, Mahwah, NJ, Lawrence Erlbaum Associates.

Crozier, G. (1998) 'Parents and schools: Partnership or surveillance?', *Journal of Education Policy*, 13(1), pp. 125–36.

Daniels, H. (2005) 'Vygotsky and educational psychology: some preliminary remarks', *Educational and Child Psychology*, 22(1), pp. 6–17.

Delgado-Gaitan, C. (1991) 'Involving parents in the schools: a process of empowerment', *American Journal of Education*, 100(1), pp. 20–46.

Dickinson, D.K, and Tabors, P.O. (eds) (2001) *Beginning Literacy with Language: Young Children Learning at Home and in School*, Baltimore, MD, Brookes Publishing Company.

Doucet, F. (2008) 'How African American parents understand their and teachers' roles in children's schooling and what this means for preparing preservice teachers', *Journal of Early Childhood Teacher Education* [Special Issue on Multicultural Teacher Education in Honor of Leslie R. Williams], 29(2), pp. 108–39.

Doucet, F. and Tudge, J.R.H. (2007) 'Co-constructing the transition to school: reframing the "novice" versus "expert" roles of children, parents, and teachers from a cultural perspective', in R. Pianta, M. Cox, and K. Snow (eds), *School Readiness and the Transition to Kindergarten in the Era of Accountability*, Baltimore, MD, Brookes Publishing, pp. 307–28.

Edwards, M. (2007) 'The depth of the exteriors, Part 2: Piaget, Vygotsky, Harré, and the social mediation of development', retrieved 15 March 2007 from http://www.integralworld.net/index.html?edwards17.html

Epstein, J.L. (1986) 'Parents' reactions to teacher practices of parent involvement', *Elementary School Journal*, 86(3), pp. 277–94.

Epstein, J.L. (1996) 'Advances in family, community, and school partnerships', *New Schools, New Communities*, 12(3), pp. 5–13.

Field, T.M. (1991) 'Quality infant day-care and grade school behavior and performance', *Child Development*, 62(4), pp. 863–70.

Freire, P. (1998) *Pedagogy of the Oppressed* (trans. M.R. Ramos), New York, The Continuum Publishing Company.

Freitas, L.B.L. and Shelton, T.L. (2005) 'Atenção à primeira infância nos EUA e no Brasil' [Young children's care and education in the USA and Brazil], *Psicologia: Teoria e Pesquisa* [*Psychology: Theory and Research*], 21(2), pp. 197–205.

Freitas, L.B.L., Shelton, T.L. and Tudge, J.R.H. (2008) 'Conceptions of US and Brazilian early childhood care and education: a historical and comparative analysis', *International Journal of Behavioral Development*, 32(2), pp. 161–70.

Gilliam, W.S., and Zigler, E.F. (2004) 'State efforts to evaluate the effects of prekindergarten: 1977 to 2003', retrieved 2 January 2006, from http://nieer.org/resources/research/StateEfforts.pdf

Graue, M.E. (1992) 'Social interpretations of readiness for kindergarten', *Early Childhood Research Quarterly*, 7, pp. 225–43.

Graue, M.E., Kroeger, J. and Prager, D. (2001) 'A Bakhtinian analysis of particular home-school relations', *American Educational Research Journal*, 38(3), pp. 467–98.

Gullo, D.F., and Burton, C.B. (1992) 'Age of entry, preschool experience, and sex as antecedents of academic readiness in kindergarten', Special issue: research on kindergarten, *Early Childhood Research Quarterly*, 7(2), pp. 175–86.

Gullo, D.F., and Burton, C.B. (1993) 'The effects of social class, class size and prekindergarten experience on early school adjustment', *Early Child Development and Care*, 88(1), pp. 43–51.

Gutman, L.M., and McLoyd, V.C. (2000) 'Parents' management of their children's education within the home, at school, and in the community: an examination of African-American families living in poverty', *The Urban Review*, 32(1), pp. 1–24.

Hart, B., and Risley, T.R. (1995) *Meaningful Differences in the Everyday Experiences of Young American Children*, Baltimore, MD, Brookes Publishing.

—— (1999) *The Social World of Children: Learning to Talk*, Baltimore, MD, Brookes Publishing.

Haynes, N.M. and Comer, J.P. (1996) 'Integrating schools, families, and communities through successful school reform', *School Psychology Review*, 25(4), pp. 501–6.

Heath, S.B. (1983) *Ways with Words: Language, Life, and Work in Communities and Classrooms*, New York, Cambridge University Press.

Hoover-Dempsey, K.V., and Sandler, H.M. (1995) 'Parental involvement in children's education: why does it make a difference?', *Teachers College Record*, 97(2), pp. 310–32.

Howes, C. (1990) 'Can the age of entry and the quality of infant child care predict behaviors in kindergarten?', *Developmental Psychology*, 26(2), pp. 292–303.

Howes, C., Phillips, D.A. and Whitebook, M. (1992) 'Thresholds of quality: implications for the social development of children in center-based child care', *Child Development*, 63(2), pp. 449–60.

James, A., Jenks, C. and Prout, A. (1998) *Theorizing Childhood*, New York, Teachers College Press.

Kohn, M.L. (1977) *Class and Conformity: A Study in Values* (2nd edn), Chicago, University of Chicago Press.

—— (1995) 'Social structure and personality through time and space', in P. Moen, G.H. Elder, Jr. and K. Lüscher (eds), *Examining Lives in Context: Perspectives on the Ecology of Human Development*, Washington, DC, American Psychological Association, pp. 141–68.

Kozol, J. (1992) *Savage Inequalities: Children in America's Schools*, New York, HarperPerennial.

Kozol, J. (2005) 'Still separate, still unequal: America's educational apartheid', *Harper's Magazine*, 311(1864), 1 September.

Lareau, A. (1989) *Home Advantage: Social Class and Parental Intervention in Elementary Education*, Philadelphia, Falmer Press.

—— (2002) 'Invisible inequality: social class and childrearing in black families and white families', *American Sociological Review*, 67(5), pp. 747–76.

Lawrence-Lightfoot, S. (2003) *The Essential Conversation: What Parents and Teachers can Learn from Each Other,* New York, Random House.

Lawson, M.A. (2003) 'School–family relations in context: parent and teacher perceptions of parent involvement', *Urban Education,* 38(1), pp. 77–133.

Lourenço, O.M. (1992) *Psicologia do desenvolvimento moral: Teoria, dados e implicações [The psychology of moral development: Theory, data, and implications],* Coimbra, Almedina.

Love, J.M., Kisker, E.E., Ross, C., Constantine, J., Boller, K., Chazan-Cohen, R., Brady-Smith, C., Fuligni, A.S., Raikes, H., Brooks-Gunn, J., Tarullo, L.B., Schochet, P., Paulsell, D. and Vogel, C. (2005) 'The effectiveness of early Head Start for 3-year-old children and their parents: lessons for policy and programs', *Developmental Psychology,* 41(6), pp. 885–901.

Lubeck, S. (1985) *Sandbox Society: Early Education in Black and White America,* London, The Falmer Press.

Lubeck, S., Jessup, P., deVries, M. and Post, J. (2001) 'The role of culture in program improvement', *Early Childhood Research Quarterly,* 16(4), pp. 499–523.

Magnuson, K.A., Meyers, M.K., Ruhm, C.J. and Waldfogel, J. (2004) 'Inequality in preschool education and school readiness', *American Educational Research Journal,* 41(1), pp. 115–57.

Mangione, P.L., and Speth, T. (1998) 'The transition to elementary school: a framework for creating early childhood continuity through home, school, and community partnerships', *The Elementary School Journal,* 98(4), pp. 381–98.

Murphey, D.A., and Burns, C.E. (2002) 'Development of a comprehensive community assessment of school readiness', *Early Childhood Research and Practice,* 4(2), retrieved 20 October 2005, from http://ecrp.uiuc.edu/v4n2/murphey.html.

National Education Goals Panel (1998) *Ready Schools,* Washington, DC, National Education Goals Panel.

National Institute for Early Education Research (2005) *The State of Preschool – 2004: State Preschool Yearbook,* retrieved 13 August 2006 from http://www.nieer.org/yearbook.

NICHD Early Child Care Research Network (2003) 'Social functioning in first grade: associations with earlier home and child care predictors and with current classroom experiences', *Child Development,* 74(6), pp. 1639–62.

Parker, F.L., Boak, A.Y., Griffin, K.W., Ripple, C. and Peay, L. (1999) 'Parent–child relationship, home learning environment, and school readiness', *School Psychology Review,* 28(3), pp. 413–25.

Pepper, S.C. (1942) *World Hypotheses: A Study in Evidence,* Berkeley, University of California Press.

Phillips, D., Mekos, D., Scarr, S., McCartney, K. and Abbott-Shim, M. (2000) 'Within and beyond the classroom door: assessing quality in child care centers', *Early Childhood Research Quarterly,* 15(4), pp. 475–96.

Pianta, R.C., and Cox, M.J. (eds) (1999) *The Transition to Kindergarten,* Baltimore, MD, Brookes Publishing.

Pianta, R.C., Rimm-Kaufman, S.E., and Cox, M.J. (1999) 'Introduction: An ecological approach to kindergarten transition', in R.C. Pianta and M.J. Cox (eds), *The Transition to Kindergarten,* Baltimore, MD, Brookes Publishing, pp. 3–12.

Ramey, C.T., Campbell, F.A., Burchinal, M.R., Bryant, D.M., Wasik, B.H., Skinner, M.L., *et al.* (1999) *Early Learning, Later Success: The Abecedarian Study,* Chapel Hill, NC, Frank Porter Graham Child Development Institute.

Scarr, S., and Weinberg, R. (1986) 'The early childhood enterprise: care and education of the young', *American Psychologist,* 41(10), pp. 1140–6.

Scrimsher, S., and Tudge, J.R.H. (2003) 'The teaching/learning relationship in the first years of school: some revolutionary implications of Vygotsky's theory', *Early Education and Development,* 14(3), pp. 293–312.

Shepard, L.A., Kagan, S.L., and Wurtz, E. (1998) 'Goal 1 early childhood assessments resource group recommendations', *Young Children,* pp. 52–4.

Shonkoff, J.P. and Phillips, D.A. (eds) (2000) *From Neurons to Neighborhoods: The Science of Early Childhood Development,* Washington, DC, National Academy Press.

Snow, C.E., Barnes, W.S., Chandler, J., Goodman, I.F. and Hemphill, L. (1991) *Unfulfilled Expectations: Home and School Influences on Literacy*, Cambridge, MA, Harvard University Press.

Tobin, J.T., Wu, D.Y.H. and Davidson, D.H. (1989) *Preschool in 3 Cultures*, New Haven, CT, Yale University Press.

Tudge, J.R.H. (2008) *The Everyday Lives of Young Children: Culture, Class, and Child Rearing in Diverse Societies*, New York, Cambridge University Press.

Tudge, J., Doucet, F., Odero, D., Sperb, T., Piccinini, C. and Lopes, R. (2006) 'A window into different cultural worlds: young children's everyday activities in the United States, Kenya, and Brazil', *Child Development*, 77(5), pp. 1446–69.

Tudge, J.R.H., and Scrimsher, S. (2003) 'Lev S. Vygotsky on education: a cultural-historical, inter-personal, and individual approach to development', in B.J. Zimmerman and D.H. Schunk (eds), *Educational Psychology: A Century of Contributions*, Mahwah, NJ, Lawrence Erlbaum Associates, pp. 207–28.

Tudge, J., Doucet, F., Kulakova, N., Snezhkova, I. and Meltsas, M. (2007) 'The transition to school in the United States, Russia, and Estonia: different impacts of preschoolers' everyday activities', paper presented at the meetings of the European Conference on Developmental Psychology, Jena, Germany, August.

Vygotsky, L.S. (1987) *The Collected Works of L.S. Vygotsky, Vol. 1: Problems of General Psychology* (R.W. Rieber and A.S. Carton, eds; N. Minick, trans.), New York, Plenum. (Original work published 1934, written between 1929 and 1934.)

—— (1993) *The Collected Works of L.S. Vygotsky, Vol. 2: The Fundamentals of Defectology (Abnormal Psychology and Learning Disabilities)* (R.W. Rieber and A.S. Carton, eds; J.E. Knox and Carol B. Stevens, trans.), New York, Plenum. (Chapters originally published or written 1924–35.)

—— (1994) 'The problem of the environment', in R. Van der Veer and J. Valsiner (eds), *The Vygotsky Reader*, Oxford, Blackwell, pp. 338–54. (Original work published 1935.)

—— (1997) *The Collected Works of L.S. Vygotsky, Vol. 4: The History of the Development of Higher Mental Functions* (R.W. Rieber, ed.; M.J. Hall, trans.), New York, Plenum. (Originally written 1931; chapters 1–5 first published 1960, chapters 6–15 first published 1997.)

Weber, E. (1969) *The Kindergarten: Its Encounter with Educational Thought in America*, New York, Teachers College Press.

Weisner, T.S. (1996) 'Why ethnography should be the most important method in the study of human development', in R. Jessor, A. Colby and R.A. Shweder (eds), *Ethnography and Human Development: Context and Meaning in Social Enquiry*, Chicago, University of Chicago Press, pp. 305–24.

Reflective questions

1 If you're a teacher of young children, your goal is probably to start providing your help from where the child is – cognitively, socially, and emotionally. But, to know that, you have to understand more than what the child seems more or less capable of within the classroom. What would you need to do to understand the child's background in more detail, including the parents' values and goals for their child and the child's strengths and weaknesses outside the classroom? How would schools need to change to give you the time to get to know these things?

2 We pointed out that the Russian word *obuchenie* has incorrectly been translated either as 'instruction' or 'learning' rather than as 'teaching/learning'. How would teacher–child interactions need to change if we wanted to create zones of proximal development in the course of teaching/learning rather than simply by providing information and assist-ance just in advance of the child's current ability level?

Further reading

For literature on the transition to school

Booth, A. and Crouter, A.C. (eds) (2007) 'Disparities in school readiness: how families contribute to transitions into school', New York, Psychology Press.

Pianta, R.C., Cox, M.J. and Snow, K. (2007) *School Readiness and the Transition to Kindergarten in the Era of Accountability*, Baltimore, MD, Brookes.

For contextualist theories

Tudge, J.R.H. (2008) *The Everyday Lives of Young Children: Culture, Class, and Child Rearing in Diverse Societies*, New York, Cambridge University Press.

For education from a Vygotskian perspective

Scrimsher, S. and Tudge, J.R.H. (2003) 'The teaching/learning relationship in the first years of school: some revolutionary implications of Vygotsky's theory', *Early Education and Development*, 14(3), pp. 293–312.

Tudge, J.R.H., and Scrimsher, S. (2003) 'Lev S. Vygotsky on education: a cultural-historical, inter-personal, and individual approach to development', in B.J. Zimmerman and D.H. Schunk (eds), *Educational Psychology: A Century of Contributions*, Mahwah, NJ, Lawrence Erlbaum Associates, pp. 207–28.

Section 3

Teachers and learners

Introduction

Harry Daniels

(Cartoon by Ros Asquith)

Scrutiny of the documents issued by many governments around the world appears to reveal an image of the teacher and the learner cast in purely cognitive terms. The affective dimensions of teaching and learning are underplayed if not ignored and the values and beliefs embedded in the practices of schooling are either unseen or unacknowledged. It would also appear that the dominant conception of learning remains that of the internalisation of content transmitted by the teacher to the individual leaner who learns in exactly the same way as all the members of the class in which she or he is placed. This solitary act of passive acquisition is often assessed through what is known as 'high stakes testing' in the USA, and the resulting data have little formative impact on the processes of teaching and learning but do serve as indicators in a free market of competition between schools.

The contributors to this section challenge these assumptions and, in slightly different ways, introduce the sociocultural turn in educational theory, which is rapidly gaining influence. In Chapter 3.1, David and Heather Wood present an interpretation of the Vygotskian sociocultural argument in the context of the tutorial or micro teaching. They advance an argument for the primacy of the social in learning. They present a case for the factors which teachers should consider in managing classrooms as environments for collective endeavour. They also suggest that education should be seen as a process in and through which children are supported as they acquire the tools that they will need to gain control of their own lives:

Children do not – indeed they could not – have lessons in all they need to learn. Well chosen starting places endow them with the means to learn how to use for themselves systems of signs to represent, problematise, work with and through situations. They can be exploited to create and solve their own problems and to make their own discoveries. The creative, generative nature of systems of signs thus lets children teach themselves and, ultimately, allows them to achieve new insights as they move away from those have taught them.

In Chapter 3.2 Anne Edwards turns her gaze towards the production of teacher identities in settings where the imperatives of 'practical experience' held sway over engagement with theories of teaching and being a teacher. She draws on recent advances in our understanding of notions of both expertise and transfer to argue that there is a need to reconsider the place of theory in the education and development of teachers for the twenty-first century. In a way that echoes David and Heather Wood's account of pupil learning she argues that 'learners move between settings and that they need to learn how to navigate them and reformulate their prior understandings so that they can act knowledgeably within different settings'. This critique of narrowly conceived notions of 'upskilling' places emphasis on the creative interplay between collective meaning and personal sense-making. She is careful not to commit the 1970s' constructivist error of abandoning the importance of subject knowledge in the flight from a model of knowledge as something that is stored by an individual for subsequent application. Her understanding of distributed expertise demands a collective conception of the practice of teaching and the organisation of schooling and practices which prepare people to act as teachers in these practices. In Chapter 3.3, Chris James adds a further dimension to this argument as he turns his attention to the affective dimensions of schooling. Importantly he does not seek to divorce an analysis of thinking and feeling in schooling. He writes of the implications of the emotional dynamics of institutions, specifically the complex institutions that are witnessed in schooling. He considers the way defences are mounted in the face of emotional challenge, reactions to change and the way emotions impact on decision making. He argues that feeling and thinking and willing are integral and intertwined aspects of participation in schooling for adults and young people alike. To pretend that such complexity does not exist and should not be a feature of discussions concerning preparation for participation in teaching is rendered naïve.

Guy Claxton considers the importance of the formation of habits of mind in successful preparation for lifelong learning. He distinguishes between different approaches to the issue and proposes an emphasis on '*learning* rather than thinking; *dispositions* rather than skills; *infusion* rather than stand-alone; *organic* rather than prescriptive methods; *involvement of students* rather than delivery of a ready-made product to them; and *culture-shifting* rather than training'. He uses the terms sand, cement and water to introduce the key elements of a strong bedrock for educational work. These terms refer to the neuroscientific and sociocultural aspects of learning to learn, the values that underpin practice and an action research orientation which turns this sand and cement into everyday reality in schooling. These elements can create the basis for a movement that may lead to the king of cultural emphasis in school improvement which he argues will lead to a form of practice which genuinely enhances and transforms the dispositions of young people alongside their teachers and the institutions in which they work.

Yolande Muschamp offers her readers a theoretical and an empirical account of the impact of change in cultural circumstance. In this she considers the changes in activities, emotions and perceptions engendered by the process of transfer from primary to secondary school. The changes in patterns of signification are experienced in making moves between institutions reveal the power of the tacit and implicit influence that schools bring to bear on all the people who work within them. These influences shape all aspects of human functioning, not just the cognitive matters which are privileged in so many forms of state education but also the social, moral and affective development of individuals and their understandings of themselves.

In Chapter 3.6 Wim Wardekker engages with the issue of moral development of the learner in education. Development, identity and, latterly, citizenship in a democratic society are all referenced to the central theme. He allows the notion of adult inconsistency into the discussion of phenomena which are, in his mind, often erroneously assumed to be consistent in the democratic citizen. The suggestion is that knowledge of these inconsistencies within ourselves is a crucial component in being prepared to accept diversity in the world around us. He concludes with a cautionary note on the limits of educational action without political will. By implication such a political will may only be formed by politicians who acknowledge the moral dimensions of Wim Wardekker's argument. Jack Whitehead takes up this issue of self-awareness of the 'I' in education. He starts from the assumption that practitioners want to know how they can improve their practice and that they see improved practices evolving in settings where individuals produce and share understandings and explanations of their own learning. He revisits his own engagement with propositional and dialectical logic and shows how this has led to his own development as an educator. Both Jack Whitehead and Wim Wardekker are making a case (albeit from somewhat different perspectives) for a more self-aware profession and professional way of being for teachers. With regard to the differences between them it is worth remembering Jerome Bruner's (1997) celebratory note concerning the differences between Vygotsky and Piaget that perception of depth requires difference.

In the final paper in this section William Lachicotte takes up the related matter of identity which in his case he relates to agency and social practice. He discusses the ways in which people take up positions in a social world which is in itself figured in such a way that it shapes the possibilities for action but is also open to change. This can, of course, be read in terms of how both teachers and young people take up positions and are positioned in the figured worlds of particular schools. A casual observation of life in different schools reveals the existence of very different institutional cultures; the same variation may be seen between the administrative districts which govern schools. Acting in these worlds becomes a 'common sense' way of being. As William Lachicotte notes, 'Identities become personal, intimate forms of self-understanding which gain salience and lose self-consciousness as actors identify and rehearse them within figured worlds.' It is this process which is reversed in the actions aimed at self-understanding which Jack Whitehead and Wim Wardekker discuss in their chapters. This is acknowledged in the conclusion.

The papers brought together in this section of the book all lean towards a sociocultural interpretation of the way a person comes to be in the social world of schooling. While it is clear that there is variation between the chapters in the detail of the assumptions that underpin the texts they share a desire to move beyond the twentieth-century accounts of the individual learner, whether this person is a pupil or a teacher. The section also signals a desire to move beyond the model of person cast not only as a lone individual learner but also a lone cognitive entity whose emotions and values do not feature in the relentless pursuit of narrowly conceived 'educational' outcomes.

References

Bruner, J.S. (1997) 'Celebrating divergence: Piaget and Vygotsky', *Human Development*, 40, pp. 63–73.

3.1 Vygotsky, tutoring and learning

David Wood and Heather Wood

Introduction

This chapter opens with a selective examination of research into individualised tutoring. We articulate theoretical and empirical evidence to support the conclusion that a set of common principles governs such tutoring. These principles apply to the provision of tutorial support for preschool-aged children through to adult learners in a number of domains. In support of these claims, the chapter brings together and relates research and theory from both face-to-face teaching and computer-based tutoring situations. In so doing the chapter will highlight some of the current limitations in our understanding. We suggest that the principles identified apply mainly to procedural learning in well-structured domains. The chapter examines the idea that other learning goals, such as the development of skills in self-regulation, need to be derived from a different model of the learning process.

Scaffolding and the zone of proximal development

Almost twenty years ago, Wood, Bruner and Ross (Wood *et al.*, 1976) introduced the metaphor of 'scaffolding' in the context of tutorial interactions between an adult and individual children. The formulation of this notion was designed to explore the nature of the support that an adult provides in helping a child to learn how to perform a task that, alone, the child could not master. Parallels between the notion of scaffolding and Vygotsky's more general theoretical concept of the *zone of proximal development* or ZPD (Vygotsky, 1978) were soon drawn (Rogoff and Wertsch, 1984).

Vygotsky's ZPD is probably so widely known as to need no definition. However, in case it remains unfamiliar to some, it refers to the gap between what a given child can achieve alone, their 'potential development as determined by independent problem solving', and what they can achieve 'through problem solving under adult guidance or in collaboration with more capable peers'.

Vygotsky's definition of the ZPD leaves open to us the task of identifying the nature of the guidance and collaboration that promotes development and a need to specify what gets learned during the course of a given history of tutor/learner interaction. These two key issues provide the main agenda for this paper.

Scaffolding can be seen as one attempt to address the first of these questions; what is the nature of help or guidance? The suggestion was that the adult could serve several key tutoring functions. These included recruitment of the child's interest in the task, establishing and maintaining an orientation towards task-relevant goals, highlighting critical features of the task that the child might overlook, demonstrating how to achieve goals and helping to control frustration. This latter role was achieved by ensuring that the child was neither left to struggle alone with too much complexity, nor, conversely, given too little scope for involvement and initiative in task activity.

Since its formulation, the scaffolding idea has been developed, extended and criticised in several different ways. For example, it was argued that the concept ignored the nature of the relationship between adult and child, was limited to a single, isolated task and said too little about the nature of the communicative mechanisms involved. Several attempts have been made to try to remedy these shortcomings, though the nature of what gets learned or internalised during the course of interaction still remains unclear and controversial.

It is not our intention to try to review here the history of scaffolding nor the formulation of related concepts such as 'cognitive apprenticeship' (Collins *et al.*, 1989), 'guided participation' (Rogoff, 1990) and 'reciprocal teaching' (Brown and Campione, 1990). Extensive, evaluative reviews of these notions have already been undertaken (Rogoff, 1986, 1990) and we have only space here to summarise some of the generalisations that have emerged.

Reviewing the literature on both adult and peer tutoring, Rogoff suggests that laboratory investigation and naturalistic observation have identified several general features of effective collaboration. These are summarised below:

1   Tutors serve to provide a bridge between a learner's existing knowledge and skills and the demands of the new task. Left alone, a novice might not appreciate the relations between what the task demands and what they already know or can do that is relevant.
2   By providing instructions and help in the context of the learner's activity, tutors provide a structure to support the learner's problem solving. For example, while focused on their immediate actions, learners, left alone, might lose sight of the overall goal of the activity.
3   Although the learner is involved in what is initially, for them, 'out of reach' problem solving, guided participation ensures that they play an active role in learning and that they contribute to the successful solution of problems.
4   Effective guidance involves the transfer of responsibility from tutor to learner.
5   Not all guided participation involves deliberate or explicit attempts to teach and learn. Often, interactions with the four characteristics just listed occur when children set out to 'help' their parents, as they participate in everyday activities, or in playful encounters.

These features of everyday interactions involving children as learners are hardly surprising and seemingly self-evident. However, on a socio-historical account of development, like Vygotsky's, it is their very familiarity which indicates their power. If they were not familiar and mundane they could not serve the functions that are claimed for them. They help to explain why, over years of childhood, small-scale 'micro-genetic' changes brought about in such social encounters serve to transmit culture from one generation to the next.

Contingent instruction

In our own work, we have focused on the issue of task responsibility and control, seeking to identify aspects of tutorial activity which lead to the progressive acquisition of task competence by the child and to the 'hand over' of task responsibility from tutor to learner. Briefly, we suggested that effective helping involved two ingredients:

1   The first concerns circumstances in which a child gets into difficulty. Here, the tutor immediately offers more specific instruction or help than was offered previously. For

instance, if the tutor had suggested a specific action or goal to the child, but the child did not understand what s/he meant by what s/he said, then the tutor steps in to point out or show the child what to work with next. By fleshing out the meaning of the (initially non-understood) utterances by showing what they entail in action, the tutor eventually negotiates the task-specific meaning of the language used and draws the child into the tutor's conceptualisation of the situation.

2   The second ingredient of effective instruction is 'fading'; providing the child with the minimal help needed to ensure joint success. For instance, if, initially, a child needs to be shown what to do in order to succeed, the contingent tutor will attempt to replace showing by telling. As the child comes to understand verbal hints, then the tutor attempts to remain silent (no easy task when teaching) ensuring that, if the child gets into no more difficulty, s/he proceeds to complete the task alone.

Patterns of instruction which are marked by these two principles – give more help when the learner gets into difficulty, and offer less help as they gain in proficiency – we have termed 'contingent' teaching. Others have found that similar principles govern the effectiveness of face-to-face instruction in other task contexts involving parents with infant learners (Heckhausen, 1987), school-aged children learning mathematics (Pratt *et al.*, 1989) and in teaching planning skills (Rogoff, 1990).

The 'rules' for contingent instruction may seem self-evident and simple. In practice, however, contingency is hard to sustain. Empirically, we have observed that many face-to-face teaching interactions involving both parents and professional teachers are almost never maximally contingent. Even an adult trained to teach contingently could not sustain 100 per cent adherence to the rules (Wood *et al.*, 1978). One clear implication is that less than contingent instructional performance is adequate to ensure learning in most cases.

The complexity of the task of achieving contingent instruction is also highlighted by our recent attempts to apply the same principles to the design of computer-based tutoring systems.

Planning and teaching

Imagine a situation in which a would-be tutor has made a suggestion to their learner about what they might try to do next. The learner does not follow the instruction but does something else. What they do, however, represents a perfectly sensible way of proceeding: another means for achieving task-relevant ends. What does the would-be contingent tutor do? It would seem inappropriate (and objectively incorrect) to act in any way that might imply to the learner that what they are attempting to do is wrong.

The contingent tutor should suspend their own initial teaching intent and offer any subsequent help in relation to what the learner is inferred to be trying to do. We have termed this aspect of effective helping 'domain contingency'. It involves decisions about what to teach next in response to local circumstances.

Achieving such flexibility in computer-based tutoring is difficult. However well the system designer understands the learning domain and how it might be learned, there is always a possibility that the learner will invent a novel means to master it. Unless computer-based systems can be made sufficiently flexible and adaptive to be able to evaluate unexpected learner activities, they will not achieve maximal contingency. More generally, the ability to integrate behaviour based on a plan with the capacity to depart from that plan as and when the situation demands is a difficult problem for Artificial Intelligence, and current AI systems are not competent at meeting such demands in real time. The implication of this for the current generation of computer-based tutoring systems is that they run the risk of classifying learner innovation as error. Of course, human tutors may also fail to appreciate learner innovation. But they do possess the potential to learn. To the best of our knowledge, no such computer-based systems yet exist.

Having decided what is to be the focus of any help to be offered, the next tutorial task is to determine how specific that help should be, as discussed earlier. Achieving this is relatively easy with a computer-based system. The system is programmed to record any level of help given to an individual learner. When the learner gets into difficulty increasingly specific help is given, up to the point where either the learner follows an instruction successfully or the system provides maximum help by doing the next part of the task itself. The system is thus 'driven' to provide increasingly specific help as a learner struggles but it is programmed always to attempt to fade the level of help offered after success. Although easy for a computer, the demands that these requirements put on human powers of observation, attention and memory are considerable, which helps to explain why contingent tutoring is easily described but hard to practise.

A third requirement concerns the timing of instruction or 'temporal contingency'. Imagine a situation in which a learner is pondering over their next move. Then think of an episode in which they are so bemused that they have not a clue what to do next. Attention to the posture, facial expression or other non-verbal features of learner behaviour would probably enable a human tutor to decide what their lack of task activity betokened. Acting contingently, they would decide to leave the learner alone in the first situation but offer help in the second. A computer-based tutoring system has no means whatsoever to make such decisions. All they can be programmed to respond to are the key-presses, mouse movements or whatever by which the learner interacts with the system. Anything that relies on more subtle aspects of non-verbal communication can play no role in human–computer interaction. In designing their systems, then, programmers must either impose some arbitrary time criterion, after which help will be given in such circumstances (wanted or not), or they must leave the learner with the task of requesting help. In either case, the system cannot guarantee temporal contingency.

From a different direction: J.A. Anderson and learning theory

The research that we have just outlined rests on attempts to describe tutoring activity in a way that relates to learning outcomes. On the basis of such analyses, it has sought to formulate principles, like instructional contingency, which are implicated in effective face-to-face tutoring. Anderson's approach is quite different; he comes from another direction. Over several years, he has developed a theory of learning that is couched in information-processing terms and implemented as a computer 'architecture'. On the grounds of the not unreasonable assumption that principles of instruction should be compatible with what one takes to be an adequate theory of learning, he has sought to make a contribution to education by drawing principles of instruction from the theory and testing these out in the design of Intelligent Tutoring Systems (ITSs) which have been evaluated in classrooms.

Anderson and ACT theory

We first encountered Anderson's work on ITSs through a 1987 paper which, written with colleagues, offered an overview of their previous work. A principal motivation for the ITS research was to provide a context for an empirical evaluation of the ACT theory of skill learning (ACT standing for the Adaptive Character of Thought).

Citing Bloom's (Bloom, 1984) comparative analysis of the relative effectiveness of conventional class teaching versus one-to-one (human) tutoring, Anderson and colleagues suggested that some of the benefits reported by Bloom might be obtained by means of computer systems designed to individualise instruction. Bloom concluded that face-to-face instruction leads to an improvement of two standard deviations over conventional class teaching (i.e. about 98 per cent of individually taught learners score above the average for group taught). If computer-based systems could be designed to capture even part of this benefit, then the educational rewards of the research could be highly significant.

What we found striking was the resemblance between the design principles that Anderson and his colleagues had drawn from their theory of learning and the notions of scaffolding and contingent instruction. Since Anderson's group was not only advocating similar tutoring principles but also justifying these in terms of their theory, then it seemed possible that they could provide an answer to the question being asked by many working with Vygotskian theory: what gets internalised during the course of interactions within the ZPD?

An information processing approach to tutoring

One of the central features of ITSs, like face-to-face tutoring, is that they can provide instruction contingently in the context of the learner's real-time activity. In Anderson's terms, they honour the principle: (1) *provide instruction in the problem-solving context*. In group situations, where a learner might, say, be talked through a mathematics problem or see a demonstration proof worked out, the teacher might offer advice and guidance about how to solve problems before asking the learners to work at some for themselves. The learner, then, has not only to remember and recall such advice but also recognise the actual problem contexts to which it relates. In face-to-face teaching, the location and timing of any help can be offered by the tutor at relevant junctures, i.e. contingently. Further, the learner can be prevented from wasting time and losing motivation by spending large amounts of time in confused and fruitless activity. To avoid such confusion, the theory advocates: (2) *immediate response to learner errors*. Within the theory, nothing is learned from errors, they only waste time. Thus, intelligent tutors should provide immediate feedback on error.

Initially, with a learner who understands little of the lesson at hand, the tutor may have to step in frequently to repair error and to show the learner what to do. However, the aim is: (3) *to support successive approximations to competent performance*. The tutor should be programmed not to interfere with successful learner activity. Thus, as the learner learns, the system fades and becomes silent.

Since learners have limited 'working memory capacity' they may overlook important features of the task at hand or lose sight of what they are trying to achieve. The system can support learning: (4) *by providing reminders of the learning goal*. They can also provide reminders by, for instance, showing, on screen, a trace of what the learner has already achieved on a given task. The learner's attention can be directed to this if and when they lose track of what they are doing.

There is much more by way of detail that the ACT theory has to say about these issues. However, the aim here is simply to draw attention to some of the resemblances between ACT theory and the findings from developmental research outlined earlier. We now need to explore the theory which justifies these instructional design principles.

Theory and practice

In designing a computer tutor, Anderson identifies three main tasks. The system must:

1   include an ideal student model (i.e. a specification of what needs to be learned);
2   include a model of where an individual learner 'is at' relative to the ideal student; and
3   include the generation of a tutoring strategy adapted to the needs of each learner.

The ideal student model is essentially a statement of the curriculum to be learned. In one sense, this model stands 'outside' the theory in that it is a specification of the 'what' rather than the 'how' of learning. However, and here comes a strong theoretical claim, that curriculum must be subjected to a cognitive task analysis to identify the rules that it embodies. According to the ACT theory, these rules must be of a specific nature, i.e. production rules. For those for whom this is a novel concept, an example of production rules for simple arithmetic problems might help to give an impression of their nature:

IF   the goal is to solve a problem and C1 is the rightmost column without an
            answer digit
THEN   set a subgoal to write an answer in C1.

IF   the goal is to write out an answer in C1 and d1 and d2 are the digits in that
            column let d3 be the sum of d1 and d2
THEN   set a subgoal to write d3 in C1.

The claim is that human knowledge includes such rules. This does not mean, of course, that when one thinks one is conscious of figuring out 'if–then' propositions. Indeed, according to the theory, procedural knowledge, i.e. what production rules model, is not consciously inspectable. It is a form of 'mentalese' which, though roughly describable in linguistic terms, is not speech per se.

In addition to production rules, knowing also involves declarative knowledge. This is knowledge that can be verbally stated or communicated in some other way such as through figures and diagrams. Such communicable or demonstrable knowledge is of itself 'inert'. Thus, a learner might be able, say, to read and even remember a verbal instruction, but until this is connected to procedural knowledge in the service of some goal, it lacks utility. Learning how to act in response to declarative knowledge, i.e. how to proceduralise that knowledge to achieve goals, is at the heart of skill learning in ACT.

The (dynamic) model of each individual learner is built up in the same language of production rules. As the tutoring system presents examples or problems for the learner to solve, it compares their performance with that of the ideal student model (hence the term 'model-based tutoring'). This analysis then provides the tutorial goals of the system. Where a learner demonstrates knowledge of a production rule and its relation to declarative knowledge, the system offers no intervention. However, an individual student may not evidence knowledge of such connections. They may also make an error which signals a lack of sensitivity to the crucial elements of a situation, or perform an action which does not take activity closer to the solution being sought. In such circumstances, problems are selected to provide instruction and practice with the rules that have yet to be learned. The system monitors the effects of practice (in terms of the learning theory) to specify when the learner can be moved on to encounter novel productions. The amount of novelty is also theoretically constrained by the theory.

Another central feature of the latest version of the theory (Anderson, 1993) concerns the nature of mechanisms for the generalisation of knowledge. Anderson argues that analogy is the key to generalisation. In a problematic situation, the learner may seek to draw analogies between their current difficulties and previous experiences with related problems. Worked examples are thus a crucial factor in learning. If and when a learner succeeds in solving a problem by analogy to a previously worked example (which, initially, may be supported by a tutor), then the example is elaborated or 'reified' to start the formation of a 'schema' or meta-procedure. To the extent that this schema supports future learning, it becomes increasingly linked (procedurally) to the class of problems that it serves. Thus, the identification of productive worked examples is central to pedagogical decision-making.

Evaluation

Judged by their own objectives, Anderson and his colleagues can claim a fair degree of success with their tutors. Classroom evaluations of systems designed to support learning in geometry and LISP programming showed evidence of benefits over conventional teaching. Improvements of about one standard deviation in performance levels were obtained (equivalent to a grade level in the US accreditation system) and learning time for computer-based students was around one-third of that taken for group teaching.

The problem with evaluating educational research, of course, is that evidence must be measured against values. Divides over assumptions about what is worth knowing and how knowledge is gained run deep throughout the history of education. Consequently, as one might expect, reactions to Anderson's findings amongst educationalists range from enthusiasm to rejection. Kaput (1992), for instance, argues that procedural learning of the type supported by Anderson's tutors is of limited relevance and value to current educational needs. However, as Anderson points out, critics seldom enter the debate armed with evidence favouring other pedagogical approaches. We will not try to adjudicate such issues here. Instead, we will explore some of the limits to the ACT theory in the next section.

Attempts have also been made to exploit ACT tutors in support of collaborative learning involving pairs of students. The benefits found for individualised tutoring were not replicated with pairs (Anderson, 1993). This result contrasts with several lines of evidence which suggest that computer-based activity can be used to support effective collaboration in learning contexts. It seems, however, that the design of environments for this purpose will need to be based on different principles from those derived from Anderson's theory.

We believe that the evidence showing that ACT tutors do not do well with more than one learner actually offers support for the theory. Since the tutorial actions of the system are derived from a detailed analysis of individual knowledge, it is not surprising that it cannot analyse and support the activities of two or more learners working in collaboration. If the system optimises to individuals, then any response designed to support one learner will clearly not be guaranteed to fit the instructional needs of another. Tutorial contingency will break down under such circumstances. This observation, we contend, generalises; it implies that any theory designed to explain how and why individualised instruction works cannot be extended without further theoretical development to a theory of scaffolding of collaborative or group learning.

Tutoring and self-regulation

Anderson's tutoring systems confront the learner with problems that are well structured and which are set by the system. They are not expected to devise their own problems, nor are they required to find out how to transform 'messy' problematical situations into a form which may enable them to be solved. The problems set by the tutor are expressed in a symbol system or language that is known to support their solution. Learners are given no experience in selecting and experimenting with different ways of representing problems for themselves. Although learners are left to their own devices so long as they are succeeding with a problem, the responsibility for regulating performance when they get into difficulties is external; it rests with the tutor. Thus, learners gain no experience in deciding for themselves when they may be going wrong, nor are they given opportunities to detect and repair their own performance. In situations where tasks are not well structured, a learner may need to decide or negotiate criteria against which their own performance can be assessed. Experience with such demands is not an integral part of the tutoring systems and no analyses or representations of these abilities are offered in the ideal student model, i.e. they are not candidates for instruction.

Such proposed limits on ACT-inspired tutoring underpin the objections that several educationalists and cognitive scientists have levelled against both the theory and the tutoring regimes that it generates. These, of course, are extremely complex issues that cannot be given due consideration here. It is worth noting, however, that we cannot assume that such competencies are typically engendered through schooling either. In relation to mathematics learning, for example, there is evidence showing that the vast majority of children do not develop the envisaged skills in transforming 'messy' situations into soluble problems. Nor are skills in self-regulation and recovery from error guaranteed. Whether these findings are telling us either (a) that learning is so situated that such proposed competencies are a myth; (b) that it takes too much time and experience to achieve the necessary knowledge and expertise for us to expect such accomplishments in the normal course of schooling; and/or (c) that we have yet to perfect curricula and teaching methods which would promote such learning, it is not possible to say.

However, returning to our theme of computer-based tutoring, there is a little evidence which suggests that the acquisition of some skills in self-regulation can be supported by one-to-one teaching. To illustrate research which leads us to such an optimistic position, we will outline work by Shute, Glaser and their colleagues. This group has been studying, among other things, the development of skills in investigation, design and decision-making in both adults and children.

Computer-simulated microworlds provide the learning environments employed. These include 'Smithtown' (Shute and Glaser, 1990) which models the economic life of a small community, and 'Daytona' (Schauble and Glaser, 1990) an environment in which adults and children were asked to design and test their own simulated racing cars. The educational objective of Smithtown is to develop the learner's understanding of basic principles of microeconomics. Daytona was created to provide detailed analyses of the learner's strategies for investigation, hypothesis testing and design. The goal is to discover how to design the fastest car possible. In both environments, the (individual) learner sets their own problems, formulates hypotheses and evaluates these by 'driving' the simulations.

The analyses of learner activity have identified features of problem-solving activities, in both children and adults, which inhibit discovery and limit the effectiveness of the design processes.

Confirmation bias

As many previous investigations of human decision-making have shown, both children and adults displayed a natural tendency to confirm their own prior beliefs. Thus, experiments or designs which might have generated evidence which could serve to test (and potentially falsify) a belief, or which might lend credence to a hypothesis that was not favoured, were seldom undertaken.

This bias restricted the range of problems set and investigated, thus limiting the extent of the space of possibilities that were searched and evaluated. In consequence, optimal solutions or designs are rarely obtained. For example, in designing racing cars, many learners start out with the assumption that the size of a car's muffler (i.e. exhaust), which influences a car's sound, also constrains its top speed. Attempts to disconfirm this (false) belief were rare.

Impulsivity

Learners often formulate hypotheses and set out to test them without first examining relevant factors or evidence (available from the system if sought) which could be used to assess the quality or potential decisiveness of the test in question. Thus, adults working with the Smithtown simulation might decide that they were going to establish a new coffee selling business without examining the demographic composition of the area in which they had elected to trade when such factors relate to consumption. The desire to 'get on with it', potentially ignoring crucially relevant information before acting, is another common failing in human exploratory activity.

Confounding variables and ignoring interactions

Another common cognitive disposition was illustrated by the finding that people conduct experiments or create designs which cannot provide decisive information because two or more potentially interacting factors are confounded. For instance, if one has designed and tested a car with, say, five main attributes, and one wants to decide if two or more are crucially important, then creating a new design in which both are changed (and leaving it at that) will not create a crucial test.

Where two factors or variables interact, most designers/explorers failed to come up with a hypothesis which led to relevant tests. For instance, in the Daytona microworld, placing a tail fin on a low-powered car will simply add to its weight, increase drag and lower its top speed. Adding the same fin to a suitably powerful car (where it increases stability at high speeds) will enable the car to travel faster without going out of control. Few designers, adults or children, came up with this idea.

Implicit (unwarranted) belief in the power of memory

Although the simulation environments provided the means to record the results of tests and designs, it was common for the learner not to exploit such facilities (to the detriment of performance). Their apparent belief in an ability to remember and reason about a complex space of possibilities without using external tools to 'amplify' their cognition further reduced the extent and quality of their search of the space of possibilities.

Replicating success: pragmatic problem solving versus scientific discovery

If one manages to bake the most superb of cakes, it seems natural that, in future culinary activities, one will strive to re-duplicate success. However ritualistic or superstitious one becomes in striving to maintain excellence, if the end result is always a superb cake, then one is likely to be satisfied. However, if the goal is to discover the minimum set of necessary and sufficient conditions which lead to a successful outcome, it may well be necessary, along the way, to bake some less than perfect cakes, i.e. one might even need to make 'errors' in order to determine whether one's current hypothesis about the ingredients of success are tenable.

Such pragmatically satisfying attempts to duplicate success were found in the investigations of Shute and Glaser. The incidence and frequency of such activities help to illustrate fundamental differences in the 'stance' that one needs to adopt in scientific investigation as opposed to everyday problem solving.

Coaching and self-regulation

The list just presented illustrates categories that can be used to record and assess learner activity. In Smithtown, the system was programmed to monitor and log key actions by a learner in the simulation environment. For example, the system recorded whether or not a given learner requested relevant information from the system before starting up some economic venture in the simulation. It also recorded and inspected sequences of activity to see if, say, the learner was attempting some economic experiment which involved confounded variables. When some criterion was reached (e.g. the learner failed to seek relevant information two or three times) the system was programmed to deliver a message to the learner pointing out, for example, information that needed to be evaluated prior to further action.

In general, then, a profile of key features of a learner's strategies for formulating goals, undertaking experiments, recording data and testing hypotheses was built up. The coach used such information to provide a critique of a learner's performance and took tutorial actions based on specific aspects of the individual profile.

Shute and Glaser (1990) report a large-scale evaluation of the Smithtown coaching system. This involved comparing the examination performances of psychology undergraduates who worked with the system for a few hours with that of economics students who had taken a semester course which was designed to teach similar economic ideas. The authors report that the Smithtown taught students fared as well as those conventionally taught. They also found that, although the Smithtown coach only commented on strategic aspects of behaviour and did not explicate the economic laws or principles upon which the simulation activities were designed, students were often able to infer and state these principles. It seems that they were able to induce or abduct explicit rules from patterns discovered in their problem solving.

Although we would require more extensive and detailed evaluations before accepting the conclusion that skills in self-regulation can be taught, including ways of thinking and acting which override well entrenched biases in decision-making, the findings cited by Smithtown's creators offer some hope that this may turn out to be the case.

Conclusions

We have argued that principles for the design of effective one-to-one tutoring systems have been identified in research arising out of different theoretical traditions. We have also explored, albeit briefly, a theory of learning which explains how and why such principles work. Though couched in terms which are not commonly heard in discussions of Vygotskian theory, we suggest that ACT needs to be taken seriously by those working in the Vygotskian tradition and that something like the process of rule-learning that it defines is a good candidate for a model of procedural skill learning. According to the theory, what is internalised during instruction is not simply speech, but rules of action, in the service of goals, which become activated by symbol systems such as language and diagrams. Whilst such rules can be described as proposition-like structures, they are not available to conscious inspection. However, they are, we suggest, plausible candidates for the 'inner speech' that Vygotsky argued arises out of social interaction to form higher mental processes.

We have also identified what we take to be important limitations on the scope of the principles of instruction as currently formulated. More specifically, where tutoring supports the development of skills in self-regulation, rather than task performance per se, we have argued that a more elaborated analysis of the learning process, one based on different aspects of the learner's knowledge and activity, needs to be taken into account. Whether or not procedural learning theory can be extended to explain the development of self-regulation remains to be seen.

The models that we have been considering are also limited in other, fundamental ways. Central to effective tutoring is a model of the learning domain, what some call the 'ideal student model'. The specification of this model lies outside the scope of the theories considered. Thus, learning theory does not bypass long-standing issues to do with curriculum analysis. For instance, recent research into mathematics learning has provided much-enriched accounts of the nature of what needs to be learned (Greer, 1992). Such research, which represents a combination of mathematical and psychological analysis, can provide tutors (human or machine) with new models of what it is that has to be learned. We have also stressed the fact that there is always the possibility of learner innovation which, far from being predictable on the basis of contemporary learning theory, cannot even be recognised by those theories. This, we suspect, indicates a fundamental aspect of human development. We may seek to reconstruct knowledge with children, but they may sometimes find their own means to achieve the goals that we set.

Acknowledgements

The preparation of this paper and our own research was supported by the Economic and Social Research Council. It was first published as 'Vygotsky, tutoring and learning', *Oxford Review of Education*, 22(1). Reprinted by permission of Taylor & Francis Ltd (http://www.tandf.co.uk/journals).

References

Anderson, J.A. (1993) *Rules of the Mind*, Hillsdale, NJ, Erlbaum.

Bloom, B.S. (1984) 'The 2-sigma problem: the search for methods of group instruction as effective as one-to-one tutoring', *Educational Researcher*, 13, pp. 4–16.

Brown, A.L. and Campione, J.C. (1990) 'Communities of learning and thinking, or a context by any other name', in D. Kuhn (ed.), *Developmental Perspectives on Teaching and Learning Thinking Skills*, Basle, Karger, pp. 108–26.

Collins, A., Brown, J.S. and Newman, S. (1989) 'Cognitive apprenticeship: teaching the crafts of reading, writing and mathematics', in L. B. Resnick (ed.), *Knowing, Learning and Instruction: Essays in Honor of Robert Glaser*, Hillsdale, NJ, Erlbaum, pp. 453–94.

Greer, B. (1992) 'Multiplication and division as models of situations', in D. Grouws (ed.), *Handbook of Research on Mathematics Teaching and Learning*, New York, Macmillan.

Heckhausen, J. (1987) 'How do mothers know? Infants' chronological age or infants' performance as determinants of adaptation in maternal instruction?', *Journal of Experimental Child Psychology*, 43, pp. 212–26.

Kaput, J.J. (1992) 'Linking representations in the symbol systems of algebra', in D.A. Grouws (ed.), *Handbook of Research on Mathematics Teaching and Learning*, New York, Macmillan, pp. 167–294.

Pratt, H., Michalewski, H.J., Barrett, G. and Starr, A. (1989) 'Brain potentials in a memory-scanning task. I. Modality and task effects on potentials to the probes', *Electroencephalography and Clinical Neurophysiology*, 72, pp. 407–21.

Rogoff, B. (1986) 'Adult assistance of children's learning', in T.E. Raphael (ed.), *The Contexts of School-Based Literacy*, New York, Random House.

—— (1990) *Apprenticeship in Thinking: Cognitive Development in Social Context*, New York, Oxford University Press.

Rogoff, B. and Wertsch, J.V. (1984) *Children's Learning in the 'Zone of Proximal Development'*, San Francisco, Jossey-Bass.

Schauble, L. and Glaser, R. (1990) 'Scientific thinking in children and adults', in D. Kuhn (ed.), *Developmental Perspectives on Teaching and Learning Thinking Skills*, New York, Karger, pp. 9–27.

Shute, V.J. and Glaser, R. (1990) 'A large-scale evaluation of an intelligent discovery world: Smithtown', *Interactive Learning Environments*, 1, pp. 51–77.

Vygotsky, L.S. (1978) *Mind in Society: The Development of Higher Psychological Processes* (eds M. Cole, V. John-Steiner, S. Scribner, E. Souberman), Cambridge, MA, Harvard University Press.

Wood, D., Bruner, J.S. and Ross, G. (1976) 'The role of tutoring in problem solving', *Journal of Child Psychology and Psychiatry*, 17(2), pp. 89–100.

Wood, D.J., Wood, H.A. and Middleton, D.J. (1978) 'An experimental evaluation of four face-to-face teaching strategies', *International Journal of Behavioral Development*, 1, pp. 131–47.

Reflective questions

To the best of our knowledge, Vygotsky never attempted to extend his theorising to provide detailed analyses of educational curricula. What he did offer, however, was a novel perspective on the culturally sustained systems of signs and symbols that play a central role in *any* domain of knowledge and skill. These, on a Vygotskian perspective, provide the major vehicles whereby knowledge and skills may be preserved over time and reconstructed across the generations. They also provide one means for the creative extension and development of knowledge by each new generation.

Consider, for example, the systems of representation we use to think about, communicate with and to solve problems when we exploit the 'language' of arithmetic and mathematics. Call to mind the written and spoken symbols we use to represent numbers, and to refer to operations on and over numbers such as those acting as instructions to perform addition or subtraction, multiplication and division. Move on to consider the elaboration and extension of these sign systems to represent, think and communicate about situations calling for the use of algebra and calculus, elaborations that took centuries and many generations of mathematicians to invent, codify and symbolise. In all branches of knowledge, systems of representation, and the procedures and situations to which they are linked, offer learners the means to perform a wide range of relevant tasks, to communicate related ideas and to meet new challenges in the domains of knowledge to which they can be applied.

Such systems – whether they are spoken, sung, or played on a musical instrument, or are written, drawn, painted, cast diagrammatically, graphically, pictorially or in bronze – are visible, audible, perhaps tactile representations of knowledge and skills constructed and communicated from previous generations. They provide repositories of invitations, challenges, tasks, problems, practices, tools and procedures by which each new generation might come to re-construct knowledge in collaboration with those who already embody and act with that knowledge.

The intellectual grasp needed to master such systems, the situations they can provide for learning, tutoring and communicating are, of course, a major focus for schooling. The laying down of a curriculum for any subject area represents a theory about how a learner's journey through a domain of knowledge and skill should be planned and enacted.

Completed, Vygotsky's theoretical account would serve to marry principles of tutoring, such as those we have been considering, with well grounded and workable curriculum theory informed by an understanding of the pedagogy of systems of signs and symbols. But this is a tough undertaking. Yet the prospect of such a synthesis offers many exciting possibilities. From our point of view, one of the most exciting is the chance to integrate a theory of children's creativity in learning with the practices vital to the social re-construction of knowledge supported by tutoring. Because systems of signs – be they those involved in mathematics, or in writing down a language, or in music, science or the arts – have a creative and generative nature. Children do not – indeed they could not – have lessons in all they need to learn. Well chosen starting places endow them with the means to learn how to use for themselves systems of signs to represent, problematise, work with and through situations. They can be exploited to create and solve their own problems and to make their own discoveries. The creative, generative nature of systems of signs thus lets children teach themselves and, ultimately, allows them to achieve new insights as they move away from those who have taught them.

In trying to make some contribution towards the remote goal of synthesising such a theory of signs and the theory of tutoring, we have looked to the expertise provided by colleagues in other fields – such as literacy and mathematics – in order to collaborate on this quest.

By exploiting the now extensive evidence base derived from investigations of children's understanding of arithmetic and mathematics, we have tried to achieve an integration of tutoring theory with insights into children's mastery of sign systems in maths (e.g. Wood and Wood, 1999; Wood, 2001; Wood and Wood, 2006). By working with experts in the field of literacy, we have also started to see if and how our theory of contingent tutoring might be developed, with Marie Clay and her colleagues, to understand the interactions between tutoring processes and children learning to read in Reading Recovery[1] lessons (Wood, 2003).

One of the challenges and rewards arising out of the attempt to extend our analysis of contingent tutoring to teaching in Reading Recovery was the need to elaborate and apply in detail the nature of what we have termed domain contingency – i.e. planning the task, challenge and demand to place on the learner at a specific point given an assessment of their current level of reading competence. We also noted that instructional contingency provided the tutor with one source of formative, dynamic assessment. Before a child fully mastered a skill or competence, evidence of learning came from the teacher's observation that, as lessons proceeded, the learner needed less specific help to succeed. Eventually, the learner manages to meet the task demand alone and the tutor is freed to move on to new activities. Clay's analysis of the knowledge and skills involved in becoming literate, combined with the assessment practices she and her colleagues have designed to help the teacher to construct appropriate learning tasks, provides the means of planning individual lessons tailored to the needs of a given learner – in our terms, to try to meet the demands for domain contingency. A more recent metaphor, perhaps, is 'personalised learning'.

One outcome of the experience of working in such a rich domain, for us, was the realisation of a deeper and more concrete, specific and extensive understanding of why and how the demands of contingent tutoring can be so difficult to realise in literacy tutoring, resting as it must on considerable experience and skills in assessment, knowledge of the complexities of the reading process and lesson design. However, we were also heartened to find that our two lines of thinking showed considerable convergence and agreement about the very nature of effective tutorial practice.

The inner game of tutoring: can you imagine how you might act as a contingent tutor?

Think of a topic or subject that you feel you know well and take on some task or aspect of it that you suspect will cause significant challenges for learners. Imagine yourself trying to tutor a learner who is obviously experiencing difficulty. Can you construct hints at different levels of specificity to help solve the problem(s) they may face? Image how an interaction might unfold if, at first, your phantom learner does not understand what you suggest by way of help.

It might be useful to repeat this thought experiment in an area where you feel less confident in your own knowledge of the task to be learned. What might you learn from the imagined contrasts between the two types of tutorial encounter?

Time to help?

We have argued that effective tutoring relies not only on the construction of activities that are relevant and suitably challenging for the learner (domain contingency) and that it demands more than the provision of hints and help at an appropriate level (instructional contingency): good timing is also vital (temporal contingency). Leaving enough time for the learner to work out, for instance, the meaning and implications of a hint, or to figure out how to answer a question; spending enough time after they appear to have got things wrong to see if they actually know what they are doing when, perhaps, they will decide to backtrack or to self-correct; waiting long enough before intervening to find out if the learner knows enough about their own learning needs to decide for themselves that they need to ask for help. Our collaborations with Reading Recovery colleagues, our research into mathematics tutoring and our collaborations with colleagues in the field of 'wait time'[2] and learning have each served to underline the connections between instructional timing and the learning processes. We have found, for instance, that learners who take more time before they decide to seek help tend to achieve better learning outcomes than those who take little time. Better outcomes are also likely to be achieved by learners who avoid error and confusion by seeking help more readily when they are in trouble. These findings, which come from studies in which learners have to decide for themselves if and when they need help from a tutor, illustrate the need to leave enough time for learners to decide if they know when they need help in order to learn. What we are not yet clear about is the extent to which what looks like ineffective help-seeking activity (a sign of poor self-regulation?) stems from persistent individual differences (that is, some learners are just generally less self-aware in knowing when to seek help) or is a more local phenomenon that arises from the simple fact that a given learner might be more confused than others are in a particular situation. Work in this area of self-regulation and learning has become an important area of research (see Aleven *et al.*, 2003) and is one field in which progress in understanding of learning and tutoring in relation to learning skills (self-regulation) promises to move on apace.

Another thought experiment

Imagine a situation in which you are tutoring a learner in a domain or task that you know well. You are finding it hard to make progress with a learner. Why? What might lead you to decide that the difficulty stemmed from the choice of activity – which might be too far out of reach or too boring? What might lead you to conclude that you are finding it difficult to decide what kind of help or instruction to try? How would you test out the possibility that your pace of activity was too fast for the learner?

Notes

1   For those unfamiliar with this term, it refers to an extremely well founded, internationally practised approach to the early identification and tutoring of children at risk of becoming poor readers and writers (for the foundations of this work, see Clay, 1985, 1993).
2   Basically, this term refers to the amount of time a teacher leaves after, for example, addressing a question to a class. Typically, as in normal conversation, the pause tends to last for around 0.5 seconds or so. Helping teachers to extend this time up to 3 or more seconds can lead to more thoughtful and insightful replies from the class. The pioneering studies in this area were by Swift and Gooding (1983).

Further reading

Aleven, V., Stahl, E., Schworm, S., Fischer, F. and Wallacode, R. (2003) 'Help seeking and help design in interactive learning environments', *Review of Educational Research*, 73(3), pp. 277–320.

Clay, M.M. (1985) *The Early Detection of Reading Difficulties*, Auckland, NZ, Heinemann.

—— (1993) *Reading Recovery: A Guidebook for Teachers in Training*, Auckland, NZ, Heinemann.

Swift, J.N. and Gooding, C.T. (1983) 'Interaction of wait time, feedback and questioning instruction in middle school science teaching', *Journal of Research in Science Teaching*, 20, pp. 721–30.

Wood, D. (2003) 'The why? what? when? and how? of tutoring: the development of helping and tutoring skills in children', *Literacy Teaching and Learning*, 7(1/2), pp. 1–30.

—— (2001) 'Scaffolding, contingency and computer-supported learning', *International Journal of Artificial Intelligence in Education*, Special edition on Modelling human teaching tactics and strategies, 12(3), pp. 280–92.

Wood, D. and Wood, H. (2006) *Meet the Problem Solvers*, Sherston, Malmesbury, Wilts, Sherston Publishing Group.

Wood, H. and Wood, D. (1999) 'Help seeking, learning and contingent tutoring', *Computers and Education*, 33(2/3), pp. 153–69.

3.2 Becoming a teacher

A sociocultural analysis of initial teacher education

Anne Edwards

Introduction

Initial Teacher Education (ITE), in most countries, highlights the importance of practical experience in schools at the same time as valuing the place of higher education in teacher preparation. We therefore find a paradox, where models of practical training, which could be justified as learning through participation in established practices, are in close alignment with the idea that knowledge acquired in one setting can be applied in another. Attempts at riding this paradox have included a focus on reflection as a way of bridging the 'theory–practice gap' (Calderhead and Gates, 1993; Korthagen, 2004); invoking the university-led discourses of critical pedagogy or democracy to ensure that individual beginning teachers learn that teaching is more than becoming acculturated to local practices (Giroux, 1983; Smyth and Shacklock, 1998; Zeichner and Liston, 1996); and asserting the particular contributions to ITE to be made by higher education (Furlong and Smith, 1996). How has the conceptual muddle, which so tightly aligns a participatory approach to learning with an acquisition one, arisen? We need to locate its roots and examine its recent development, before looking at the implications for the learning experiences of beginning teachers and an alternative way of considering them.

Gaining university status for ITE over the latter part of the last century was a triumph both for the profession and for a view of knowledge about teaching as a commodity to be acquired and applied. However, over the last two decades or so in England, the freedom of professional action that its higher education status implied has been eroded and alongside that erosion has been a downplaying of the acquisition and application view of learning in ITE. This destabilising of higher education's warrant for involvement in ITE makes England a useful case study within which we can begin to see ways forward for early professional learning.

By the early 1980s all English courses for the education of beginning teachers included periods of school-based experience, while the higher education components necessary for a degree or postgraduate certificate were relatively idiosyncratic but tended to cover both the academic study of education and practical preparation for school-based work. The 1980s saw a gradual tightening of government control over the curricula offered by training programmes in England and Wales and in 1992 and 1993 government circulars (DfE, 1992, 1993) made training partnerships between schools and universities mandatory, with the expectation that student teachers would spend more time in schools and that schools would take the lead in those partnerships. As Furlong *et al.* (2000) explain, schools did not seize the opportunity to be leading partners and university departments ran training partnerships on bureaucratic lines. Nonetheless, these circulars and the various statutory guidelines that had preceded them ensured that the academic autonomy coupled with strong associations with professional bodies that have characterised other university-based routes to professional accreditation were not an option for intending teachers.

The 1990s saw English teacher education coming even more firmly under the grip of modernising governments which regarded existing forms of teacher education as the problem rather than the solution to improving standards in schools (Gilroy, 1998; Mortimore and Mortimore, 1998). The period witnessed the introduction of national standards for beginning teachers; regular inspections of ITE which directed funding for student places; and rigid guidance on the content of training programmes. Both schools and higher education departments of education became agents in strongly directed government education reform programmes. These programmes gave scant room for manoeuvre, requiring little more than bureaucratic links between schools and universities and ensuring that established and beginning teachers became adept at curriculum delivery. Compliance was the dominant mode of engagement for both schools and university departments of education. The programmes were a huge success (Edwards and Protheroe, 2003, 2004), with student teachers learning how to deliver curricula at the required pace.

In the process the intellectual role of university departments of education became less clear, as the pedagogic knowledge being applied in schools was found in policy documents produced by government. The value of the knowledge acquisition and application model as a rationale for university involvement in teacher education was seriously weakened. Indeed it now provides so fragile a rationale that those who still see the link between ITE and universities as a triumph are needing to rethink that relationship.

The case study of the English system has been given in some detail because it highlights the paradox of the alignment of two distinct beliefs about teaching and learning within one training experience; and it reveals quite starkly how the rationale offered for a university base for ITE could not withstand the policy onslaught, with the result that teacher education is at risk of loosing its professional ties with higher education. While the particular context of England and the vigorous focus of English governments on education is not completely replicated elsewhere, this analysis of partnerships does resonate more widely with concerns about ITE in the same period: in the US (Bullough and Kauchak, 1997); Australia (Chadbourne, 1995); and New Zealand (Openshaw, 1999).

The implications for the professional preparation of beginning teachers

There were excellent training partnerships in place in England prior to the 1992 and 1993 circulars (Benton, 1990). They had developed carefully over time to ensure a common purpose; a shared understanding of the practices of teacher education; and the roles of each participant in the training programmes. The imperatives of the two circulars, however, meant that new partnerships, if not entirely shotgun arrangements, were certainly constrained by government expectations and short time-scales so that partnerships often lacked the careful interweaving of purposes and practices which characterised the earlier versions.

There were considerable implications for the preparation of beginning teachers in these new partnerships. In our early research on the experiences of student teachers and their mentors in primary schools (Edwards and Collison, 1995, 1996; Edwards, 1997) we found that student teachers were frequently isolated or 'desert-islanded' in schools, working mainly with their allocated mentors; classrooms were not seen as places where adults were legitimate learners; and student teachers were the pivotal connection between school and university with all the personal stress that this role implied. The stressful isolation of student teachers in primary schools was also evident in contemporary studies of secondary school training experiences (Head *et al.*, 1996).

There have been changes. Many schools are now embracing teacher education enthusiastically. Mutton and his colleagues found that schools were increasingly working with more than one university with some working with more than four (Mutton and Butcher, in press). Among the 60 schools which responded to their survey were secondary schools which offered 30, 38 and 47 placements. Schools dealt with the potential complexity by having increasingly tenuous links with the universities which provided the core courses and instead developed their own tailored courses which played to the strengths of each school and which were offered to all student teachers regardless of their university. The problem, of course, was that within-school consistency was at the expense of within-programme consistency when this occurred (Edwards and Mutton, 2007), with new forms of tension for beginning teachers.

The developing identity of beginning teachers

As Furlong has observed, in England the government Department for Education and Skills (DfES) and university-based teacher educators have different aims for teacher education (Furlong, 2002). The DfES, he notes, wants a modern labour force with flexible working practices responsive to changing national priorities; while teacher educators want autonomous professionals with their own expert knowledge and values able to make their own independent judgements. The rich strand of work on the identity of beginning teachers that has emerged over the last thirty years (Carter and Doyle, 1996; Darling-Hammond and Sclan, 1996; Knowles, 1993; Korthagen, 2004) reflects, in part, the need to attend carefully to the nature and purposes of teacher identity in the context of increasing government control over the teaching profession in different parts of the world.

The new and changing landscape of teacher education outlined so far makes huge demands on individual student teachers. As well as learning to teach alone in public, where small slips can lead to breakdown in the precariously balanced social practices of classrooms (Doyle, 1986; Edwards and Protheroe, 2003, 2004), student teachers do most of the boundary crossing between school and university and therefore are the primary mediators of their own learning as they try to make connections between these two sites and their actions within them. That it is commonplace for student teachers to judge their university courses as irrelevant to what they are meeting in schools is hardly surprising: they are often getting little or no help with making these connections (Boag-Munroe, 2007).

What kinds of teacher identities are therefore being produced? The demands of public teaching and individual boundary crossing, together with the emphasis on attention to national curricular policies, have led to an understandable but regrettable propensity for caution and avoidance of complexity among English student teachers in order to protect their vulnerable embryonic teacher identities (Desforges, 1995; Edwards and Protheroe, 2003, 2004). This propensity is unfortunate because unless student teachers learn to recognise complexity, for example why a teenage carer is not able to concentrate, or why some children cannot easily understand how to translate fractions to decimals, they are not going to learn how to teach. That is, they are not going to be able to reposition themselves in relation to a more complex reading of a problem of practice and seek ways of responding to it. As a result they remain efficient deliverers of a curriculum but do not learn to become responsive teachers of children.

The erosion of the special place in ITE that English universities used to claim means that it is timely that we examine the structure and purposes of initial training. In doing so we need to maintain a focus on the identities of student teachers in order to understand how they negotiate the worlds of school and university; interpret the problems of practice in ways which might allow them to seek out complexity and thereby learn; and draw on the resources available to help them to respond to that complexity. The last point is particularly important as I shall be suggesting that teacher educators' aspiration to produce the autonomous decision-maker may need some re-working.

The analytic lens I am bringing to this examination is sociocultural theory augmented by activity theory (Engeström, 1999). Both approaches are based on the ideas of Vygotsky, who worked in Moscow in the late 1920s and early 30s to develop a pedagogical psychology which would enable people to understand their worlds and to act on them and shape them for the better. Understanding and acting on was described by Vygotsky as the processes of internalisation and externalisation: i.e. we take on the ideas and practices that matter in our worlds and use them to act on and shape those worlds. Vygotsky's legacy has been constantly reworked to now allow, for example, a combined focus on individuals and the systems or activities they inhabit (Cole, 1996); the dynamics that drive both individual and systemic learning (Engeström, 1999); and a rethinking of the problem of transfer which lies at the heart of an acquisition and application rationale for current versions of teacher education (Beach, 1999; Greeno, 2006).

The problem of transfer

As so many writers have pointed out (Beach, 1999; Bereiter, 2002; Greeno, 1997, 2006; Hager, 2004; Lobato, 2006; Tuomi-Gröhn and Engeström, 2003) the idea that knowledge acquired in one setting can be applied in another is simplistic, probably only having currency because it is part of collective common-sense having formed the basis of schooling for so long. Solutions to the problem of transfer do, however, vary. For example, Greeno's sociocultural analysis proposes, among other things, that transfer is helped by the existence of common or recognisable patterns of participation in the various sites experienced by the individual; while Tuomi-Gröhn and Engeström, taking the activity theory view of learning as a collective activity, see it as the proliferation of collective practices across sites. Beach's notion of 'consequential transitions' is perhaps the most helpful when considering ITE and the complementary roles of schools and universities.

One of Beach's starting points is that transfer cannot be explained away by locating knowledge in the head of the individual who moves between settings, neither can it simply be off-loaded onto the design of learning contexts. Beach's sociocultural approach to transfer recognises the interweaving of mind and context over time, and that we are propelled forward by what matters to us. In other words, we mindfully navigate different settings and shape and are shaped by them. He explains:

> Any sociocultural reconceptualization of transfer should be true to the premise that underlies all sociocultural approaches to learning and development: that learners and social organizations exist in a recursive and mutually constitutive relation to one another across time.
>
> (Beach, 1999, p. 111)

For Beach, transfer or continuity and transformation across time and place is an outcome of the relation between person and situation. Learning involves a changing relation between individuals and situations which is driven by the intentions of the individual for whom the change has consequences. Beach's examples of what he terms 'consequential transitions' include a college student becoming a teacher, becoming a parent or writing to a newspaper for the first time. These transitions are 'consequential for the individual', 'developmental in nature' and 'located in the changing relations between individuals and social activities' (Beach, 1999).

Transitions involve the 'reconstruction' of new knowledge and skills as people move across space and time, rather than 'reproduction'; and they often involve a change in identity (Beach, 2001). Let's look at each of these changes in turn and consider what they mean for ITE partnerships. Beach's examples of reconstruction of knowledge include the Nepalese high school students who adapted their school maths to the maths used by the shopkeepers to whom they were apprenticed. They intended to become shopkeepers and therefore needed to adapt to the practices of the market place. We can see student teachers doing the same when they find themselves conforming to the practices of the schools in which they are placed rather than applying the models of, for example, behaviour management that are offered in university courses. They want to become teachers and in school they see what teachers do, their own agentic intentions tell them that they should work with those practices and not against them. In their identity formation as beginning teachers they aim at being 'encompassed' (Beach, 1999) by the relatively stable practices of the schools in which they are placed.

The consequential transitions of student teachers as they move from university to school, where practices are geared at keeping order, are therefore characterised by the caution and identity protection that was discussed earlier, rather than by a seeking of the complexity that might lead to learning. Beach recognises the problem. His answer (Beach, 2001) is that we should think of differences between, for example, school and work as opportunities for learning rather than as 'boundaries to transfer across'. We should not be simply aiming at making patterns of participation in different settings as similar as possible. Rather we should see the processes of 'reconstruction' and the consequential transitions of which they are part as 'important pedagogical opportunities'. In ITE it means that there is an intervention or mediating role to be played which lifts the burden of self-mediation from the shoulders of the boundary-crossing student teachers.

Let us speculate a little further on that role in ITE and its implications. Helping student teachers to become metacognitively aware of the practices to which they are adapting and how they negotiate them in order to accomplish the tasks of teaching has a great deal to commend it. It would allow teacher education to meet both governments' needs for flexible workforces and teacher educators' hope that teachers will become informed decision-makers. But how might that mediation occur?

One example is the DETAIL project led by Ellis at Oxford (Ellis, in press). Ellis has been working with one English specialist teacher mentor from each of four different schools. Each mentor in turn works with four English specialist interns (student teachers) who are placed with the mentor. All four teachers and sixteen interns, with Ellis, work together to use the tools of activity theory to try to understand the settings and practices in which they provide learning opportunities for school pupils. Activity theory comes into play as they identify (a) the problem of practice to be worked on and changed; (b) what they think has shaped their existing practices and what they might need to do in their schools to make their new practices feasible; (c) what new ideas about teaching and learning are arising from their fresh ways of working; and (d) how these ideas connect to other research in the area of teaching English. Ellis's role is a mediating one; he is a resource for the mentors and for the interns, and all the participants, including Ellis, are learning.

DETAIL is more than a matter of mentors modelling inquiring teaching. It requires mentors and interns to make their thinking and reconstruction of practices and research-based knowledge visible and open to scrutiny and, importantly, it requires attention to the within-school practices that shape how problems of practice are both interpreted and responded to. Teachers and interns are required to seek complexity, reposition themselves in relation to their new readings of an aspect of practice and then draw on a range of resources, including each other, to respond to those interpretations. DETAIL is therefore true to the Vygotskian and Marxist legacies to activity theory: that the scientific constructs of psychology should be used to help people to work on their world to understand it better and to shape it. DETAIL also offers one example of how a 'third space' (Gutiérrez *et al.*, 1999) between school and university, like a collaborative research and development project, can provide the opportunity for 'important pedagogical opportunities' for both mentors and interns. These opportunities do not only involve re-cognising practices and being aware of how they are navigated, they also involve acknowledging that sometimes new interpretations of practical problems call for changes in established practices and the rules that sustain them. As Beach has reminded us, a sociocultural view of learning cannot disentangle individuals from the organisations or settings in which they act.

Is a sociocultural approach the way forward for ITE?

From what I have suggested so far, the answer would seem to be, yes, it is. However, much depends on how a sociocultural approach to learning is understood and what implications for the design of ITE are drawn. There have been several attempts to make a case for a sociocultural framing of ITE. In 1995, for example, I drew on the Vygotskian ideas of learning as a gradual internalisation of collective understandings and a subsequent externalisation of those personal understandings in action, to map how universities and schools might work together to support the learning of student teachers. The analysis called for more attention to the interactive support that mentors offered student teachers while they were in school than was happening at the time (Edwards, 1995), and a recognition of what students teachers might offer schools. In discussions of ITE in the USA particularly, sociocultural understandings of mindful action have often become intertwined with accounts of situated cognition where knowledge is seen as a resource which is located or situated within specific settings and their practices.

In 2000 Putnam and Borko discussed what they termed the 'situative perspective' in ITE in the USA, saying that they had based their discussion on the defence of 'situated learning' as framework for understanding human cognition made by Greeno in 1997. They took, however, a relatively narrow line on situated cognition, saying for example that 'the situative perspective holds that all knowledge is (by definition) situated'. The important question therefore is 'in what contexts they are situated'. This analysis led them to suggest that more attention should be paid to the places where student teachers learn to 'think, talk, and act as a teacher'. Putnam and Borko were, however, concerned that some schools were not offering good models for beginning teachers; for example, they may offer restricted 'mini-discourses'. Perhaps more attention should therefore be paid to placing training in professional development schools which have strong ties with universities and are places where new practices can be developed.

Putman and Borko's reading of situated cognition, as knowledge located in settings and accessed through participation in those settings, is commonly made, in part because early understandings of situated cognition were developed by anthropologists who were fascinated by the way in which knowledge was embedded in rituals and artefacts within traditional communities (Lave, 1988; Scribner and Tobach, 1997). However, their reading connects only tangentially with the more complex points that had been made by Greeno in 1997 when he discussed situated cognition.

Greeno's arguments were more closely aligned to those of Beach with a focus on how people acted intentionally in different settings. The core of Greeno's case was (a) that 'people learn adaptively in situations where they engage in activities' and teaching in schools needs to acknowledge this; (b) in order to understand what people know we need to look at their knowing in a range of situations and see how they interact with those situations; (c) a focus on knowing allows us to think of a 'generality of knowing' rather than a 'transfer of knowledge'; (d) a generality of knowing involves the learner in being attuned to the constraints and opportunities for action in a setting so that they can take action within it; (e) attuning will involve the use of abstract representations that people carry with them from setting to setting, i.e. situated learning is not context specific and dependent only on the knowledge embedded in that context; and (f) individual cognition and behaviour can be explained 'in terms of their contributions to interactive systems'.

It is worth spelling out Greeno's somewhat complex argument for two reasons. First, it allows us to see how much it echoes Beach's view of learning as an active transaction between individual and context and Vygotsky's emphasis on the processes of both internalisation and externalisation in the processes of learning. Second, it should dispel any idea that a recognition of learning as situated is simply a matter of becoming acculturated into existing practices. It is premised on the expectation that learners move between settings and need to learn how to navigate them and reformulate their prior understandings so that they can act knowledgeably within different settings.

Relating Greeno's analyses to ITE, Edwards *et al.* (2002) argued that they called for an understanding of mind which was very different from the filing cabinet model of effective storage that provided the rationale for an acquisition and application notion of ITE. We suggested that teacher educators should move from a focus on developing minds that were good at encoding and storing knowledge to include an additional focus on developing a capacity to decode the sites of action. That is, student teachers need to be able to read and interpret situations in order to be able to act knowledgeably within them and should also develop a disposition to do so.

We compared what we described as an encoding information-processing model of mind with a more outward-looking decoding connectionist model. The decoding mind, we argued, was a mechanism for 'interpreting the potential for action in an environment' and was 'primed to look for familiar patterns when it moves to a new environment and tries to interpret it'. One of the challenges for teacher educators, as we saw it, was to help learners interpret and respond to new experiences in ways that encouraged them to see the complexity in them. Though we did not draw on activity theory in that suggestion, we were encouraging teacher mentors to help student teachers to expand the 'object of activity' (Engeström, 1999) that they were working on; and to respond with help from their mentors to their expanded interpretations.

Recently van Huizen *et al.* (2005) turned more directly to the work of Vygotsky to consider how student teachers develop as professionals, and highlighted the importance of professional values to the development of teacher identity. Their starting point is, like Beach's, that a Vygotskian perspective 'concentrates on the connections between individual functioning and development *and* the sociocultural practices in which individuals take part' (p. 271). Referring to A.N. Leont'ev, a close colleague of Vygotsky in Moscow in the late 1920s, they point to a particularly Russian stand on personality and identity, seeing it as a process of involvement with public cultural meanings which, in the process of working with them, people transform into personal sense. This distinction and dialectic between collective meaning and personal sense-making is central to understanding learning from a Vygotskian viewpoint. It lies behind his emphasis on internalisation and externalisation, or our both being shaped by and shaping our worlds. Echoing the emphasis placed on intentionality by both Beach and Greeno, van Huizen and his colleagues argue that the 'assignment of meaning to teaching' as part of what is needed by society is central to the development of professional identity.

Their analysis, like that offered here, starts with the meanings to be found at the societal level and how these are mediated within teacher education environments. Like Ellis in his DETAIL project, they suggest that student teachers should be placed in a variety of roles as learners, researchers and teachers to explore possible meanings; and, like Beach and Greeno, they see each individual teacher as ultimately responsible for their own sense-making. Their paper concludes with an outline of professional preparation as a process of 'guided development of professional identity'. The analysis is particularly useful because it places ITE as part of a process of people-making which connects with Northern European notions of *Bildung* or responsible personal development and contribution to society.

Developing expert practitioners

As we have seen, developing a responsible professional identity, from a sociocultural perspective, also involves being able to knowledgeably navigate the terrain of schooling. Holland and her colleagues help us to see this navigation as knowing how to act within what they describe as the 'figured worlds' or implicitly understood social practices of specific settings (Holland *et al.*, 1998). They don't look at schools, but their analyses of the social practices and implicit rules of a range of social environments alert us to the ways that practices and expectations in schools can restrict certain responses while encouraging others; and that not only do schools differ but the figured worlds of departments within the same school can vary. For example, in some departments student teachers may be expected to contribute to planning discussions, while in others they receive the plans that were drawn up elsewhere and are expected to implement them efficiently. Being able to navigate these practices and mould one's identity to them is a part of becoming a teacher.

But there is more to becoming an expert teacher than the cautious negotiation of existing local practices. In abandoning the idea of knowledge as something that is stored and applied, the sociocultural approach to ITE may also appear to have relinquished a major warrant for teachers' expertise: subject knowledge and its delivery through the curriculum. That is not the intention. However, most subject knowledge is now so complex that much of it is off-loaded on to artefacts or is distributed among groups of teachers who have specialist areas of expertise (Childs and McNicholl, 2007). Becoming a teacher now involves becoming resourceful: good at knowing how one's own subject knowledge can be augmented by artefacts or working with colleagues. Resourceful practice is, therefore, perhaps a better way of looking at expertise in schools, than the idea of the all-knowing pedagogue who is mistress of all aspects of her subject.

Teachers' expertise could perhaps be summarised as *knowing what* needs to be taught, i.e. curriculum content; *knowing when* to teach it, i.e. in what sequence and possibly to what age group; and *knowing how* to teach it, i.e. what Shulman referred to as 'pedagogic content knowledge' (Shulman, 1987). A sociocultural perspective on expertise adds a fourth kind of knowing: *knowing who* can augment one's practice. The 'who' may be another colleague in the science department with a different subject specialism; an ICT resource;

pupils' knowledge of the neighbourhood or use of the web. Teaching can therefore be seen as 'resourceful practice' (Edwards, 2005) in which teachers recognise how others can help them expand the problems of practice and also help them respond to those expanded understandings.

This view of expertise therefore does not place expertise solely within the mind of the practitioner, though it does recognise that being an expert practitioner involves some knowing what, when and how. It suggests that expertise crucially involves reading the figured worlds of classrooms, departments and schools; understanding the pedagogic tasks as part of those worlds; and knowing how to use the resources available to work on those tasks. This analysis connects closely with Beach's idea of learning through examining the differences that people observe when they move from setting to setting: if student teachers have difficulty in reading a classroom, the difficulties become an opportunity for analysing the difficulty, the resources available and how they can be used.

The emphasis on analyses and resourceful practice is important. Engeström and Middleton (1996), for example, describe an activity theory perspective on expertise as the 'collaborative and discursive construction of tasks, solutions, visions, breakdowns and innovations' within and across systems (p. 4) rather than as individual mastery of specific areas of relatively stable activity. Their description of expertise acknowledges the complexity of ever-changing knowledge bases and, when applied to teaching, relieves teachers of the burden of classroom omniscience, which, as I've already indicated, can lead to student teachers filtering out complexity. At the same time their description calls for an expanded notion of professional autonomy. The autonomous practitioner is not the isolated performer engaged in efficient curriculum delivery. Rather, she is located within a network of expertise located within and beyond the school, which she draws on and contributes to in her practice. Such a practitioner is also likely to be the kind of flexible worker who Furlong (2002) noted was what governments required, but a worker who is expert in unpicking pedagogic complexity with others and able to work with others to respond to the problems of practice to take forward children as learners.

The sociocultural view of becoming a teacher that I have presented here recognises that action is mindful and not simply a matter of being swept along by the established social practices of a school or department. Neither is it just a convenient way out of the conceptual muddle outlined at the start of this chapter. Rather it allows us to see teaching as a process of informed decision-making in complex situations and to argue for ITE programmes which prepare teachers to read that complexity and to know how to respond resourcefully to it.

References

Beach, K. (1999) 'Consequential transitions: a sociocultural expedition beyond transfer in education', *Review of Research in Education*, 24, pp. 101–39.

—— (2001) 'Transitions between school and work: some new understandings and questions about adult mathematics', in M. Schmitt and K. Safford-Ramus (eds), *Adults Learning Mathematics-7: A Conversation between Researchers and Practitioners,* International Conference of Adults Learning Mathematics. Downloaded from ERIC 13 May 2007.

Benton, P. (1990) *The Oxford Internship Scheme*, London, Calouste Gulbenkian Foundation.

Bereiter, C. (2002) *Education and Mind in the Knowledge Age*, Mahwah NJ, Lawrence Erlbaum Associates.

Boag-Munroe, G. (2007) A Commerce of the Old and New: How Classroom Teacher Mentors Work in Multiple Activities, unpublished PhD Thesis, University of Birmingham.

Bullough, R. and Kauchak, D. (1997) 'Partnerships between higher education and schools: some problems', *Journal of Education for Teaching,* 23(3), pp. 215–33.

Calderhead, J. and Gates, P. (eds) (1993) *Conceptualising Reflection in Teacher Education*, London, Falmer.

Carter, K. and Doyle, W. (1996) 'Personal narrative and life history', in J. Sikula (ed.), *Handbook of Research on Teacher Education*, New York, Macmillan.

Chadbourne, R. (1995) 'Student reluctance to take up school-based teacher education: one university's experience', *Journal of Education for Teaching*, 21(2), pp. 219–26.

Childs, A. and McNicholl, J. (2007) 'Science teachers teaching outside of subject specialism: challenges, strategies adopted and implications for initial teacher education', *Teacher Development*, 1(1), pp. 1–20.

Cole, M. (1996) *Cultural Psychology*, Cambridge MA, Harvard University Press.

Darling-Hammond, L. and Sclan, E. (1996) 'Who teaches and why: dilemmas of building a profession for twenty-first century schools', in J. Sikula (ed.), *Handbook of Research on Teacher Education*, New York, Macmillan.

Desforges, C. (1995) 'How does experience affect theoretical knowledge for teaching?', *Learning and Instruction*, 5(4), pp. 385–400.

DfE (1992) *Initial Teacher Training: secondary phase – Circular 9/92*, London, Department for Education.

—— (1993) *The Initial Training of Primary School Teachers: new criteria for courses – Circular 14/93*, London, Department for Education.

Doyle, W. (1986) 'Classroom organization and management', in M.C. Wittrock (ed.), *Handbook of Research on Teaching*, New York, Macmillan.

Edwards, A. (1995) 'Teacher education: partnerships in pedagogy?', *Teaching and Teacher Education*, 11(6), pp. 265–79.

—— (1997) 'Guests bearing gifts: the position of student teachers in primary school classrooms', *British Educational Research Journal*, 23(1), pp. 27–37.

—— (2005) 'Relational agency: learning to be a resourceful practitioner', *International Journal of Educational Research*, 43, pp. 168–82.

Edwards, A. and Collison, J. (1995) 'What do teacher mentors tell student teachers about pupil learning in primary schools?', *Teachers and Teaching; Theory and Practice*, 1(2), pp. 265–79.

—— (1996) *Mentoring and Developing Practice in Primary School*, Buckingham, Open University Press.

Edwards, A. and Mutton, T. (2007) 'Looking forward: rethinking professional learning through partnership arrangements in initial teacher education', *Oxford Review of Education*, 33(4), pp. 503–19.

Edwards, A. and Protheroe, L. (2003) 'Learning to see in classrooms: what are student teachers learning about teaching and learning while learning to teach in schools?', *British Educational Research Journal*, 29(2), pp. 227–42.

—— (2004) 'Teaching by proxy: understanding how mentors are positioned in partnerships', *Oxford Review of Education*, 30(2), pp. 183–97.

Edwards, A., Gilroy, P. and Hartley, D. (2002) *Rethinking Teacher Education: Collaborative Responses to Uncertainty*, London, Falmer.

Ellis, V. (in press) 'More than soldiering on: realizing the potential of teacher education to rethink English in schools', in V. Ellis, C. Fox and B. Street (eds), *Rethinking English in Schools: A New Constructive Stage*, London, Continuum. See also www.edstud.ox.ac.uk/research/detail

Engeström, Y. (1999) 'Activity theory and individual and social transformation', in Y. Engeström, R. Miettinen and R.-L. Punamäki (eds). *Perspectives on Activity Theory*, Cambridge, Cambridge University Press.

Engeström, Y. and Middleton, D. (eds) (1996) *Cognition and Communication at Work*, Cambridge, Cambridge University Press.

Furlong, J. (2002) 'Ideology and reform in teacher education in England', *Educational Researcher*, 31(6), pp. 23–5.

Furlong, J., Barton, L., Miles, S., Whiting, C. and Whitty, G. (2000) *Teacher Education in Transition – Reforming Professionalism?*, Buckingham, Open University Press.

Furlong, J. and Smith, R.D. (eds) (1996) *The Role of Higher Education in Initial Teacher Training*, London, Kogan Page.

Gilroy, P. (1998) 'New Labour and teacher education in England: the first 500 days', *Journal of Education for Teaching*, 24 (3), pp. 221–230.

Giroux, H. (1983) *Teachers as Intellectuals: Towards a Critical Pedagogy of Learning*, Westport CT, Praeger-Greenwood.

Greeno, J. (1997) 'On claims that answer the wrong questions', *Educational Researcher*, 26(1), pp. 5–17.

—— (2006) 'Authoritative, accountable positioning and connected general knowing; progressive themes in understanding transfer', *Journal of the Learning Sciences*, 15(4), pp. 537–47.

Gutiérrez, K., Baquedano-López, P., Alvarez, H.H, and Chiu, M. M. (1999) 'Building a culture of collaboration through hybrid language practices', *Theory into Practice*, 38(2), pp. 87–93.

Hager, P. (2004) 'Conceptions of learning and understanding at work', *Studies in Continuing Education*, 26(1), pp. 3–17.

Head, J., Hill, F. and Maguire, M. (1996) 'Stress and the post-graduate secondary school trainee: a British case study', *Journal of Education for Teaching*, 22(1), pp. 71–84.

Holland, D., Skinner, D., Lachicotte, W. and Cain, C. (1998) *Identity and Agency in Cultural Worlds*, Cambridge, MA, Harvard University Press.

Knowles, J.G. (1993) 'Life-history accounts as mirrors: a practical avenue for the conceptualization of reflection in teacher education', in J. Calderhead and P. Gates (eds), *Conceptualizing Reflection in Teacher Education*, London, Falmer.

Korthagen, F. (2004) 'In search of the essence of a good teacher: towards a more holistic approach in teacher education', *Teaching and Teacher Education*, 20(1), pp. 77–97.

Lave, J. (1988) *Cognition in Practice: Mind, Mathematics and Culture in Everyday Life*, Cambridge, Cambridge University Press.

Lobato, J. (2006) 'Alternative perspectives on the transfer of learning: history, issues, and challenges for future research', *Journal of the Learning Sciences*, 15(4), pp. 431–49.

Mortimore, P. and Mortimore, J. (1998) 'The political and professional in education: an unnecessary conflict?', *Journal of Education for Teaching*, 24(3), pp. 205–19.

Mutton, T. and Butcher, J. (in press) 'More than managing? The role of the ITT coordinator in schools in England', *Teacher Development*.

Openshaw, R. (1999) 'Forward to the past in New Zealand teacher education', *Journal of Education for Teaching*, 25(2), pp. 111–22.

Putnam, R. and Borko, H. (2000) 'What do new views of knowledge and thinking have to say about research on teacher learning?', *Educational Researcher*, 29, pp. 4–15.

Scribner, S. and Tobach, E. (1997) *Mind and Social Practice: Selected Writings by Sylvia Scribner*, Cambridge, Cambridge University Press.

Shulman, L. (1987) 'Knowledge and the foundations of the new reform', *Harvard Educational Review*, 57, pp. 1–21.

Smyth, J. and Shacklock, G. (1998) *Re-Making Teaching: Ideology, Politics and Practice*, London, Routledge.

Tuomi-Gröhn, T. and Engeström, Y. (eds) (2003) *Between School and Work: New Perspectives on Transfer and Boundary Crossing*, Oxford, Pergamon.

van Huizen, P, van Oers, B. and Wubbels, T. (2005) 'A Vygotskian perspective on teacher education', *Journal of Curriculum Studies*, 37(3), pp. 267–90.

Zeichner, K. and Liston, D. (1996) *Reflective Teaching: An Introduction*, Mahwah, NJ, Lawrence Erlbaum Associates.

Reflective questions

1   Identify two settings which you move between and where you are expected to draw on the knowledge developed in one to inform your actions in another. To what extent do the ideas of 'transition' rather than 'transfer'; 'the knowledgeable navigation of a terrain'; and 'figured worlds' of social practices reflect what happens in the second setting?

2   Beach suggests that we should look for what is consequential for people when they make the transition from one setting to another. What do you think is consequential for beginning teachers and how does that seem to impact on how they deal with complexity? If you are learning to teach, how does your analysis reflect your own experience?

3   Is there a case for a university element in ITE? If so, what is it?

Further reading

The publications by Beach and Greeno together with Edwards *et al.* (2002), which are all listed in the references, expand the arguments presented here.

Among writing not referenced the following pursue similar themes:

Roth, W.-M. and Tobin, K. (2004) 'Co-teaching: from praxis to theory', *Teachers and Teaching: Theory and Practice*, 10(2), pp. 161–80.

Sfard, A. and Prusak, A. (2005) 'Telling identities: in search of an analytic tool for investigating learning as a culturally shaped activity', *Educational Researcher*, 34(4), pp. 14–22.

Wilson, E. (2005) 'Powerful pedagogical strategies in initial teacher education', *Teachers and Teaching: Theory and Practice*, 11(4), pp. 359–78.

3.3 Teaching as an affective practice

Chris James

Introduction

Schools and colleges are places where strong feelings are continually sensed and shown. They are locales of considerable affective intensity (James, 1999). All good teachers experience powerful feelings as part of their work and they also need to recognise, understand and engage their feelings if they are to be successful (Hargreaves, 1998; James and Connolly, 2000; Day, 2004). Teaching is therefore an affective practice and the intention of this chapter is to explore it from that standpoint.

The chapter starts by discussing the relationship between affects and other mental processes, the notion of affect, and why schools are places where feelings run high. In the sections that follow, there is a discussion of the ways in which the affective experience of work in schools can be considered. The chapter then explores the consequences of the affective nature of work in schools and some of the implications for educational organising and change; individual and organisational defences against the negative affective aspects of educational work; and the importance of affective containment.

Starting points

Affect, cognition and conation

The relationship between thinking (cognition) and feeling (affect) has long fascinated Western philosophers, from as far back as Aristotle through to St Augustine, Descartes, Pascal, and Kant (Forgas, 2000; Oatley and Jenkins, 1996). During the Enlightenment in the eighteenth century, this interest broadened. Mental life was distinguished into three distinct and complementary domains, the so-called 'trilogy of the mind' (Hilgard, 1980): affect, cognition and conation, which are those psychological processes that tend towards activity or change.

The distinction between affect, cognition and conation was a feature of much of twentieth century psychology arguably under the domination of behaviourism, which focuses on a simplistic view of conation as goal-oriented action, and cognitivism, which has sought to separate thinking from affect. To a large extent, those distinctions still persist. Affect, cognition, and conation are often still viewed as fundamentally distinct and importantly the significance of feelings has been underplayed. Individual and collective thinking and action were 'de-emotionalised' (Fineman, 1993), perhaps because feelings were thought to get in the way (Etzioni, 1988; Argyris, 1990), and there was generally little interest in feelings in organisations.

Only relatively recently has it become clear that in everyday life thinking, feeling and action are inextricably intertwined and the importance of affect been recognised. Many would argue, see for example Forgas (2000), that affects are as significant rationales for, and outcomes of, actions as are cognitions, if not more so. So, although there may be a cognitive rationale for actions, there will also be an underlying and possibly stronger affective rationale. We are moved to act by our feelings (Gabriel, 1999) and we are also moved to think by our feelings. In addition, the significant interconnection between the unconscious parts of the psyche and conscious feeling, thought and action are also now more widely acknowledged.

Feelings, emotions and moods

Affects are the particular mental states we experience and include feelings, emotions and moods (Forgas, 2000). Distinguishing between those three states is problematic, and differentiating between feelings and emotions is particularly so. Fineman (2003) takes the view that feelings are what we experience while emotions are feelings that are shown. Emotions are thus the physical manifestations of feelings, such as facial expressions that are apparent to others (Oatley and Jenkins, 1996). It has to be said that some authors, for example Niendenthal *et al.* (2006), do not distinguish between feelings and emotions in this way and use the term 'emotion' to describe both feelings (the experience) and emotions (the apparent expression).

The nature of feelings raises important ontological questions which are concerned with 'the very essence of the phenomena under investigation' (Burrell and Morgan, 1979, p. 1). Feelings are subjective phenomena, a notion which may be difficult to acknowledge because they are so often socially embedded as familiar, intrinsic and expected parts of interactions with others. Even so, feelings are substantively different from other objects, such as hospitals, the sky or children, which we generally accept do really exist in our external world. Feelings do not exist in that way. Only when feelings are shown as emotions do they become apparent to others as objects – a notion which raises important epistemological issues (How do we understand and communicate knowledge about feelings?) and methodological concerns (How do we study feelings?).

One additional complication with distinguishing between feeling as experience and emotion as apparent expression is that not all feelings are experienced consciously and not all feelings are made apparent as emotions consciously. Feelings may be projected unconsciously to others who may 'take them in' or introject them. The recipients of projected feelings may experience them, consciously or unconsciously, a process known as transference. They may even begin to identify with them, through a process called projective identification. Those who have projected the feelings may themselves behave towards the object on the basis of those projected feelings. The experience of transference may cause an individual to start acting on the basis of the projected feelings they have introjected. This process is called counter-transference.

Generally emotions and moods are distinguished on the basis that emotions are temporary and intense and usually have an identifiable cause and clear content such as sadness or disgust. Moods on the other hand are low intensity, diffuse and persistent feelings that often have no identifiable rationale and little cognitive content. They may or may not be apparent to others (Forgas, 2000; Fineman, 2003).

There is a wide range of names for feelings – shame, contempt, sadness, pleasure – and feelings can be made apparent in an enormous variety of ways. Arguably, anxiety is a particularly significant feeling. First, it is a primitive response to a threat. It has a deep evolutionary origin in human ancestry as Darwin first pointed out in the nineteenth century (Darwin, 1872). Second, anxiety calls up a whole range of sometimes powerful physiological responses many of which are reflexes and not under conscious control. These so-called fight or flight reflexes are largely protective and gear the body up for an appropriate response to the threat – to fight it or to run away. Third, anxiety is often associated with other feelings, or the prospect of those feelings. This association may not only be with unpleasant feelings. Anxiety may also accompany positive feelings, for example, an anxiety that a feeling of happiness may not last, in addition to the anxiety that results from a specific threat. The fact is, although we may not notice, anxiety is likely to be ever present (Obholzer, 1994). Without it we would lack an important aspect of our motivation, although of course, with too much of it we may freeze and be unable to act at all.

Schools and colleges as locales for high levels of affect

For a variety of reasons, schools and colleges are particular locales for high levels of affect (James, 1999; James and Connolly, 2000). Any teacher will probably say that schools are places where almost all feelings can be experienced. Learning is inextricably associated with change, which is always associated with feelings of some kind (see below). It is also linked with risk and uncertainty and therefore possibly anxiety and excitement, as is the process of teaching. Educational relationships with pupils, parents and close working colleagues have a powerful affective aspect. Changes in the expectations on teachers resulting from changes in policy or management, dynamic models of professional working such as reflective practice, and curriculum changes, all increase the affective intensity of work in schools. One important reason for this high level of feelings in schools is the centrality of educational institutions as organisations with a foundational social purpose. Schools and colleges are important institutions that are concerned with processes that are central to people's lives such as maturation into adulthood and the preparation for adult life. They are places where skills and capabilities are to be learned which may then enable a pathway to lifetime success and security. Failure in this important task has significant implications for the pupils, so schools carry a heavy responsibility, which brings with it strong feelings and high levels of anxiety.

The affective dimensions of work in institutions

The affective experience of working in schools and colleges can be studied from a number of standpoints. It can be described and mapped (Hargreaves, 1998, 2001) and it can be analysed from different theoretical perspectives such as Marxist (Hochschild, 1983), feminist (Boler, 1999) and social constructionist perspectives (Fineman, 2000). The affective experience of work in schools can also be considered from a systems psychodynamics standpoint (Obholzer and Roberts, 1994; Neumann, 1999; James and Connolly, 2000; Gould *et al.*, 2001; James *et al.*, 2006). This perspective argues that our conscious and unconscious affective experience is deeply grounded in our inherited dispositions and our early affective experience and is highly significant and very powerful.

The exploration of the affective nature of the work of teachers has been brought to the fore in recent times by the work of Hargreaves (1998, 2001). While he argues that 'Good teaching is charged with positive emotion' (Hargreaves, 1998, p. 835), it is also true to say that teaching – good or bad – is charged with a whole range of often contradictory emotions. Hargreaves uses the root metaphor of emotional geography to characterise teaching as an emotional practice. Emotional geography consists of 'the spatial and experiential patterns of closeness and/or distance in human interactions and relationships' (Hargreaves, 2001, p. 1061). These patterns help to establish and influence the feelings we experience. Hargreaves distinguishes the notion of emotional geography from emotional understanding (Denzin, 1984) which he argues teachers draw upon to make sense of the affective experiences and responses of others. In that sense, this emotional understanding compares with the notion of emotional intelligence first identified by Salovey and Mayer (1990) and subsequently popularised by Goleman (1996). To characterise the notion of emotional geography, Hargreaves uses the organising metaphor of 'distance' – sociocultural, moral, professional, physical and political – to characterise teachers' affective experience. The shorter the distance the greater the affective effect. He argues that there are no universal rules for appropriate distance – they will be culturally conditioned – and that distance is not a physical phenomenon. He also asserts that closeness is an active accomplishment requiring emotional work or even emotional labour (see below). The emotional geography concept is a social constructionist view of feelings; they are largely culturally and socially conditioned. A psychodynamic perspective would argue that affective experience is much more deeply founded, in our genetic histories, in our early affective experience and in our unconscious. From that standpoint, James *et al.* (2006) have argued that the emotional geology – the underlying influences – is as important as the surface geography: 'Just as the forces under the Earth's crust shape the surface topography, unconscious forces shape people's surface terrain, have colossal and unmanageable power, and are impossible to predict' (James *et al.*, 2006, p. 45).

Hochschild's (1983) study of the working lives of the cabin crew of Delta Airlines revealed much about the affective nature of the work. Her substantially Marxist analysis revealed that the work of the stewards and air hostesses in managing the considerable stresses and strains of their work with 'genuine' smiles and a 'real' feeling of warmth when dealing with the passengers took a considerable emotional toll. The cabin staff clearly did emotional work, which is the kind undertaken when employees need to control their emotions in carrying out their duties and responsibilities. But Hochschild argued that the cabin crew also undertook emotional labour, that is, they had to engage in emotional work as a specific work requirement and importantly their remuneration depended on it. Arguably, emotional work and labour are characteristics of many occupations and from Hochschild's perspective teachers undertake both emotional work *and* emotional labour. They are required to control their emotions – the feelings they show – as part of their work. There is certainly a strong expectation and a condition of employment that they will do so, even though their remuneration may not directly and immediately depend on it. Thus, both emotional work and emotional labour come with the territory of teaching. For many teachers their emotional labour is important and a positive aspect (Hargreaves, 1998). But it also makes them vulnerable especially when the working conditions make it difficult for them to undertake their emotional labour properly and in a way that gives them satisfaction (Blackmore, 1996).

Boler (1999) developed Hochschild's perspectives from a feminist perspective and explored feelings as sites of social control in educational practices. She argued that the organisational discourse in schools is filled with emotion and that this discourse controls pupils and teachers. Boler further argued that feelings and emotions in schools are gendered, a point which others such as Parkin (1993) have made about affective aspects of organisations generally. The rhetoric is that women experience feelings strongly and express their feelings powerfully, whereas men do not and this discourse is employed to shore up a male hegemony where male 'non-emotional rationality' takes precedence over female 'emotional irrationality'. Hearn (1993) takes a different view arguing that men are no more immune from feelings than women and in particular circumstances experience and express their feelings just as strongly. He argues that both men and women seek out different 'emotional zones', which are places where emotions can be expressed in a way that is culturally acceptable. This notion of the emotional zone is interesting in the context of schools and teaching. There are various emotional zones in schools, such as the staff room, the science preparation room, the playground or the headteacher's office where particular feelings are expressed and where such expression is deemed acceptable.

From a social constructionist standpoint, the feelings we experience and the feelings we show as emotions are governed by social and cultural influences (Fineman, 2003). Over time, we learn to over-ride the powerful genetic influences upon us, reconfigure our early emotional experiences and learn what is socially and culturally acceptable and respond accordingly. Our feelings are thus largely governed by social conventions, cultural mores and the impression we want to convey to others. The social constructionist perspective stresses the effects on our affective experience of our experience and expectations, the parts we play in everyday life, our language and how we make sense of the world (Fineman, 2003). In organisations such as schools, affective experience is conditioned by 'feeling rules' (Hochschild, 1979), which are the socially shared guidelines that govern how we want to try to feel. Such rules are often hidden and tacitly agreed. An example of feeling rules in a school would be a teacher trying to motivate and inspire a class while feeling exhausted and 'burned out'. The feeling rules are governing how the teacher wants to feel. Similarly, the display of feelings as emotions is governed by 'display rules' (Rafeli and Sutton, 1989; Ashforth and Humphrey, 1993) that guide which feelings are to be publicly expressed. Again, these rules are often unspoken and covert. An example of display rules in practice would be a headteacher not expressing her dismay at a colleague's forgetfulness while in the presence of pupils. It would be inappropriate to display such feelings with pupils present.

One feature of the social and cultural influence on affective experience and display is its role in micropolitics. From a social constructionist standpoint, micropolitical behaviour is a complex net of individual explanations and agendas, initiated and constructed by the mobilisation of self-interest (Fineman, 2003). So micropolitics includes engaging in one-upmanship, being competitive – overtly or maybe more subtly – and spreading malicious gossip about a colleague. The micropolitics of schools has received some attention by researchers in, for example, Hoyle (1986), Ball (1987), Blase and Anderson (1995), Bennett (1999), Vann (1999) and Busher (2001) but arguably it has not received as much as one might expect given its prevalence in schools and the complex nature of educational work. It is in a consideration of micropolitics that social constructionist and psychodynamic perspectives can be distinguished. The psychodynamic micropolitical perspective sees organisational politics as arising from individual and collective, conscious and unconscious fears about identity, worth and vulnerability. These anxieties can be at the heart of very powerful emotions such as anger and euphoria and can be the basis of more commonplace feelings such as annoyance and happiness. So, micropolitics is more than advancing self-interest, as a social constructionist perspective would see it. Micropolitical activity may be much more deeply seated, which is the line that systems psychodynamics takes. In both the social constructionist and psychodynamic perspectives, symbols and what they represent are important although from the psychodynamic viewpoint symbols can be especially significant since they may represent 'the visible tips of wholly unconscious processes' (Gabriel, 1999, p. 309). So the large desk in the headteacher's office at one level is a signal of his status, which is to his advantage. At another level, it is a signal that he has 'made it' (though he can't quite believe it), that he has reached the top (so he must after all be OK), and that despite his anxieties he must be up to the task. It may also be a useful barrier, preventing members of staff getting too 'close' to him and allowing him to keep his distance. Given the powerful nature of the feelings and the responses they engender, it is no surprise that individuals and organisations seek to protect themselves from threatening feelings by protective behaviours know as social defences (Hirschhorn, 1988; Gabriel, 1999; James and Connolly, 2000; James *et al.*, 2006).

Defences against feelings

Social defences are a group of mental processes and actions aimed at reducing the pain of emotions, most notably anxiety, or eliminating forces that are experienced as threatening a person's mental survival (Gabriel, 1999). While they offer protection, they also distance the individual from reality, so they can also be very unhelpful. Social defences may take the form of patterns of behaviour that can be recognised and typified and include the following.

Regression is when people behave in ways that have been learned earlier in their lives in the face of unacceptable feelings and anxieties. These behaviours may be 'childlike', signalling a regression to dependency and helplessness, and lacking maturity and authority in the face of difficulties.

Covert coalitions are when people resort to familiar relationship patterns, such as parent–child or sibling relationships, to protect themselves from painful feelings. So, for example, a young and inexperienced teacher may seek to view the older and more experienced headteacher as a father figure and treat him in that way to gain protection from work-related difficulties. The headteacher may well collude in the coalition.

Denial is when an aspect of experience is put aside because of its unpleasant affective connotations. For example, a headteacher may put off dealing with the school budget or will repeatedly assert to himself and others that the financial situation is 'fine' when in fact he is in denial and is not facing up to a serious (and therefore threatening) problem.

Resistance is when people endeavour to resist being controlled by expressing their opposition. Often the resistance is in response to a proposed or imposed change and is underpinned by a desire to continue with existing practice. As explained below, changing practice can call up very powerful feelings.

Splitting and projection is a very powerful and frequently encountered defence against unbearable feelings, particularly contradictory ones that generate painful or threatening internal conflicts (Halton, 1994). In the face of these threats, individuals and groups may split their feelings into different elements. The unacceptable elements are then located in other individuals, inanimate objects, groups, or institutions through the process of projection (Likierman, 2001). So, a school blaming 'the government' for all its problems, or seeing all the difficulties the school faces as being the fault of a distinct group of pupils, or criticising a particular department for low pupil attainment levels may all be examples of splitting and projection. Splitting and projection can be the origin of a blame culture, where mistakes are always deemed to be the fault of others, bullying where individuals are repeatedly picked upon, and scapegoating where the recipient of the difficult projected feelings eventually leaves the organisation taking the difficult feelings with them, much to the pleasure – and relief – of those left behind (Dunning *et al.*, 2005).

Organisational rituals, which are the routines that then become the taken for granted ways of working, also offer protection against difficult feelings. Such behaviours may have little apparent connection to any rational understanding of experience or may have a cognitive rationale that overlays their deeper affective purpose. The 'regular seat' set aside for a senior teacher in the staff room avoids any conflicts and difficulties that might ensue if there was a free-for-all for seats at lunchtime. In times gone by (mostly), pupils would be known by their surname, arguably to distance them from the staff and to reduce the affective (and therefore perhaps difficult) content of teacher–pupil relationships. The long established tradition of referring to teachers as 'Sir' and 'Miss' is another way of reducing the affective content of pupil–teacher relationships. Perhaps school uniform is simply a way of protecting against the difficult feelings that may result from pupils being allowed to wear what they like.

When social defences – the 'desires to defend' against work-related feelings and anxiety – become habitual and rationalised, they can become very durable organisational practices. For individuals in any work institution, defensive behaviours of all kinds can give structure, security and a sense of order to a potentially unstructured, insecure and chaotic working life. However, because of their durability and their purpose of protecting against pain, they can be very difficult to change and can inhibit learning and limit creativity.

Emotions and change

Educational change and emotion are inextricably linked and the emotional response to change can be very powerful (Hargreaves, 1998; James and Connolly, 2000). The affective response may be particularly strong if the change requires altering defensive behaviours especially when those defensive behaviours are deeply founded (James and Connolly, 2000). The difficulty of educational change can be explained from an affective standpoint in the following way. First, much educational practice, although it may have an explicit cognitive rationale, is actually intended to protect against difficult feelings; it is defensive in nature. Second, any behaviour change, regardless of whether it is defensive or not, is likely to be accompanied by a feeling of loss, insecurity and inadequacy, experiences which may bring distressing feelings of dismay, fear and even terror in extreme cases. Third, educational change may involve changing behaviours, which can be associated with difficult feelings and anxieties, those behaviours that are explicitly intended to protect against other difficult feelings and anxieties. So, change can bring with it two sets of difficult feeling and anxieties – a 'double dose of difficult dreads' (James *et al.*, 2006).

Emotions and decision-making

One important way in which feelings 'interfere' in the process of teaching is by creating a disparity between the 'espoused' and the 'in use' theories. An espoused theory is 'the theory of action that is advanced to explain or justify a given pattern of activity', whereas a theory in use is 'the theory of action which is implicit in the performance of that pattern of activity' (Argyris, 1985: 13). The distinction here is not between theory and action. It is between two different theories of action (Argyris *et al.*, 1985, p. 82). Argyris (1980) argues that individual and organisational effectiveness is the consequence of congruence between in-use and espoused theories. The affective experience of teaching and organising in schools can play a significant part in both separating and bringing together the espoused and the in-use (James and Jones, 2007; James and Vince, 2001), which can have significant organisational implications. So a teacher may well espouse being child-centred and creative in her approach to teaching but her anxieties about the forthcoming examinations may lead her to teach to the test and to stick to some very tried and tested ways of working. James and Jones (2008) argue that allowing feelings to surface and reflecting on them can help to bring the espoused and in-use feelings together and enhance individual and organisational effectiveness.

Feelings, emotions and individual and organisational boundaries

Boundaries represent inconsistencies and discontinuities in individuals, organisations and social structures and systems (Heracleous, 2004) and they can be very important in social systems and organisations such as schools. Boundaries can be internal to the individual's psyche as well as external in the social world (Roberts, 1994). One of the first boundaries to develop in individuals is the one that separates them from the external world – the boundary of the ego (Gabriel, 1999). Later, the ego itself acquires boundaries which separate conscious and unconscious mental activities and other internal entities, and the ego becomes co-extensive with the part of the mental personality that stands at the boundary with the external world (Gabriel, 1999).

In organisations, boundaries are not incidentally shaped by organisations but are inherent to the organisation itself and indeed to the process of organising (Hernes, 2004). Thus, organisations evolve through the process of boundary setting and schools as organisations evolve through their boundary setting processes. For example, the 'teacher and the class' as an organisation will evolve over time as boundaries are set – the teacher telling a class not to talk while he is talking – and broken – pupils arriving late for a lesson when they have been told to arrive on time. Many boundaries in schools are continually changing, variable, unclear and, to varying degrees, permeable, a view supported by a number of other studies, for example Weick (1979, 1995), Perrow (1986) and Scott (1998).

Czander (1993) argues that all organisational conflicts are boundary issues of some kind. As points of dissimilarity, distinction and interruption (Heracleous, 2004), boundaries will be places where feelings are experienced and may be zones of anxiety and tension (Hernes, 2004). Boundary violations are typically experienced as conflicts and have the potential to escalate into major battles, which is why there may be reluctance to protect boundaries, or indeed, a desire to over-protect them (Czander, 1993). So, for example, noise coming from a neighbouring class is likely to be experienced as a boundary incursion by the teacher whose class is affected, and is likely to become a source of conflict. A pupil being cheeky to a teacher is a boundary incursion – the pupil has not respected the teacher's professional and personal boundary. The same would apply if a teacher was over-familiar with a pupil. An irate parent striding into the headteacher's office to complain about an incident involving her child is a boundary incursion. The point is, one way or another, feelings, emotions and moods are involved in all boundary setting, changing, attacking and defending. So, for example, the teacher whose class is disrupted by noise from the neighbouring class is likely to experience feelings of anger and frustration, which may lead him to over-react. The teacher of the 'noisy class' may dislike the teacher next door so is secretly pleased to have caused the irritation. The cheeky pupil may be experienced as a significant threat to the teacher, who may then dwell on the incident, and subsequently over-react 'so it doesn't happen again' or under-react for fear of provoking another threatening event. The irate parent in the example above has assailed the headteacher's boundary because of her anger. How the headteacher responds to the incident will depend on his feelings. Boundaries are therefore important and will always be emotionally charged. The more secure the individual and organisational boundaries are in a school, the more healthy a school is likely to be from an affective standpoint. It is here that the notion of affective containment comes in.

Affective containment and the transformation of feelings into creativity

There is a good case for arguing that the more difficult feelings there are in an organisation, the more likely it is to resort to defensive behaviours (Dunning *et al.*, 2005). So, it is likely that schools – places of high affective intensity – are likely to be places where social defences abound. On that basis it may appear important to minimise or even eradicate the difficult feelings including anxiety which are part of the work of teachers and schools. But there is a paradox here. We know that very high levels of emotion and anxiety inhibit the motivation to act. People and groups become 'paralysed with fear' in such situations. At the other end of the scale, with very low levels of feeling, there is no motivation to act. In those situations people are simply not moved to action. The central issue is that feelings motivate actions (and vice versa) and are a prerequisite for acting but they are very difficult to control. An alternative to emotional control is emotional containment.

Containment is the organisational process of providing the conditions that facilitate effective and authentic receptiveness and reflection. The term was first coined by Wilfrid Bion (1961) in the context of psychoanalysis and it describes an environment in which the experience of emotion and anxiety can be held, surfaced and reflected upon. An important feature of a containing environment is the secure management of boundaries and in particular the management of the time, task and territory boundaries. So for a teacher, the time of the start and end of the lesson is important and is adhered to, as is the internal time structure of a lesson. The task boundary is also important – what work is task related and what is not? The teacher has a role ensuring that the pupils work within the task boundary. The territory boundary which secures 'place' – the classroom, the location of working groups within the group, and the layout of the classroom – is similarly important. In such a containing environment, feelings can be allowed to surface in a structured, secure and safe way and can be brought to the tasks of teaching and learning. A containing environment for feelings contrasts with a controlling environment where feelings are restrained, hidden and not allowed to become apparent. In such controlling environments, emotions and anxieties have to be dealt with in other ways and may need to be defended against. Controlling environments may therefore call up social defences against emotional pain and energy is spent suppressing the display of feelings as emotions, energy in a class which could be used on the tasks of teaching and learning. Moreover, 'being controlled' can itself feel very threatening, which may create emotional responses of its own. As a result, controlling environments may create more difficult feelings than they prevent. The final outcome of affective containment is that it can create an authentic working environment where feelings can be expressed genuinely, risks taken appropriately, and ideas can be worked with in new and creative ways.

Concluding comments

This chapter started from the point of view that all work in schools is imbued with feelings and that teaching is an affective practice. By asserting the close connection between affect, cognition and conation (feeling and thinking and willing), it becomes clear of course that teaching is not just an affective practice, it involves all three domains. The point remains however, that of all the three domains, feelings are dominant, and have a significant effect on both thinking and will. Importantly, the feelings associated with teaching are not experienced solely at the level of the social and the cultural, they are grounded deeply in our genetic history and early life experiences. The affective experience of teaching cannot be properly addressed without a consideration of those influences.

References

Argyris, C. (1980) *Inner Contradictions of Rigorous Research*, New York, Academic Press.
—— (1985) *Strategy, Change and Defensive Routines*, Boston, Pitman.
—— (1990) *Overcoming Organizational Defences: Facilitating Organizational Learning*, London, Allyn and Bacon.
Argyris, C. and Schon, D. (1996) *Organisational Learning II*, New York, Addison-Wesley.
Argyris, C., Putnam, R. and McLain Smith, D. (1985) *Action Science: Concepts, Methods and Skills for Research and Intervention*, San Francisco, Jossey Bass.
Ashforth, B.E. and Humphrey, R.H. (1993) 'Emotional labour in service roles', *Academy of Management Review*, 18, pp. 88–115.
Ball, S. (1987), *The Micro-politics of the School*, London, Methuen.
Bennett, J. (1999) 'Micropolitics in the Tasmanian context of school reform', *School Leadership and Management*, 19, pp. 197–200.
Bion, W.R. (1961) *Experiences in Groups and Other Papers*, London, Tavistock.
Blackmore, J. (1996) 'Doing emotional labour in the education market place: stories from the field of women in management', *Discourse: Studies in the Cultural Politics of Education*, 17(3), pp. 337–49.
Blase, J. and Anderson, G. (1995) *The Micropolitics of Educational Leadership: From Control to Empowerment*, London, Cassell.
Boler, M. (1999), *Feeling Power*, London, Routledge.
Burrell G. and Morgan G. (1979) *Sociological Paradigms and Organisational Analysis*, Aldershot, Ashgate Publishing.
Busher, H. (2001) 'The micropolitics of change, improvement and effectiveness in schools', in N. Bennett and A. Harris (eds), *School Effectiveness and School Improvement: Searching for the Elusive Partnership*, London, Cassell, pp. 75–97.
Czander, W. (1993) *The Psychodynamics of Work and Organisations*, New York, Guilford Press.
Darwin, C. (1872) *The Expression of the Emotions in Man and Animals*. Chicago, University of Chicago Press.
Day, C. (2004) *A Passion for Teaching*, London, Falmer.
Denzin, N. (1984) *On Understanding Emotion*, San Francisco, Jossey Bass.
Dunning, G., James, C. and Jones, N. (2005) 'Splitting and projection at work in schools', *Journal of Educational Administration*, 43(3), pp. 244–59.
Etzioni, A. (1988) *The Moral Dimension: Towards a New Economics*, New York, The Free Press.
Fineman, S. (1993) *Emotions in Organisations*, 1st edn, London, Sage.
—— (2000) *Emotions in Organisations*, 2nd edn, London, Sage.
—— (2003) *Understanding Emotion at Work*, London, SAGE.
Forgas, (2000) *Feeling and Thinking: The Role of Affect in Cognition*, Cambridge, Cambridge University Press.
Gabriel, Y. (1999) *Organizations in Depth*, London, Sage.
Goleman, D. (1996) *Emotional Intelligence*, London, Bloomsbury.
Gould, L.J., Stapley, L.F. and Stein, M. (eds) (2001) *The Systems Psychodynamics of Organisations: Integrating the Groups Relations Approach, Psychoanalytic and Open Systems Perspectives. Contributions in Honour of Eric J. Miller*, London, Karnac.
Halton, W. (1994) 'Some unconscious aspects of organisational life', in A. Obholzer and V.Z. Roberts (eds), *The Unconscious at Work*, London, Routledge, pp. 11–18.
Hargreaves, A. (1998) 'The emotional practice of teaching', *Teaching and Teacher Education*, 14(8), pp. 835–54.
—— (2001) 'The emotional geographies of teaching', *Teachers College Record*, 103(6), pp. 1056–80.
Hearn, J. (1993) 'Emotive subjects: organisational man, organisational masculinities and the (de) construction of emotions', in S. Fineman (ed.), *Emotions in Organisations*, 1st edn, London, Sage.
Heracleous, L. (2004) 'Boundaries in the study of organisations', *Human Relations*, 57(1), pp. 95–103.

Hernes, T. (2004) 'Studying composite boundaries: a framework of analysis', *Human Relations,* 57(1), pp. 9–29.

Hilgard, E. R. (1980) 'The trilogy of the mind: cognition, affection and conation', *Journal of the History of the Behavioural Sciences,* 16, pp. 107–17.

Hirschhorn, L. (1988) *The Workplace Within: Psychodynamics of Organisational Life,* Cambridge, MA, MIT Press.

Hochschild, A.R. (1979) 'Emotion work, feeling rules and social structure', *American Journal of Sociology,* 85, pp. 551–75.

Hochschild, A.R. (1983) *The Managed Heart: Commercialisation of Human Feeling,* Berkeley, University of California Press.

Hoyle, E. (1986) *The Politics of School Management,* London, Hodder and Stoughton.

James, C.R. (1999) 'Institutional transformation and educational management', in T. Bush, L. Bell, R. Bolam, R. Glatter and P. Ribbins (eds), *Educational Management: Redefining Theory, Policy and Practice,* London, Paul Chapman Publishing/Sage, pp. 142–54.

James, C.R. and Connolly, U. (2000) *Effective Change in Schools,* London, Routledge Falmer.

James, C.R. and Jones, N. (2008) 'A case study of the mis-management of educational change: an interpretation from an affective standpoint', *Journal of Educational Change,* 9(1), pp. 1–16.

James, C.R. and Vince, R. (2001) 'Developing the leadership capability of headteachers', *Educational Management and Administration,* 29(1), pp. 307–17.

James, C.R., Connolly, M., Dunning, G. and Elliott, T. (2006) *How Very Effective Primary Schools Work,* London, SAGE.

Likierman, M. (2001) *Melanie Klein: Her Work in Context,* London, Continuum.

Neumann, J. E. (1999) *Systems Psychodynamics in the Service of a Political Organisational Change,* Oxford, Oxford University Press.

Niendenthal, P.M., Krauth-Griber, S. and Ric, F. (2006) *The Psychology of Emotion: Interpersonal, Experiential and Cognitive Approaches,* New York, Psychology Press.

Oatley, K. and Jenkins, J.M. (1996) *Understanding Emotions,* Oxford, Blackwell.

Obholzer, A. and Roberts, V.Z. (eds) (1994) *The Unconscious at Work,* London, Routledge.

Obholzer, A. (1994) 'Afterword', in A. Obholzer and V.Z. Roberts (eds), *The Unconscious at Work,* London, Routledge, pp. 11–18.

Parkin, W. (1993) 'The public and the private: gender, sexuality and emotion', in S. Fineman (ed.), *Emotion in Organisation,* London, Sage, pp. 167–89.

Perrow, C. (1986) *Complex Organisations – A Critical Essay,* 3rd edn, New York, McGraw-Hill.

Rafeli, A. and Sutton, M. (1989) 'The expression of emotion in organisational life', in L.L. Cummings and B.L. Straw (eds), *Research in Organisational Behaviour, Vol. 11,* Greenwich, CT, JAI Press.

Roberts, V.Z. (1994) 'The organisation of work: contributions from open systems theory', in A. Obholzer and V.Z. Roberts (eds), *The Unconscious at Work,* London, Routledge.

Salovey, P. and Mayer, J.D. (1990) 'Emotional intelligence', *Imagination, Cognition and Personality,* 9(4), pp. 158–211.

Scott, W.R. (1998) *Organisations – Rational, Natural and Open Systems,* Englewood Cliffs, NJ, Prentice-Hall.

Vann, B.J. (1999), 'Micropolitics in the United Kingdom: can a principal ever be expected to be "one of us"?' *School Leadership and Management,* 19, pp. 201–4.

Weick, K.E. (1979) *The Social Psychology of Organising,* 2nd edn, New York, Random House.

—— (1995) *Sensemaking in Organisations,* Thousand Oaks, CA, Sage.

Reflective questions

1   What is the difference between affect, cognition and conation? Are you able to distinguish between them in practice?
2   Why is anxiety important as a feeling? What effect do you think 'feeling anxious' may have on a teacher?
3   Compare schools as places of 'high affective intensity' with other institutions such as hospitals, law courts and prisons.
4   The affective experience of teaching can be studied from Marxist, feminist, social constructionist and systems psychodynamics standpoints. Compare and contrast two of these perspectives and evaluate them in terms of their usefulness for considering the affective nature of teaching.
5   How do people in work organisations such as schools protect themselves from experiencing difficult feelings?
6   Some people argue that some feelings at work cannot be controlled, they are just too powerful. More importantly, attempts to control or suppress feelings simply make matters worse. The feelings will 'come out' sooner or later. As you read the sections on feelings and change, decision-making, boundaries and creativity, think of five rules that might help teachers in schools work more productively with their feelings.

Further reading

James, C. R., Connolly, M., Dunning, G. and Elliott, T. (2006) *How Very Effective Primary Schools Work*, London, SAGE.
Bowler, M. (1999) *Feeling Power*, London, Routledge.
Hochschild, A.R. (2003) *The Managed Heart: Commercialisation of Human Feeling*, Berkeley, University of California Press.

3.4 Cultivating positive learning dispositions

Guy Claxton

Why do I come to school? To develop my learning power, of course! They give us interesting things to explore that get harder and harder. In finding out how to grapple with them, we develop the 'learning muscles' and learning stamina that will enable us to get better at whatever we want, for the rest of our lives. People like scientists and historians have figured out special-purpose ways to learn: as we get older, we practise those, and think about how they might help us in everyday life. As powerful learners, we will be better able to learn new skills, solve new problems, have new ideas and make new friends. We know that learning itself is the one ability that will never go out of date – guaranteed – (unlike programming your iPod!). And learning power is learnable. No matter how so-called 'bright' you are, everyone can get better at learning. Even professors sometimes have learning difficulties! Oh, and by the way, as we learn the tricks of the learning trade, so we naturally do better on examinations too! It's a no-brainer, really.

Kyle, 14, Cardiff

Introduction

Approaches to the development of young people's habits of mind vary along a number of dimensions. Some foreground intellectual habits, and tend to prefer speaking of developing 'thinking' rather than 'learning'; others take a broader view of what lifelong learning involves, and include experiential, emotional and imaginative factors. Some focus on the development of 'skills' while others argue that we need to think of attitudes, values and interests – the fashionable word is 'dispositions' – as well. Some seek to develop stand-alone materials and activities, while others look for ways to infuse regular classrooms and schools with features that lead to the strengthening of desirable habits of mind. Some tend to be prescriptive, having done all the planning, as it were, behind the scenes, while others are more organic, encouraging teachers to evolve their own methods in a more critical and creative fashion. Some are designed to be strongly 'delivered' by teachers to students, while others see essential value in involving students themselves in understanding and developing their own local knowledge and preferred methods for habits-of-mind development. And finally, some think of teachers as being 'trainers' of these habits, while others emphasise their role as 'culture-change agent', creating an environment that systematically invites and stretches the habits. This chapter describes a range of approaches that stress *learning* rather than thinking; *dispositions* rather than skills; *infusion* rather than stand-alone; *organic* rather than prescriptive methods; *involvement of students* rather than delivery of a ready-made product to them; and *culture-shifting* rather than training. It is argued that such approaches offer a more effective foundation for lifelong learning.

Enhancing the capacity to learn

Apart from food, shelter and love, more than anything else today's young people need strong minds. They need minds that are supple and robust enough, as Kyle says, to deal well with the challenges and uncertainties that are coming their way. Whether it be mastering complicated new technology, mixing with different kinds of people, moving to a new country, or coping with a baby without any Aunties or Grannies to support and advise you ... the one thing we can be sure of is that today's students will need to be up to living a learning life.

If they are not – if they do not feel equipped to do so – then we are only too well aware of the escape routes that are open to them. When fighting, drinking, shagging, getting stoned or blowing yourself up become the only apparent alternatives to facing complicated reality – because you have not learned how to – we all suffer the consequences. 'My ex-boyfriend takes drugs to escape from reality,' said one young woman. 'It was his inability to cope with insecurity'. Another said: 'If you're insecure anyway, or you've got a problem, and you're out with your mates, and somebody says to you, you know, I've got something, what do you want ... It's just a way of escaping' (Industrial Society, 1997).

So much is common knowledge. There is no shortage of fine words and good intentions along these lines, as education systems around the world try to engage with these issues. In the UK we are currently surrounded by rhetoric about 'lifelong' and 'personalised' learning. 'Our ultimate goal is to promote and value learning as a rewarding lifelong experience', says one recently launched Local Authority policy document on Teaching and Learning. '21st century teaching needs to [develop] learning how to learn in preparation for a lifetime of change', declares the UK Government. A report from the think-tank Demos, commissioned by the Minister for School Standards in June 2004, declares that:

> Successful lifelong learners need the ability to learn new material quickly in both their working lives and their personal development. Those who cannot learn well face educational, economic and social exclusion. The more learning can be personalised to meet the needs of individuals, the more successful and enduring their education will be.
>
> (Demos, 2004)

'Young people need to be provided with educational experiences that will enable them to deal successfully with current and future change with optimism and resilience' says Tasmania's widely admired and copied *Essential Learnings Framework*. And so on.

Until recently, however, practical responses to these calls for educational reform have often been disappointing. Students have been exhorted to plan their revision carefully; to organise their knowledge using spider or tree diagrams instead of linear notes; to use mnemonics and imagery to help them remember lists of facts; to drink water constantly, lest their brains dry up and stop learning. Teachers have tried to address issues of 'self-esteem' or 'emotional literacy' that are thought to interfere with learning. Or they have tried to sort their students into various boxes according to their 'learning style' or 'multiple intelligence profile' – mental characteristics that have often been assumed to be immutable, and readily discernible on the basis of simple pencil-and-paper questionnaires – and to differentiate their teaching style accordingly. Despite a good deal of enthusiasm, many such approaches have turned out to be piecemeal, short-lived, scientifically dubious, and largely ineffective at either raising standards or changing students' learning attitudes. A recent comprehensive meta-analysis of studies of learning styles, commissioned by the Learning and Skills Research Council, for example, concludes that:

Some of the best known and commercially most successful instruments have such low reliability, poor validity, and *negligible impact on pedagogy*, that we recommend their use in research and in practice should be discontinued.

(Coffield *et al.*, 2004, emphasis added)

Even many of the sounder attempts to teach 'thinking skills' have had equivocal results, often being greeted enthusiastically by teachers and students alike, sometimes producing some short-term gains, but frequently showing a disappointing lack of transfer, or a failure to last or embed in spontaneous thinking and learning (Perkins, 1995).

While it is possible, as we shall see, to improve on such pioneering efforts, progress over the last 20 years has been hampered by a number of factors. Educational 'traditionalists' have consistently rubbished all such attempts to explore skill development, caricaturing it as 'trendy' or 'laissez-faire', and as jeopardising the central aim of transmitting knowledge. Teachers have often been sceptical about skills-based approaches that have not been clearly articulated, while some of the proponents of 'brain-based learning' and the like have been rather over-enthusiastic and uncritical in promoting simplistic slogans and models, and 'handy hints' that are ill founded. Commercial imperatives have sometimes driven out proper scientific caution.

The foundations of learning to learn: sand, cement and water

Recently there have been a number of attempts to construct a sounder and more coherent conceptual and empirical platform from which to launch innovative approaches to pedagogy and school organisation. The three main ingredients of these foundations – the sand, cement and water, if you like – are the *learning sciences, futures thinking*, and school-based *action research*. Let me say a little about each.

Cognitive sand

The scientific 'sand' comes in a variety of colours, of which three of the most important are cognitive science, neuroscience, and sociocultural studies. From cognitive science comes, crucially, a reappraisal of our understanding of the nature of 'intelligence'. Out has gone the idea that young people's learning is largely determined by a fixed-sized pot of general purpose resource which they inherited from their parents – a factor over which teachers therefore have no control. And in has come a growing realisation of the extent to which *learning reflects habits of mind that have themselves been learned*, and which are therefore amenable in principle to further growth or change. On this new view, it becomes possible for teachers to see themselves as 'mind coaches': people who are in the business not only of transmitting 'bodies of knowledge, skill and understanding' but of expanding the capacity to learn itself. What matters here, from a practical point of view, is not the technical niceties of the 'nature vs. nurture' debate (which have been exhaustively discussed elsewhere) but the shift of attention from that which is fixed about youngsters' minds to that which is capable of development.

This shift is of very much more than academic interest. Children's learning lives depend on it. The work of Carol Dweck, for example, has shown that culturally transmitted beliefs about 'the fixity of ability' have a direct, deleterious effect on students' willingness to persist intelligently in the face of difficulty (Dweck, 1999). Crudely, if you believe that 'finding things difficult' means you 'lack ability' (i.e. are (relatively) stupid) then, from that point of view, it looks smart to give up. There is no point in needlessly distressing yourself by banging your head painfully against a brick wall that you 'lack the ability' to penetrate. In general, this strand of cognitive scientific work has shown that dispositions like determination, recovery from frustration, willingness to take risks and 'have a go' are all capable – at least in principle – of being influenced by teaching methods, classroom cultures and school ethos.

Another recent trend in cognitive science has implications for the way in which 'learning to learn' programmes are developed. It challenges a pervasive belief about the way the mind is organised, which assumes that kernels of useful 'skills' and 'concepts' are readily extracted from the shells of particular materials and experiences, and then stored in the mind in a general, free-floating kind of way, so that they will (potentially at least) be called up by any subsequent problem to which they are relevant. Sadly, it turns out that the sense of 'relevance' is not given; it has to be learned. Our heads are full of useful ideas and skills that do not come to mind when they are needed: that is the norm. We are all capable of much better thinking than we usually deploy, for example (Perkins, 1995). Thus acquiring the 'skill' is only a part of the learning that is required; the rest involves slowly discovering when and how and for what purpose it can be used. We need to be not only 'able', but 'ready' and 'willing' as well. It is no surprise, therefore, that many kinds of short-term and/or stand-alone training in 'thinking skills' do not spread; do not deepen; and do not last. To achieve this, longer-term, more sustained, strategies are required.

Cognitive science tells us a range of other useful things, that there is not space here to go into in detail. We know there are smart and not-so-smart ways to 'practise', and that some forms of coaching make a positive difference, while others can even be deleterious. We know that 'mental rehearsal' is a powerfully effective learning tool – for learning a wide range of things from sports skills to handling stressful encounters – and that with encouragement people become more ready, willing and able to make use of such a strategy. We know that creativity involves, amongst other things, the ability to move fluently between focused, purposeful cognition and relaxed, receptive cognition, and that there are simple methods for encouraging young people to do so (see Claxton, 1999, for a review).

Neuroscientific sand

Integral to the construction of strong foundations for educational practice is the second kind of 'sand', which comes from neuroscience. Here we have to be careful, however, as it has become contaminated. There is a good deal of uncritical hype about 'brain-based learning' at the moment. There is no good evidence that you can make youngsters smarter by giving them short bursts of tricky exercises designed to expand the bundle of fibres that connect the 'analytical' left hemisphere of the brain to the 'holistic' or 'imaginative' right. There is no good evidence that an hour without water turns a smart plum of a brain into a dried-up prune. There is still very little evidence that so-called 'smart pills' will actually make you smarter.

On the other hand, there is very good evidence indeed that 'thinking too much' interferes with learning. Hard thinking focuses the brain's attentional field on that which is probable, plausible or 'sayable', and thus makes it miss more intricate or unexpected details and patterns in experience. For example, the effort to describe a face – to render down all that patterned subtlety into a few words – interferes with one's ability to recognise it again in a crowd. And thinking aloud can interfere with creative problem-solving. Once they know these things, teachers can be more alert to the disadvantages of 'trying too hard' and 'thinking too much', and help their students to develop an appreciation of when and how to pay wordless attention, as well as when and how to analyse and explain (Claxton, 1997).

Another important area of brain research for education is the new field of 'affective neuroscience'. While popular approaches to 'emotional intelligence' have focused on crude categories such as 'anxiety' and 'self-esteem', and bland nostrums such as 'Feel good, learn good!', the neuroscientists have been finding that emotions are not antagonists of 'intelligence' but essential aspects of it. Without feelings, intellectual cleverness becomes abstract and disembodied, and people who have lost emotional capacities through brain injury (or mental illness) are inclined to 'think clever and act dumb'. Emotional intelligence seems to be much more a matter of understanding the vital functions of emotions, and heeding their messages, than of trying to 'manage them away'. Emotions do not block learning so much as colour or nuance it in a variety of useful ways (Panksepp, 2005).

Sociocultural sand

The third kind of scientific sand comes from the sociocultural studies that have developed out of the pioneering work of Russian psychologist Lev Semyonovich Vygotsky (1978). His insights were twofold. First, minds consist largely of internalised habits, strategies and attitudes that are first developed in interaction with other people, and which therefore substantially reflect *their* habits and values. Minds are contagious, in other words. Thus one of the most powerful influences that teachers can have, especially on younger minds, is not so much what they are teaching, but what learning characteristics they are modelling as they do so. When things go slightly wrong, does the teacher model calm, patient inquisitiveness, or do they model an anxious concern to re-establish control as quickly as they can? Do they welcome and enjoy challenge and uncertainty, and thus foster a climate in which their students can welcome them too, or do they, inadvertently, reinforce the idea, by their reflex behaviour, that it is *knowing* we want round here, not *finding out,* and that 'not knowing' is an aversive state to be rid of fast?

Vygotsky's second insight is that, whatever habits of mind you bring with you to learning, these are always selected, shaped and skewed by whatever unique predicament you happen to find yourself in. The 'intelligent learning agent', we might say, is never the person alone, as they can be described in abstract, but always 'person plus': me plus my laptop, plus my modem, plus my books ... and most importantly, plus the intricate, evanescent web of human resources in which I am always enmeshed. How I learn reflects who I'm with – and that includes who I might be with in my memory and imagination – as well as who's currently around, on my team. Knowing this, teachers can help students make the best use of the material and human resources that surround them, and to learn how to move skilfully around in the social space of learning – knowing when to go for a walk by yourself, when to dash off an email for advice, and to whom, and how to contribute to groups in ways that maximise the collective learning power of all (Wells and Claxton, 2002).

Visionary cement

The 'cement' of these learning-to-learn approaches adds well-thought-out values to scientifically informed theory. We cannot decide what is 'good practice' until we are clear about what are we educating young people *for*. Education is, after all, the systematic attempt to cultivate in all young people whatever-it-is that we think they are going to need to thrive in the twenty-first century. We can't know what and how to teach them unless we have some idea what the challenges and opportunities are which we imagine they are going to meet. Education draws on the past in order to anticipate the demands of the future. If it only focuses on transmitting what is known, without paying serious attention to what it is that students will need, it risks – especially in times of change – becoming a waste of young people's precious time.

The bald insistence that 'they must study Shakespeare and algebra' (or whatever is your favourite subject) because we are agreed that these are exemplary products of human learning and achievement, without paying any attention to the *habits of mind* that are being cultivated by 'studying' them in a particular way – and without asking whether those habits of mind are the ones they are going to need – is wildly irresponsible. The tedious to and fro between 'traditionalists' and 'progressives' that has passed for educational debate, and the woeful poverty of imagination that manifests as the current fascination with 'personalisation' and 'choice', are costly distractions because they usually leave the vital, prior questions of 'Why?' and 'What for?' unasked and unanswered. Young people know that what they need – what they have a right to expect from their education – are strong minds, up to the challenge of coping with all the complexities of twenty-first-century life. Many of them know they are not getting it, and that fiddling around with fractions and formulae, analysing literary works and historical motives, is not developing what they need – unless it is done in a very particular way. The compliant may learn to walk the narrow plank of examination success, or simply the art of keeping out of trouble. The less docile learn how to avoid challenges and subvert authorities. It is an open question, regardless of the qualifications they do or don't get, which strategies develop life skills of greater real-world currency.

The history of educational reform is a chronicle of failed innovation. The rusting scrap-heap of tinkerings, once so hotly contested, now so quickly superseded, reflects the fact that such reforms invariably involve tinkering with what exists, rather than asking the 'What for?' question and working back. They barely scratch the surface. It seems likely that young people will not re-engage with their schooling until they can see how it will help them not just in the job market – a dubious rationale, as they know – but with the central challenge of their lives: insecurity in the face of ambiguity and complexity.

Practical water: the role of action research in educational change

The third foundation of what we might call 'expansive education' – the 'water', without which the other two ingredients would not 'set' – is action research: a wide range of small-scale, low-cost, low-risk, highly practical activities and interventions that turn the 'in principle' of science, and the ideals of vision, into concrete realities, accessible and appealing to large numbers of teachers. The action research foundation places more value on such practitioner-generated ideas than it does on large-scale, costly Research with a capital R, which so often in the past has had disappointingly weak effects on practice. These approaches also value grass-roots dissemination over the laborious construction of fine-sounding 'policies', which again have little effect unless they are cashed out in practical suggestions that both inform and inspire. They draw on the science to give depth and coherence to its ideas, and on the vision to acknowledge the social realities and social needs that teachers see around them every day. Combined, at best, these two ingredients fire educators' imaginations about what is both possible and desirable. But this enthusiasm can all too easily fizzle out if the science and the vision are not immediately backed up with 'And here's something you could try'.

It is central to the dispositional approach, therefore, that local experiments are communicated within and between schools, and that this creative ownership is publicly acknowledged and celebrated. The low-key approach of 'here's something you could try' is, we feel, much more likely to appeal to busy teachers than the deluge of glossy materials, full of fine words, to which they have become used. But any classroom-tested ideas and illustrations that are passed on must be quickly and continually 'hedged' with encouragement to 'try them out', customise them, and make them their own. Indeed, it may well be central to the sustained success of any 'learning to learn' initiative that not only teachers, but students themselves, are continually involved in critical and creative reflection on whatever they are trying out. No 'magic bullets'; no 'prescriptions': only seeds of practical ideas that have 'worked' for at least one other teacher, to be played with, adapted and discussed (Horne, 2001).

The dispositional approach thus rests on the working assumption that effective, sustained change in the ethos and effects of schooling, to develop stronger positive learning dispositions, only happens when all three of these ingredients are present.

The dispositional framework

Taken together, these three kinds of consideration have steered the development of a more 'cultural' approach to school improvement that is distinct from some of the other approaches to 'learning to learn'. Let me draw out and make explicit some of the key dimensions along which such approaches may differ.

Learning rather than thinking

Many current approaches to 'learning to learn' describe their intentions in terms of the development of thinking. Though different authors define the scope of what counts as 'thinking' differently, the usual emphasis is on processes that are explicit, intellectual, precise, justifiable, rigorous and logical. Improving the construction and evaluation of explicit, reasoned argument is the central concern. Often the word 'learning', when it is used, is taken to be co-extensive with this kind of thinking. However, it is clear from the scientific literature that I have illustrated, that learning involves far more than rational cogitation – for example, patient, unthinking attention to immediate experience; daydreaming and reverie; active visualisation and mental rehearsal; sensitivity to creative inklings and hunches; a nuanced understanding of the relationship between emotion and learning; and sensitivity to different rhythms and phases of learning. Dispositional approaches deliberately incorporate these less rational aspects of learning, seeing their cultivation as a vital balance to models of education that have largely ignored them.

Dispositions rather than skills

Conventional approaches to learning to learn also make use of the word 'skills' – 'thinking skills', 'critical skills', and so on. More broadly, it is now commonplace for the goals of education to be described as 'key skills or 'core competencies'. It is, of course, welcome to see the traditional preoccupation with knowledge transmission balanced with an explicit concern for the development of mental capability (even to the point where we had until recently a government Department for Education *and Skills*). However, there are two pitfalls in the skills notion. First, it suggests that complex performance can be broken down into component 'skills', which can then be 'trained' (and then somehow re-integrated inside a person's head as a complex assembly of cognitive sub-routines). Second, it falls into the trap, of which we spoke earlier, of assuming that such training experiences can rapidly result in the creation of the free-floating mental capacities. Neither of these assumptions is valid. Nor is their corollary: that you can tell, on the basis of a quick test, whether someone 'has' the skill or not. They may have it but do not feel ready or willing to show it. Or they may display it in a familiar and predictable setting, but have failed to realise the wider range of situations to which it is potentially applicable.

To counteract some of these over-simplifications, many recent approaches prefer to speak of the cultivation of 'dispositions' – though this is not without risks in its own right (Carr and Claxton, 2002; Perkins *et al.*, 1993). The abstract noun 'disposition' seems to point to a class of mental entities distinct from 'skills' (as well as 'knowledge'). This can create bogus and unnecessary worries about which category to place particular capacities – kindness? imaginativeness? – into. Whereas actually all that is at stake is the recognition that people are differentially 'disposed' to make use of *any* putative skill or ability; that their degree of disposed-ness changes over time and place; and that education can influence the development of these inclinations, as well as the sophistication of the 'skill' itself. It is of little use 'having' a skill that never comes to mind. The dispositional approach assumes that to help someone become a more effective all-round learner, you have to help them disembed any ability from its context of acquisition, and to develop the 'meta-disposition' to drive that disembedding process for themselves.

Capability rather than attainment

Many of the pioneering learning-to-learn approaches were focused on raising students' school attainment. Mnemonics will help your students remember their French verbs. Spider diagrams will help them organise and retrieve conceptual knowledge – and thus do better in their exams. Thinking skills will help them write better-argued and better-structured essays. Dispositional approaches, however, may derive from their future-oriented values a more ambitious aim: to help students become better learners – curious, tenacious, thoughtful, imaginative and so on – out of school as well as within (Claxton, 2002). The goal of dispositional development cannot be pursued at the expense of the 'standards agenda' – these days, no headteacher could afford to ignore the latter. But it does mean that we have to take the transfer issue doubly seriously, and deny ourselves the comforting assumption that aiming to raise examination performance will – should? – automatically inculcate useful real-life learning dispositions. The science tells us that 'traditional good teaching' is more likely to stunt the development of dispositions such as resilience and resourcefulness, than it is to strengthen them.

Some approaches do not distinguish clearly between the aim of helping young people 'become better learners', and helping them 'learn better'. Yet a moment's reflection reveals their difference. A traditional good teacher may well create close to an optimal environment in the classroom for students to focus on their set tasks, and by doing so, she will help them learn better. But her very success at creating and maintaining a calm, orderly, pleasant, purposeful environment deprives students of opportunities to develop the social and cognitive dispositions to do this optimising for themselves. Thus they become more, not less, dependent on the continual presence of the teacher. (Teachers are familiar with inheriting classes who cannot regulate themselves but can only 'work well' under the firm hand of a controlling authority.) Dispositional approaches set themselves the task of helping teachers to support the development of positive learning dispositions that will stand young people in good stead wherever they find themselves.

Infusion rather than add-on

Many of the earlier learning-to-learn approaches left 95 per cent of school and classroom life unaltered, and added on something different. Some of these add-ons were small-scale hints and tips to be used within ordinary lessons. Some were stand-alone lessons in 'thinking skills', 'creative thinking' and so on. Some sectioned off a few days, or even a whole week, at the end of term, for a feast of 'creativity'. Many of these activities were very well received by students. However, the evidence for any abiding impact on students' learning dispositions, let alone on their school attainment, has been very thin, and often disappointing. There are several possible reasons why this might be so. Bolt-ons often underestimate the transfer problem, and so do not attend to it. The initial novelty can pall quite rapidly. There is sometimes very little progression in the activities, so they quickly become stale. And sometimes they are presented to students in an unquestioning, 'God's Gift' kind of way, that does not invite their critical involvement or ownership.

More recently, dispositional approaches have tried to find ways in which the learning-to-learn intention can become more deeply rooted, more gently cumulative, more organic and experimental, and more involving of students' critical and creative energies (e.g. Claxton, 2002). Such approaches try to find practical ways of seeding a culture change in the classroom (or the school as a whole) that nurture, value and steer students' development in the direction of the positive learning dispositions. A beautiful laminated 'Stuck poster' – a display of ideas about what students can do when they are stuck – may well have less impact on dispositional development than a more scruffy home-made version that is a continual source of debate and up-grading by students themselves. The idea that learners are predominantly Visual, Auditory or Kinaesthetic in their learning is better presented not as an established truth (which it isn't), but as a subject for critical discussion and experimentation in the classroom. The idea of 'learning styles' becomes a device for stimulating the development of students' self-awareness, rather than another label to hang around their necks.

Infusion approaches also make use of some of the sociocultural insights outlined above. If ideas about how to learn effectively are contagious, as Vygotsky argued, then the classroom and the school can become a place where positive contagion is maximised, and negative diminished. Orchestrating opportunities for students to learn together, discussing hard problems, sharing ideas, swapping between the roles of 'learner' and 'teacher' amongst themselves, becomes a higher priority for a dispositional teacher. So-called 'reciprocal' and 'peer' teaching have been shown to be effective at building the knowledge and the confidence of both the 'tutor' and the 'learner'. The nature of learning conversations, and the vocabulary that is used to articulate the process of learning, are also important. And dispositional teachers quickly come to see that opportunities for them to model positive learning dispositions are also valuable. It becomes part of their professional role to seize and create chances to say 'I don't know', 'Could you explain that to me again: I didn't get it', or 'That's a good question: I've never thought of that'.

Though they are still in their infancy, our guiding hypothesis is that pedagogical approaches that

- involve infused culture-change,
- are organic and evolving rather than static, and
- involve students in enquiring about learning rather than learning to use someone else's Handy Hints

will be more effective in the long run.

Whole-school rather than just classroom-based

The heightened recognition of the importance of language, modelling, student involvement and ownership, and other tell-tale aspects of cultural value – as well as pedagogy – draws attention to the impact that the whole-school environment can have on the development of students' 'learning power'. Where the earlier approaches to learning-to-learn focused exclusively on what the teacher was doing in the privacy of her classroom, more recent approaches, such as 'building learning power', are on the look-out for opportunities to embed learning-to-learn messages in the life of the whole school. For example:

- Do displays of students' 'work' acknowledge and celebrate their Learning Journey, with all its ups and downs, or only the Wonderful Product?
- Do you show a video of the collapsing scenery and the drying up, as well as the last night of the school play when everything finally went right?
- Do you invite members of the community in to the school to talk not about their achievements, but about their struggles, difficulties and failures?
- Do teachers dare to display themselves as learners, both to each other and to the students?
- Can teachers ask each other for help without feeling threatened?
- Can the head make a fool of herself without getting uptight?
- Do the governors appoint an observer to help them improve the quality of their meetings?
- Are parents (and students) privy to the doubts and uncertainties that the school is facing, or are they continually presented with the Illusion of Total Control?
- Are sports about Learning, or are they all about Winning?

Conclusion

These are pioneering days. For over a hundred years, schools have mimicked the industrial production line. Students progressed down the conveyor belt in batches, with a variety of 'experts' bolting packages of 'knowledge, skill and understanding' on to them as they went. Every so often they went through Quality Control to be graded and stamped, as a result of which they were sent into different sets or streams or schools, or they left altogether. A student could no more question the bit of Maths that was being welded on than an egg could question being imprinted with a little lion. Things *have* changed since the nineteenth century – but surprisingly little, given the massive changes in the surrounding society. But finally, with a lot of creaking, and some complaining, we are realising that education is about becoming a Learner rather than a Knower, and that the idea of school as Knowers' Ark has had its day. We are coming to see that developing positive, transferable learning dispositions is a subtle but achievable goal that takes time, finesse, and a change of heart by those who run and work in our schools. And we are also coming to realise that Learning involves much more than Thinking, and that powerful learners need to know how and when to watch and dream, as well as how to pick holes in an argument.

References

Carr, M.A. and Claxton, G.L. (2002) 'Tracking the development of learning dispositions', *Assessment in Education*, 9(1), pp. 9–37.

Claxton, G.L. (1997) *Hare Brain, Tortoise Mind: Why Intelligence Increases When You Think Less*, London, Fourth Estate.

—— (1999) *Wise Up: The Challenge of Lifelong Learning*, London, Bloomsbury.

—— (2002) *Building Learning Power*, Bristol, TLO Ltd.

Coffield, F., Mosely, D., Hall, E. and Ecclestone, K. (2004) *Learning Styles and Pedagogy in Post-16 Learning*, London, Learning and Skills Research Centre.

Demos (2004) *About Learning*, London, Demos.

Dweck, C.S. (1999) *Self-Theories: Their Role in Motivation, Personality and Development*, Philadelphia, Psychology Press.

Horne, M. (2001) *Classroom Assistance*, London, Demos.

Industrial Society (1997) *Speaking Up, Speaking Out*, London, The Industrial Society.

Panksepp, J. (2005) *Affective Neuroscience*, Oxford, Oxford University Press.

Perkins, D. (1995) *Outsmarting IQ: The Emerging Science of Learnable Intelligence*, New York, Free Press.

Perkins, D., Jay E. and Tishman S. (1993) 'Beyond abilities: a dispositional theory of thinking', *Merrill-Palmer Quarterly*, 39(1), pp. 1–21.

Vygotsky, L.S. (1978) *Mind in Society*, Cambridge, MA, Harvard University Press.

Wells, G. and Claxton, G.L. (eds) (2002) *Learning for Life in the 21st Century: Sociocultural Perspectives on the Future of Education*, Oxford, Blackwell.

Reflective questions

1   The chapter argues that young people's mental health is a challenge for education, as much as for families, social services or politicians. To what extent is this argument well made, and do you agree?

2   What is the difference between training a skill and cultivating a disposition? Do you think the latter is an achievable aim in schools?

3   Can you critique and develop the list of ways, above, in which schools could embody a culture of 'learning to learn'?

Further reading

Claxton, G. (1999) *Wise Up: Learning to Live the Learning Life*, Bloomsbury, London. Reprinted 2001, London, Network/Continuum.

Dweck, C. (1999) *Self-Theories: Their Role in Motivation, Personality and Development*, Philadelphia, Psychology Press.

Perkins, D. (1995) *Outsmarting IQ: The Emerging Science of Learnable Intelligence*, New York, Free Press.

3.5 Continuity and discontinuity in school transfer

Yolande Muschamp

Introduction

This chapter explores how pupils experience change as they transfer from the primary (elementary) to the secondary (high) school. It examines the practical and theoretical perspectives which have shaped the transfer process over the last two decades. It questions the efficacy of transfer and identifies the discontinuities which remain, despite unprecedented reform of schooling in England designed to ensure curriculum continuity, progression and social support for pupils as they move between schools.

Transfer has long been a key concern of governments. However, despite the realisation that there needs to be continuity in experience for pupils as they move between schools in England, research into the experience of pupils at transfer has shown that:

> Pupils are enjoying their final year in primary school to a lesser extent than 5 years ago and by the end of their first year after transfer they find school an even less enjoyable experience.
>
> (Galton *et al.*, 2003)

These findings have led to a call for a reassessment of the value of continuity of experience at transfer and prompted suggestions that perhaps discontinuity rather than continuity could be more beneficial to pupils. These more recent arguments build on complex accounts of the learner and are often wider ranging, going so far as to challenge the traditional curriculum experience of many pupils in the middle years of schooling where, despite higher achievement in the primary school, a dip in attainment is still the norm during the first two years of secondary school.

A contemporary examination of continuities and discontinuities reveals a complex picture. At a macro level, the structure and organisation of classrooms bring discontinuities which create anxieties in children as well as excitement. The worry of getting lost in a new school, the fears of adapting to new ways of working, being responsible for arriving at the right room with the correct books at the correct time are often outweighed by the excitement of more sophisticated equipment. Many studies have revealed the 'Bunsen burner effect' as children anticipate experiments in science laboratories. The first experiences of art studios, drama spaces, sport facilities, craft workshops and the school cafeteria suggest, for the children, a move to an adult world. They also suggest a move towards authentic experiences of the real world of work, greater independence, and new forms of pedagogy. Such hopes, unfortunately, are rarely sustained.

Many research projects have studied pupils' experiences as they transfer from their primary (elementary) school to secondary (high) school. In England this usually happens at age 11, although researchers have noted the same pattern of a drop in attainment in the first year of a new school at different ages of transfer (Hargreaves and Galton, 2002). (The term transfer is used to describe the process of moving between schools, and a second term, transition, is used to describe the movement between classes in the same school.) We use the findings from one of our own projects, the Independent Learning in the Middle Years (ILMY) Project[1] to provide examples of the typical concerns of pupils at transfer. The aim of the ILMY project was to explore the strategies that pupils use in their approaches to schoolwork and to examine how these change as they move from primary to secondary school. Within the study 24 children from four primary schools were interviewed in the final term before transfer and again after moving to two secondary schools.

What pupils say

This chapter uses the views of children (from our own and other projects) before and after transfer to secondary schools to amplify and reinterpret what is known about the transfer process. Discontinuities are identified and explored revealing how, despite many efforts to the contrary, the pedagogies of the primary and secondary schools are still very different and pedagogical development has had very little impact in these important middle years of schooling.

The first account is from a girl who explained what she had learned about the secondary school after an orientation visit where she had spoken with children who had transferred the previous year. She focused at first on the topic of homework but soon reflected on her preoccupation with social issues and the behaviour of other children:

> Most people said homework, homework, because every lesson you're going to get homework, so you'll have perhaps five pieces of homework every day. So that will be quite hard because it has to be back on a certain day. So you've got this diary where you write down all the things that your homework is, you tick it. And people say that at Chimneys School people get their heads flushed down the toilet.

The rumours were partly the result of horror stories handed down from pupils within the secondary school and from legitimate fears of the unknown as in this dramatic, and hopefully exaggerated, account of the threat of violent behaviour from peers from a second girl.

I   What are you looking forward to at secondary school? Are you looking forward to going to Chimneys School?
P   No, not really. Because last year someone from downstairs called S— has a friend of hers who she calls her sister and I got beaten up by her and her friends are in Chimneys School so I'm a bit worried I'm going up. Every time my sister comes home, because she's at Chimneys, she goes 'Everyone in Yr. 8 hates you' so I'm worried about going up in case they beat me up and everything. My brother is in Yr. 5 now and he's going up the year after me and he got pushed into a river and cracked his head and it was S—'s friend who done it. It was her boyfriend. And I've got beaten up all the time, so I'm a bit worried.

The fears were widespread and the norm even when school induction programmes had helped children to rationalise their fears. This boy was able to reflect on how violent behaviour would have an impact on his progress. He was worried about bullies and how they would affect his learning:

> ...but knowing that most secondary schools have loads of bullies in them, I think if I get distracted I won't learn so well because in my old school as I got bullied more and more my work began to go down, and my reputation.

There were, however, many features of the secondary school which were received with more optimism. The different resources available at the secondary schools had excited some of the children, particularly the science equipment. This boy was a little mistaken but nevertheless was one of many who spoke of the science laboratories:

> You're going to get things like petrol and all that and play with it and experiment with it. And practical things like that. It's going to be different because they've got labs there. They've got better things probably for the school because everyone uses it.

These girls looked forward to a different pattern of work as well as more sophisticated resources when they moved to their secondary school:

> Because you'll have like more responsibility, which will be quite good. You're not being told everything, exactly this is the set way to do it. Stuff like, moving round from different classrooms rather than staying and having more equipment and things. Like in science, all the Bunsen burners.

> I think I'm looking forward to having more responsibility and having a wider range of lessons I think. You have the different types of science, like biology, chemistry and stuff. I know we do them here, but it's all like one thing and they're the same thing, but I think in Chimneys it will be different.

After transfer, the majority of students were positive about their move to the senior school. Some identified the work as more challenging and for most the expectation of greater responsibilities was realised:

> The teacher we have tells you what to do and then if we want to do something else, but still do the same thing but adding it in, we'd ask her and she'd either say yes or no. She sort of sets out a template, like a recommendation, but if you want to add stuff or take away stuff you can. Teachers here they're a lot stricter.

None indicated any serious nostalgia for their previous primary school. Although one boy explained:

> You have one teacher in primary school so you develop a friendship. Here there are lots of teachers. It's a good thing to develop a relationship. It's good for learning. I miss that in secondary school.

There were admissions of still not liking a particular subject but this confession was nearly always qualified by the reassurance that the subject was better in secondary school. Although part of the primary curriculum, subjects like physical education, design and technology and science were perceived differently and depicted as new and motivating. On the other hand two core subjects, English and mathematics, appeared to suffer from being lodged within the same pedagogies and classroom organisations.

> [Maths is] not really different but we're doing things in more detail. We've got a special maths teacher this time.

> Maths is doing harder things, not simple things. Like if you were in Year 6 you'd normally do adding or take away and that's all you'd ever do. In my class now we do like adding As and Bs and doing letter maths in algebra. We have to do bigger numbers, adding them and taking them away without using calculators.

> We've been doing range, mean and median. We're doing stuff that's different but we're not doing it in a different way.

I   Have you learnt more since being here about English?
P   If I had to be completely honest, no. My reading skill I suppose has gone up a bit because I'm doing slightly more reading now, but apart from that I don't really think I've learnt many more skills, apart from a few things such as – actually that doesn't really help because I can't remember what it's called!!

However positive comments were not restricted to curriculum related issues. This girl thought that the different classroom structure would offer more opportunities for social activity:

> The school is much bigger. And you don't stay in one classroom during the day. You have to walk round. I think it will be a good thing because while you're walking round you could see your friends quickly and go back to your classroom.

While a top ability boy observed:

> Teachers expect more from us in the way we behave, how much work we do, how we co-operate with each other … We mostly work in small groups in secondary … that's good because we're allowed to talk and everything. We talk about other things as well as work.

Such timeless and universal anxieties and anticipations have been found in many research projects and are not unique to England (Anderson *et al.*, 2000; Pinnell, 1998; Noyes, 2004, 2006) and these pupils' views confirm what we know about transfer. Researchers have attempted to identify the significant changes that children experience at transfer and how these can be managed by the school to alleviate the stress that is caused. The views above are typical of children in many different settings in that the social aspects of transfer dominate their concerns. This is unsurprising as the transfer coincides with transition from childhood to adolescence and is seen as one of the most important status passages experienced in a lifetime. Researchers have found that it has been raised to a 'rite of passage' (Measor and Wood, 1984) who also reported the frightening and mythical accounts from peers who have already made the transfer. Lucey and Reay (2000) examined the impact of such anxieties in their study of transfer and show ways in which such anxieties can lead to helpful and even constructive experiences for the year six pupils. They argue that the anxieties can mobilise children to think ahead and to anticipate future possibilities. For many children the very idea of a secondary school could

> open up a space in their imagination that ... provided a highly fertile ground in which half-formed ambiguous and contradictory fears, fantasies and hopes of their own could be planted.
>
> (Lucey and Reay, 2000, p. 192)

From our research and that of others, therefore, it appears that transfer issues can be clustered around three main pupil concerns. These are social networks, curriculum continuity and classroom organisation and language. Practice and policy initiatives have tended to focus on the first two, but it may be in coming to grips with the latter where the real challenges occur. We consider the continuities and discontinuities that are evident in each of these areas and reflect on the implications for progression.

Social networks

The first year of secondary education provides a unique context for learning, as can be seen from the comments from children in the ILMY project above, where pupils are generally positive, albeit nervous, about the rite of passage and a strange environment. Rudduck *et al.* (1996) observed that students experienced the transfer from primary to secondary school with a healthy mixture of excitement and apprehension that was fuelled by practical and social concerns rather than worries about learning.

The social concern extends beyond the children themselves and children's anxieties about transfer are shared by their families. Worries may be exacerbated by the changing family relationships during this time as the children move towards greater independence. In the IMLY project this was demonstrated by an increased preference in secondary school for a child experiencing a problem in class to ask a friend for help, rather than their mother or father.

Hargreaves and colleagues have examined the transition that children make from family orientation to identification with a peer group and the difficulties they experience as they begin to make personal and educational decisions which will have a long lasting impact on their lives (Hargreaves *et al.*, 1996). They argue that the struggle to establish identity and affiliation is the most dramatic and problematic shift for adolescents as value systems move from being defined mostly by parents to being more strongly influenced by peers. At the same time this move reflects the movement from the top of one institution to the bottom of another and leads to the renegotiation of friendships. Pratt and George (2005) show this realignment results in an intensified desire by children to conform to a peer group and this in turn results in the development of more differentiated gender identities. The role of friendships becomes very important in order to support the children in making sense of their new situation (Pratt and George, 2005, p. 24).

This re-orientation from a well-known community to a large unfamiliar environment and the reforming of the social mix within a more complex culture with its impact on the emotions and perceptions of the young is largely understood and well managed by schools. Galton *et al.* (2003) in their survey of transfer found the teachers were aware of the pupils' anxieties and recognised that these anxieties were shared by the children's families. In their review they found that attempts to address the impact of this social discontinuity had resulted in a range of transfer activities which often included both the involvement of parents and pupils alike. Teachers increasingly managed the social aspects of the transfer process and supported children and their families with open evenings, visits, induction programmes, buddy schemes and summer programmes. The children we interviewed in Year 7 suggested that pre-transfer fears were unfounded and the following comment was typical.

> I felt a little bit nervous, but excited at the same time ... about making new friends and new teachers. I made friends quite quickly and I settled down within a week.

Curriculum continuity

Many of these transfer and induction programmes also attempted to address the anxieties which related to curriculum issues. Unlike the focus on the social aspects of transition, the effectiveness of programmes to reduce curriculum discontinuity has not been as great (Galton *et al.*, 2003; Schagan and Kerr, 1999; Ofsted, 2002; Osborn *et al.*, 2006; Braund and Hames, 2005). Surveys and research findings have consistently shown that around 40 per cent of pupils fail to make educational progress during the year immediately following the change of schools and attainment dips continue into the second year of the secondary school (Galton and Willcocks, 1983; Galton *et al.*, 2000; Ofsted, 2002; Howson, 2002). The figure of 40 per cent has varied little over the years and in the current age of targets and accountability has been a source of some concern in England. Despite changes in policy in the form of curriculum and organisational innovations, the learning dip has persisted and it seems that the lack of educational progress is not ameliorated by considerations of subject continuity or styles of pedagogy (Galton *et al.*, 2003).

> In literacy here we're doing what we did in primary – in primary school we looked at the poem 'The Highwayman' and we're reading that again, so we're doing pretty much the same thing. Makes it boring!

The response from practitioners has been an increased focus on learning as process, which has moved the curriculum debate within many schools away from content. An increased interest in such approaches as accelerated learning, learning styles and multiple intelligences, building on Gardner's work (1999), has underpinned this move and conveniently allows the debate to complement discussion of the National Curriculum. It also fulfils the pressure on schools to focus on the individual. Despite evidence to the contrary, the conceptualisation of intelligence as inborn, unchangeable and fixed has persisted. Developments in the study of the brain are unhelpfully contributing to this underlying view, as in the debate over dyslexia, gifted and talented and dyscalculia, and are closely linked to multiple intelligence and learning styles. The theory of multiple intelligences expressed as ways of knowing and closely matching traditional subjects has widened our general understanding of intelligence but has, by promoting teaching as a response to individual characteristics, done very little to challenge a view of intelligence as fixed.

Classroom organisation and language

Opportunities for different forms of pedagogy do exist and become apparent when primary and secondary school are compared at the level of the classroom. The regulated subject lessons of the secondary school provide a contrast to the informal and less structured pedagogy of the primary school. Research into transfer which has focused on observations of the classroom has shown that the greatest discontinuities are to be found in the organisation of teaching groups in these two phases (Galton *et al.*, 2000; Beverton, 2003; Ferguson and Fraser, 1998; Lucey and Reay, 2000; Noyes, 2004). The primary school continues with the family-oriented whole-class structure for both teaching and pastoral care, in contrast to the secondary school where the curriculum is delivered by as many as 10 subject specialists and the pastoral role is provided by the form tutor. Primary school children face an experience of whole-class teaching punctuated by individual activities while grouped around tables (Alexander, 2000; Galton *et al.*, 1999; Reason, 2002). Individual sustained engagement with their teacher is likely to be during plenary didactic activities increasingly organised as question and answer activities. Individual support is likely to be provided through short exchanges measured in seconds. The activities will range over the days and weeks from the tightly controlled to completely relaxed where children choose activities themselves. Group work will be encouraged but only in the most effective classrooms will this go beyond the seating arrangement and common task. The children will undertake individual work which provides consolidation, revision and practice but the children are unlikely to be challenged until they encounter a session of individual support from the teacher as she circulates among the groups.

The introduction of a session begins with exposition and continues with question and answer; the conclusion reverses this. The typical day is spent in individual activities dominated by worksheets and carried out alongside peers streamed and grouped by ability. Teachers will spend five hours a day in the same room for 36 weeks in the school year. While the social interaction within the primary classroom remains informal and teachers attempt to recreate the atmosphere of a family, familiar to the children, it is important to ask if this will militate against the child's development of an understanding of their role within the classroom. Will children's understanding of the learning process, and therefore their role as a learner, be confused by the expectations raised by the mixed messages of the family conventions of the child-centred classroom. One girl explained the differences in classroom organisation:

> You can do it your own way [in secondary school], rather than having to follow the teacher's way, which we had to do more in primary school. In Year 6 we had set groups so you weren't necessarily with who you wanted to be with, so that made it more difficult because you weren't necessarily friends.

When Year 7 children were asked what makes a good learner, most replied in a similar vein:

> People who mess around are not good learners because they get distracted.

A rare insight came from a top ability boy:

> Good learners are people who think things through after they've done them and look at them instead of thinking it's all good.

A less researched area within the transfer process is the difference in the language of the classroom. Although there is often recognition of the need for a shared language, the English primary classroom is not characterised by the purposeful language of instruction (Alexander, 2000). What is more, the interest and promotion of authentic experience of activities for primary-age children, which build on their everyday lives, may even militate against the transition to technical vocabularies. The classroom is likely to be dominated by approaches which build on everyday vocabularies, representing lay knowledge as the starting point for tasks which aim to be child-centred (Alexander, 2000). This approach has long been promoted and characterised as an 'own words' philosophy where children are given the opportunities to explore ideas by using their own language – language they understand and use comfortably (Watts, 1980, quoted in White and Welford, 1988, p. 5). Although this 'own words' philosophy is regarded by many as common sense it has not always been valued and in extreme cases it is seen as a barrier to learning. The debates about standard English and the introduction of linguistic terms such as 'phoneme' and 'grapheme' to replace 'sound' and 'shape' of letters are examples of attempts to move away from this philosophy in recent primary policy.

In one sense the move to new terms is inevitable and synonymous with learning for both the teachers and the child, and the secondary school with its specialist subject curriculum is well placed to capitalise on this learning. The introduction of the specialist vocabulary can have a similar impact to the science laboratories, art studies and drama halls:

> We've been doing circuits and stuff and acids and alkalis. In English we're learning about similes and metaphors.

Implications of classroom organisation and language for transfer and progression

The new experience of facilities and specialist knowledge is underpinned by an acceleration (rather than a discontinuity) in the move towards a system of knowledge which, despite the introduction of the National Curriculum, has not been possible in the generalist primary school. Minick describes the process for the child: 'the child learns word meanings in certain forms of school instruction, not as a means of communication, but as part of a system of knowledge' (Minick, 2005, p. 45). Minick argues that this is an acceleration of a process that children have begun as they first acquire language. A failure to see the different pace of secondary school as an acceleration of the experience of the primary school can have negative effects. Braund and Hames show how a misunderstanding can lead teachers to offer pupils a 'fresh start' and in so doing to fail to build on earlier achievement and even fail to recognise what work has been carried out before. Primary pupils therefore experience repeated tasks and receive little or no bridging to the different teaching environments, teaching styles and teacher language of the secondary school (Braund and Hames, 2005, p. 782).

Braund and Hames' own science project illustrates the complexity of balancing the advantages and disadvantages of continuity and shows the practical realities of aspects of acceleration. Their STAY project (Braund and Hames, 2005, p. 785) framed an investigation of canned fizzy drinks from within the 'considering and evaluating evidence' strand of the science curriculum in an industrial and commercial context. The project started in the last year of the primary and continued in the secondary and aimed to provide continuity of approach through the three-part lesson structure. However the procedural and conceptual demands ensured a discontinuity which both excited and challenged the pupils in the first year at the secondary school and built on the Bunsen burner effect. The industrial context provided opportunities to make direct contact with drinks companies and establish the authentic real-life settings which the pupils anticipated. The pupils' reactions to the project were overwhelmingly positive and showed how the bridging can provide comfort and familiarity without repeating work carried out in the primary school. The practical procedures used gave immediate access to the science facilities and nurtured confidence in the children. The practical nature of the activity particularly supported those children who had worried about not coping with large amounts of reading and writing. The project demonstrated an acceleration in the pupils' understanding of the scientific approach and entry to the subject of science.

Our research (Bullock and Muschamp, 2006) suggests that the pupils recognise and want to enter into the authentic experiences offered by experts. It is the rich detail, idiosyncrasies and unpredictability of authentic experiences which provide the disequilibrium essential to effective learning. In this context, Vygotsky's (1934/1986) theoretical account of learning is helpful. He described a lay vocabulary (Vygotsky's term is 'natural') as representative of a lay understanding which is the first stage in a process of transition from natural to mediated forms of cognitive processes. He argued that the school curriculum is the mediated form and comprises a discrete body of knowledge which is composed of 'scientific' or 'true' concepts which are different from the everyday or lay concepts of the home. He explains learning as the transition from this lay understanding to the mediated form, knowledge structured by technical concepts. The vocabularies used to describe and explain the lay and scientific concepts may overlap, but words take on new and more specific meaning as they transfer from one to the other.

This acceleration from a lay to a technical vocabulary will involve the correction of erroneous and idiosyncratic understanding of concepts. However this is not always the case. Engeström (2005) makes the point that misconceptions are not necessarily an 'indication of immature thinking. They are culturally produced artefacts which often persist regardless of maturation' (p. 161) which reminds us that 'the act of naming is not a mental activity but a means of social interaction' (Minick, 2005, p. 45) and that 'it is essential to keep in mind that the actual and potential levels of development correspond with the intra-mental and inter-mental functioning' (Wertsch and Tulviste, 2005, p. 63). The transition from the learning which has resulted from this 'inter-mental functioning' for some children will be a radical move to a different way of knowing; for others it will be an enhancement characterised by progression and continuity.

This process of transfer is not very visible in the English primary classroom. In relation to the curriculum the new school can therefore offer a challenging and accelerating discontinuity from the comfortable traditions of the primary school.

Conclusion

In order to comprehend the development of understanding and skills related to learning, it is important to unravel the activities, emotions and perceptions of young people as they experience the transfer from primary to secondary school. At the time of our second interviews, towards the end of the first term in Year 7 in secondary school, students' excitement at the novelty of the new institution was plain. Practical concerns about the transfer had been short-lived. Many students had worried about getting lost in the larger school, or had been alarmed by hearsay about the behaviour of other pupils, but these anxieties had only lasted for the first week or so. When asked about their feelings about learning in Year 7, students thought that they were doing harder work in secondary school. They appeared more aware of a responsibility for their own learning and stressed the belief that for them to be fully engaged, learning needed to be fun.

There were three main differences between primary and secondary schools that appeared to have an impact on children's learning and identities. These were mainly related to the language and organisation of the classroom. First, the curriculum is expanded. In Year 7, it extends to a variety of topics, environments and resources offering children a range of styles and complexities of learning. While this diversity is well appreciated by most, some may find it daunting and regret the loss of the once familiar primary classroom and teacher. The need to establish educational relationships with several teachers rather than one 'parent-like' figure may involve inconsistencies in rules and roles that can undermine capability and motivation in less confident children. Second, the loss of the single class teacher means that children come to accept responsibility for their own learning. However, although most acknowledge and 'know' this, only a few understand the reality in terms of self-organisation and -evaluation. Third, the language of instruction becomes more specialised and authentic: the language of adults. Children need space and time to accommodate the social changes, more sophisticated organisation, language and weight of information. While the majority of our respondents claimed to have adjusted within the first term of transfer, for an important minority this emotional reorganisation is likely to take much longer.

Ultimately, no matter how well transfer is eased by pastoral care, cross-phase liaison, preparation and induction strategies, for the child it will always be a momentous change and an episode of turbulence. However, coping with change is a key life skill. How children cope with uncertainties and setbacks, readjust their identities and form new friendship groups may, therefore, be the most important learning experience for 11- and 12-year-olds. Monitoring and tracking attainment by subject-based targets may be less important than individual support and guidance for managing change and creating positive self-identities as good learners.

Note

1   These data were collected during the project by Muschamp and Bullock carried out with a cluster of schools in the south-west in 2003 and funded by the British Academy. The names of schools and pupils are fictitious. A fuller account of the ILMY project can be found in Bullock and Muschamp, 2006.

References

Alexander, R. (2000) *Culture and Pedagogy*, Oxford, Blackwell.

Anderson, L.W., Jacobs, J., Schramm, S. and Splittgerber, F. (2000) 'School transitions: beginning of the end or a new beginning?', *International Journal of Educational Research*, 33(4), pp. 325–39.

Beverton, S. (2003) 'Can you see the difference? Early impacts of the primary national literacy strategy on four secondary English departments', *Cambridge Journal of Education*, 33(2), pp. 217–35.

Braund, M. and Hames, V. (2005) 'Improving progression and continuity from primary to secondary science: pupils' reactions to bridging work', *International Journal of Science Education*, 27(7), pp. 781–801.

Bullock, K. and Muschamp, Y. (2006) 'Learning about learning in the primary school', *Cambridge Journal of Education*, 36(1), pp. 49–62.

Engeström, Y. (2005) 'Non scolae sed vitae discimus: towards overcoming the encapsulation of school learning', in H. Daniels (ed.), *An Introduction to Vygotsky*, Hove, Routledge, pp. 157–76.

Ferguson, P. and Fraser, B. (1998) 'Student gender, school size and changing perceptions of science learning environments during the transition from primary to secondary school', *Research in Science Education*, 28(4), pp. 387–97.

Galton, M. and Willcocks, J. (1983) 'Changing teachers and changing schools', in M. Galton and J. Willcocks (eds), *Moving from the Primary Classroom*, London, Routledge & Kegan Paul.

Galton, M., Gray, J. and Ruddock, J. (1999) *The Impact of School Transitions and Transfers on Pupil Progress and Attainment*, London: DfEE.

Galton, M., Hargreaves, L., Comber, C., Wall, D. and Pell, T. (1999a) 'Changes in patterns of teacher interaction in primary classrooms: 1976–96', *British Educational Research Journal*, 25(1), pp. 23–37.

Galton, M., Gray, J. and Rudduck, J. (2003) *Transfer and Transition in the Middle Years of Schooling (7–14): Continuities and Discontinuities in Learning*, Nottingham: DfES Publications.

Galton, M., Morrison, I. and Pell, T. (2000) 'Transfer and transition in English schools: reviewing the evidence', *International Journal of Educational Research*, 33(4), pp. 341–63.

Gardner, H. (1999) *Intelligence Reframed: Multiple Intelligences for the 21st Century*, New York: Basic Books.

Hargreaves, A., Earl, L. and Ryan, J. (1996) *Schooling for Change: Reinventing Education for Early Adolescents*, London, The Falmer Press.

Hargreaves, L. and Galton, M. (2002) *Moving from the Primary Classroom: 20 Years On*, London, Routledge.

Howson, G. (2002) 'Yet more maths problems', *National Institute Economic Review*, 179, pp. 76–86.

Lucey, H. and Reay, D. (2000) 'Identities in transition: anxiety and excitement in the move to secondary school', *Oxford Review of Education*, 26(2), pp. 191–205.

Measor, P. and Woods, P. (1984) *Changing Schools*, Milton Keynes, Open University Press.

Minick, N. (2005) 'The development of Vygotsky's thought: an introduction to Thinking and Speech', in H. Daniels (ed.), *An Introduction to Vygotsky*, Hove, Routledge, pp. 33–58.

Noyes, A. (2004) 'Learning Landscapes', *British Educational Research Journal*, 30(1), pp. 27–41.

—— (2006) 'School transfer and the diffraction of learning trajectories', *Research Papers in Education*, 21(1), pp. 43–62.

Office for Standards in Education (Ofsted) (2002) *Changing Schools: An Evaluation of the Effectiveness of Transfer Arrangements at Age 11*, London, Ofsted.

Osborn, M., McNess, E. and Pollard, A. (2006) 'Identity and transfer: a new focus for home-school knowledge exchange', *Educational Review*, 58(4), pp. 415–33.

Pinnell, P. (1998) *Middle Schooling: A Practitioner's Perspective*, IARTV Occasional Paper 57, Victoria, IARTV.

Pratt, S. and George, R. (2005) 'Transferring friendship: girls' and boys' friendships in the transition from primary to secondary school', *Children and Society*, 19(1), pp. 16–26.

Reason, R. (2002) '"Good practice" in group work', Reading 10.5 in A. Pollard (ed.), *Readings for Reflective Teaching*, London, Continuum.

Rudduck, J., Chaplain, R. and Wallace, G. (1996) *School Improvement: What Can Pupils Tell Us?*, London, David Fulton.

Schagen, S. and Kerr, D. (1999) *Bridging the Gap?* Slough, NFER.

Stir, J., Renshaw, P. and Meerman, R. (2003) 'Science as "edu-tainment": a socio-cultural analysis of a nation-wide school science competition', paper presented at European Association for Research on Learning and Instruction (EARLI) Annual Conference, Padova.

Vygotsky, L.S. (1986[1934]) *Thought and Language*, Cambridge, MA, MIT.

Wertsch, J.V. and Tulviste, P. (2005) 'L.S.Vygotsky and contemporary developmental psychology', in H. Daniels (ed.), *An Introduction to Vygotsky*, Hove, Routledge.

White, J. and Welford, G. (1988) *The Language of Science*, London APU/DES.

Reflective questions

1   During the process of transfer, schools work hard to ensure continuity in both curricular and social aspects of a pupil's experience while at the same attempting to offer the opportunity for a 'fresh start' for pupils. How do your own experiences of transfer influence your view of these conflicting demands?

2   Analyse the difficulties faced by the schools in attempting to accommodate parental wishes and to address their concerns while at the same time nurturing the growing independence of the pupil. Reflect on your own experiences and consider when and how you reached a stage of independence.

Further reading

Lucey, H. and Reay, D. (2000) 'Identities in transition: anxiety and excitement in the move to secondary school', *Oxford Review of Education*, 26(2), pp. 191–205.

Pratt, S. and George, R. (2005) 'Transferring friendship: girls' and boys' friendships in the transition from primary to secondary school', *Children and Society*, 19(1), pp. 16–26.

3.6 Moral development and education

Willem L. Wardekker

Introduction

In many (Western) countries a feeling exists at the moment that there is no longer a shared 'expectation horizon', a basis of values, norms and ways of acting and reacting that we can expect to share with unknown others. Although the feeling of a decline in 'good manners' and shared values seems to be more or less of all times, the process of globalisation has certainly given a new impetus to these feelings. Globalisation expresses itself, for instance, in a large influx of fugitives and other migrants from very different cultures, and a waning power of nation states coupled with a rising movement striving towards regional independences. Governments react to this, among other things, with an increased emphasis on re-establishing a shared value base. Part of the burden of transmitting such values falls on schools. If for no other reason, this should lead schools, teachers and other stakeholders in education to rethink the possibilities and problems of moral education. For it is by no means obvious how, or even if, values can be 'transmitted', or which values should be chosen, i.e. if the emphasis on 'shared values' is an acceptable aim for moral education.

In this chapter, I sketch the outlines of a theory of moral education and its relation to child development, loosely based on neo-Vygotskian (sociocultural) theory. Although the sociocultural view has become rather popular as a theory for the more intellectual aspects of education, its explicit application to moral development and moral education has been all but neglected until now, the most important exception being the work of Mark Tappan (2006). Still, I expect that looking from a Vygotskian point of view can contribute both to our insight in moral development and to the practice of education.

Morality

First, let's make clear what we are talking about here. Most people react to the expression 'moral education' with thinking of values and norms for behaviour. The concept of value, though, is tricky. It exists in a way, just like other concepts, on two levels. On the one hand, there are the rather abstract ideas, or rather ideals, held by some community, and for which you can find a description in a thesaurus. On the other hand, values can be described as those persons, things, or ideas that a specific person values, that are valuable to her. Such valuations are not always explicit and well formulated; they represent commitments this person has made, whether she is aware of them or not, in the course of her life. It is these emotional commitments, not the abstract principles, that guide our behaviour in a way that will be discussed later on. One goal of education might be described as bringing a person to become aware of such valuations and restructuring them, possibly with the help of the first form of values, the explicit and abstract form. Such abstract values form a means of structuring our thinking and our communication with others, but as long as they are not 'internalised', that is, coupled with a personal valuation or commitment, they do not function in our action decisions.

There is a second point we need to remember about valuations: they are not all of them of the same kind. One can value peanut butter, or being rich, or swimming, or truth, or respect. In the community, people may value decent clothing, or being honest. Turiel (1983) and Nucci (2001, 2006) distinguish three domains of social judgement:

- the personal domain: this is not so much about liking peanut butter (which is not in itself a social judgement), but primarily about seeking pleasure and avoiding unpleasantness and pain;
- the conventional domain: social rules like dress codes that could be different in a different community without harmful consequences, but which can be felt to be very important;
- the moral domain: rules and ideals that are related to the well-being of other people, such as respect or honesty.

It should be kept in mind that the boundaries between the domains are rather fuzzy, and depend partly on the feelings of the community. For some, especially for adolescents, clothing is in the personal domain, for others it is an important matter of convention. In some societies, homosexuality is considered a moral problem, in others it is seen as belonging to the conventional or even the personal domain.

Now we can be more precise about the aims of moral education: it is not only about bringing children in contact with moral values and rules, but also about re-building their commitments such that in situations of conflict, moral values will tend to be prioritised above those in the personal and conventional domain, and a course of action is chosen that is beneficial rather than harmful to others. However, education can never ensure that a pro-social action decision will be made; acting morally is never totally determined by emotional commitments or by thinking. One reason for that is exactly that in most situations, many wishes and commitments play a role at the same time, and it depends on a lot of factors what decision is finally made – be it consciously or intuitively. Another reason is that many situations that require action are too complex for us to be able to determine clearly what the 'right' course of action is.

For the same reasons, it is problematic to consider morality or moral education as a separate field, in which for instance separate lessons could be given in schools. Many moments in actual life where action has to be taken have a moral component, because nearly always other people are involved in some way. In almost none of those moments are moral considerations the only ones to be taken into account, because situations are always complex. Thus, morality is normally a component, or a quality, of actions. When we speak about a 'moral action', we normally mean an action that has moral quality. However, it is possible to distinguish a separate 'moral activity': when we explicitly consider the morality of a projected course of action, morality becomes the focal point of our activity. This is a 'moral action' in a different sense.

Moral development

The development of the human ability to make moral action decisions is not something that happens apart from general development. Rather, it is gradually differentiated out of other aspects of development. Moreover, it does not develop all by itself in an isolated individual. Every human being is from the moment of birth a member of some community, and moral development depends on that community. Bowlby's attachment theory (1984) makes clear how development in general depends on the formation of emotional attachment to caregivers from the first moment after birth. This is an important element in moral development too, because later commitments to other persons, to causes and values, develop as a differentiation from these early attachments. The need to belong, to be accepted by others, may be regarded (along with the need for autonomy and competence, as Deci and Ryan, 1985, theorise) as a prime need of all human beings and as the beginning of all aspects of development. At the same time, the differentiation of attachment into the moral and other domains is only possible as a result of development in other areas.

There is a complicated interaction between general development and education. Some theorists have maintained that development comes first, and education can do no more than fill the spaces that autonomous development has created with 'content'. Sociocultural theory, however, holds that development combines growth and stimuli from the environment, especially the social and cultural environment, in such a way that mental functioning reaches a higher plane by the incorporation of culturally available 'mental instruments', the most important of which is language. The first step that is important for moral development, however, occurs before the child is able to use language. It is the gradual acquisition of self-control. As Carr (2006, p. 452) notes, 'it seems hard to see how children or young people might acquire more complex virtues of practical wisdom, justice and even courage, in the absence of some appropriate degree of control over their desires, passions and appetites'. Physical and neural development make control possible; but the form it takes, and the specific incentives, come from the social environment, especially from the persons the child is attached to. Some authors writing about early years development hold that self-control is mainly the product of disciplining measures by others, resulting in the child trying to avoid the accompanying negative emotions by complying. However, such a view disregards the importance of attachment and the child's wish to belong. From an early age, children want to be and to do just like the persons that are important to them. This brings them to imitate the actions of those persons, mostly without understanding why these actions are performed. The caregivers will often play along, giving help and directions, and generally accepting the child *as if* it was a participant in the activity. In such interchanges, learning takes place, certainly including learning self-control, based on positive emotions related to being able to participate.

A second point is that, as Dunn (2006) argues, even young children have already some insight into the feelings of others, and will (with the help of others) try to avoid causing them distress. In this beginning empathy we can also see the interaction between the child and its social environment as the driving force of moral development. For next to self-control, empathy and the ability to take the perspective of the other that develops out of it are prerequisites for morality.

Such learning processes form the beginnings of the acquisition of pro-social valuations. This is not to say that small children can already act morally. They cannot make informed choices, nor can they be held fully responsible. But when they participate in social practices, the moral aspect of their actions (together with many of the more technical aspects) will be taken care of by more adult participants. It is exactly in this way, where novices are treated 'as if' they could fully participate in social practices, that they learn to become more central participants (Lave and Wenger, 1991); this principle holds true for the moral aspects of behaviour too.

It should be clear from this description that the valuations a child builds in the course of her life are not totally idiosyncratic. Other people with whom the individual interacts point out the objects and so forth to which a value is to be attached, they show their own valuations and their valuation of the individual's valuations, they value the individual's developing identity in a certain way. And in doing so, they in turn express not just idiosyncratic valuations but at least partly those a community of practice has developed in its history of creating ways to realise its goals in a resisting world. (Such practices are not only those of work or school; any human goal-directed activity takes the form of a cultural practice, that is, has a historical and cultural form.) 'In our self-definition and self-evaluation we have to take as a background a sense of what is significant independently of our autonomous will', Bonnett and Cuypers (2003, p. 334) say, paraphrasing Charles Taylor. Learning about the world and building an identity are fundamentally social processes. This on the other hand should not be taken as a strict socialisation process: the commitments and interpretations of the world an individual makes depend also on prior experience, connect with earlier valuations, and are also related to pre-existing (but not necessarily unchangeable) personality characteristics. Growing up and education are a matter neither of (creating opportunities for) autonomous self-realisation nor of passive socialisation; they are best seen as a process of individuation in which the individual identity gradually takes shape.

Development and language

From birth, development and learning processes take place in a language environment. Disciplining, imitating participation, and other learning situations are almost invariably, if not totally expressed in language, then at least accompanied by it. The same principle is at work as in imitative participation: the child probably does not understand fully, but caregivers treat it as if it understood, which provides a challenge for the child to participate more fully, with better understanding and better language use.

An important point in development is reached when a child gradually learns to use language not only as a means of communication but as a means to regulate its own behaviour. For this signifies the advent of what Vygotsky called the 'higher psychological functions', which develop out of the 'lower' functions when these are restructured by language. This implies that a child can now 'talk to itself', representing within itself the dialogue it otherwise conducts with adults. This concept of mediated functioning, or mediated activity, is central to a neo-Vygotskian view of development, and indeed of human activity itself. Although mediation is not limited to representations in language but can make use of anything that can be used as an 'instrument', language is certainly the most important medium. An example of the restructuring that occurs can be seen in the way memory works: young children probably remember things more or less pictorially, while older children and adults remember mainly by the use of language aids and other means, such as the famous knot in a handkerchief.

This kind of restructuring by the use of mediational means, especially language, is true of morality too. As Tappan (2006, p. 354) says, real 'moral functioning (like all "higher psychological functioning") is necessarily mediated by words, language, and forms of discourse'. Language makes it possible to give meaning to existing valuations. It is the growing command of language that makes reflection possible and, with it, the capability of directing one's own behaviour and taking responsibility for it, and also of reconsidering and changing the original valuations – in short, of real moral action. Thus, the advent of language also provides education with a new kind of starting point. But before we can analyse what exactly those opportunities for education look like, we have to go into the question of what is meant by 'the capability of directing one's own behaviour'.

Identity stories

Human beings, at least in Western cultures, learn to organise their valuations and the inter-pretations of (their position in) the world attached to them into more or less coherent images of themselves, or rather, given the language-based character of thinking, into stories about themselves. As Tappan (2006) points out, such stories are not couched in the language of abstract ideas, but 'in the vernacular'. They are constructed out of reminiscences of the past, of projections of the future using models that are available in the culture in which one lives (e.g. wanting to be like a television personality, a football player, not wanting to be like your dad, and so on), of interpretations of 'ascribed' elements of identity (what does it mean *to me* to be a man, a Russian, ...) and so on. These stories are constructed and reconstructed as interactions with other people and with situations demand; experiences are integrated into them; new choices are made and obtain a place. Although adolescence is the period in which young people are explicitly involved in (re)constructing their identities, it is a process that begins much earlier and goes on over the life span.

We use such stories as an instrument, as a sort of mirror, to ask ourselves who we are (or want to be) and what that means for how we want to act in a given situation. The answer we find in this way can always only be a heuristic: we do not *need* to act in a way we see as consistent. How we really act will depend on many factors: on the strength of our convic-tions about ourselves, on the quality of the analysis of the situation, but also maybe on our mood or our physical well-being. (This is always supposing that there are multiple courses of action open to us, which is not always the case.) Also, the mirror does not always give us the same image: we have many stories about ourselves, directed at different publics, and some of them inconsistent with each other.

Identity stories can be said to have moral qualities (Wardekker, 2004). These may be stronger or weaker, and more or less integrated, according to the nature and the strength of the valuations that underlie them, and to the extent to which a person has tried to give conscious attention to the moral side of the identity stories. One goal of moral education, then, would be to get students to re-examine their valuations, to make them think about these and about the stories they use about themselves, in the light of their moral aspect – that is, to re-structure their identities with a view to their relations to other people and to the world they live in.

Of course, in many situations we do not really first refer to a more or less elaborated story and then use it as a mirror to make a decision. Like many other actions, in well-known situ-ations the process will have become automated – compare it with writing or with riding a bicycle. We might talk here about 'moral intuition'. Narvaez (2006) calls it moral expertise, and rightly says that reaching moral expertise is the proper aim of moral education. Learning to become an expert requires training under the guidance of others. Also, expertise is never fully unconscious: like writing, it can be made conscious again when the automatic response does not suffice: in a new situation, or when the normal course of action is challenged, for instance by an educator. Such moments call for a restructuring of our identity stories and perhaps of the underlying valuations. This restructuring can be done in several ways, one of which is by systematically referring to the abstract value concepts that we normally think of as 'values'. Learning to do that *can* be the subject of a systematic course of learning – but it will only be effective if there is an underlying need to restructure one's identity. Such a need occurs, for instance, when the situation in which a person knows how to behave undergoes major changes – which some would say is almost a defining characteristic of the present world. This is one reason that moral education in this sense has become a priority.

Other theories of moral development

The theory outlined above, which emphasises the development of the moral qualities of identity stories, differs in a number of ways from other theories that have been proposed in the field of moral development. In fact, there are so many theories that it is impossible to mention all of them here. But certainly the most influential has been the cognitive developmental approach of Kohlberg. Based on Piaget's paradigm of general cognitive development, it concentrates on the types of arguments children of different ages are able to use in discussions about moral issues. Part of its popularity undoubtedly stems from the fact that it is non-relativistic, placing values like justice at the top of the developmental trajectory. According to Kohlberg, arguments of personal pleasure or pain, and conventional arguments, make place in the course of development for genuinely moral arguments, so using the former kind of arguments is seen as a sign of unripeness. This aspect of the theory has been challenged by Turiel and Nucci's domain theory, which holds that development in each of these three domains (personal, conventional and moral) is relatively independent. According to Nucci (2006, p. 661), this 'social-cognitive domain theory' allows for a more pluralistic view, while not becoming relativistic.

Another problem with Kohlberg's model is its concentration on explicit reasoning and verbal interaction. This has three implications. For one, it tends to interpret morality as a product of moral reasoning instead of as an aspect or quality of actions. Morality thus becomes a separate area of life. In its applications to curriculum, correct reasoning tends to become more important than acting morally. Second, the theory is overly rationalistic: it supposes that moral decisions ought to be well-considered and grounded in the best reasoning available to a person in a certain developmental stage. But coming to a decision is not just a matter of sound reasoning, and in making decisions we do not refer to value concepts as such, but to our identity narratives in which our experiences 'personalise' these concepts with affects. The third implication then is that the theory tends to ignore the affective anchoring of moral convictions in the person. Kohlberg himself has tried to remedy this aspect by promoting the concept of the 'just community school', where the school community is the place where commitment to moral values is fostered; this concept, however, remains relatively unintegrated with the rest of his theory.

Kohlberg's theory is a developmental interpretation of a class of theories about ethical behaviour in general called 'rule ethics'. Such theories hold that in acting morally, people refer to more or less explicit rules of behaviour. Another class of theories can be called 'character ethics' (Narvaez, 2006; Carr, 2006). In such theories, in contrast, emotional commitment is all important. In 'character education' theories, the idea is that acting in a moral way rests on more or less implicit dispositions leading to 'automatic' responses. In trying to establish these dispositions, students are tackled about conduct that does not conform to norms that are supposedly uncontested, they are given stories and other examples of morally acceptable behaviour, and teachers are supposed to act as role models. Moreover, individuals are seen as embedded in a supportive community which makes it possible for them to thrive and realise a full life.

However, this type of education does hardly take its point of departure in the learner's own pre-existing valuations, and thus runs a real risk of becoming oppressively moralising.

The effect of this may well be that learners resist this pressure, either because it comes from teachers who represent the type of school tasks that they have learned to dodge as much as possible, or because they see that in their actual behaviour, not a lot of people do realise this kind of values unrestrictedly. Also, a 'person of character' is clearly not somebody who has learned to reflect critically on their own behaviour or that of others, which implies the risk that the values that constitute the 'character' are those chosen by a powerful group. Also, learners may not acquire the kind of reflective abilities directed at their own identity narratives that are necessary in a pluralistic and rapidly changing society. In such a society they may be confronted with real moral dilemmas which cannot be solved by relying on automatic responses (and neither, for that matter, by abstract reasoning with general moral principles). The attractiveness of this model seems rooted in nostalgia for a life in a warm and caring community and in conservatism.

There are many theories that try to combine the best of both worlds, so-called hybrid or integrative models, the most elaborate of which was developed by the Child Development Project (Solomon *et al.*, 1988). But as Nucci (2006, p. 660) says, 'The effort to coordinate paradigms with such divergent underlying assumptions is always difficult and generally problematic.' Probably the most interesting new effort is a model called Integrative Ethical Education (Narvaez, 2006). It is 'built on the notion of expertise development. Expertise refers to a refined, deep understanding that is evident in practice and action. [...] Expertise harnesses the full capacities of the individual' (Narvaez, 2006, p. 716). Moral expertise is gained not through mindless repetition or endless reasoning, but is constructed by 'apprenticeship under the guidance of others' in the community. Narvaez adopts a constructivist perspective based on Piaget, but at the same time emphasises the fact that most often, action is guided by subconscious insight and thought comes only after the fact. Therefore, educators should create caring environments and also make sure that ethical knowledge is integrated into 'naive' insights.

Narvaez's theory is an example of a third class of theories of ethical behaviour called 'virtue ethics'. This term may be somewhat confusing, since 'virtue' is also used by proponents of character ethics in the sense of habits formed by repeating a behaviour over and over. But both Narvaez and Carr interpret 'virtue' as 'patterns of behavior developed with practice, effort, and guidance from parents, teachers and mentors, until external guidance is unnecessary. In other words, virtue development requires apprenticeship under the guidance of others' (Narvaez, 2006, p. 719).

Although Narvaez's model has much to commend it, it concentrates on the cognitivist view of mind as an information processing facility. This is a 'monological' interpretation of the working of the mind. Because of that, it remains somewhat unclear how the unconscious insights acquired in experience are integrated with the explicit rules the community has into a consistent pattern of virtues. A discursive theory of mind (Harré, 1983) might be better suited as a background for thinking about morality.

Such a discursive theory is advocated by Tappan (2006), who is working to develop a sociocultural (Vygotsky-based) theory of moral education. On this view, human thinking, once it is transformed into a 'higher psychological process', i.e. has become language-based, consists of 'internalised' dialogue with significant others. In this internal dialogue, multiple 'voices' or points of view are represented (it is polyphonic), so for instance, a person can hold both a justice-oriented and a care-oriented view of morality. This is because we construct stories about ourselves out of examples, analogies, ideas, that seem to express some of our affective commitments and can serve to centre our thinking about ourselves on. Thus, young children want to be like their caregivers; adolescents try on different identities based on movie or football stars, peer cultures, and so on. Such examples are culturally available. Thus, how we see ourselves depends on the possibilities that a specific culture affords. (This implies that identity is not something found deep inside us; it is more like the stick of a blind person.) One consequence of this is that the way we see ourselves can only be a unity inasmuch as the culture in which we live is a unified whole, because the elements of our identity have been taken from that culture at different times and for different needs. However, virtually no culture is such a unity. There are always different points of view, different interests, different groups. And in a world that becomes increasingly multicultural, our identities will be based on different cultures too. That is, identities can be understood as *bricolages* that contain all manner of inconsistencies.

Tappan's views seem to take rule ethics as their point of departure. And indeed, at many points he speaks of moral functioning and morality in the same way as do the proponents of rule ethics: as a separate field or activity concerned with the moral justification of actions:

> Moral functioning is the higher psychological process (in Vygotsky's terms) that a person invokes in order to respond to and resolve a specific problem, conflict, or dilemma that requires a moral decision and a moral action – that is, when one is faced with the question 'What is the "right" or "moral" thing to do in this situation?'
>
> (Tappan, 2006, p. 355)

However, Tappan emphasises that morality is not a system of rules that one refers to, but a number of stories in everyday language, based on dialogue with others. These stories are polyphonic, that is, they represent different points of view, causing the person to engage in an inner dialogue. Therefore, it is perhaps more adequate to interpret Tappan as saying that virtues (in the sense of Narvaez) are and remain necessarily language-based. The consequences of such a position have yet to be explored. I do not think however that it implies that morality is always a function of, or even limited to, explicit inner dialogue about the question of what is right. But it does have to do with being able to take explicit responsibility for one's actions, whether they are premeditated or 'intuitive'.

Interpersonal morality or citizenship

Philosophers of morality tend to speak of the ideal to be reached in moral development and education in terms of personal flourishing or 'the good life'. Given that morality has always to do with one's relationships with other people, these terms should not be taken as exclusively individualistic as they may sound. Human beings are dependent on others to lead a good and flourishing existence. Exactly what this means in terms of moral valuations to be made is contested between different writers. Whether the emphasis should be on justice (Kohlberg) or on care (Gilligan) as a paramount value or on something else entirely, whether morality consists in the reflective development of one's own pre-existing values (which leads to a relativistic view), in the adoption of the values shared by the community, or in arriving at universal values, all these are issues that are hotly discussed. I will not go into those discussions here, but rather pay attention to a somewhat different point, raised (among others) by Nucci (2006, p. 662). Nucci states that morality can never be confined to the interpersonal relations a person enters upon, because this excludes what happens at the level of social systems. A moral person is also someone who is able to reflect on, and if necessary criticise, the workings of the social systems of which he or she is a member, and to act on such an evaluation. Many of the great evils in the world are not to be located on the interpersonal level; they more often than not start with an emphasis on differences between groups, leading to the exclusion of the group with less power (Schuyt, 2006). Democracy is the only answer we have against such processes, because it inherently values differences instead of condemning them. However, it is a difficult answer. Thinking in terms of the exclusion of differences and even of antagonisms between groups is alluring, especially for those belonging to a dominant group, exactly because it provides a feeling of belonging and makes it possible to overlook differences within one's own group. Therefore, Schuyt emphasises that a democracy requires members with a strong sense of personal identity and who have acquired what he calls 'democratic virtues', among which are openness to differences and a love for truth. It is for such reasons that I think we should speak of the aims of moral development and education in terms of democratic citizenship. And because inclusiveness and openness to differences imply that this concept be extended to every human being, it cannot be limited to those countries where democracy is actually supposed to exist. We must strive for global democratic citizenship. Nussbaum (1996) states that three elements are necessary for this: a critical examination of oneself and one's traditions; to see oneself as a human being bound to all other human beings by ties of recognition and concern; and the ability to think what it would be like to be in another's shoes.

But clearly there are numerous countries that have no history of such democratic ideals, and no intention to convert to them. What does citizenship mean in a dictatorship, or in a country where the highest political value is submission to its leaders? Is it realistic to interpret democratic citizenship as a universally valid ideal, and if so, what would its propagation in non-democratic countries mean? Can we really expect people in such countries, who have a long history of looking at the proper authorities for important decisions, to suddenly embrace ideals such as autonomy and responsibility? And, on the other hand, can we afford to leave them out of our considerations when the whole point of global citizenship is inclusiveness? At this point, Stevenson (2003) points at the importance of 'civil society', which he interprets as a sphere of agency where criticism against vested powers can become institutionalised, exactly because this sector now also exists of global organisations or at least global networks. Such structures, according to Stevenson, could be organised in such a way that they ensure the voice of minorities and repressed groups be heard. This implies that global citizenship is not only dependent upon learning processes of individuals. It also requires certain organisation forms that afford its being put into practice.

Education for democratic citizenship

Education for citizenship, as Schuyt (2006) implies, is primarily a matter of helping young people to establish strong personal identities, with due attention paid to the moral qualities of the commitments they build, especially in the form of democratic virtues, and to their abilities to reflect on their own commitments. This immediately implies that moral education cannot stand alone; it is an aspect of the whole educational endeavour, because education as a whole can be said to direct itself to the formation of personal identity. We can, however, point to some aspects of education and to some problems that are particularly relevant in the context of establishing 'democratic virtues'.

First of all, we have seen that identity formation has to do with the integration of emotion in the form of affective commitments and cognitions. The starting point for this integration lies in the experiences students make. To a certain extent, schools can make relevant experiences happen. Providing such experiences, however, requires a curriculum that does not aim just at the acquisition of knowledge and skills but at the introduction of learners in selected cultural and societal practices. This is what such approaches as dual learning, project method, and the like are, or ought to be, about. In other words, ideally moral education supposes a transformation of the curriculum such that learners are enabled to have authentic experiences and valuate the things they learn in relation to their possible position in such practices. If the curriculum is organised around the participation in practices, moral questions related to the complexities, problems and conflicts in such practices will present themselves along with opportunities to learn knowledge and skills. This gives learners opportunities to encounter real moral problems (for instance, which faction to support and for what reasons) and to take a critical stance toward the proceedings in and the future development of a practice. Adequate education should help learners to discern such complexities, to find words, stories and images to talk about them, and to handle them adequately in their actions with the help of all kinds of 'instruments' provided.

Of course, such a curriculum is not the same thing as learning directly in a workplace. Educational institutions have a dual obligation here: to ensure that learners are safe and also feel safe, both physically and emotionally; and to ensure that there is adequate time and opportunity to reflect on and discuss experiences. These conditions are necessary for learners to be able to see themselves as part of a practice on the one hand, and not be totally immersed in it on the other hand. If an actual practice does not provide such opportunities, they may be simulated in school. Also, the school should whenever necessary, offer opportunities to concentrate on learning necessary knowledge, skills, and attitudes. These are conditions under which students may learn not just to belong to a certain group that endorses certain values, but also to take an informed critical stance. Both are necessary for participating in a democracy.

Integration of cognition and affect, however, does not imply that personal identity becomes an integrated unity. It will always remain a polyphonic and dialogic process. We all have multiple and conflicting loyalties and commitments. Everybody has to do work to handle such inconsistencies when they surface – a task that is more pressing in present Western multicultural societies (Giddens, 1991; Sennett, 1998; Kegan, 1994), but is also there in more stable and traditional societies. In such tasks, we recognise that we have in our own conceptions of ourselves elements that seem strange and alien to us, that we are surprised and often afraid to discover in ourselves.

In that sense, we do not just live in multicultural societies; each of us is a multicultural being, each of us is in that sense already a world citizen. But many are afraid to admit this, to discover such a pattern of inconsistencies in themselves, partly because the cultural ideal of an adult person has always been consistency. It may be this fear, the fear of chaos in ourselves, that drives many people to deny it, to try and see themselves as wholly belonging to one consistent cultural pattern. But how can we recognise and accept cultural differences between people and between cultures if we are afraid of accepting them within ourselves? The problem of global democratic citizenship is partly a problem of self-knowledge. We need to know ourselves in order to understand the world. We need to accept the diversity and the conflicting commitments within ourselves in order to form a commitment to a diverse and conflict-ridden world.

This is not a task that education can fulfil on its own. As Basil Bernstein famously said, education cannot compensate for society. In a world ridden with exclusionary practices, war, and poverty, education is at a disadvantage. Creating the conditions for democratic citizenship is a political as well as an educational task.

References

Bonnett, M. and Cuypers, S. (2003) 'Autonomy and authenticity in education', in N. Blake, P. Smeyers, R. Smith, and P. Standish (eds), *The Blackwell Guide to the Philosophy of Education*, Oxford, Blackwell, pp. 326–40.

Bowlby, J. (1984) *Attachment and Loss, vol. 1: Attachment*, 2nd edn, Harmondsworth, Penguin.

Carr, D. (2006) 'The moral roots of citizenship: reconciling principle and character in citizenship education', *Journal of Moral Education*, 35, pp. 443–56.

Deci, E. and Ryan, R. (1985) *Intrinsic Motivation and Self-determination in Human Behavior*, New York, Academic Press.

Dunn, J. (2006) 'Moral development in early childhood and social interaction in the family', in M. Killen and J.G. Smetana (eds), *Handbook of Moral Development*, Mahwah, NJ, Lawrence Erlbaum Associates, pp. 331–50.

Giddens, A. (1991) *Modernity and Self-identity; Self and Society in a Late Modern Age*, Cambridge, Polity Press.

Harré, R. (1983) *Personal Being*, Oxford, Blackwell.

Kegan, R. (1994) *In Over Our Heads: The Mental Demands of Modern Life*, Cambridge, MA, Harvard University Press.

Lave, J., and Wenger, E. (1991) *Situated Learning: Legitimate Peripheral Participation*, Cambridge, Cambridge University Press.

Narvaez, D. (2006) 'Integrative ethical education', in M. Killen and J.G. Smetana (eds), *Handbook of Moral Development*, Mahwah, NJ, Lawrence Erlbaum Associates, pp. 703–32.

Nucci, L. (2001) *Education in the Moral Domain*, Cambridge, Cambridge University Press.

—— (2006) 'Education for moral development', in M. Killen and J.G. Smetana (eds), *Handbook of Moral Development*, Mahwah, NJ, Lawrence Erlbaum Associates, pp. 657–81.

Nussbaum, M.C. (1996) *For Love of Country: Debating the Limits of Patriotism*, Boston, Beacon Press.

Schuyt, K. (2006) *Democratische deugden* [Democratic virtues], Amsterdam, Leiden University Press.

Sennett, R. (1998) *The Corrosion of Character: The Personal Consequences of Work in the New Capitalism*, New York, NY, Norton.

Solomon, D., Watson, M., Delucchi, K., Schaps, E. and Battistich, V. (1988) 'Enhancing children's prosocial behavior in the classroom', *American Educational Research Journal*, 25, pp. 527–54.

Stevenson, N. (2003) *Cultural Citizenship: Cosmopolitan Questions*, Maidenhead, Berks., Open University Press.

Tappan, M.B. (2006) 'Mediated moralities: sociocultural approaches to moral development', in M. Killen and J.G. Smetana (eds), *Handbook of Moral Development*, Mahwah, NJ, Lawrence Erlbaum Associates, pp. 351–74.

Turiel, E. (1983) *The Development of Social Knowledge: Morality and Convention*, Cambridge, Cambridge University Press.

Wardekker, W. (2004) 'Moral education and the construction of meaning', *Educational Review*, 56(2), pp. 183–92.

Reflective questions

1 Educators thinking about moral education have often come up with more or less elaborate lists of values that they want children to acquire. (In many of these, *respect* figures prominently.) What, in your opinion, is the actual value of such lists?

2 Restructuring the curriculum to provide more 'authentic experiences' is a daunting task. How could you bring elements of moral education into the curriculum on a smaller scale? And are there curriculum areas, e.g. maths, that are unrelated to moral education?

3   Teaching, even if not explicitly concerned with moral education, has been called an inherently moral enterprise. Can you think of examples of this inherent morality? Would schools and teachers benefit from discussing such instances of the morality of teaching?

Further reading

Nucci, L. (2001) *Education in the Moral Domain*, Cambridge, Cambridge University Press. (An account of moral development based on the domains theory.)

Holland, D., Lachicotte, W., Skinner, D. and Cain, C. (1998) *Identity and Agency in Cultural Worlds,* Cambridge, MA, Harvard University Press. (About personal identity and its development, not especially about morality.)

Narvaez, D. (2006) 'Integrative ethical education', in M. Killen and J.G. Smetana (eds), *Handbook of Moral Development*, Mahwah, NJ, Lawrence Erlbaum Associates, pp. 703–32. (Gives a good overview of the field.)

Stengel, B.S., and Tom, A.R. (2006) *Moral Matters: Five Ways to Develop the Moral Life of Schools*, New York, Teachers College Press. (Discusses five models of the relation between 'the academic' and 'the moral'.)

3.7 The significance of 'I' in living educational theories

Jack Whitehead

Introduction

This chapter is based on two assumptions about ourselves as persons and the evolution of the social formations in which we live and work. The first is that everyone reading this chapter has something in common. That is, each of us has explored the implications of asking ourselves an 'I' question of the kind, 'How do I improve what I am doing?' The second is that a world of educational quality can be created through individuals producing and sharing explanations of our educational influences in our own learning, in the learning of others and in the social formations in which we are living and working (Whitehead, 2007). I call these explanations living educational theories to distinguish them from the propositional and dialectical theories of disciplines of education.

The chapter is organised into three parts. The first explains the influence of a 'disciplines' approach to educational theory that *replaces* the principles individuals use, to explain their educational influences in 'I' enquiries, with principles from propositional and dialectical theories. It explains my break with this approach because of its limitations and because of a commitment to generate living educational theories in a way that retains a direct relationship with the conscious lived experience of the individual 'I'. The second part is focused on the significance of including 'I' in living educational theories in the generation of a world of educational quality. The theories are constituted by doctoral theses of individuals working and researching in a range of professional, social and cultural contexts. While the generation of living theories is not restricted to doctoral research programmes, I have chosen to focus on successfully completed doctorates because they have passed through rigorous legitimation procedures of examination in terms of their contributions to educational knowledge. The final part explains how insights from propositional and dialectical theories of educational influences in learning can be used in the generation of living educational theories from a perspective of inclusionality. This perspective includes a new epistemology for educational knowledge.

Because of past experiences (Whitehead, 2008) of miscommunication I want to take care to avoid misunderstandings about the nature of my criticism of limitations and mistakes in both a disciplines approach to educational theory and in the sole use of propositional and/or dialectical logics in explanations of educational influences in learning. I want to be clear that I value and use insights from the disciplines of education in the generation of living educational theories in enquiries of the kind, 'How do I improve what I am doing?' I also use and value the propositional and dialectical logics that give form to most theories of education. However, the central point of this chapter is to reveal the errors and limitations in thinking that valid explanations of the educational influences of individuals in learning can be generated from the sole use of the disciplines of education and the propositional and dialectical logics that structure the majority of academic theories and research methods programmes in education.

Explaining how I permitted the colonising influences of propositional and dialectical theories of education

Some 42 years ago I began my studies of educational theory as a 22-year-old on my initial teacher education programme at the University of Newcastle in the UK. I read the works of John Dewey (1916) on *Democracy and Education* and Richard Peters (1966) on *Ethics and Education*. Between 1968 and 1970, in my initial studies of educational theory for the Advanced Diploma in the Philosophy and Psychology of Education at the Institute of Education of London University, I agreed with the view of educational theory, known as the disciplines approach. In this view, educational theory was constituted by the disciplines of the philosophy, psychology, sociology and history of education. Using a Kantian form of transcendental deduction Peters would justify his claims that any rational person who was seriously asking themselves questions of the kind 'What ought I to do?' must necessarily be committed to living values of fairness, equality, justice, consideration of interests, worthwhile activities and to the procedural principles of democracy. I continue to be inspired by Peters' (1966, p. 319) advocacy of learning to participate more actively with zest and humanity in democratic forms of government.

Looking back on my initial acceptance of the disciplines approach I can see my error in permitting the colonisation of my mind through the pedagogic power of my teachers in the communication of the ideas. Here is my explanation of how I permitted the colonising influences of the disciplines approach to educational theory. I permitted this influence by accepting the move (Peters, 1977, p. 140) to replace the principles I used in explaining my educational influences in learning as I explored the implications of asking 'How do I improve what I am doing?' In 1968 I found myself asking this question daily, in the context of my educational relationships with my pupils at Langdon Park School in London's Tower Hamlets. I would then attend weekly sessions at the Institute in which the living 'I' in such questions was replaced by the abstract concept of a 'person', as the adherents to the disciplines approach ignored the living 'I' in their pedagogic adherence to the disciplines approach. It is my initial acceptance of this replacement that I am distinguishing as my mistake in accepting this colonising influence. It violates my understanding of the relation in education described by Martin Buber as the humility of the educator (1947, p. 122). In 1971 I rejected this assumption of 'replacement' because I could not produce a valid explanation for my educational influences in my own learning and in the learning of my students by applying any theory, individually or collectively from any of the disciplines of education that constituted the disciplines approach to educational theory.

In 1983 Paul Hirst acknowledged a similar mistake, in believing that principles developed in the context of immediate practical experience would be replaced by principles with more theoretical justification, when he said that much understanding of educational theory will be developed

> in the context of immediate practical experience and will be co-terminus with everyday understanding. In particular, many of its operational principles, both explicit and implicit, will be of their nature generalisations from practical experience and have as their justification the results of individual activities and practices.
>
> In many characterisations of educational theory, my own included, principles justified

in this way have until recently been regarded as at best pragmatic maxims having a first crude and superficial justification in practice that in any rationally developed theory would be replaced by principles with more fundamental, theoretical justification. That now seems to me to be a mistake. Rationally defensible practical principles, I suggest, must of their nature stand up to such practical tests and without that are necessarily inadequate.

(Hirst, 1983, p. 18)

My purpose in coming to the University of Bath in 1973 as a Lecturer in Education was to contribute to the generation of educational theories that could produce valid explanations for the educational influences of individuals in their own learning and in the learning of others. I call the explanations that individuals produce for their educational influence in their own learning, in the learning of others and in the learning of social formations, living educational theories (Whitehead, 1989; Whitehead and McNiff, 2006), to distinguish them from the propositional and dialectical theories that constitute the disciplines of education. I have been exploring the implications of asking myself 'How do I improve what I am doing?' in the context of my life in education. In supporting others in their enquiries I have resisted the severance of the living 'I' through reification into the linguistic concept 'person'.

Schroyer made a similar point about the work of Heidegger that 'the "I" remains formal and yet pretends that the word contains content in-itself. For Adorno, Heidegger's existentialism is a new Platonism which implies that authenticity comes in the complete disposal of the person over himself – as if there were no determination emerging from the objectivity of history' (1973, p. vvii).

I am claiming that the generation and legitimation of living educational theories in the Academy require the acceptance of a living inclusional logic and living standards of judgement. Present regimes of truth in the Academy are structured mainly through the propositional logics of Aristotle and the dialectical logics of Hegel, Marx and Ilyenkov. These logics eliminate the inclusional logics of living individuals from the explanations of the educational influences of individuals in learning. In the following section I shall present evidence that shows how creative spaces have been opened in the Academy for the legitimation of living educational theories that do offer valid explanations for these educational influences. Lest you think the above claims about present regimes of truth are ungrounded I point to a requirement of the research committee of Kingston University in the early 1990s, when I was acting as a consultant to promote action research, that the personal pronoun be removed from the title of a research enquiry, because a self-study involving 'I' had no place in academic research!

The idea of logic as the mode of thought that is appropriate for comprehending the real as rational (Marcuse, 1964, p. 105) appeals to me. If someone says of my writings that they aren't logical I take this as a fundamental criticism of the validity of my ideas. I want my ideas about the nature of educational theory to be logical in the sense that they are comprehensible to a rational mind. Yet even as I use the words 'rational mind' I am aware of at least three logics that can distinguish very different forms of rationality. Here is a brief clarification of the distinguishing characteristics of the three forms of logic I use in my educational enquiries into the nature of educational knowledge and theory.

The first logic I learnt to use in my studies of educational theory was a logic with a 2,500-year history in the Western Academy. It is the Aristotelean logic that eliminates, through the Law of Contradiction, the possibility that two mutually exclusive statements, such as

I am free/I am not free, can be true simultaneously. In my engagement with theories in the philosophy, psychology, sociology, history, economics, theology, politics, management and leadership of education they all abide by this Law of Contradiction in eliminating such contradictions between statements.

The second logic I learnt to use was a dialectical logic, again with a 2,500-year history, from the ideas of Socrates expressed through the writings of Plato. In the *Phaedrus*, a dialogue on love, Socrates explains the art of the dialectician in holding both the One and the Many together. Socrates explains to Phaedrus that human beings have two ways of coming to know, they can break things down into separate components as nature directs (and not after the manner of a bungling carver!) and we can hold things together in a general idea. Socrates holds in high esteem the art of the dialectician in holding both together these apparently contradictory perspectives of holding something as both One and Many.

The third logic I am learning to use is a living logic of inclusionality (Rayner, 2005), which emerges in the course of creating one's own form of life with responses to the possibilities that life itself permits in particular environmental, global, social and cultural contexts. Inclusionality is a relationally dynamic awareness of space and boundaries as connective, reflexive and co-creative. Living logics of inclusionality, in the sense of a mode of thought that is appropriate for comprehending the real as rational, emerge in the course of giving form to life itself.

Having benefited in the growth of my educational knowledge from insights from both propositional and dialectical theories and understanding this growth of educational knowledge through the production of my living educational theory with its living logic, I do not deny the value of the forms of rationality in both propositional and dialectical logics. However I do understand the 2,500-year-old arguments in which both propositional and dialectical logicians deny the rationality of the other's logic.

For example, in the 1960s Karl Popper demonstrated, using two Aristotelean laws of inference, that any propositional theory that contained contradictory statements was entirely useless as a theory because he could demonstrate using the two laws how any such theory that claimed something to be true could also claim with equal validity that the opposite was true. Herbert Marcuse (1964) in his book *One Dimensional Man* explained that propositional theories that abide by the Law of Contradiction are masking the dialectical nature or reality with its nucleus of contradiction. One of the great dialectical thinkers of the twentieth century, Edvard Ilyenkov sought to explicate the nature of dialectical logic by 'writing' Logic (Ilyenkov, 1977, p. 9). Because of his decision to 'write' logic without a 'living' logic Ilyenkov was still left with the problem of living contradictions at the end of his life, in his questions, 'If any object is a living contradiction, what must the thought (statement about the object) be that expresses it? Can and should an objective contradiction find reflection in thought? And if so, in what form?' (Ilyenkov, 1977, p. 320).

When Polanyi (1958) developed his views on personal knowledge as a post-critical account he advocated the making of a decision to understand the world from our own points of view as individuals claiming originality and exercising judgement responsibly with universal intent. He developed a logic of affirmation that does not have a nucleus of contradiction yet can include contradictions in the working out of the implications of affirmation. Rayner has worked out some of implications of such a logic in his living logic of inclusionality. Working from within a living logic of inclusionality Rayner (2004, 2005) avoids the conflict between formal and dialectical logicians through seeing that a mode of thought that is appropriate for comprehending the real as rational is living with a relationally dynamic awareness of space and boundaries:

> Inclusionality is an awareness of space and the variably permeable boundaries – ultimately formed by what physicists refer to as 'electromagnetic energy' – that inseparably line it, as connective, reflective and co-creative, rather than divisive.
>
> (Rayner, 2005)

I now want to move the ground of my communication from words on a page into responses to multi-sensorial experiences and multi-media representations to communicate the vital significance of developing a new epistemology for educational knowledge that can contribute to the creation of a world of educational quality.

The significance of including 'I' in living educational theories in the generation of a world of educational quality

In advocating the inclusion of 'I', I am aware of a serious limitation in printed, text-based representations of my meanings. I am thinking of limitations in lexical understandings where meanings are communicated solely in terms of the definitions of the meanings of words in terms of other words. Lexical definitions can sever a relationship with the expression of meanings in lived experience that require ostensive understandings. I am thinking of understandings, particularly in the communication of the meanings of the expression of embodied ontological values, that need the showing of what is being talked or written about. To develop adequate communications in the generation of living educational theories I have been using multi-media forms of representation (Eisner, 1988, 1993, 1997, 2005) to communicate the meanings of the expression of ontological values in educational relationships and in explanations of educational influence.

The visual data, used as evidence in visual narratives of educational influence enables the communication of meanings that flow non-verbally through embodied expressions in living educational relationships. To show what I mean you can access video-clips and visual narratives at this url: www.jackwhitehead.com/jack/sigI.htm, with video-clips linked to the images.

These visual narratives include video-clips of my own educational relationships in tutoring master's students, supervising doctoral students and presenting ideas on a new epistemology for educational knowledge at international conferences. They include explanations by practitioner-researchers of their own educational influences in their own learning, in the learning of others and in the learning of social formations. They differ in the meanings that can be communicated through printed text-based media such as this chapter. Consider, for example, the communication of the meanings of a flow of life-affirming energy in explanations of educational influence. Vasilyuk (1991, pp. 63–4) has pointed out that conceptions involving energy, while current in psychology, have been very poorly worked out from a methodological standpoint. As Vasilyuk says, we know how 'energetically' a person can act when positively motivated but we have little understanding of the conceptual links between energy and motivation, energy and meaning and energy and value. I am suggesting that to understand the vital influence of energy and values in explanations of educational influences in learning, ostensive expressions are required that include visual records of the living relationships of practice.

The meanings that can be communicated through lexical definitions and ostensive expression also differ, especially in the meanings of the receptive and responsive communicative relationships, in explanations of educational influence. Marian Naidoo shows these differences clearly in the multi-media communication of her emergent living theory of her responsive and inclusional practice in her doctoral thesis (Naidoo, 2005). Hymer (2007) contributes his living theory to the flow of living theories through web-space in answering his question *How do I understand and communicate my values and beliefs in my work as an educator in the field of giftedness?* (http://www.actionresearch.net/hymer.shtml). Farren and Crotty (2007), in the eLife Connecting People Project at Dublin City University, are exploring the nature of the new living standards of judgement in the development of a relationally dynamic epistemology of educational enquiry. They are developing the use of streamed video in visual narratives. From www.jackwhitehead.com/jack/sigI.htm you can connect to the visual narrative on 'Creating a world of educational quality through living educational theories' (Whitehead, 2007), which integrates ostensive expression of the meanings of flows of life-affirming energy, with values in explanations of educational influence. The explanations use the three logics above with relationally dynamic standards of judgement that emerge from educational relationships. The educational relationships include such receptively responsive qualities as love, compassion and justice. The meanings of these qualities differ in relation to the different logics and languages used to express them and to form the rationality of the explanation.

The significance of 'I' in living educational theories is that a living 'I', exploring the implications of answering questions of the kind 'How do I improve what I am doing?', can produce an explanation of educational influence (McNiff and Whitehead, 2006; Moustakim, 2007) that includes insights from propositional and dialectical theories within a living logic of inclusionality. In the final part of this chapter I now want to show how such insights can be drawn into a living educational theory with a living logic of inclusionality without excluding either propositional or dialectical logic.

Using insights from propositional and dialectical theories in the generation of living educational theories from a perspective of inclusionality

Researching the person, the individual 'I' in the enquiry 'How do I improve what I am doing?' from an inclusional perspective, means researching with a relationally dynamic awareness of space and boundaries that are connective, reflexive and co-creative (Rayner, 2005). The insights from propositional and dialectical theories that I use in the inclusional evolution of my educational theory are too numerous to include here. They are acknowledged in other publications (Whitehead, 1989, 1993, 2007; Whitehead and McNiff, 2006). What I want to do here is to illustrate how some of these insights from propositional and dialectical theories have been integrated within my living educational theory.

In stressing the importance of both personal and social validation in enhancing the validity of explanations of educational influences in learning, I draw on Habermas's ideas (2002, 1987, 1976, 1975). He says that 'Not *learning*, but *not*-learning is the phenomenon that calls for explanation at the socio-cultural stage of development' (Habermas, 1975, p. 15). In enhancing the validity claims of living theories I ask the individuals who constitute validation groups in responding to my explanations to use Habermas's four principles of social validity of comprehensibility, truth, rightness and authenticity (Habermas, 1976, pp. 2–3). In doing this I am also drawn to Habermas's (1987) point about refraining from critically evaluating and normatively ordering totalities, forms of life and cultures, and life-contexts and epochs as a whole. I agree with his emphasis on an orientation to a range of learning processes that are opened up at a given time by a historically attained level of learning. Where the generation of living educational theories differs from the generation of such social theories is that the genesis of living theories, with their questions 'How do I improve what I am doing?'

does begin with an awareness of concrete ideals immanent in an individual's form of life. For Habermas, a social theory can no longer start by examining concrete ideals immanent in traditional forms of life. In the generation of his social theory Habermas abstracts cognitive structures from the historical dynamics of events and abstracts the evolution of society from the historical concretion of forms of life (p. 383).

While Habermas, and other social theories decouple (i.e. sever) their concepts from the conscious lived experience of individuals, their conceptual abstractions can be of great value in extending the understandings of the individual in the growth of their educational knowledge. For example, Habermas (2002) emphasises the importance of engaging with the contents of an intersubjectively shared social world to which individuals do not have access 'simply through the epistemic authority of the first person singular' (p. 25). However, living educational theories are created in the relational dynamic of the epistemic authority of the first person singular and the contents of intersubjectively shared social worlds.

A dialectical theory that has influenced the growth of my educational knowledge is Ilyenkov's (1977) theory of dialectical logic. The tension between propositional and dialectical theorists can be appreciated in Popper's (1963, pp. 316–17) rejection of dialectical theories as being entirely useless as theories on the grounds that they contain contradictions. For Ilyenkov the concretisation of a general definition of Logic consists in disclosing the concepts composing it, especially the concept of thinking. For Ilyenkov to define this concept fully, i.e. concretely, also means to 'write' Logic, because as he says, 'a full definition cannot by any means be given by a "definition"' but only by 'developing the essence of the matter' (Ilyenkov, 1977, p. 9). In developing the essence of dialectical logic Ilyenkov points out that contradiction as the concrete unity of mutually exclusive opposites is the real nucleus of dialectics, its central category. He also recognises the difficulty of expressing in statements the meanings of 'subjective dialectics', on dialectics as the logic of thinking when he says, 'If any object is a living contradiction, what must the thought (statement about the object) be that expresses it? Can and should an objective contradiction find reflection in thought? And if so, in what form?' (Ilyenkov, 1977, p. 320).

The experience of 'I' as a living contradiction in answering the question 'How do I improve what I am doing?', when experienced from a perspective of inclusionality in the generation of living educational theories, is in a flow-form of experiencing that can be understood rationally in a living logic of inclusionality. In my view Ilyenkov's difficulty with expressing contradictions between statements emerged from seeking to 'write' logic, rather than including the writing within a living logic of inclusionality. Living logics of inclusionality, as each living educational theory shows (www.actionresearch.net/living.shtml), can draw insights from ideas in both propositional and dialectical theories without denying the rationality of either logic. In the growth of my educational knowledge (Whitehead, 1989, 1993; Whitehead and McNiff, 2006) I show the educational influences in my learning of my engagement with ideas from both kinds of theory. I want to stress the importance of this learning. At the same time I am holding to the validity of my experience-based resistance to the idea that an individual's explanation of their educational influence in their own learning, in the learning of others and in the learning of social formations can be reduced to any explanation offered by any discipline of education either individually or in any combination.

In conclusion I want to continue to highlight the tension between those researchers who are developing a discipline of education and those who are generating their own living educational theories from disciplining their 'I' educational enquiries. The tension can be appreciated in the differences between education research and educational research. I work in a Department of *Education*. My most memorable professional development as an educator took place in the Institute of *Education* of London University. The two research associations I belong to are the American *Educational* Research Association and the British *Educational* Research Association (my emphasis). I have spent the last 35 years of my professional life seeking to contribute to educational theory at the University of Bath. In doing this I see myself contributing to a draft Mission of the University which includes having a distinct academic approach to the education of professional practitioners. I am offering the ideas about the nature of living educational theories as such a distinct approach. Yet I am aware that the field of educational research continues to be dominated by researchers in education research. Geoff Whitty is a former President of the British Educational Research Association who explains very clearly why the distinction he makes between education research and educational research leads him to advocate a change in the name of the British Educational Research Association, presumably to the British Education Research Association.

> One problem with this distinction between 'education research' as the broad term and 'educational research' as the narrower field of work specifically geared to the improvement of policy and practice is that it would mean that BERA, as the British Educational Research Association would have to change its name or be seen as only involved with the latter. So trying to make the distinction clearer would also involve BERA in a re-branding exercise which may not necessarily be the best way of spending our time and resources. But it is at least worth considering.
>
> (Whitty, 2005)

Given what I have been saying about the significance of generating living educational theories for the creation of a world of educational quality, I wish to keep the focus on educational research with the recognition that education research has a vital part to play in the generation of living theories, but must not be permitted to dominate the field of educational research. Unlike Whitty I would subsume insights from education research within educational research and retain the focus on educational in both the British and American Educational Research Associations. The significance for me of including 'I' in living educational theories is that this prevents the reification of living individuals into the conceptual abstraction 'person'. The inclusion of 'I' works for me in preventing the severing of the embodied knowledge of a living 'I' from the expression of the life-affirming energy and values of individuals in their educational relationships. In particular the use of visual narratives that show the forms of life of individuals in their social, global and cosmic contexts can avoid the omission of life-affirming energy and the expression of embodied values in explanations of educational influence, especially in explanations for educational influences in the learning of social formations.

My present emphasis on understanding the educational influences of individuals and groups in the learning of social formations is related to Bourdieu's understandings of the automatisms of the habitus in analysing social formations (Bourdieu, 1990, p. 145). What I am seeking to do in enhancing the flow of living educational theories through web-space is to enhance their educational influence, as cultural artefacts, in the learning of social formations as well as individuals. I believe that living educational theories in the education of social formations can explain transformatory influences that go beyond the influences of the automatisms of the habitus in reproducing social formations. In doing this I wish to demonstrate that the living standards of judgement (Laidlaw, 1996) of living theories can be seen as guiding rules that can make a significant contribution to the generation of a world of educational quality. I acknowledge the value of Butler's (1999) desire to 'open up possibilities' in her research into gender where she says that 'the aim of the text was to open up the field of possibility for gender without dictating which kinds of possibilities ought to be realized' (Butler, 1999, p. viii). For the past 34 years I have held together, in a dialectical tension, this open field of possibility at the University of Bath for the creation and legitimation of living educational theories, with an exploration of the constraining and emancipatory influences on what is possible related to culture, history and the material conditions of a social order. In facing this tension through the creative responses of 'I' in the enquiries, 'How do I improve what I am doing?' individuals have shown, in their living educational theories, how they have avoided the determinations of performativity by resisting the anticipation of an authoritative disclosure of meaning (Butler, 1999, p. xv). In stressing the importance of 'I' in the generation of living educational theories I am conscious of Lyotard's point about the postmodern condition in which the writer is 'working without rules in order to formulate the rules of what will have been done' (Lyotard, 1986, p. 81).

In the course of generating living educational theories I am drawn to Bakhtin's insight about the 'I' being 'radically singular' and 'responsible' (Emerson and Morson, 1989, p. 13). In stressing the significance of 'I', as radically singular and responsible in generating living educational theories and providing access to the flow of living theories through webspace, (Whitehead, 2008a and b) I am stressing the importance of each individual's responsibility for making a contribution to the generation of a world of educational quality. I am suggesting that educational researchers, as distinct from education researchers have a responsibilty to undertake self-studies that make public their educational influences in their own learning, in the learning of others and in the education of social formations as we seek to live our ontological values as fully as we can. I am thinking of these values as those that give meaning and purpose to our existence and agree with Bullough and Pinnegar (2004, p. 319) that 'The consideration of ontology, of one's being in and toward the world, should be a central feature of any discussion of the value of self-study research'. This is not to deny the value of being an education researcher. It is to acknowledge the value of the creative engagements of the individual 'I' with the ideas produced by education researchers in generating living educational theories that are contributing to the creation of a world of educational quality.

I hope my writings have captivated your imaginations in seeing the validity of the case I have made for educational researchers, as distinct from education researchers, to produce valid explanations for the educational influences of themselves in their own learning, in the learning of others and in the learning of social formations. I do hope that you will access the visual narratives at www.jackwhitehead.com/jack/sigI.htm and in the *Educational Journal of Living Theories* (EJOLTS) at http://ejolts.net/index.php which communicate, much better than my words alone, the meanings of the expression of the life-affirming energy and embodied values of humanity that are contributing to enhancing the quality of our living spaces in enquiries of the kind, 'How do I improve what I am doing?'

References

Bourdieu, P. (1990) *The Logic of Practice*, Stanford, CA, Stanford University Press.
Buber, M. (1947) *Between Man and Man*, London, Kegan Paul, Trench, Trubner and Co. Ltd.
Bullough, R. and Pinnegar, S. (2004) 'Thinking about the thinking about self-study: an analysis of eight chapters', in J.J. Loughran, M.L. Hamilton, V.K. LaBoskey, and T. Russell (eds), *International Handbook of Self-Study of Teaching and Teacher-Education Practices*, Dordrecht, Kluwer Academic Publishers.

Butler, J. (1999) *Gender Trouble: Feminism and the Subversion of Identity*, New York and London, Routledge.

Dewey, J. (1916) *Democracy and Education*, London, The Macmillan Company.

Eisner, E. (1988) 'The primacy of experience and the politics of method', *Educational Researcher*, 17(5), pp. 15–20.

—— (1993) 'Forms of understanding and the future of educational research', *Educational Researcher*, 22(7), pp. 5–11.

—— (1997) 'The promise and perils of alternative forms of data representation', *Educational Researcher*, 26(6), pp. 4–10.

—— (2005) *Reimaging Schools: The Selected Works of Elliot W. Eisner*, Oxford and New York, Routledge.

Emerson, C. and Morson, G.S. (1989) *Rethinking Bakhtin*, Evanston, Northwestern Press.

Farren, M. and Crotty, Y. (2007) 'The eLife Connecting People Project at Dublin City University'. Retrieved 21 May 2007 from www.jackwhitehead.com/farren/eLife.htm

Habermas, J. (1975) *Legitimation Crisis*, Boston, Beacon Press.

—— (1976) *Communication and the Evolution of Society*, London, Heinemann.

—— (1987) *The Theory of Communicative Action, Vol 2: The Critique of Functionalist Reason*, Oxford, Polity.

—— (2002) *The Inclusion of the Other: Studies in Political Theory*, Oxford, Polity.

Hirst, P. (ed.) (1983) *Educational Theory and its Foundation Disciplines*, London, Routledge and Kegan Paul.

Hymer, B. (2007) *How do I understand and communicate my values and beliefs in my work as an educator in the field of giftedness?* DEdPsy thesis, University of Newcastle, retrieved 3 December 2008 from http://www.actionresearch.net/hymer.shtml

Ilyenkov, E. (1977) *Dialectical Logic*, Moscow, Progress Publishers.

Laidlaw, M. (1996) *How can I create my own living educational theory as I offer you an account of my educational development?* PhD thesis, University of Bath, retrieved 19 February 2004 from www.actionresearch.net/moira2.shtml

Lyotard, F. (1986) *The Postmodern Condition: A Report on Knowledge*, Manchester, Manchester University Press.

Marcuse, H. (1964) *One Dimensional Man*, London, Routledge and Kegan Paul.

McNiff, J. and Whitehead, J. (2006) *All You Need To Know About Action Research*, London, Sage.

Moustakim, M. (2007) 'From transmission to dialogue: promoting critical engagement in higher education teaching and learning', *Educational Action Research*, 15(2), pp. 209–20.

Naidoo, M. (2005) *I am because we are (A never ending story): The emergence of a living theory of inclusional and responsive practice*, PhD thesis, University of Bath, retrieved 3 December 2008 from http://www.actionresearch.net/naidoo.shtml

Peters, R.S. (1966) *Ethics and Education*, London, Allen and Unwin.

—— (1977) *Education and the Education of Teachers*, London, Routledge and Kegan Paul.

Polanyi, M. (1958) *Personal Knowledge: Towards a Post-Critical Philosophy*, London, Routledge and Kegan Paul.

Popper, K. (1963) *Conjectures and Refutations*, Oxford, Oxford University Press.

Rayner, A. (2004) 'Inclusionality: the science, art and spirituality of place, space and evolution', retrieved 9 March 2007 from http://people.bath.ac.uk/bssadmr/inclusionality/placespaceevolution.html

—— (2005) 'Space, dust and the co-evolutionary context of *His Dark Materials*', retrieved 2 August 2006 from http://people.bath.ac.uk/bssadmr/inclusionality/HisDarkMaterials.htm

Schroyer, T. (1973) 'Foreword', in T.W. Adorno, *The Jargon of Authenticity* (trans. K. Tarnowski and F. Will), London, Routledge and Kegan Paul.

Vasilyuk, F. (1991) *The Psychology of Experiencing: The Resolution of Life's Critical Situations*, Hemel Hempstead, Harvester Wheatsheaf.

Whitehead, J. (1989) 'Creating a living educational theory from questions of the kind, "How do I improve my practice?"', *Cambridge Journal of Education*, 19(1), pp. 41–52.

—— (1993) *The Growth of Educational Knowledge*, Bournemouth, Hyde Publication; retrieved 24 May 2007 from http://www.actionresearch.net/writings/jwgek93.htm

—— (2007) 'A new epistemology for educational knowledge', presentation for AERA in Chicago on 13 April 2007; retrieved 9 March 2007 from www.jackwhitehead.com/jack/jwaera07dr0903.htm

—— (2008a) 'An epistemological transformation in what counts as educational knowledge: responses to Laidlaw and Adler-Collins', *Research Intelligence*, 105, pp. 28–9.

—— (2008b) 'Using a living theory methodology in improving practice and generating educational knowledge in living theories', *Educational Journal of Living Theories*, 1(1), pp. 103–26, retrieved 30 December 2008 from http://ejolts.net/node/80.

Whitehead, J. and McNiff, J. (2006) *Action Research Living Theory*, London, Sage.

Whitty, G. (2005) 'Education(al) research and education policy making: is conflict inevitable?', Presidential Address to the British Educational Research Association, University of Glamorgan, 17 September 2005.

Reflective questions

1   How do you explain to yourself and others your educational influences in your own learning, in the learning of others and in the learning of the social formations in which you live and work?

2   In your explanations of your educational influences what forms of representation most appropriately communicate the expressions of your life-affirming energy and values?

Further reading

Biesta, G. (2006) *Beyond Learning; Democratic Education for a Human Future*, Boulder, Paradigm Publishers.

Connelly, M.F. and Clandinin, D.J. (1990) 'Stories of experience and narrative inquiry', *Educational Researcher*, 19(5), pp. 2–14.

McNiff, J. (2007) 'My story is my living educational theory', in J. Clandinin (ed.), *Handbook of Narrative Inquiry: Mapping a Methodology*, Thousand Oaks, London, New Delhi, Sage.

3.8 Identity, agency and social practice

William Lachicotte

Introduction

In American universities of the 1970s and 1980s, women students took three basic orientations to academic work, according to the anthropological research of Dorothy Holland and Margaret Eisenhart.[1] The first perspective, 'getting over', was named by the students themselves. Here the significance of academic work was the certification it provided – the degree achieved, not the knowledge gained. The point was to 'get over' the hurdle (jump through the hoops, go through the motions) of college to gain the B.A. that admitted one to the work world at a higher level. What counted (the 'capital') was accreditation, in the form either of time invested in work (on the part of students) or of grades given (on the part of instructors). In this ritualistic orientation, college education was only tokenly related to one's later work and life. Students expected no real connection of substance or skill.

Holland and Eisenhart called the second orientation 'doing well'. Academic life was regarded as a place to shine, to reveal one's inherent abilities and intellect. The point of attending college was a kind of self-discovery or recognition (its 'capital') confirmed by those who had the ability to see it (faculty who had already 'done well'). 'Doing well' is an aesthetic perspective, but the artist, and not the work, is its focus. The substance of learning is valuable only as a token of one's worth. Doing well was its own reward, regardless the subject. As with many constitutional or naturalist notions of intelligence, 'doing well' was not a matter of work, but of the ease with which one mastered the work. Effort was to be concealed, because it should be unnecessary.

Only the third orientation conceived the substance of learning as the significance of college life. Holland and Eisenhart called this perspective, 'learning from experts'. Mastery of a particular branch of knowledge was the reason one came to college, though the particular subject might only come clear to students as they experimented with the variety of courses offered. This mastery was directly and intimately connected to one's future life. It was the basis of a career begun in apprenticeship with professors who had painstakingly accumulated knowledge of real affairs. One's academic work was neither the sacrifice which brought credit, nor the easy sign of inner merit. It was the laboratory of knowledge achieved. 'Learning from experts' was a professional orientation.

What is the point of these 'orientations'? In the terms I will use, they are different ways to figure (to conceive and play out) the meaning of academics expressed in the 'peer culture' of university students. They propose different visions of students and instructors and different ground rules for academic actions. From the standpoint of 'getting over', those who identify themselves as learning from experts are naïve 'ear'oles'.[2] The latter believe that 'book learning' will actually take them somewhere, and waste their time in real comprehension, rather than in learning simply enough to get them past the next test, the next course, the next level. From the standpoint of 'learning from experts', those who identify themselves as getting over are 'slackers', whose minimal effort will never get them anywhere but to the next day and the next paycheck in the next meaningless job. Instructors too change sense according to framework, becoming, in turn, officials who grant 'marks', aesthetic judges who validate inherent skill (confirming an elite of taste), and masters of craft who labor to impart expertise. In sum, orientations provide a framework, what I will call a 'figured world', that organizes the significance and course of social action and social actors. Identity is key to such an understanding, the transit point between activity and actor.

This essay discusses a particular approach to *identity* as a constitutive feature of human experience and factor in another critical element of social life, human *agency*. Identity is a relatively recent notion of sociologists and psychologists that has gained currency with scholars and the general public.[3] It was first popularized by the psychologist, Erik Erikson, in the 1940s and 1950s, and has since gained wide circulation, first in popular psychology and then in popular sociology and cultural studies.[4] It has always had to do with the relations between people and society, and I will argue that it still has considerable value as a means to understand contemporary social action in fields such as education.

The approach I will take to understand identity is called social practice theory. It is a variant of the practice theories that were elaborated in the 1970s and 1980s by Pierre Bourdieu and other social theorists.[5] My collaborators and I (Holland *et al.*, 1998) have attempted to wed practice theory to the American (and sociological) pragmatism of George Herbert Mead, the sociocultural psychology of Lev S. Vygotsky and the semiotics and sociolinguistics of M.M. Bakhtin.[6] Our goal is to understand what identity has long pointed to, the relations of people to society, in a way that responds to the developments in social theory that follow on post-structuralism, and revives a social psychology intimately tied to cultural forms and historical contexts. Our notion of identity is, unlike many contemporary cultural studies, not founded in psychoanalytic or ego psychology.[7] It does however insist (with 'depth psychology') that intimate or interior processes must be taken into account in any analysis of identity as a force in human experience. Too often cultural identity has been read *onto/into* people prescriptively, which misses both the variability and dynamics of cultural discourses and practices and the relative autonomy of the person and psyche. In this sense, our approach is true to Bourdieu's intent that practice theory attend to the objective and subjective aspects of human experience.

What is identity?

In our framework, put simply, an identity is a sense of self-as-actor, where the sense is always relative to a particular frame of activity.[8] People have many identities, fashioned according to their engagements in different sectors of social life.

This idea of identity squares with the presentation of society that confronts people in the writing of George Herbert Mead and his followers. Mead presumes that we do not experience social life as a kind of abstract spectacle of institutions and classes, statuses and objective roles. Instead we enter into social interaction practically, with people we come to recognize as collaborators in tasks that preoccupy us. Humans are always doubly engaged in activities: instrumentally, with an eye toward the task, and socially, with an eye toward the relationships, the team which does the work. For Mead, language and meaning are necessary to conduct – indeed to *create* – both aspects of social life. Hence the social theory developed from Mead's social psychology has been called 'symbolic interactionism'. Similarly, his philosophy is a brand of American pragmatism, for it regards human knowledge and being as founded in social practice, in doing things with others.[9]

Even nearer to the point of this essay, Mead famously regarded self-knowledge and self-consciousness as the product of others' responses to us.[10] The subject-in-action, the 'I', has no (in fact, cannot have) immediate knowledge of itself. In order to understand oneself, one must respond to oneself as an object, as a 'me'. Yet the only models in experience for such self-response are the responses of other people. Hence one's sense of self is empirically and inevitably based upon what others say about and how they act toward one. Because interaction is framed and differentiated by the variety of activities/practices into which one enters, senses of self vary according to those contexts. Each of us conceives many 'me's as one responds to oneself in different life activities in concert with others' apprehensions of us, there and then. Though Mead did not use the term, the symbolic interactionists who followed him called such senses of self, 'identities' or role-identities.

This understanding of identity differs from Erikson's idea of it.[11] Both locate identity between the person and society. Yet Mead's approach works from the outside in. It understands identity as a product of social interchange, and is oriented more to the problem of coordination with others in ongoing social activities. Erikson's idea of identity works from the inside out. That is, identity is first and foremost a personal effort to create continuity, or 'self-sameness', in the face of various engagements of 'me' in different social fields and with different (cultural) kinds of folk. It is an imperative of a psychic economy that must grow toward adulthood in the complex and varied social world of today, a world that cannot be denied and that has no ready external measure. Erikson conceived identity as the definitive accomplishment (or failure) of adolescence. By contrast, Mead was less concerned with personal integrity and self-sameness than with learning to take part in those social fields that Erikson mostly presumed to be already accessible. The two scholars emphasized different problems.[12]

Presumptions

The notion of identity depends upon certain common presumptions about social practice. I will assert and not defend these assumptions here. First, social life and self-understanding depend upon the capacity to make the sensible world meaningful through representations. 'Semiotic mediation' (Vygotsky's term) directs attention, gives structure to perception and objective to action.[13] Representation remakes the 'nature' of reality in the purposes of human activity.

Signs and symbols only make sense in their interrelations. One aspect of meaning-as-relation concerns the formal systems of contrast, 'codes', proposed by structuralism. The second aspect involves the ways signs are used together in practical contexts of social activity – what Wittgenstein called language-games. Practical meaning relates signs along lines of activity, as sign systems that capture the unfolding of entire scenes: virtual, if limited, worlds.[14] Understanding responds to the scene of action which the sign indexes and evokes.[15]

For Vygotsky, signs and the social actions they make possible are internalized to create the psyche and its capacities. The 'intrapersonal' is first the interpersonal: 'all the higher [psychological] functions originate as actual relations between human individuals' (Vygotsky, 1978, p. 57).[16] Psychological phenomena, like 'identities', are historical and developmental, dependent upon social experience as it is internalized and embodied. This kind of development is reiterated across the life cycle as people enter new fields of activity. As we rehearse our responses to things outwardly (as act, speech or gesture), we learn to produce the signs which organize action internally, as 'sign-image' (inner speech and 'in-sight'). Internalized mediators become imperceptible first to others and then to ourselves. As we become expert with the routine of response, we no longer even look to internal signs. Behavior becomes fossilized, as Vygotsky called it; all that is left is the response, the trace and not the learned, *signal* process of its generation. Behavior becomes automated as habit.[17]

Vygotsky's notion of the unconscious is thus a 'habitus'. Humans embody social history together, as what Bourdieu called a structure of disposition: a generator and regulator of relationships, orientations toward others, of perceptual and cognitive schemes, and of predispositions, inclinations to action, which are learned by doing. *Habitus* is a bodily product of repeated, instrumental learning, cultural because its settings are so organized, or because its parts are fossilized, symbolic learning abbreviated to the point of erasure. It is 'history in person', a ground for social practice.

Habitus has a partner, an additional ground of practice, in what Bourdieu called 'fields'. Fields are the ways activity is depicted and organized among participants in the various sectors of social life spun off by the division of labor. They consist of positions for action (occupations) that hold a recognized cachet, a store of resources (symbolic capital), which in turn permit (invest) a range of interaction and exchange (strategies) whose goal is to enlarge one's productive means. Each field has a specific 'capital' which is both a means of transaction and form of accumulation or capacity. Fields are objective phenomena only insofar as people represent and recognize them and reproduce them through actions. They are games whose terrain, player-positions, rules, strategies and outcomes are commonly understood and yet continually negotiated.[18]

Fields are interrelated in what Bourdieu called the field of power. Fields interact, are formed and dissipate according to relations of power. Just as positions within fields are ranked by their access to symbolic capital, so too fields are ranked according to the convertibility of their capitals. The dominance of the economy is expressed by the general value of its (monetary) capital: its capacity to convert to other forms of capital at 'advantageous rates of exchange'.

Yet power, the capacity to instigate and organize action, does not exist for us in the abstract. Its expression has face and voice. Bakhtin and his colleague, V.N. Voloshinov carried the pragmatic aspect of meaning to its ultimate ends. In their view, signs and sign-complexes (words and utterances), whether spoken or thought, retain the sense of the practices in which they are learned and most commonly used. Words come to us in development, first and foremost, as other people's words. They carry the voice/image of the kinds of people who mouth them and are colored (connoted) by their ideological position and authority.[19]

Speaking and thinking are not socially neutral forms of (self-)expression. They are instead kinds of social-relational work, acts of affiliation, disaffiliation and 'indifference'. Beyond the shaping of word and deed by immediate social context (Voloshinov does emphasize this sociolinguistic fact),[20] this work of communication is a measure of the social weight and marking which imbues its very media. Speaking and imagining are marked by social accent and voice (or speaking personality). They position partners in dialogue (even if the dialogue is silent!), cast them as certain kinds of people according to the styles of expression used. Speaking is a tool of self-fashioning because it comes to us with social identification. Society, for Bakhtin, inhabits us, socializes us, to the extent that it is already impersonated.

These propositions form the basis of our understanding of identity. The remainder of the essay summarizes our view with respect to the four sites or contexts which frame identity formation. These are figured worlds, positioning, spaces of authoring and cultural world-making.

Figured worlds

Let us begin by picturing the landscape in which identity makes sense. Imagine yourself in a social activity, a setting of social interaction, but imagine this setting as if it were a scene from a play.[21] You join an ensemble of fellow actors engaged in a common task, framed by a collection of conventional materials arranged in recognizable scenes – stage sets – and following a generally known path toward that objective – a storyline or script. The play is a kind of allegory, in which the characters represent general types of people in the form of particular roles. The script is, you will discover, sketchy and much of the performance is improvised. The entirety of these elements, the whole staging of actions, provides an obvious basis for players' performances.

It may be easier for one to imagine this scene in such formal or institutionalized activities as schooling. Here recognized 'roles' – teacher, student and many others; settings – classrooms, offices, school buildings; subjects (mathematics, literature, chemistry, even anthropology); activities – lectures, tutorials, exercises; and courses of events – curricula and class schedules: all serve to frame what people learn and do together in schooling. Yet more informal and everyday activities, like students' performance of academic or even romantic relationships, are also conducted with reference to a 'field-lore' or knowledge of how things happen. That is, we understand romance (and school work) by reference to frameworks that tell us what to expect: who the actors may be, what kinds of events and interactions may happen among them, where such events may occur, and how these interactions may unfold, toward what conclusions.

These frameworks, which guide the interpretation and realization of actions and actors, have been called 'cultural worlds'. They are popular today, when social scientists have lost faith in older and grander notions of culture as a shared basis for whole societies or subsocieties. My colleagues and I prefer to use the term, 'figured world', for it emphasizes the presence of human figures, of people, as elemental features of social life as it is pictured culturally.[22] Statuses, roles, subject-positions – however one names the components of interaction – are more than niches in an abstract field of activity. In line with Mead and Bakhtin, we conceive them to have residences, bodies, faces and voices. There were model strategists of getting over, prototypically clever well-doers and unfailingly persistent apprentice learners at each university locale. They were emblems of what they did – and what one strives to do, or not. Figured worlds step around the abstract idea of a society which in effect acts 'through' us and for which people are only pretext. They depict the familiarity of social life inhabited by recognizable figures, places, storylines and objectives. From their basis, we look to understand how everyday life is shaped historically by forces, discourses, institutions and 'systems' – and how it reacts upon these powers.

Entering an activity informed by a figured world, one learns directly from more knowledgeable participants, from their responses to one's own efforts, how to sense the framework which organizes the activity. One learns practically the 'moves' one might make and the possible roles that one might play. That is, one identifies with 'getting over' or 'doing well' and with the people who play those games.[23] One gradually assumes, as one is cast by co-actors in, a certain part among these possible roles – as one must in order take one's place, to participate legitimately, in what plays out. One learns to direct one's actions in terms of the possibilities accorded this role. For instance, a savvy student learns it is acceptable to study hard for a test to 'get over', but absurd to study hard to master molecular biology. As one invests in the activity and rehearses one's actions over and over, one comes to a sense of oneself – Vygotsky called it an 'imagined I' – in this particular arena. One develops an intimate sense of self, an identity, in terms of the social identities figured by the cultural world. Personal identity is rooted in social performance.[24]

Figured worlds are opened by artifacts or markers (as a *specific* playing field is shown by the boundary lines and facilities that ring it). Vygotsky called such evocative signs, pivots; they shift activities from scene to scene as a stage on a roundtable. They materialize 'code-switching' – the movement between frames of interpretation, in sociolinguistics – in perceptible form. Virtually any element of a figured world – from characters and costumes to mimicked acts or settings – can signal the whole framework. Practically, however, certain artifacts gain definitive force in order to distinguish the game from others. 'Defining the situation', as sociologists of the 1970s might term the problem, is not automatic; it usually consists of contestation and negotiation. Still it is no mystery which cultural world is in play – unless one is new to the field.

Positioning and relational identity

Personal identity is also doubly informed. This sense of self-as-actor, this identity, has the figurative dimension cast within the 'vision' or imagination of the activity itself. But it also has a relational dimension. Activities must be peopled, not just conceived – and whether one gets to play a role or part is not necessarily a matter of choice.[25] People strive for position and strive to position one another in one role or another first according to the objectives of the activity, the trajectories and strategies designed to take a participant from beginner to primary player.[26] Such competition is a recognized aspect of activity within figured worlds – variants of storylines both learned and improvised in response to the current situation of the field.

Yet, beyond this lore of the activity, there is a second dimension of positioning emphasized by both Bakhtin and Bourdieu. This dimension cuts across figured worlds according to pervasive lines of social division and is learned most often tacitly or at best peremptorily. Subject-positions and spaces of activities are tinged with, voiced and imagined with, certain understandings of the kinds of person who may (most) legitimately take them up, or even get an 'audition'. It is a commonplace of social life that access to status, resources, activities and settings is not open. It depends upon who you are (socially), relative to one's fellow actors and to what is going on. In and across activities, one learns – through practices of (obligatory) inclusion and exclusion, of monopolization and marginalization, of invocation and silencing, of privacy and surveillance – a relative sense of self as privileged or disadvantaged, proper or improper, 'in' or 'out', free or restrained, comfortable or tense.[27] This relational or positional dimension of identity invokes the familiar lines of class, gender, race, age – as performed, not conceived. It is not accidental that 'getting over' was more common among African-American students, whose *learning* was treated, by teachers and others, as less relevant to career (and school), and whose life prospects were dictated by forces that education did not vitiate. Nor was it surprising that 'doing well' prevailed among white women, for whom the showing of (principally symbolic) merit was a key value.

I do not mean that privilege and rank cannot be figured. We are all familiar with ideologies, figured worlds of gender and sexuality, caste and class, race and ethnicity, generations and 'eras' – the stuff of stereotype, prejudice and mother wit. It is simply that our first encounters with these divisions, as they occur to us as children, immigrants, and novices, are rarely explained. We learn – by doing and erring, by praise and punishment, by having the run of the place and being shown the door – that some things are, and others are not, for the likes of us. We learn it in virtually everything we do. Gradually we infer, though that may not be the right term for developing 'sense', our limits and freedoms. We sense from the trappings, the signs of status materialized in most human settings and in the costumes of its characters, where we can go, when we can speak, how we should act. As Michel Foucault would say, we become our own governor. The force of this relational sense of self is, according to Bourdieu, habitual and anonymous to the extent that social domination takes the form of common sense. The more contested, the less hegemonic and more 'ideologized' is cultural privilege, then the more conscious and reflectively strategic is our relational sense of self.[28]

Figured worlds inflect the salience and modulate the force of social hierarchies. Some, as we shall see, can in effect thematize, point to, the bases of relational identities, though they cannot entirely divert their power to inform people's actions. Yet such experimental activities, like the figured worlds of Courtly Love in high medieval Western Europe or of the 'Bohemian' avant-garde in fin-de-siècle Paris, are modest forms of agency. Before I discuss them, I need to describe one more context of identity.

Spaces of authoring

Humans are, Bakhtin maintained, addressed by and answerable to a social world of constituencies. These 'consociates' become part of us: voices (speaking personalities) in a chorus of consciousness, intrapersonal because they are interpersonal points of address. The image of self-consciousness as polyphonal dialogue echoes Mead's discussion in his classic article, 'The Social Self', and Vygotsky's analyses of inner speech. Inner activity doubles (but does not mirror) interaction. Within as well as without, humans are hailed and condemned to answer, for life as well as understanding is responsiveness.[29]

The struggle is to find a voice of our own, when we have no choice but to speak with other people's words. If we are to avoid simply being a mouthpiece for discourse that makes us up in its own terms, then we must somehow make those words our own. The struggle is one of authoring. Yet it cannot be a matter of neutralizing these voices. Instead we must 'refract' them, impart our own spin to the continuous colloquy that is human life. Agency, the control we have over the conditions of our own actions, is tied up in this authoring, but we must understand agency in its old sense. It is founded in 'agents' that work for us. It is the argument of social practice theory that identities constitute such agents.[30] The question remains: how do, how can, we deploy identities to make a difference in our situations?

One crucial fact is the diversity of voices that address us. Rare are the situations in which we answer to only one audience. Instead, because of the variety of speech genres, from whole languages to dialects, accents, and registers (a condition Bakhtin named 'heteroglossia'), invested with a variety of social values and intentions, and invoked by a variety of speakers who simultaneously address us, we find ourselves drawn in different terms toward different objectives. The positional force of discourse(s) is not concordant, not aligned. Human situations comprise a field of possible frames for multiple activities. They evoke several figured worlds – and constituencies who interpret action and respond through these worlds. Remember too that some of these voices and operant worlds are interior and some exterior. This practically complex field is what we call the space of authoring.

Under such conditions, Bakhtin maintained, the dialogue that is self-consciousness and our identities, the voices of inner speech which seem to be mine, are created in 'orchestration', i.e., from the arrangement struck among the socially-identified voices that comprise the twinned circuits of inner and social speech. So, if it is true that we always speak and think through the words of others, still we may deploy these voices, combine them, sequence and orient them in time and space. Here lies a possibility for authorship. We respond to such a world like the author of a novel, said Bakhtin, by representing and reworking what is said and acted, even to style, to articulate a synthetic/syncretic voice.[31] In the modern world, personal identities are particular only in the nature of their organization and orchestration of 'characteristic' elements.

Yet it is by such arrangements, by the choral voices which are our speaking personalities, that we refract the authority of those who would pin us down. We alter the conditions of our response and give play to, free our actions by a kind of jiujitsu. For instance, students 'getting over' grafted the utterly pragmatic (and bureaucratic) voice of business with the street-smart cleverness of the powerless in order to deflect (while mimicking) the authority of the educational establishment. They worked to pass, not to learn, taking pleasure in the parody. Like them, we may use power against itself at the same time that we engage it legitimately, in (at least partly) its own terms. Identities, conceived as these 'recombinant' senses of self-as-actor, are points of leverage – pivots – in the cultural worlds and social contests that shape us.[32]

World-making

Sometimes the innovation of identity becomes more than a transient creation or standpoint of the moment. When the rough orchestration of activities that frames this identity attracts fellow actors, they may take it up experimentally, extending and reworking the framework as they rehearse it, and together create an incipient figured world. Though they begin as moments of improvisation, novel cultural worlds are the work of 'communities of practice' (as Lave and Wenger, 1991, termed the constituencies organized by common activity). They gain purchase and claim on new generations of actors only if they are materialized in social life, instituted by artifacts that mediate interaction and ground the imagination.

New visions of social life are most often double-voiced; they speak simultaneously in two (or more) identifiable styles, twisting relations among different constituencies. They frame speech and action with 'a sideways glance', in irony, satire or parody, and are articulated against dominant cultural worlds, in ways that invert or shift the usual relations of power, the usual terms of taste.[33] They constitute, in short, 'subcultures' or 'countercultures', organized around new forms of value, new symbolic capitals. Such world-making is not new.

Our book (Holland *et al.*, 1998) discussed the example of Courtly Love. If the historical argument is correct, it is one of the most successful social experiments in European history. Courtly Love began as a form of amusement among the nobility of old Occitans[34] in the eleventh century. It worked by recasting feudal relations as gender relations, with ladies as lords, men as vassals and carnal love as the honor-bond between them – the wellspring of civility in service. Spread by troubadours and the currency of courtly etiquette (not to mention intermarriage and conquest), even to the great works of romance that comprise the Arthurian cycle, the social vision of Courtly Love ended as the image of cross-gender (and arguably same-sex) sexual relationships. It was the foundation of romantic love as we know it today.

Courtly Love founded no political revolution, though it had its political entanglements. Instead it framed new gender practices and identities in ways that played off and subverted political power. It offered a culturally hybrid, transformed image of domestic relations, a parlor revolution. By borrowing the trappings of political power, the standing of its noble conversants, the popularity of its poetry and song, and the rivalry among regional dynasts, Courtly Love shaped the desire to adopt its practices and made 'space' for its transactions. Today we might call Courtly Love a 'new social movement'. Its objective, or at least its outcome, was not political but cultural. It did not take power, rather it remade power 'by other means'. In the process, it instituted a new field of social life and articulated new ways of being human.

In this sense, of course, world-making is also a means toward agency. It is, in fact, the only real basis for transformative agency, the capacity to make over, in ways that endure, the social conditions that inform activity. Efforts to institute new figured worlds are at the root of contemporary social struggles, whether they are about feminism, environmentalism, human rights, anti-racism, or anti-capitalism ('anti-globalism'). The 'identity politics' so character-istic of our time is about identity not simply because our cultural politics vests political rights in social identities, but also because change must happen through us, not to us. Its difficulty, as Raymond Williams clearly saw, lies in the too rarely won emergence of a positive practice of human social life that escapes the limits of its oppositional origins.[35]

Conclusion and critique

Social practice theories conceive identities as senses of self that serve as agents: symbolic means to organize activity that legitimate and manage its effects. They are features of interac-tion in social fields, subject-positions that are more than formal loci of activity (in a division of labor). They are 'signatures' in practice, styles of action imbued with image and voice: character sketches. Identities become personal, intimate forms of self-understanding which gain salience and lose self-consciousness as actors identify and rehearse them within figured worlds. The symbolic economy of the psyche derives from social experience and history, but has its own history-in-person, whose dynamics differ from social interaction. The person is, in effect, a relatively autonomous, though fully social, site of activity. The problem of 'socio-cultural studies' is to understand human experience as the production of social beings that are simultaneously 'intersubjects' and subjects.

Any relatively new approach to the human sciences has its problems. Social practice theory is no exception. I will list several issues and leave further exploration to the reader. First, as with many 'anti-foundationalist' theories, the question of what/who it is that acts or orchestrates has no 'original' answer. Why do people seek to create space for their own voice, image or peculiar signature in practice; what moves us toward agency?[36] The only answer that we are willing to give is historical rather than final. Vygotsky would perhaps have answered that it is human being – human drives and instinct – which founds the impetus toward self-fashioning, though he was always quick to assert that social and personal history give content (objective) and higher organization to instinct. Today we are even less willing to posit 'human nature' because we have more evidence of the cultural shaping of drives and desires. So we seek an answer in the historical dynamics of social practice that lead us to 'our' signal forms of agency. The necessity is the empirical happenstance of unfolding social life – and it is history all the way down. At no point do we reach the pure motivations of human essence.

A second version of this quandary concerns personal identity. In our theory, there is no final reason a person has to take a social role or social identity to heart. It is perfectly possible and perfectly normal for people to act superficially in a figured world, according to the rules or directions of others, never to internalize the identification as a fully personal identity. Our actions might remain largely mechanical, and irritatingly literal to those who are personally vested in the activity, but there is no compulsion to personalize the identification, to develop the intuitive (fully internal and automated) sense of self-as-actor. Again, one needs to reconstruct the social history and history-in-person to gain some understanding of the 'suturing', as Stuart

Hall (1996) called it, of person to social field. It asks a lot of any social analysis to accumulate information in this detail. Moreover, in contrast to identity theories founded in psychoanalysis, social practice theory lacks the (nearly) universal dramas of development that are lynchpins of explanatory accounts. There are common social struggles and contradictions that may be presumed as important landmarks, but it is even less a given that they have sufficient force to 'hail' us personally. Hence, an exhaustive account of human social practice is unlikely.

Finally, as social practice theory now stands, two faces of what Homi Bhabha (1996) called 'culture's in-between' remain ill-defined. First, as Dorothy Holland and Jean Lave have argued (2001), there is theoretical work to be done, effectively to link intimate and local practice ('intrapersonal' and face-to-face) to the institutional and historic scale of fields. The middle ground is not well mapped.[37] Second, beyond the protean quality of figured worlds which divide and recombine at variable scales, Bhabha's 'in-between' marks the common point of dialogism, in which person and society lose their distinctiveness. There is no sanctuary for society that is closed off from the person – and vice versa. There are only human activities, which tend to a 'we-pole' or an 'I-pole', in different degrees according to 'circumstances'.[38] We must work to catalogue those circumstances that identities bear for us and to us. You and I are found in this in-between.

Notes

1 Published in the monograph, *Educated in Romance*, Holland and Eisenhart, 1990.
2 The reference is of course to those conforming students in Willis's *Learning to Labour* (1981), who (putatively) sought upward mobility through education, rather than joining 'the lads' in contesting the class-based, 'official' school culture.
3 For a history of the concept of identity, see Gleason, 1983.
4 Cultural studies were given impetus by the advent of 'multiculturalism' and the so-called 'identity politics' associated with it. Witness, in the UK alone, the various collections of essays on cultural identity: Rutherford, 1990; Hall and du Gay, 1996; Woodward, 1997; to name only a few.
5 Major works (in English) are Bourdieu, 1977a, 1990; de Certeau, 1984; Lefebvre, 1991. Ortner, 1984, offers an early discussion of practice theories from an anthropological perspective.
6 See Mead, 1934; Vygotsky, 1978, 1986; Bakhtin, 1981, 1986, 1990, for extended presentations of these perspectives. Their works have inspired other scholars of identity. Symbolic interactionists, such as McCall and Simmons, 1978 (and many others), extended Mead's ideas about 'selves' to concepts of identity and role-identity. Lee *et al.*, 1983; Penuel and Wertsch, 1995, and Holland and Lachicotte, 2007, have outlined Vygotskian approaches to identity. Hermans and Kempen, 1993 (and in numerous other works), have drawn on Bakhtin to articulate an influential, cultural-psychological, theory of the self.
7 As, for example, are the writings of Stuart Hall and Judith Butler or the works of French feminist thinkers influenced by Lacan – Cixous, Irigaray and Kristeva.
8 Sense, as we use it here, refers both to perception and to intuition (apperception). These meanings correspond, respectively, to the ways Hochschild (1983) discusses emotion and Bourdieu (1990) describes 'practical sense' (*sens pratique*).
9 For an extended discussion of Mead's philosophical and social/psychological import, see Joas, 1985.
10 See Mead, 1912, 1913.
11 Erikson, 1963, 1968.
12 For an extended discussion of the contrast between Mead's and Erikson's working conceptions of 'identity', see Holland and Lachicotte, 2007.
13 See Vygotsky, 1978, 1986, for his discussions of semiotic mediation, meaning and sense, and the culturally 'real' worlds that humans inhabit. Vygotsky held a pragmatic or heuristic, rather than 'representational', understanding of sign use. See Wertsch, 1985, for commentary.
14 Later linguistic philosophers would argue that meaning derives from 'world-making'. See Nelson Goodman, 1978.
15 From this angle, it is somewhat nonsensical to say that 'The Pope is a bachelor'. Since the Pope exists in a social world for which marital status is not telling – the Pope's significance does not play out in cross-

gender relationships – bachelor is an impractical characterization for him. The example is drawn from Fillmore, 1975.

16 A classic example is 'inner speech', the voice-over in our (adult) head which directs and comments on what we do. It begins as social speech, the directive comments of our elders or peers. We then appropriate this speech stream and voice it to ourselves in 'egocentric speech'. Finally, the voiced aspect falls away, so that only we 'hear' (as sound-image) what we say to ourselves. See Vygotsky, 1986. Compare Voloshinov's idea of the sign as an 'extraterritorial' constituent of the psyche (Voloshinov, 1986).

17 See Vygotsky, 1978, pp. 52–7 for this developmental history of the sign. Cf. Mead's theory of the gesture (Mead, 1934) and also Foucault's idea of the inscription of habits through exercise and examination (Foucault, 1979).

18 See Bourdieu, 1985, and the collected essays on fields in Bourdieu, 1993.

19 My favorite discussion of this idea of 'language' as social work and social operator is in the essay, 'Discourse in the novel', collected in Bakhtin, 1981. It is, however, found throughout Bakhtin's writings.

20 In Voloshinov, 1986. The value of this work for the student lies partly in Voloshinov's ability to epitomize Bakhtin's skeins of associations as declarations of a lucid argument.

21 The drama was Mead's metaphor (Mead, 1913), though it was more than metaphor. Bakhtin preferred the novel as analogue, though he had an idiosyncratic notion of the genre. See below.

22 See Holland *et al.* (1998), chapter 3, for a more complete discussion of the concept.

23 Both Vygotsky, 1978, and Bourdieu, 1977a, use the idea of the game, and, more generally, of play, to emphasize the social bases of what we learn to imagine ourselves to be. These 'games' operate, however, by 'rules of thumb', not by the codified rules of games that are officiated.

24 As Judith Butler (1990, 1994) insists, though one must remember the primacy she accords to 'performativity', the capacity of discourse to produce what it names. Insofar as the 'subject' derives from, rather than is presumed by, social practice, we would agree.

25 In Althusser's (1971) words, people are hailed (interpellated) by society.

26 See Davies and Harré, 1990, and Harré and van Langenhove, 1991, for an influential discussion of discursive positioning. See also Smith, 1988.

27 The foregoing makes this learning of social position seem far too clear. In fact, it is often marked by ambivalence and ambiguity. See the discussion of 'spaces of authoring' which follows.

28 See the discussion in Holland *et al.*, 1998, chapter 6. Our 'sense' of relational identity depends greatly on Bourdieu's ideas. See Bourdieu, 1977b, for a concise presentation of position as it becomes disposition and Bourdieu, 1984, for his most complete discussions of habitus, field and social divisions.

29 See Voloshinov, 1986, for an exposition of addressivity, and Bakhtin, 1990, for the idea of answerabililty. Holquist, 1990, provides an extended discussion of these concepts and of the centrality of responsiveness in Bakhtin's imagination of human life and understanding.

30 This is not to deny 'agency' (in the element of choice) in our formation of identities – the point usually raised by scholars of identity (e.g. Woodward, 2000). It is to suggest that such control may already depend upon the standing accorded one.

31 Again, see his essay, 'Discourse in the novel', in Bakhtin, 1981, for his most condensed presentation of authorship as orchestration.

32 Or take the case of Roger, a psychiatric patient whom I interviewed. Roger acted from his recognized diagnoses – his therapeutic identities – in his everyday dealings with wife and family (as husband and son), drawing on medical authority to counter their ways of identifying him. See Lachicotte, 2002, for the complete discussion.

33 The 'sideways glance' is Bakhtin's phrase. He was fascinated by inversions of power in ritual, play and the arts. See his studies of 'carnival' (1984a, 1984b) in the works of Dostoyevsky and Rabelais.

34 A cultural/economic area consisting of the 'Mediterranean rim' of northeastern Spain, southern France and far western Italy.

35 The search for the emergent is part of Williams's investigations of hegemony and the 'structure of feeling'. See, e.g., Williams, 1977.

36 The point recalls Hirst's (1979) criticism of Lacan, that his 'subject' must already have the faculties of a subject to become itself. See also Hall, 1996. Vygotsky's concept of development vests these faculties of subjectivity in transaction before they are embodied 'in person'.

37 Or should I say, well timed? Wortham (2006) has begun to treat the problem in terms of the different time scales along which actions unfold (as their material, artifactual tokens circulate).

38 The terms (we-pole or I-pole) and characterization are Voloshinov's (1986).

References

Althusser, L. (1971) *Lenin and Philosophy, and Other Essays*, London, New Left Books.

Bakhtin, M.M. (1981) *The Dialogic Imagination: Four Essays by M.M. Bakhtin* (ed. M.E. Holquist, trans. C. Emerson and M.E. Holquist), Austin, University of Texas Press.

—— (1984a) *Problems of Dostoevsky's Poetics* (ed. and trans. C. Emerson), Minneapolis, University of Minnesota Press.

—— (1984b) *Rabelais and his World* (trans. Helene Iswolsky), Bloomington, University of Indiana Press.

—— (1986) *Speech Genres and Other Late Essays* (eds Caryl Emerson and Michael Holquist, trans. Vern McGee), Austin, University of Texas Press.

—— (1990) *Art and Answerability* (ed. M. Holquist and V. Liapunov, trans. V. Liapunov), Austin, University of Texas Press.

Bhabha, H. (1996) 'Culture's in-between', in *Questions of Cultural Identity* (eds S. Hall and P. du Gay), London, Sage, pp. 53–60.

Bourdieu, P. (1977a) *Outline of a Theory of Practice* (trans. R. Nice), Cambridge, Cambridge University Press.

—— (1977b) 'The economics of linguistic exchanges', *Social Science Information*, 16(6), pp. 645–68.

—— (1984) *Distinction: A Social Critique of the Judgement of Taste* (trans. Richard Nice), Cambridge, MA, Harvard University Press.

—— (1985) 'The genesis of the concepts of "habitus" and "field"', *Sociocriticism*, 2(2), pp. 11–24.

—— (1990) *The Logic of Practice* (trans. R. Nice), Palo Alto, CA, Stanford University Press.

—— (1993) *The Field of Cultural Production: Essays on Art and Literature*, New York, Columbia University Press.

Butler, J. (1990) *Gender Trouble: Feminism and the Subversion of Identity*, New York, Routledge.

—— (1994) 'Gender as performance: an interview with Judith Butler', *Radical Philosophy*, 67(Summer), pp. 32–7.

Certeau, M. de (1984) *The Practice of Everyday Life* (trans. S. Rendall), Berkeley, University of California Press.

Davies, B. and Harré, R. (1990) 'Positioning: the discursive production of selves', *Journal for the Theory of Social Behaviour*, 20, pp. 43–63.

Erikson, E. (1963) *Childhood and Society*, 2nd edn, New York, Norton.

—— (1968) *Identity: Youth and Crisis*, New York, Norton.

Fillmore, C. (1975) 'An alternative to checklist theories of meaning', in *Proceedings of the First Annual Meeting of the Berkeley Linguistics Society* (ed. C. Cogne *et al.*), Berkeley, University of California Press, pp. 123–31.

Foucault, M. (1979. *Discipline and Punish: The Birth of the Prison* (trans. A. Sheridan), New York, Vintage Books.

Gleason, P. (1983) 'Identifying identity: a semantic history', *Journal of American History*, 69(4), pp. 910–31.

Goodman, N. (1978) *Ways of Worldmaking*, Hassocks, UK, Harvester Press.

Hall, S. (1996) 'Introduction: who needs identity?', in S. Hall and P. du Gay (eds), *Questions of Cultural Identity*, London, Sage Publications, pp. 1–17.

Hall, S. and du Gay, P. (eds) (1996) *Questions of Cultural Identity*, London, Sage.

Harré, R and Van Langenhove, R. (1991) 'Varieties of positioning', *Journal for the Theory of Social Behaviour*, 21, pp. 391–407.

Hermans, H.J.M., and Kempen, H. (1993) *The Dialogical Self: Meaning as Movement*, San Diego, Academic Press.

Hirst, P. (1979) *On Law and Ideology*, London, Macmillan.

Hochschild, A. (1983) *The Managed Heart: Commercialization of Human Feeling*, Berkeley, University of California Press.

Holland, D.C. and Eisenhart, M. (1990) *Educated in Romance: Women, Achievement and College Culture*, Chicago, University of Chicago Press.

Holland, D.C. and Lachicotte, W.S. (2007) 'Vygotsky, Mead, and new sociocultural studies of identity', in H. Daniels, M. Cole and J. Wertsch (eds), *The Cambridge Companion to Vygotsky*, Cambridge, Cambridge University Press, pp. 101–35.

Holland, D.C., Lachicotte, W.S., Skinner, D.G. and Cain, C. (1998) *Identity and Agency in Cultural Worlds*, Cambridge, MA, Harvard University Press.

Holland, D.C., and Lave, J. (2001) 'History in person: an introduction', in D. Holland and J. Lave (eds), *History in Person: Enduring Struggles, Contentious Practice, Intimate Identities*, Santa Fe, NM, SAR Press, pp. 3–33.

Holquist, M. (1990) *Dialogism: Bakhtin and his World*, New York, Routledge.

Joas, H. (1985) *G.H. Mead: A Contemporary Re-Examination of his Thought* (trans. Raymond Meyer), Cambridge, MA, MIT Press.

Lachicotte, W.S. (2002) 'Intimate practices, public selves: Bakhtin's space of authoring', in J. Mageo (ed.), *Power and the Self*, Cambridge, Cambridge University Press, pp. 48–66.

Lave, J. and Wenger, E. (1991) *Situated Learning: Legitimate Peripheral Participation*, Cambridge, Cambridge University Press.

Lee, B., Wertsch, J. and Stone, A. (1983) 'Towards a Vygotskian theory of the self', in B. Lee and G. Noam, *Developmental Approaches to the Self*, New York, Plenum Press, pp. 309–41.

Lefebvre, H. (1991) *Critique of Everyday Life* (trans. John Moore), London, Verso.

McCall, G.J. and Simmons, J.L. (1978) *Identities and Interactions: An Examination of Human Associations in Everyday Life*, rev. edn, New York, Free Press.

—— (1912) 'The mechanism of social consciousness', *Journal of Philosophy, Psychology and Scientific Methods*, 9, pp. 401–6.

—— (1913) 'The social self', *Journal of Philosophy, Psychology and Scientific Methods*, 10, pp. 374–80.

—— (1934) *Mind, Self and Society*, Chicago, University of Chicago Press.

Ortner, S. (1984) 'Theory in anthropology since the sixties', *Comparative Studies in Society and History*, 26(1), pp. 126–66.

Penuel, W. and Wertsch, J. (1995) 'Dynamics of negation in the identity politics of cultural other and cultural self: the rhetorical image of the person in developmental psychology', *Culture and Psychology*, 1, pp. 343–59.

Rutherford, J. (ed.) (1990) *Identity: Community, Culture, Difference*, London, Lawrence and Wishart.

Smith, P. (1988) *Discerning the Subject*, Minneapolis, University of Minnesota Press.

Voloshinov, V.N. (1986) *Marxism and the Philosophy of Language* (trans. L. Matejka and I.R. Titunik), Cambridge, MA, Harvard University Press.

Vygotsky, L.S. (1978) *Mind in Society: The Development of Higher Psychological Processes* (eds M. Cole, V. John-Steiner, S. Scribner and E. Souberman), Cambridge, MA, Harvard University Press.

—— (1986) *Thought and Language*, rev. edn (ed. A. Kozulin), Cambridge, MA, Harvard University Press.

Wertsch, J.V. (1985) *Vygotsky and the Social Formation of Mind*, Cambridge, MA, Harvard University Press.

Williams, R. (1977) *Marxism and Literature*, Oxford, Oxford University Press.

Willis, P. (1981) *Learning to Labour: How Working Class Kids Get Working Class Jobs*, New York, Columbia University Press.

Woodward, K. (ed.) (1997) *Identity and Difference*, London, Sage Publications.

—— (2000) 'Questions of identity', in K. Woodward (ed.), *Questioning Identity: Gender, Class, Nation*, London, Routledge, pp. 6–41.

Wortham, S.E.F. (2006) *Learning Identity: The Joint Emergence of Social Identification and Academic Learning*, New York, Cambridge University Press.

Reflective questions

1   Consider two cultural activities, framed by different figured worlds, in which you regularly participate. (E.g., for argument's sake, 'romance' vs. 'schoolwork'.) Choose one of importance to you, and another of little importance. Now:

   a   Try to reconstruct how you learned to take part in both activities. How did you learn the meaning of the settings and 'props' of action, what was expected to happen and what roles were set out for which sorts of people? How did you achieve a characteristic place in the activity (following 'role models' or defining your place against others) – if you did? Did your sense of self in the 'game' (the imaginary 'I' that Vygotsky talked about) reflect how others acted toward you and felt about you? Did it match how you felt about yourself?

   b   Contrast the outcomes of your learning in the two activities. How would you characterize your performance in both settings? What, if anything, is different about your sense of action and your sense of self in the two settings? What about the activities strikes you differently? Can you say why the first activity intrigues and draws you in and the other leaves you indifferent? Why do you continue to participate?

   c   Does a social practice theory of identity seem to make sense in terms of your experience? Where does it fall short?

2   The chapter argues that human interaction often takes place in 'spaces of authoring', where several frames of meaning, several figured worlds, are pertinent to the course of action. As an ethnographic exercise, describe any extended interaction / conversation in which you took part in terms of the self-expression and 'positioning' (role-taking and role-casting) of the participants. Can you distinguish multiple 'definitions of the situation' through which participants figured the interaction, the identities actors assumed and the strategies of action they pursued? [Look for points where you asked yourself: where is (s)he coming from? What could (s)he possibly mean?] How did participants signal their various perspectives (identities) and negotiate a sense of what was happening in the situation? Was a 'consensus view' achieved, or some other outcome?

Further reading:

Hall, S. and du Gay, P. (eds) (1996) *Questions of Cultural Identity*, London, Sage Publications.

Holland, D.C., Lachicotte, W.S., Skinner, D. and Cain, C. (1998) *Identity and Agency in Cultural Worlds*, Cambridge, MA, Harvard University Press.

Holland, D.C. and Lave, J. (eds) (2001) *History in Person: Enduring Struggles, Contentious Practice, Intimate Identities*, Santa Fe, SAR Press.

Penuel, W. and Wertsch, J. (1995) 'Dynamics of negation in the identity politics of cultural other and cultural self: The rhetorical image of the person in developmental psychology', *Culture and Psychology*, 1, pp. 343–59.

Index

CPSIA information can be obtained at www.ICGtesting.com
Printed in the USA
LVOW110934161111

255215LV00004B/4/P